जीवंत साहित्य

LIVING LITERATURE

वाणी प्रकाशन

जीवंत साहित्य
LIVING LITERATURE

A TRILINGUAL DOCUMENTATION OF INDO-GERMAN LITERARY EXCHANGE

DEUTSCH - INDISCHER LITERATURAUSTAUSCH IN DREI SPRACHEN

भारतीय-जर्मन साहित्यिक विनिमय का त्रिभाषीय संकलन

Edited by
Barbara Lotz and Vishnu Khare

संपादन
बार्बरा लौट्स और विष्णु खरे

VANI PRAKASHAN

4695, 21-A, Daryaganj, New Delhi 110 002

Branch

Ashok Rajpath, Patna 800 004

Phone : +91 11 23273167 Fax : +91 11 23275710

www.vaniprakashan.in
vaniprakashan@gmail.com

LIVING LITERATURE
Edited by Barbara Lotz and Vishnu Khare

ISBN : 978-93-5072-248-0
Literature/Linguistics

First Edition 1998
Second Edition 2012

Cover Design : Barbara Lotz and Debu Sarkar

Price : ₹ 795

Printed at New Krishna Offset, Delhi 110 093

Vani Prakashan's logo is a creation of the strokes from M.F. Husain

भारतीय स्वतंत्रता की 50वीं वर्षगांठ पर

FIFTY YEARS OF INDIAN INDEPENDENCE

CONTENTS

FOREWORD XIII
Georg LECHNER

INTRODUCTION XV
Barbara LOTZ

एक जीवंत आदान-प्रदान का दस्तावेज़ XIX
Vishnu KHARE

PART I FROM INDIAN LANGUAGES INTO GERMAN AND ENGLISH

PROSE

Manzoor AHTESHAM 2
दास्तान-ए-लापता / Geschichte eines Verlorenen / Tale of The Lost

U.R. ANANTHA MURTHY 12
ಸೂರ್ಯನ ಕುದುರೆ / Ein Pferd für die Sonne / A Horse for the Sun

Satyen KUMAR 28
झरना / Wasserfall / Waterfall

Uday PRAKASH 40
छप्पन तोले का करधन / Der goldene Gürtel / The Golden Waist Chain

Krishna SOBTI 50
मित्रो मरजानी / Verflixte Mitro / Wretched Mitro

Krishna Baldev VAID 72
अंधेरे की आत्मा / Die Seele der Dunkelheit / The Soul of Darkness

Nirmal VERMA 78
लन्दन की एक रात / Eine Nacht in London / A Night in London

POETRY

Kumar AMBUJ 88

नए अपराधी / Die neuen Verbrecher / Neo-Criminals
बिजली का खंभा / Der Lichtmast / The Electric Pole
अकस्मात् एक दिन / Unerwartet eines Tages / Mother Will Arrive

Shaista ANWAR 98

बचपन / Kindheit / Childhood
आदत / Gewohnheit / Habit
बाजार बहुत दूर है / Der Bazar ist ganz schön weit weg / The Far-Away Bazar

Sanjay CHATURVEDI 104

लुटेरे बनकर इतिहास / Die Räuber, Geschichte geworden / Marauders Becoming History
पैसे के दाँत / Die Zähne des Geldes / The Fangs of Money

Dilip P.CHITRE 110

अंधळ्याला दिसणारे देखावे / Was der Blinde sieht / Sights the Blind View
The House of my Childhood / Das Haus meiner Kindheit
चवथा ब्रांडेनबुर्ग काँचेर्तो / Viertes Brandenburgisches Konzert / Fourth Brandenburg Concerto

Mangalesh DABRAL 116

पत्तों की मृत्यु / Der Tod der Blätter / The Death of Leaves
सपना / Traum / A Dream
कुछ देर के लिए / Eine Weile / For a While
शहर / Die Stadt / City

Alokeranjan DASGUPTA 124

ত্বরান্বিত / Hast / Accelerated
গোধুলিময় একটি যুগল / Ein Paar in der Dämmerung / Couple Charged with Dusk
চিত্রিত আছো, নিসর্গ / In Japanischen Wasserfarben / Painted Nature
কাগজের গাড়ি / Zeitungswagen / Paper Coach

Nida FAZLI 132

سلیقہ / Das richtige Benehmen / Discipline
نئی ڈائری کا ایک ورق / Eine Seite im neuen Tagebuch / Page from the New Diary
راستے کی منطق / Das Gesetz der Strasse / On the Road
بس یونہی جیتے رہو / Leb einfach so weiter / Just Keep on Living

Gagan GILL 140

मछली / Der Fisch / The Fish
आधे सिर का दर्द–2 / Migräne-2 / Migraine-2
किसी दूसरे का प्रेम / Die Liebe eines anderen / Somebody Else's Love

Pramod KAUNSWAL 146

दुकानें 1-4 / Läden 1-4 / Shops 1-4
गाँव के दो दिन / Zwei Tage im Dorf / Two Days in the Village

Vishnu KHARE 152

दिल्ली में अपना फ्लैट बनाने के बाद... / Einer der es in Delhi zu einer eigenen Wohnung gebracht hat... / Having Built a Flat in Delhi...
सिंगल विकेट सीरिज़ / Kricket / Single Wicket Series

Sitakant MAHAPATRA 162

ସମୟ ବହିଯାଏନି / Nicht die Zeit fliesst / Time does not fly
ଧାଙ୍ଗଡ଼ାର ପ୍ରେମ ସଙ୍ଗୀତ / Dhangras Liebeslied / Dhangra's Love Song
ପବନ / Der Wind / The Wind

MOHANJEET 172

1984 / 1984 / 1984
ਸੰਵਾਦ-ਚਿਤਰ / Gespräch / Dialogue

Kunvar NARAYAN 178

सरकस / Zirkus / Circus
अयोध्या 1992 / Ayodhya 1992 / Ayodhya 1992
स्पष्टीकरण / Klarstellung / Clarification

Sutinder Singh NOOR 184

ਪਿਆਰ ਤੇ ਕਿਤਾਬ / Lieben und Lesen / Love and a Book
ਏਨੀ ਵੀ ਉਡੀਕ ਨਾ ਕਰੇ / Warte nicht solange / Don't Wait So Much
ਕਵਿਤਾ ਨੂੰ ਉੱਗਣ ਦਿਉ ਅਪਣੇ ਅੰਦਰ / Lass Gedichte blühn / Let Poetry Grow

Surjeet PATAR 190

ਇਕ ਪਸ਼ੂ-ਕਥਾ / Eine Fabel / An Animal Tale
ਪਰਦੇਸ / Ausland / The Alien Land
ਦੋ ਰੁਖਾਂ ਦੀ ਗੁਫ਼ਤਗੂ / Zwei Bäume im Gespräch / Dialogue Between Two Trees
ਕਵੀ ਸਾਹਿਬ / Herr Dichter / Mr. Poet

Bhagwat RAWAT 200

सच पूछो तो / Um die Wahrheit zu sagen / If You Ask Me the Truth

कचरा बीनने वाली लड़कियाँ / Mädchen, die im Abfall wühlen / The Rag-Picking Girls
इस शोर में / In diesem Lärm / In this Din

Padma SACHDEVA 208
राजा के महल / Königspaläste / The Raja's Palaces
कबूतर / Tauben / Pigeons

Prayag SHUKLA 216
खंडहर होते एक महल को देखते / Beim Anblick eines zur Ruine verfallenden Palastes / On Visiting a Palace Turning into a Ruin
ये लिखता हूँ / Das schreibe ich / This I Write
व्यंजन बनाने की विधियाँ / Arten zu kochen / The Ways of Cooking
दिल्ली में / In Delhi / In Delhi

Kedarnath SINGH 224
कविता क्या है / Was ist ein Gedicht / What is Poetry?
एक प्रेम कविता को पढ़कर / Nach dem Lesen eines Liebesgedichtes / Reading a Love Poem
बनारस / Benares / Banaras

Varyam SINGH 236
कृताब / Das Buch / Book
बोली / Sprache / Language
ऊड़दी रौहें / Flieg weiter / Keep Flying

Nitin Nema SUBODH 242
वह औरत / Die Frau dort / That Woman
सीताफल / Sitafrüchte / Custard Apples
बँटवारा / Trennung / Partition

Ashok VAJPEYI 248
देह की पुकार सुनती है देह ही / Den Ruf des Leibes hört nur der Leib / A Body is Heard by a Body
तलाश / Suche / Search
संभावना / Möglichkeit / A Possibility

PART II FROM GERMAN INTO INDIAN LANGUAGES AND ENGLISH

PROSE

Jurek BECKER 256

New Yorker Woche / न्यूयॉर्क के पांच दिन / A Week in New York

Hans-Christoph BUCH 274

Rede des Toten Columbus am Tag des Jüngsten Gerichts / फ़ैसले के दिन मृत कोलम्बस का बयान / Dead Columbus Speaks on Judgement Day

Uwe TIMM 286

Die Entdeckung der Currywurst / मसालेदार गुलमे का आविष्कार / The Invention of Curried Sausage

POETRY

Gottfried BENN 296

Was schlimm ist / बुरा क्या है / What's Bad
Kreislauf / सिलसिला / Circle
Ein Wort / एक शब्द / A Word

Bertolt BRECHT 302

Ich sage ja nichts gegen Alexander / मैं सिकंदर के खिलाफ़ तो कुछ नहीं कह रहा / I'm not Saying Anything Against Alexander
Schlechte Zeit für Lyrik / प्रगीत के लिए बुरा वक़्त / Bad Time for Poetry
An die Nachgeborenen / अनुजों के लिए / To Those Born Later
Fahrend in einem bequemen Wagen / आरामदेह कार में जाते हुए / Travelling in a Comfortable Car
Der Rauch / धुआँ / The Smoke

Paul CELAN 314

Dein Haar überm Meer / तुझे केस अध्धर समुद्रावर / Your Hair Above the Sea
Espenbaum / एस्पन्च्या झाडा / Aspen Tree

Günter EICH 318

En attendant / सेवा में / En Attendant
Tauben / कबूतर / Pigeons
In anderen Sprachen / दूसरी भाषाओं में / In Other Languages

Hans Magnus ENZENSBERGER 324

Zukunftsmusik / भविष्यरागिणी / Dreams of the Future

Erich FRIED 326

Vielleicht Allende / नहीं थका हूँ / Allende Perhaps
Fragen nach der Poesie seit Auschwitz / आउश्वित्स के बाद कविता के बारे में सवालात / Questions about Poetry since Auschwitz
Rückblick / पुनरावलोकन / Retrospect

Günter GRASS 336

Zunge zeigen / जीभ दिखाना / Show Your Tongue

Sarah KIRSCH 344

Kalt / गाराठा
Ferne / दूरत्व
Der Chronist / बखरक्र्ता
Wach / जागी
Flüchtig / पलायमान

Tadeus PFEIFER 354

Spaziergang im Winter / सर्दियों में घूमना / A Walk in Winter
Sammler toter Gedichte / मृत कविताओं का संकलनकार / Collector of Dead Poems
A,B,C... / क, ख, ग... / A, B, C...
Eins und anderes / एक और दूसरा / One and the Other

AFTERWORD 363
Lothar LUTZE

NOTES ON CONTRIBUTORS 364

ACKNOWLEDGEMENTS AND COPYRIGHT STATEMENTS 385

LIST OF EVENTS 389

FOREWORD

When I set sails for India to take up my second posting in New Delhi in 1992, I had a most reassuring asset in my luggage: I had learned that Lothar Lutze, old India hand like myself, would head the Delhi office of the South Asia Institute again and share my new tenure as director of Max Mueller Bhavan.

Soon after arrival we sat down, along with MMB programme officer Petra Matusche, to line out broad guidelines for a series that we agreed to name "Living Literature". The basic idea was to invite, at loosely regular intervals, poets and writers of Indian literatures to present their works in their own languages, accompanied by selective German translations, and to establish a dialogue with German colleagues and their works, whenever possible. The choice of the invitees was half as difficult as it would seem, what with Lothar Lutze's intimate knowledge and personal contacts helping from the beginning. This is how representatives from literatures in northern Indian languages filled the programme agenda early on and Hindi, Urdu, Bengali set the tone, followed by Marathi and Oriya. Vishnu Khare joined the organizers' team enthusiastically and formed an inseparable tandem with Lothar Lutze. Luckily, some German writers, like the late Jurek Becker and Hans Christoph Buch, came our way and participated in the series. Vishnu Khare was tempted into translating "Zunge zeigen" by Günter Grass into Hindi and generously accepted Petra Matusche's and my own assistance in the endeavour. Even Günter Grass himself helped to clear many a passage through correspondence. The resulting publication became the subject of a lively and controversial debate between Indian and German readers of the book and its translation within the series.

After Lothar's retirement and departure from Delhi, his successor, Barbara Lotz, vigorously took over the reins on this literary voyage and has never looked back since. With the continued assistance of Vishnu Khare she brought in new voices - young, female and lesser known Indian languages among them - and succeeded in giving the series a new lease of life.

Although I have kept alive in my memory many an inspiring evening, I would rather not single out individual names and works and leave it to the discretion of the readers of this volume to make their own choice. But it is heartening to know, that the spoken word of so many literary gatherings at MMB and SAI within the series "Living Literature" also finds its way to a general public through the written form of this volume. This is perhaps also the most adequate sign of gratitude to the participating authors.

Georg Lechner
Goethe-Institut München

INTRODUCTION

This volume documents a series of of literary events conceived and organized between 1992 and 1997 by the New Delhi branches of Goethe Institute (Max Mueller Bhavan) and the South Asia Institute Heidelberg, as part of a larger project to promote a meaningful exchange between the German and Indian worlds of letters. The series had two goals: to present Indian authors through a reading of their original texts followed by German translations and to provide a forum for German authors visiting India for a joint reading with their Indian counterparts, followed by selective translations and a discussion on mutual concerns. The series also sought to present works of German authors translated into Indian languages and to discuss the problematics of translation between the two language groups.

Although these were the broad parameters along which the series was organized, each individual event differed from the other and was marked by its own distinct bearing and character. As with any creative process, some events were the spontaneous outcome of the personal relationship and interaction between organizers, translators and authors. No literary strait-jackets were visible. Subsequently, the series unfolded, not with a pre-planned, all-encompassing objective of covering a representative section of Indian and German writers for later compilation in an anthology, but in a rather organic and instinctive manner. If one construes the term 'living' as something that not only reflects contemporariness but also variation, change and all the other dynamics of life, "Living Literature", as the series was called, was worthy of its name.

Presentations sometimes consisted of two authors (as in the case of N.Fazli and K.N. Singh), three (as in "Triveni", "Punjab Poetry" and "Voices from Bhopal") or even five ("Yuva Kavita"). Individual writers too, featured during a given evening (Dasgupta, Chitre, Mahapatra, Khare, Anantha Murthy, Sobti, Gill, Shukla). Further, there were combined readings of German and Indian authors (Prakash/Buch, Verma/Becker, Vaid/Pfeifer) and one evening with a single German author (Timm), presented in selected translations followed by a panel discussion. Some of the Indian authors read their own poetry as well as their translations of German poets (Khare: Benn, Eich and Fried; Dasgupta: Hölderlin and Goethe; Chitre: Enzensberger, Kirsch and Celan). Publications of German authors in Hindi translations by Indian authors also featured in the series (Rathi: Brecht; Khare: Grass). A mixed poetry reading in lesser known languages was held on the periphery of a conference on South Asian languages at Jawaharlal Nehru University, and there were lectures on literary topics (Riemenschneider; Lutze). One evening saw an elaborate performance of old devotional songs in Bengali and Maithili translated into German and set to Odissi and Manipuri dance and music. There was also the additional pleasure of Polish translations by Prof. K.M. Byrski and Dr. D. Stasik on two evenings ("Triveni" and "Yuva Kavita"). All in all, each evening of the series was organized under different circumstances and consisted of contrasting material, variant perspectives.

Of course, one of the consequences of the heterogeneous nature and the 'living' dynamics of the series is that to many, this collection may seem imbalanced and incomplete, the selection wilful and arbitrary. The imbalance is not one-sided: it applies just as much to the dominance of the 'Hindi-belt' over South Indian languages, as to the selection of German writers who appear

here in Hindi and Marathi translations. While both the Indian and the German section carry some famous names, they include some lesser known writers as well.

Further, the selection contains more poetry than prose, and the section on texts translated from Indian languages into German and English is much larger than the one on Hindi translations of German writing. Unfortunately, time constraints hindered the inclusion of a large number of outstanding Indian authors from participating in the series and therewith being included in this selection. The apparent neglect of South Indian languages can only be stated and regretted, not excused. In no way does the omission reflect on the richness, originality and variety of these literatures. We hope to find able German translators to present the vibrant literary scene elsewhere in the subcontinent, at a future date.

As with the choice of language groups, the respective lengths of the contributions in no way reflect a ranking or hierarchical importance of the authors included. This aspect too, emerged from the nature of the series itself, which consisted of events with single authors or several writers, the latter resulting in individually less translated material. Also, the allotted lengths differ in regard to poetry or prose contributions. Poetry, which has the advantage of reflecting the wide spectrum of an author's consciousness within a relatively taut selection, formed the major genre during our evenings. Prose readings, on the other hand, must - and often did - comprise of extracts of novels or short stories. Keeping this aspect in mind, prose extracts, which always tend to appear mutilated without their natural context, were granted slightly more individual space in this volume. Since we had the privilege of choosing the shorter story of two read out one evening, K.B. Vaid's prose is the only short piece presented in its entirety in this volume. (The other story has, in the meantime, been published in its German translation).

In spite of all these shortcomings and room for improvement, we decided to take up the challenge and publish this collection based on the compilation over the years. However, the idea to put together such a publication emerged only towards the later stages of the series and was never a primary objective. Many participating writers, loathe to let the texts and translations lie forgotten in a desk drawer, themselves supported the idea.

It is our hope that this collection will be seen as a relevant representation of the many facets and tendencies of modern Indian writing. It is also our earnest wish to make a small contribution towards filling the glaring void that some critics recently said exists in the publication of Indian 'vernacular' literature, by including some examples of *real existing* contemporary writing, other than in English: these range from the harshly realistic, such as Uday Prakash' stories to the melancholically detached like some of Prayag Shukla's poems; the poets from Punjab reflect on contemporary political affairs while others, like the authors from Bhopal and also Kunvar Narayan and Nida Fazli, paint grim but witty pictures of a society by distancing themselves from it. The classic piece by Krishna Sobti communicates a refreshing new attitude towards the feminine self, as also do the subtle and finely crafted poems by Gagan Gill. Some of the finest poems by Mangalesh Dabral and Vishnu Khare reflect the rural background of today's modern, urban intellectuals. The moving cheerfulness of U.R. Anantha Murthy's short story also represents the same conundrum.

Elsewhere, dense, symbolic language is in evidence, as in the works of Dilip Chitre and Alokeranjan Dasgupta. The poems of Ashok Vajpeyi and Sitakant Mahapatra craft a mosaic of fleeting emotions, personal memories and fragmented images. Nirmal Verma's short story is of intense personal perception, while K.B. Vaid's piece is replete with allegory. The poems of Padma Sachdeva or Varyam Singh articulate a concern for one's endangered language and culture. Finally, the poems

of Shaista Anwar, Kumar Ambuj, Nitin Nema Subodh, Sanjay Chaturvedi and Pramod Kaunswal mark the emergence of a whole generation of writers equipped with a new awareness, evolving sensibilities and style.

In order to lend a focus to the multifariousness of the material, the selection concentrates on modern prose and poetry from Germany and India. Certain older works presented during the series, such as the songs of Vidyapati and Chandidas as well as the poems of Heine, Hölderlin and Goethe, or the material presented by C.P. Zoller and R.K. Reddy in the context of oral folk traditions were in danger of appearing isolated in this selection and were therefore put aside for a future project. It is for the same reason that not all lectures and talks delivered during the series have been included. Regretfully, technical constraints prevented us from carrying the Polish translations in this selection too.

The main challenge and incentive for the German translators to take on these literary works lay in avoiding the English version and presenting instead, a direct link between Indian languages and German. The obvious dominance of North Indian languages in this selection is partly because the organizers and translators are predominantly scholars of Hindi. In the case of Kannada, Oriya, Marathi, Dogri and Punjabi texts, we had to compromise and rely on texts translated into English and Hindi by the authors themselves and worked under their close supervision. We were lucky in the case of Urdu, due to the participation of Christina Oesterheld and equally fortunate to have translations from Bengali by Hans Harder and Christian Weiss.

A further dimension was added to the subject of translation by the inclusion of the English versions of the respective texts in this volume. Though English was omitted in the process of translation itself, it still formed the working *lingua franca* and often emerged as the only mode of interaction between the authors and the public of mixed origin. Since English proved the most popular medium of communication with Indian, English and German *listeners*, the English texts were included to enlarge the number of potential *readers* too. Based on pragmatism and marketability, the decision had to take into consideration the limited international readership of both the Indian languages and German and thereby overlook the ideological debate on the colonial dominance and role of the English language in India.

At the same time, the inclusion of the English versions caused a great deal of delays and difficulties, as not all the material read out in the series had been translated into English. Collecting the texts already published and obtaining the copyright was one task, getting texts translated and edited, the other. Thanks to the committed efforts of translators like Rupert Snell, Harish Trivedi, Vishnu Khare, Girdhar Rathi, Jaidev, Shrinath, Kuldip Singh, R.P. Dixit and many others, the problem of translating Indian languages into English could be overcome. For some texts to be translated from German into English, we are grateful to Michael Hamburger and Padma Rao, who worked on several pieces especially for this selection. Though we tried our best to procure them, the poems of Sarah Kirsch included here are not available in English translation at present. The trilingual endeavour also created technical problems relating to layout and format, which had to be tackled with patience and dedication.

All material presented here is based on the texts read out during the series. Occasional variations in the translation from the original version stem partially from the fact that while the German translation still corresponds to the text presented at the reading itself, the handwritten Hindi texts were published after the series with slight alterations. Where possible, translations already published were included with their original spelling, footnotes, layout etc.

I wish to express my sincere and heartfelt thanks to the many people involved in organizing the series and this publication. My mentor and predecessor, Prof. Lothar Lutze heads the list, as also do Dr. Lechner and Petra Matusche who provided unstinting support for the evenings. Their respective successors, Tilmann Waldraff as Director and Peter Sewitz as programme officer of the MMB, were equally committed and took great interest in the uninterrupted and smooth progress of the events. Besides the 'official' organizers, Aruna George was always busy behind the scenes, arranging our post-event receptions on the beautiful lawns of MMB. More than once, I returned to Bettina Radner, MMB librarian, for her patient advice and useful hints concerning copyrights and translations. Jayashree Joshi of MMB lent a helping hand by typing some of the texts on floppies. Manish of Vinayak Computers arranged the vast material attractively with interest and patience. My staff at the South Asia Institute displayed great diligence in collecting the material and hunting down the missing details. Vishnu Khare, whose multi-faceted contributions as co-organizer, translator and editor alone were responsible for the series and this volume, calls for a special mention. Last but not least, I wish to express my gratitude to Tilmann Waldraff, Director of Max Mueller Bhavan, New Delhi, and to Professor Monika Boehm-Tettelbach, Director of South Asia Institute, Heidelberg, for granting financial support to bring out this book.

In conclusion, it is my hope that readers of this volume will be able to share some of our enthusiasm, inspiration and fun while preparing and holding the evenings with all the authors presented here, many of whom have become dear friends (or even dearer ones) during the process. It is in this spirit, that we wish to thank all the contributors and dedicate this volume to the celebrations of India's fiftieth year of Independence.

Barbara Lotz
New Delhi

एक जीवंत आदान-प्रदान का दस्तावेज़

इस संकलन की बनावट और स्वरूप को पूरी तरह से तभी समझा जा सकता है जब इसके लिए जिम्मेदार संस्थाओं और कुछ व्यक्तियों तथा उनके उद्देश्यों और सोच के बारे में कुछ जान लिया जाए।

जिस तरह भारत में 'भारतीय सांस्कृतिक संबंध परिषद' नामक एक आधिकारिक संस्था है जिसका प्रमुख कार्य भारतीय संस्कृति का विदेशों में प्रसार करना है उसी तरह जर्मनी की संस्था 'गोएठे इंस्टिटूट' (गोएठे संस्थान) है, जिसका नाम जर्मन विश्वकवि तथा चिंतक गोएठे पर रखा गया है और जिसकी शाखाएँ विश्व के प्रमुख नगरों में जर्मन भाषा तथा जर्मन संस्कृति के प्रसार का काम करती हैं। भारत में सभी जानते हैं कि गोएठे कालिदास के 'अभिज्ञानशाकुंतल' से परिचय प्राप्त कर कितने अभिभूत हुए थे और तब से जर्मनी में भारत के प्रति एक विशेष आकर्षण बना हुआ है। किंतु भारत में गोएठे उतने लोकप्रिय नहीं हो पाए हैं जितने उनसे कनिष्ठ मक्स म्युलर, जिन्होंने अनेक भारतीय ग्रंथों का अनुवाद किया, 'वॉट कैन इंडिया टीच अस ?' (भारत से हम क्या सीख सकते हैं') सरीखी पुस्तक तब लिखी जब भारत अंग्रेजों का गुलाम था और भारत की प्राचीन आध्यात्मिक तथा ज्ञान-परंपरा को विश्व-भर में स्वीकृत होने में अभूतपूर्व योगदान दिया। इसलिए यह उचित ही था कि गोएठे संस्थान के संचालकों ने भारत में अपनी शाखाओं का नाम 'मक्स म्युलर भवन' रखा और उनकी गतिविधियों को मात्र एकतरफा जर्मन संस्कृति के प्रचार-प्रसार तक सीमित नहीं रखा बल्कि इन शाखाओं को भारत-जर्मन सांस्कृतिक आदान-प्रदान का सक्रिय मंच बनाया। मक्स म्युलर भवन की बहुविध गतिविधियों में जाना यहाँ न संभव है, न वांछनीय—यही कहना पर्याप्त है कि भारतीय तथा जर्मन साहित्यों के बीच संवाद स्थापित करना उनमें से एक है। यदि 'मक्स म्युलर भवन' अर्थात् 'गोएठे इंस्टिटूट' एक विश्वव्यापी संस्था है तो जर्मनी के हाइलेडबेर्ग विश्वविद्यालय का 'सूडाजिएन इंस्टिटूट' (दक्षिण एशिया संस्थान), जैसा कि उसके नाम से ही स्पष्ट है, भारत सहित पाकिस्तान, नेपाल, श्रीलंका तथा बांग्लादेश के लगभग संपूर्ण अध्ययन को समर्पित एक लघु-विश्वविद्यालय की तरह है जहाँ अन्य विषयों के अलावा आधुनिक भारतीय भाषाओं और साहित्यों की पढ़ाई भी होती है। दक्षिण एशियाई क्षेत्र से इसके प्राध्यापकों और छात्रों का इतना घनिष्ठ संबंध है कि उसे भी 'गोएठे इंस्टिटूट' की तरह दिल्ली में एक विशेष शाखा स्थापित करनी पड़ी है जिसके निदेशक के रूप में दक्षिण एशिया संस्थान के किसी प्राध्यापक-प्राध्यापिका को समय-समय पर भारत भेजा जाता है जो दक्षिण एशिया संबंधी किसी भी विषय के विशेषज्ञ-अध्येता हो सकते हैं किंतु सामान्यतः भारतीय संस्कृति एवं साहित्य से परिचित होते ही हैं। संस्थान की दिल्ली शाखा 'मक्स म्युलर भवन' की इमारत में ही है इसलिए दोनों के निदेशकों के बीच तालमेल अपरिहार्य है क्योंकि दोनों संस्थाओं के उद्देश्य तथा हित काफी हद तक समान हैं और परस्पर पूरक भी हैं।

चूँकि दोनों संस्थाएँ जर्मन हैं इसलिए वे अंग्रेजी के रोब और मुँहजोई से मुक्त हैं। ज्ञान के क्षेत्र में अंग्रेजी के महत्त्व से कोई इन्कार नहीं कर सकता और ऐतिहासिक कारणों तथा भाषाई तनाव के कारण भारत में अंग्रेजी विदेशियों की सुविधा तथा मजबूरी दोनों बनी हुई है फिर भी 'मक्स म्युलर भवन' और 'दक्षिण एशिया संस्थान' न तो अंग्रेजी को अपरिहार्य मानते हैं और न भारत में लिखे जा रहे अंग्रेजी साहित्य को भारत का एकमात्र साहित्य मानते हैं। इसलिए जब भाषायी या साहित्यिक आदान-प्रदान की बात चलती है तो यह दोनों संस्थाएँ मूल भारतीय भाषाओं और उनमें लिखे जा रहे साहित्यों को ही प्राथमिक महत्त्व देती हैं। वे चाहती हैं कि जब जर्मन-भारतीय साहित्यिक कार्यक्रम हों तो सिर्फ जर्मन को प्रमुख

न माना जाए बल्कि भारतीय भाषाओं को उसके समकक्ष रखा जाए, जर्मन साहित्यिक सामग्री का सीधा अनुवाद संबद्ध भारतीय भाषाओं में हो और ऐसा ही विपरीत भी हो, अंग्रेजी अनुवाद तभी उपलब्ध करवाया जाए जब अनिवार्य हो। जर्मन लेखक अकेला अपनी रचनाएँ न पढ़े या सिर्फ जर्मन सामग्री उपलब्ध न कराई जाए बल्कि साथ में एक या एक से अधिक भारतीय लेखक हों और उनकी मूल रचनाएँ पढ़ी जाएँ। इससे भी आगे जाकर यह भी किया गया कि भारतीय साहित्यों पर कार्यक्रम किए गए और उनके जर्मन तथा अन्य भारतीय भाषाओं में अनुवाद प्रस्तुत किए गए, और जरूरत होने पर अंग्रेजी भी।

किंतु कोई संस्था उतनी ही उत्कृष्ट, गतिशील तथा कल्पना-प्रवण होती है जितनी कि उसे चलानेवाले लोग। 'मक्स म्युलर भवन' का तो काम ही सांस्कृतिक कार्यक्रम आयोजित करना है इसलिए उसमें उस तरह की योग्यता रखनेवाले व्यक्ति ही रखे जाते हैं। उधर दक्षिण एशिया संस्थान का मुख्य कार्य अध्यापन तथा शोध है किंतु चूँकि उसके प्राध्यापकों को कई भारतीय विषयों का ज्ञान होता है इसलिए उसकी भारतीय शाखा के निदेशकगण भी 'मक्स म्युलर भवन' सांस्कृतिक कार्यक्रमों में सलाह से लेकर सक्रिय सहयोग तक देते हैं। संस्थान में हिंदी, मराठी, बांग्ला, उर्दू, कन्नड, तमिल आदि आधुनिक भारतीय भाषाएँ पढ़ाई जाती रही हैं। इसलिए वहाँ के शिक्षकों का सीधा संपर्क आधुनिक भारतीय साहित्यों तथा साहित्यकारों से रहा है क्योंकि विदेशों में यह माना जाता है कि साहित्यकारों से संपर्क विदेशी साहित्यों के अध्ययन-अध्यापन का एक अनिवार्य अंग है। जर्मनी जैसे भारतविद्या के गढ़ में, जहाँ प्राचीन भारतीय भाषाओं और साहित्यों के अलावा कुछ और भाषाएँ और साहित्य भी हैं यह मानने में अब भी कुछ विश्वविद्यालयों और बुद्धिजीवियों को दिक्कत होती है, समसामयिक भारतीय लेखकों का पढ़ाया जाना एक छोटी-मोटी क्रांति थी जिसे 50 के दशक के बाद के कुछ प्राध्यापकों ने संभव किया। इनमें भारतीय लेखकों के सुपरिचित डॉ. लोठार लुत्से अन्यतम हैं। उनकी सेवा-निवृत्ति के बाद प्रो. डॉ. मोनीका बोएम-टेटेलबाख अब उस परंपरा को निबाह रही हैं।

लोठार लुत्से 60 के दशक में 'जर्मन अकादमिक आदान-प्रदान सेवा' के अंतर्गत जर्मन पढ़ाने भारत आए थे। साहित्य में उनकी रुचि थी इसलिए वे हिंदी साहित्य की ओर मुड़े और विधिवत हिंदी में शोध-उपाधि प्राप्त की और नए-नए स्थापित दक्षिण एशिया संस्थान में हिंदी पढ़ाने लगे। फिर जब वे पहली बार भारत में दक्षिण एशिया संस्थान की शाखा के निदेशक नियुक्त हुए तो उन्होंने हिंदी तथा अन्य भारतीय भाषाओं के साहित्यकारों से परिचय बढ़ाना शुरू किया। प्रारंभ में डॉ. लुत्से मंचीय हिंदी कविता, गीतकारों और आधुनिक ढंग की कविता के बीच फर्क नहीं करते थे। उन्होंने 'मक्स म्युलर भवन' के तत्त्वावधान में जब पहला कवि-सम्मेलन आयोजित किया तब वे 'अज्ञेय', कैलाश वाजपेयी, श्रीकांत वर्मा, सर्वेश्वर दयाल सक्सेना तथा रघुवीर सहाय के व्यक्तित्व और कृतित्व से परिचित हुए। उसके बाद वे तीस वर्षों के अपने प्राध्यापक-जीवन में फणीश्वरनाथ रेणु, मोहन राकेश, निर्मल वर्मा, राजेंद्र यादव, कमलेश्वर, कुँवर नारायण, नागार्जुन, त्रिलोचन, शमशेर बहादुर सिंह, प्रभाकर माचवे, भारतभूषण अग्रवाल, मनोहर श्याम जोशी, मन्नू भंडारी, अशोक वाजपेयी, चंद्रकांत देवताले, विनोदकुमार शुक्ल, गोविंद मिश्र, गिरिराज किशोर, ज्ञानरंजन, मंगलेश डबराल, असद जैदी आदि अनेक प्रौढ़ तथा युवा हिंदी रचनाकारों या उनकी रचनाओं के सघन संपर्क में आए। इनके साथ दिलीप चित्रे, यू.आर. अनंतमूर्ति, सुनील गंगोपाध्याय, विजयदान देथा, सीताकांत महापात्र, नवकांत बरुआ सरीखे अहिंदीभाषी लेखक भी उनके मित्र बने। 1970-71 में जब अशोक वाजपेयी ने 'पहचान' सीरीज का संपादन-प्रकाशन शुरू किया तो डॉ. लुत्से ने उसमें सम्मिलित सभी नए-पुराने लेखकों को पढ़ा। 1966 के बाद यदि कोई भारतीय लेखक जर्मनी गया है तो हाइडेलबेर्ग के दक्षिण एशिया संस्थान में उसका रचना-पाठ या भाषण जरूर हुआ है। इसी तरह यदि दक्षिण एशिया संस्थान से कोई जर्मन भारतीय भाषाविद् अथवा साहित्यिक भारत आया है तो वह भारतीय लेखकों से बिना मिले जर्मनी नहीं लौटा है।

इस विवरण से पाठक समझ गए होंगे कि हालाँकि प्रस्तुत संकलन **जीवंत साहित्य** 1992-97 के जर्मन-भारतीय सम्मिलित साहित्यिक कार्यक्रमों को समेटता है किंतु ऐसे कार्यक्रम पिछले तीस वर्षों से हो रहे हैं, भले ही वे नियमित न रहे हों, उन्हें कोई औपचारिक नाम न दिया गया हो या उनकी संख्या बहुत बड़ी न हो। अन्य शोध-ग्रंथों के अलावा डॉ. लुत्से हिंदी कविताओं के जर्मन-अनुवादों के दो संग्रह, बांग्ला कविता का एक संग्रह, हिंदी कहानियों का एक संकलन, 'अज्ञेय' की रचनाओं का एक संकलन अनूदित तथा 'नोइए इंडिशे बिब्लियोठेक' (नया भारतीय पुस्तकालय) के नाम से भारतीय

साहित्य के जर्मन अनुवाद की एक पुस्तक-शृंखला संस्थापित-संपादित कर चुके हैं। 1986 का फ्रांकफुर्ट विश्व पुस्तक मेला यदि भारतीय साहित्य पर केंद्रित था तो उसके पीछे लोठार लुत्से, गुंटर ज़ोंठाइमर, प्रो. श्टीटनक्रोन आदि ही प्रेरणा तथा सक्रिय उपस्थिति थी।

1971 में डॉ. लुत्से से संपर्क में आने के बाद हम दोनों के बीच आपसी समझ और दोस्ती इस तरह बनी और विकसित हुई कि 1973 से लेकर आज तक मैं डॉ. लुत्से के ही कारण 'दक्षिण एशिया संस्थान' तथा 'मक्स म्युलर भवन' की गतिविधियों से अनौपचारिक किंतु घनिष्ठ रूप से जुड़ा हुआ हूँ और इसीलिए दिल्ली स्थित दक्षिण एशिया संस्थान की शाखा तथा मक्स म्युलर भवन के पिछले 25 वर्षों के अधिकांश निदेशकों को व्यक्तिगत रूप से जान सका हूँ। अपने स्वल्प जर्मन-ज्ञान के बावजूद जर्मन से अनुवाद करने का मेरा शौक जाता नहीं और इसलिए अक्सर जर्मन लेखकों के भारत आगमन या जर्मन साहित्य की किसी विशेष तिथि पर मुझे अनुवादक के रूप में दोनों संस्थानों में मुझे याद किया जाता है। दिल्ली के हिंदी जगत से जो भी थोड़ा-बहुत मेरा परिचय है उसके चलते मैं हिंदी लेखकों और कुछ अहिंदीभाषी रचनाकारों का सहयोग भी ऐसे कार्यक्रमों में ले पाया हूँ। 1992 के पहले के दो स्मरणीय जर्मन-हिंदी साहित्यिक आदान-प्रदान आयोजनों का उल्लेख यहाँ अनुचित न होगा। 1983 में डॉ. लुत्से द्वारा अनूदित तथा मेरे साथ संपादित सातवें और आठवें दशक की हिंदी कविता के जर्मन संकलन 'डेअर ओक्सेनकरेन' ('बैलगाड़ी', जो मुक्तिबोध की एक कविता से लिया गया रूपक है) का दिल्ली के विमोचन हुआ जिसमें त्रिलोचन, रघुवीर सहाय, प्रयाग शुक्ल, मंगलेश डबराल, विनोद भारद्वाज, सौमित्र मोहन, असद जैदी, गिरधर राठी आदि कवियों ने भाग लिया। फिर 1988 में ग्युंटर ग्रास दिल्ली आए और डॉ. लुत्से और मैंने बहुत फुर्ती से उनके उपन्यास 'डी रैटिन' ('चुहिया') से एक काव्यांश का अनुवाद किया जिसे अंग्रेजी अनुवाद के साथ उनकी उपस्थिति में सुनाया गया। मैं समझता हूँ कि ये दोनों आयोजन ऐतिहासिक थे।

इस संकलन की अपनी छोटी-सी भूमिकाओं में डॉ. लुत्से तथा डॉ. गेओर्ग लेष्नर लिख चुके हैं कि 1992 से जर्मन-भारतीय साहित्यिक आयोजनों को कैसे 'जीवंत साहित्य' या 'लिविंग लिटरेचर' का नाम दिया गया और उसे एक स्थायी कार्यक्रम मान लिया गया। संपादिका श्रीमती बार्बरा लौत्स नाम के 'जीवंत' या 'लिविंग' के औचित्य के बारे में अपनी भूमिका में लिख चुकी हैं तथा सारे प्रासंगिक ब्यौरे दे चुकी हैं। 'जीवंत साहित्य' के कई कार्यक्रमों में मेरी हिस्सेदारी रही है और अन्य में मैं उपस्थित रहा हूँ। दिल्ली के अंतर्राष्ट्रीय सांस्कृतिक आदान-प्रदान कार्यक्रमों का मैं कई वर्षों से गवाह रहा हूँ और मैं कह सकता हूँ कि दिल्ली के अनेक विदेशी संस्थानों द्वारा आयोजित कार्यक्रमों में अव्वल तो साहित्यिक अवसर बहुत कम आते हैं और जो आते भी हैं उनमें भारतीय अंग्रेजी साहित्य का वर्चस्व रहता है और जो भारतीय भाषाओं को केंद्र में रखते भी हैं उनमें 'जीवंत साहित्य' जैसा वैविध्य नहीं रहता—सिर्फ हंगारी सांस्कृतिक केंद्र ही हिंदी को लेकर कुछ सक्रिय रहता है और कुछ गतिविधियों के कारण पूर्व-बुल्गारियाई तथा पूर्व तथा वर्तमान रूसी सांस्कृतिक केंद्र उल्लेखनीय हैं।

'जीवंत साहित्य' या इससे पहले के भारतीय-जर्मन साहित्यिक विनिमय की कई स्मृतियाँ हैं किंतु एक अत्यंत सुखद तथा त्रासद याद है उपन्यासकार यूरेक बेकर की। बेकर उन चमत्कारिक व्यक्तियों में थे जो यहूदी होने के कारण बचपन में पोलैंड के एक नात्सी यातना-शिविर में रखे गए थे किंतु किसी तरह जीवित बच गए थे। उनके ये अनुभव उनके सुप्रसिद्ध उपन्यास 'याकोब डेअर ल्यूग्नर' ('झूठा याकोब') में अमर हैं। बाद में उन्होंने और भी उपन्यास लिखे और टेलीविजन के लिए सार्थक धारावाहिक भी। मेरा उनसे परिचय दिल्ली में 'जीवंत साहित्य' के अंतर्गत उनके रचना-पाठ के कारण ही हुआ और अच्छी मित्रता भी हो गई। 1995 में मैं बर्लिन में उनके घर भी गया और उनकी (दूसरी) पत्नी तथा बहुत छोटे बेटे से भी मिला। बेकर अपने उस नए घर, अपनी पत्नी तथा अपने बेटे के नजदीक के ही एक स्कूल में दाखिले से बहुत खुश थे। टेलीविजन पर अपने धारावाहिक की अपार सफलता पर उन्हें गर्व था। वे रचना-पाठ तथा भाषणादि के लिए विदेश यात्राओं का कार्यक्रम भी बना रहे थे। इसलिए अचानक पिछले वर्ष जब उनकी मृत्यु का समाचार सुना तो विश्वास ही नहीं हुआ। अब कई लोगों से पूछ चुकने और मृत्यु-आलेख पढ़ने के बाद ही यकीन के खिलाफ यकीन हो पाया है कि यूरेक बेकर वाकई नहीं रहे। इसमें सबसे मार्मिक बात यह है कि मुझे बताया गया है कि जब वे भारत आए थे तभी उन्हें मालूम था कि उन्हें असाध्य कैंसर है। लेकिन वे सदा हँसते रहे और किसी को यह बताया नहीं।

मैं नहीं जानता कि यह पुस्तक औपचारिक रूप से किसी को समर्पित की जाएगी या नहीं लेकिन इसमें यत्किंचित् हिस्सा जो मेरा है उसे मैं जीवितों में लोठार लुत्से को और दिवंगतों में अपने मित्र यूरेक बेकर की जीवंत स्मृति को समर्पित करना चाहूँगा।

1997-98 का यह वर्ष भारतीय स्वतंत्रता का पचासवाँ वर्ष है। युद्धोत्तर जर्मनी और स्वातंत्र्योत्तर भारत के संबंध लगातार घनिष्ठ हुए हैं—संसार में तत्कालीन पश्चिम जर्मनी को सबसे पहले मान्यता देनेवाले राष्ट्रों में भारत प्रमुख था। प्रस्तुत संकलन भारत-जर्मन सांस्कृतिक आदान-प्रदान का एक ठोस प्रतीक तो है ही, बहुत आंशिक रूप से ही सही किंतु भारतीय तथा जर्मन साहित्यों की प्रगति तथा वर्तमान स्थिति की एक बानगी भी प्रस्तुत करता है। जर्मन साहित्य विश्व के प्रखरतम वांग्मयों में गिना जाता है और भारतीय साहित्य का वैविध्य तथा सांस्कृतिक-सामाजिक महत्त्व असंदिग्ध है। 'जीवंत साहित्य' जैसे कार्यक्रमों और संकलनों की समृद्ध उपयोगिता शंकातीत है। भारतीय स्वतंत्रता की स्वर्ण-जयंती पर इस बहुभाषीय ग्रंथ का प्रकाशन महाकवि गोएठे के 'वेल्टलिटेराटूअर' (विश्व साहित्य) की अवधारणा को विनम्रता से पुष्ट तथा रेखांकित करता है और भारत-जर्मनी की परस्पर दिलचस्पी की 'मक्स म्युलर परंपरा' की एक छोटी किंतु मजबूत कड़ी है।

दिल्ली, नववर्ष दिवस, 1998

विष्णु खरे

PART I

FROM INDIAN LANGUAGES INTO GERMAN AND ENGLISH

मंजूर एहतेशाम

प्रस्तावना : एक हस्तक्षेप

[उपन्यास *दास्तान-ए-लापता* का एक अंश]

सामान्यतः प्रस्तावना उपन्यास के बिलकुल शुरू में होती है जिसमें लेखक पाठकों से अपने लेखन के बारे में दो शब्द कहता है। प्रायः उस तरह की प्रस्तावनाओं का विषय वह उपन्यास (या लेखन की कोई अन्य विधा) तो रहता ही है लेकिन वह मूल लेखन का अंश नहीं होतीं। जिसका दिल चाहे उन्हें पढ़े, जो चाहे छोड़ दे। दोनों सूरतों में मूल लेखन की सेहत पर कोई अंतर नहीं पड़ता। इस प्रस्तावना को लिखते हुए उस रिवायत का उल्लंघन शायद इसी कारण हुआ है कि यह लेखक की ओर से मूलकथा में बाहरी हस्तक्षेप होते हुए भी, है दरअसल उसी का एक अखंड भाग। अपने लेखकीय दायित्व का निर्वाह करते हुए मैं अपनी बात कुछ और विस्तार के साथ पाठकों के सम्मुख रखना चाहूँगा। अपनी सीमा और सामर्थ्य दोनों को समझते हुए मैं ऐसा करने के लिए खुद को नैतिक रूप से बाध्य पाता हूँ।

सबसे पहले मैं यह स्वीकार करना चाहूँगा कि मेरा यह लेखन एक ऐसा उपन्यास लिखने का (सफल या असफल—यह पाठक पूरा उपन्यास पढ़कर तय करें) प्रयास है जिसके चरित्र, घटनाएँ, यहाँ तक कि काल तक

Manzoor AHTESHAM

VORWORT: EIN EINSCHUB

[Auszug aus dem Roman *Dastan-e-Lapata* (Geschichte eines Verlorenen)]

Normalerweise steht das Vorwort ganz am Anfang eines Romans, und der Autor wendet sich darin mit ein paar Worten an seine Leser. Meistens ist das Thema solcher Vorworte der Roman selbst (oder ein anderer literarischer Text), aber es stellt keinen Teil des eigentlichen Werkes dar. Man kann es lesen, wenn man will, man kann es aber auch überspringen. Beides beläßt die Verfassung des Haupttextes unverändert. Wenn diese Konvention nun außer achtgelassen wurde und das Vorwort an dieser Stelle eingeschoben wird, dann nur, weil es eigentlich ein unverzichtbarer Bestandteil des Textes ist, auch wenn es wie eine Intervention des Autors erscheinen mag. Ich betrachte es als einen Teil meiner schriftstellerischen Aufgabe, meinen Lesern einige Dinge etwas näher zu erläutern. Das Bewußtsein meiner Fähigkeiten und Grenzen verpflichtet mich dazu.

Zuerst möchte ich eingestehen, daß ich mich beim Schreiben dieses Romanes darum bemühte, (ob erfolgreich oder nicht, muß letztlich der Leser entscheiden), Charaktere, Handlung und Zeitraum zu Hundert Prozent imaginär zu gestalten. Es wäre reiner Zufall (oder Pech für den

---

Manzoor AHTESHAM

PREFACE : AN INTERVENTION

[Extract from a novel entitled *Dastan-e-Lapata* (The Tale of The Lost)]

Usually the preface in which the writer has a word with his readers occurs at the very beginning of a novel. The subject-matter of such a prefatorial note is often the novel itself (or some other literary genre) but it does not form part of the body of the work. You may or may not read it. Either way it hardly affects the health of the book. If that tradition has been dispensed with in this case, the reason perhaps is that this apparently outside intervention by the author is in fact an inalienable part of the text. In discharge of my responsibility as a writer, I'd like to put before the reader in so far as I can what needs to be said. That I consider my moral duty.

At the outset I must admit that I have tried to write a novel (successfully or unsuccessfully – it's up to the reader to decide) in which the characters and the incidents, even the time

सौ फ़ीसदी काल्पनिक हैं। यह महज़ एक संयोग (और लेखक का दुर्भाग्य) होगा कि इस उपन्यास में वर्णित विषयवस्तु और चरित्र किसी ज़िंदगी या ज़माने की याद दिलाएँ या उनमें कुछ जाने-पहचाने लोगों और घटनाओं का अक्स दिखाई दे। इसके लिए लेखक किसी भी प्रकार की ज़िम्मेदारी क़बूल करने को बाध्य नहीं। इसी बात को मैं थोड़ा और स्पष्ट करते हुए कहूँ तो उपन्यास का चरित्र—'वह' या 'ज़मीर एहमद ख़ान'—जो है, वह मैं नहीं हूँ। इस बात को मैं इतना ज़ोर देकर इसलिए कह रहा हूँ क्योंकि मैं जानता हूँ कई लोगों को यह स्वीकार करने में आपत्ति हो सकती है। वे लोग भी पूर्णतः ग़लत नहीं होंगे, यह बताना भी मैं खुद अपना ही ज़िम्मा समझता हूँ। क्यों ? क्योंकि जिस काल्पनिक चरित्र और उसकी दुनिया की मैंने यहाँ स्याहो-सफ़ेद में रचना करने की कोशिश की है उसकी धूप-छाँव उन लोगों ने मेरे इर्द-गिर्द फैलती-सिमटती देखी है और उसे मेरे ही व्यक्तित्व का एक हिस्सा समझते रहे हैं। मैं खुद कब-कब और किस-किस को ऐसा करने से मना कर सकता हूँ, ख़ासकर ऐसी परिस्थिति में जबकि अक्सर खुद मुझें भी नहीं पता चलता कि कब मेरी कल्पना यथार्थ पर हावी होकर खुद मुझको एक काल्पनिक अस्तित्व में बदल देती है और मैं एक ऐसे व्यक्ति की तरह साँस लेने, देखने-सुनने और बोलने लगता हूँ जिसने कभी जन्म ही नहीं लिया। स्थिति ख़ासी जटिल इसलिए है कि मुझे सही-सही यह भी नहीं मालूम कि मैं ऐसा खुद अपनी मर्ज़ी से करता हूँ या कोई मजबूरी मुझसे ऐसा कराती है। कारण जो भी हो मगर मुझे ऐसा करने में अगर मिठास मिलती है तो कड़वाहट के मज़े से भी छुटकारा नहीं, पीड़ा होती है तो उसके साथ-साथ आनंद का अनुभव भी, पछतावा हाथ लगता है तो किसी उपलब्धि की अनुभूति भी होती है। आइए, इस काल्पनिक ज़मीर एहमद ख़ान के बारे में कुछ ऐसी बातें आपके सामने रखी जाएँ जो अभी तक के लेखन में पूरी तरह खुलकर सामने नहीं आ पाई हैं। क्योंकि स्वभाव से यह तलघर का आदमी है, इसलिए कुछ बातें तलघर की ही, थोड़े विस्तार से।

Autor), wenn das in diesem Roman behandelte Thema und die Charaktere die Erinnerung an irgendeinen Lebenslauf oder Zeitabschnitt hervorriefe, oder zum Abbild einer bekannten Persönlichkeit oder Begebenheit geriete. Allerdings ist der Autor nicht gehalten, dafür verantwortlich zu zeichnen. Um es etwas klarer auszudrücken: es handelt sich bei der Hauptfigur des Romans, dem *er* oder *Zamir Ahmad Khan*, nicht um mich selbst. Ich sage das deswegen so deutlich, weil ich weiß, daß einige Leute das nicht wahrhaben wollen. Und ich muß gestehen, daß sie damit nicht einmal völlig unrecht haben. Warum? Weil sie meinen, den Charakter, den ich hier in schwarz-weiß entworfen habe, schon um mich herum als Schattenriß mit diffusen Konturen wahrgenommen zu haben und ihn als Teil meiner Persönlichkeit betrachten. Ich kann sie schlecht vom Gegenteil überzeugen, besonders da ich selbst oft nicht gewahr bin, wann meine Phantasie die Oberhand über die Wirklichkeit gewinnt und mich selbst zur imaginären Gestalt macht, und ich wie ein Mensch zu atmen, sprechen, hören und sehen beginne, der nie existiert hat. Komplizierter wird die Sache noch dadurch, daß ich nicht ganz sicher bin, ob dies meiner Willenskraft unterliegt oder eine fremde Macht mich dazu zwingt. Wie auch immer, selbst wenn ich es genieße, dann immer mit einem Hauch süßer Bitterkeit, quält es mich, dann doch gemischt mit Glücksempfinden, suche ich die Distanz, habe ich doch das Gefühl, etwas Wertvolles aufzugeben. Lassen Sie mich Ihnen ein paar Dinge über den imaginären Zamir Ahmad Khan näherbringen, die im bisherigen Textverlauf nicht ausgeführt wurden. Seiner Natur nach ist er ein tiefgründiger Charakter, deswegen seien einige tiefgründigere Worte gestattet.

Gesicht, Größe, Statur und andere Äußerlichkeiten kommen in etwa den meinen nahe. Die imaginäre Stadt Bhopal ist dem wirklichen Bhopal recht ähnlich, und den Zeitraum kann man zwischen dem Ende der vierziger Jahre und dem Ende der achtziger Jahre dieses Jahrhunderts

period, are a hundred per cent imaginary. It will be a mere coincidence (or the writer's sheer bad luck) if the theme or the character described in the novel brings to mind a certain individual and his life, or if someone sees in it shadows of people well known, of events quite familiar. For this, however, the writer is not obliged to accept any responsibility. Let me make it clear that the protagonist of the novel – that 'he' or 'Zameer Ahmad Khan', whoever it is – is not me. I wish to emphasize this because as it is I expect many to disagree.

And they would not be entirely wrong, either – this too, I think, it's my duty to concede. Why? Because the fictional character and his world that I have tried to put in black and white may well be taken for a reflection of my own personality by people who have witnessed a similar play of light and darkness around me. But how many of them can I convince when I myself often do not know when it is that my imagination comes to dominate over the reality, rendering me into somewhat of a fictional character, into someone who begins to breathe, hear, see and speak like a person who never was. The situation is indeed complex, for I am not sure if what I do I do of my own accord or if there is some hidden force that compels me to do it. Be that as it may, but if I savour all this then there will be no escape for me from the pleasure of bitterness, joy will be tinged with pain, a sense of achievement will go hand in hand with regrets. Come, let me tell you at some length what so far has not come through about the fictional Zameer Ahmad Khan because by temperament he is a creature of the underground.

You can presume that his looks, height and built, the way he carries himself, are all similar

सूरत-शक्ल, क़द-काठी और अन्य हाल-चाल उसके आप लगभग मेरे जैसे ही मानकर चल सकते हैं। काल्पनिक शहर भोपाल काफ़ी कुछ वास्तविक शहर भोपाल से मिलता-जुलता एक शहर, और काल बीसवीं सदी की पाँचवीं दहाई के आख़िरी कुछ सालों से लेकर नवीं दहाई के अंतिम वर्षों (सन् 1947 से 1987) से समानता रखता हुआ एक काल। इतना तय करने के बाद बाक़ी चीज़ें समझना कहीं आसान हो जाता है।

ज़मीर एहमद ख़ान दरअसल एक ऐसा चरित्र है जो वास्तविक जीवन में पल-भर को भी मेरे साथ होता तो डॉक्टर तो ख़ैर बड़ी चीज़ होता है मैं उसका इलाज बहुत आसानी से कर सकता था। मेरी मान्यता है कि संसार में हर व्यक्ति अपनी कल्पना के एक ऐसे चरित्र के साथ जीने पर मजबूर होता है जिसकी कल्पना और उस कल्पना को करनेवाले के दरमियान तमीज़ कर पाना कभी-कभी उतना ही मुश्किल साबित हो सकता है जितना सूफ़ी-संतों या पहुँचे हुए लोगों के लिए ईश्वर और अल्लाह के बीच अंतर करना होता होगा। मैं अपने इस चरित्र को खुद का 'लापता' कहता हूँ क्योंकि मेरी खुद की कल्पना का फूल होते हुए भी शायद इसकी खुशबू से सबसे ज्यादा अनजान मैं ही हूँ। कभी-कभी इसके बिलकुल विपरीत यह भी महसूस होता है कि यह 'लापता' कोई और नहीं बिलकुल यक़ीनी मेरा ही हमज़ाद है जो जैसा कि बाक़ी सारी बातों से फिर प्रमाणित होता है, पूरा सच नहीं। सरलीकरण की थोड़ी और कोशिश की जाए तो वास्तव में हम सब अपने एक ऐसे 'लापता' के साथ अपनी ज़िंदगी गुज़ारते हैं, जो 'हम' होते हुए भी 'हम' नहीं होता। एक और दिलचस्प बात यह कि विभिन्न व्यक्तियों के बीच बहुत ही स्पष्ट रूप से नज़र आनेवाली असमानताओं के बावजूद लगता है सबके 'लापता' आपस में एक-दूसरे से बहुत मिलते-जुलते और एकसमान होते हैं और किसी भी 'लापता' को समझना हड्डी-बोटी के इन्सान को समझने की निस्बत कहीं आसान काम है।

तो यह उपन्यास दरअसल 'दास्तान-ए-लापता' है, जिसे दीगर 'लापताओं' से अलग शनाख़्त करने को हम

(von 1947 bis 1987) annehmen. Mit diesen Voraussetzungen wird das weitere Verständnis erleichtert.

Wenn die Person des Zamir Ahmad Khan mir tatsächlich jemals begegnet wäre, hätte ich ihn, ohne daß es dazu eines Arztes bedurft hätte, mit Leichtigkeit selbst kurieren können. Meiner Überzeugung nach muß jeder auf dieser Welt mit einem imaginären Charakter zusammenleben, und den Unterschied zwischen der imaginären Person und ihrem Erschaffer zu benennen mag ebenso schwer fallen, wie die Trennung zwischen Hindugott und Allah für die Sufi-Heiligen oder andere Erleuchtete. Ich selbst nenne diese Person den 'Verlorenen' oder 'Unbekannten', denn obwohl meine eigene Phantasie diese Blüte hervorgebracht hat, bin ich doch vielleicht am wenigsten ihres Duftes gewahr. Manchmal kommt es mir umgekehrt so vor, als sei der 'Verlorene' gar nicht fremd, sondern eine mir sehr nahestehende Person, was jedoch, wie sich anhand einiger Tasachen aufzeigen läßt, auch nicht ganz zutrifft. Schlicht gesagt, verbringen wir alle unser Leben mit einem 'Verlorenen', der wie wir zu sein scheint und es doch nicht ist. Interessant dabei ist, daß sich trotz vieler augenfälliger Unterschiede von einzelnen Menschen ihre 'Verlorenen' untereinander verblüffend ähneln, ja nahezu identisch erscheinen, und es vergleichsweise leichter fällt, diese 'Verlorenen' zu verstehen, als die wirklichen Menschen aus Fleisch und Blut.

So ist dieser Roman die Geschichte eines Verlorenen, den wir, um ihn von anderen zu unterscheiden, Zamir Ahmad Khan, '*Lapata Bhopali*' oder 'den Verlorenen aus Bhopal' nennen wollen, auch deswegen, weil er nicht nur ab und an Erzählungen schreibt und unter ähnlichen Pseudonymen veröffentlicht, sondern auch der Versuchung zum Verseschmieden (was er als Poesie bezeichnet) nicht widerstehen kann.

to mine. The fictional city of Bhopal resembles the real one, and the period corresponds to the years between the fag end of the fifth and of the ninth decades of the 20th century (from 1947 to 1987). This behind us, we can understand the rest of it better.

As a matter of fact Zameer Ahmad Khan is a character I myself, what to say of a physician, could have readily treated for his disorder had I but run into him in real life. I believe every man on earth is fated to live with a persona of his imagination which is as difficult to distinguish from the person who imagined it all as it must be for Sufis and saints to tell Allah from God. I call this persona of mine The Lost, because even though it is a flower of my own creation, I am the least aware of its fragrance. On the contrary, sometimes it seems to me that The Lost is none other than my exact counterpart – my twin, which, as borne out by the rest of the facts, is not really completely true. Were one to oversimplify it, one could say that all of us in truth live our lives with a Lost One who, though a lookalike of 'I', is not 'I'. Another interesting thing is that, despite the obvious differences between man and man, the Lost Ones of all are almost alike so that it is far easier to understand The Lost rather than the man of flesh and blood.

So, this novel is actually the story of The Lost, whom, to give him a separate identity, we can call Zameer Ahmad Khan 'Lapata'* Bhopali, for not only does he occasionally publish stories under different pseudonyms but also he cannot resist the temptation of producing rhyming lines in the name of poetry.

A confession is here called for: I am myself fond of writing poetry. I have at times tried

ज़मीर एहमद ख़ान 'लापता' भोपाली कह सकते हैं। इसलिए भी कि न सिर्फ़ यह वक़्तन-फ़वक़्तन काल्पनिक नामों से कहानियाँ लिखता और छपवाता रहा है, शायरी के नाम पर तुकबंदी के लोभ से भी यह मुक्त नहीं।

यहाँ एक इक़रार करना ज़रूरी है। शायरी करने या कविता लिखने का मोह खुद मुझे भी है। मैंने समय-समय पर अपने शेर कह सकने की क्षमता को आज़माने की कोशिश भी की है और अंततः इस नतीजे पर पहुँचा हूँ कि यह बार इस नातवाँ के बूते का नहीं। अपनी और अपने संसार की सीमाओं को एक बार समझ लेने के बाद मैंने कविता पढ़ने से तो नहीं लिखने से तौबा कर ली। मैंने तो कर ली लेकिन 'लापता' भोपाली को कौन समझाए, वह आज भी वज़न-बेवज़न की चिंता से मुक्त, रदीफ़-काफ़िया-छंद-मीटर की कैद से आज़ाद, तुकबंदी में लगा रहता है, कहीं इस निष्ठा के साथ कि वह सचमुच कवि है। कोई भी अच्छी कविता मुझे जितना सहमाती है और कवियों के लिए मन में आदर-भाव जगाती है, 'लापता' भोपाली को हड़काती और ज़िद पर आमादा करती है। कुछ ऐसी ही स्थिति कहानियाँ लिखने को लेकर है। वह तमाम चरित्र और घटनाएँ जिन्हें मैं सात पर्दों में छिपाकर जीना चाहता हूँ, इसे कहानियाँ लिखने पर उत्तेजित करती हैं।

सही या ग़लत, समस्या 'लापता' भोपाली के साथ यह है कि जितना-जितना मैं ज़िंदगी से प्यार करना चाहता हूँ, उतना ही वह उसके प्रति उदासीन होता जाता है। मैं ज़िंदगी की जिन-जिन घटनाओं को भूलना, नज़रअंदाज़ करना चाहता हूँ, अतीत और भविष्य के बीच कहीं एक 'समझौता एक्सप्रेस' चलाने की कोशिश में, उन्हीं को यह 'लापता' मील के पत्थर मानकर गिनना और हर जगह रुककर सुस्ताना चाहता है। लोग जिनके बग़ैर ज़िन्दगी अच्छी-भली चल रही है, उसे आत्मा के पैवंद नज़र आते हैं। भूलें जो मुझसे हुईं, या ग़लतियाँ और बेईमानियाँ जो मैंने कीं और जिनको देखने या जिनकी गवाही देनेवाला जहान में आज दूसरा कोई मौजूद नहीं और जिन्हें, और तो और, खुद मैं बड़ी हद तक भूलने में कामयाब हो गया हूँ, उसे अपने सिर पे इतना भारी बोझ लगती

Hier muß ich ein Geständnis machen. Seine Lust am Gedichteschreiben und Reimen ist mir nicht ganz fremd. Ich habe mich hin und wieder als Dichter versucht, bin aber schließlich zu der Überzeugung gelangt, daß ein Leichtgewicht wie ich sich nicht mit solchen Lasten überheben sollte. Als ich realisiert hatte, wo meine Grenzen liegen, habe ich zwar nicht der Lektüre von Gedichten, wohl aber dem Verfassen von solchen abgeschworen. Ich möchte betonen, daß es dabei um *mich* geht, denn wer wollte das dem Verlorenen aus Bhopal begreiflich machen, der sich heute noch der Versproduktion hingibt, – gänzlich unbekümmert um Einschränkungen wie Hebung und Senkung, gelöst von den Fesseln von Endreim, Versfuß, Rhythmus und Metrum, im sicheren Gefühl eben, ein geborener Dichter zu sein. Während mich ein gutes Gedicht einschüchtert und sogar so etwas wie Ehrfurcht gegenüber dem Dichter hervorruft, bedeutet es für den Verlorenen aus Bhopal nur eine Herausforderung, auf die er mit hartnäckiger Verbissenheit reagiert. So ähnlich verhält es sich mit Kurzgeschichten: sämtliche Charaktere und Vorfälle, die ich in meinem Leben unter sieben Hüllen verborgen halte, drängen ihn dazu, sie in Geschichten zu exponieren.

Wie dem auch sei, das ganze Problem mit dem Verlorenen aus Bhopal ist, daß er sich in dem Maße zurückzieht, wie ich mich optimistisch dem Leben zuwenden möchte. All die Ereignisse im Leben, die ich am liebsten vergessen oder in den Hintergrund verbannen möchte, die registriert er sorgfältig wie Meilensteine und hält sich an jedem von diesen endlos auf, während er sich bemüht, zwischen Vergangenheit und Zukunft eine Art "Verständigungs-Express" verkehren zu lassen. Leute, ohne die ich gut und gerne auskommen könnte, hat er fest ins Herz geschlossen. Fehler, Versäumnisse oder Grobheiten, die ich mir zuschulde habe kommen lassen, für die es jedoch heute keinen einzigen Zeugen mehr gibt und die ich darüberhinaus weitestgehend erfolgreich verdrängt

my hand at couplets but eventually reached the conclusion that my frail shoulders cannot bear the enormous burden of verse. I gave up writing, though not reading, poems once I knew my limitations. I have learned my lesson alright and said No to versifying but who can make 'Lapata' Bhopali understand: unhampered by subtleties of matter-metre-rhythm, he keeps going blithely on in the unspoken belief that he is a true poet. As much as a good poem inspires me with awe and rouses in me feelings of respect for the poet, it makes a miffed 'Lapata' Bhopali all the more determined. The same applies to stories. All those characters, all the incidents, which I strive to keep under wraps, only provoke him into writing about them in his stories.

Right or wrong, the problem with 'Lapata' Bhopali is that the more I want to reach out to life, the more apathetic he becomes. The incidents which I want to overlook, to put behind me, in an effort to run a *Samjhauta Express*** between my past and the future, he takes each one of them for a milestone to stop by for a rest. People without whom one is better off are stuck as in a patchwork to his soul. The mistakes I made, all my errors of omission and commission, the petty acts of dishonesty I indulged in, which there is no one around today to see or bear witness to, which I have largely succeeded in forgetting, so weigh him down as to make him unsteady on his feet. Indeed, he finds it difficult to walk even a few steps. And so naive is he that he still does not understand what ails him. Casting his helplessness into the mould of a couplet, he says: 'This world is not without its reason / Yet I know not what it is I await'. This is a specimen of his poetry, a verse not off the cuff but concocted

हैं कि ज़मीन पर उसके क़दमों का संतुलन गड़बड़ा दें ! उसका चंद क़दम चलना दूभर कर दें ! और वह खुद इतना मासूम कि अपनी बीमारी का कारण तक न समझ सके। अपनी लाचारी और विवशता को जब वह शेर के साँचे में ढालता है, तो कहता है—'यह दुनिया यूँ ही बेसबब तो नहीं / मगर हमको है जाने क्या इंतज़ार।' यह नमूना है उसकी शायरी का जो मेरे एक कवि-मित्र की ग़ज़ल सुनकर कहा नहीं बल्कि गढ़ा गया है।

दरअसल 'लापता' भोपाली वह दीमक है जो मेरे व्यक्तित्व, देह और आत्मा की रद्दी चाट-चाटकर पला है। उसमें प्यार की जगह पश्चात्ताप क़ंदीलें बनकर रौशन है। उसे 'जो शेष है' में रुचि इसलिए नहीं कि वह तो है ही, 'जो नहीं है' का ग़म इसलिए है कि उसे दोबारा कभी नहीं पाया जा सकता। सादा मुहावरे में कहें तो यह उन लोगों में से एक है जिनकी झोंपड़ी ढाकर अगर पुख़्ता इमारत बना दी जाए तो वह महलों में रहते हुए भी झोंपड़ी के ख़्वाब देखने से बाज़ नहीं आते।

'लापता' ने अपने होने को लेकर खुद एक शेर कहा है—'हस्ती है कि बस्ती है, सीना कि सफ़ीना है /इक दिल है जो मक्का है, इक दर्द मदीना है।'

इसके आगे किसी का कुछ कहना सूरज को चिराग़ दिखाने की मिस्ल लगता है !

[...]

habe, machen ihm den Kopf so schwer, daß es ihm den Boden unter den Füßen wegzieht. Er ist wie gelähmt und unfähig, den kleinsten Schritt zu tun. Und dabei ist er so naiv, daß ihm nicht einmal der Grund für sein Leiden auffällt. Wenn er seine Schwäche und Hilflosigkeit in ein Gedicht verpackt, dann klingt das so: "*Wohl entbehrt die Welt nicht ganz ihres Sinns / doch ich weiß nicht, worauf mein Warten sich richtet*". Das ist eine Kostprobe seiner Dichtkunst, die er als Antwort auf das Gazal eines befreundeten Dichters hervorgebracht, oder besser gesagt, ersonnen hat.

Im Grunde ist der Verlorene aus Bhopal wie eine Termite, die sich am Abfall meines Körpers, meiner Seele und Persönlichkeit gütlich getan hat und dabei prächtig gediehen ist. In ihm brennt nur das Licht der Reue, nicht das der Liebe. Deswegen zeigt er nie Interesse an dem, was geblieben ist, eben weil es ja noch da ist. Im Gegenteil beschäftigt ihn immer das, was *nicht* da ist, aus dem einfachen Grund, daß es unwiederbringlich verloren ist. Mit einem einfachen Beispiel gehört er zu den Leuten, die nach ihrer Umsiedlung aus dem Slum in eine richtige Siedlung nie aufhören, ihrer alten Hütte nachzutrauern, selbst wenn sie inzwischen in einem Palast wohnen. Einmal hat der Verlorene seine Gedanken über sich in Verse gefaßt: "*Einer Massensiedlung gleicht mein Dasein/ einer Barke mein Herz/ meine Seele ist wie Mekka/ wie Medina ist mein Schmerz*". Dem noch etwas hinzuzufügen hieße schon, mit einer Kerze gegen die Sonne antreten zu wollen.

[...]

(*Tr. from Hindi by Barbara Lotz*)

"Verständigungs-Express": Der Samjhauta-Express ("*Samjhauta*" heißt wörtl. Übereinkunft, Kompromiss) ist ein Zug, der seit dem Shimla-Abkommen von 1972 zwischen Pakistan und Indien verkehrt.

on listening to a ghazal of my friend's.

In point of fact, 'Lapata' Bhopali is a white ant feeding on the waste of my being, my soul. In him regrets rather than love burn bright. He is not interested in that which 'remains', for it *is* there; whereas he is saddened by that which is 'no more', because it cannot be regained. In simpler words, he is one of those who, even while living in concrete houses, refuse not to dream of their shacks pulled down to make way for those houses.

'Lapata' has written a couplet about himself: 'My being is a conglomerate of other beings, my ribs a boat / The heart is Mecca and pain Medina.

To say anything more will be like holding a candle to the sun!

[...]

(*Translated from Hindi by Kuldip Singh*)

*Used here as a pen-name, *Lapata* (*La*, without; *pata*, address: 'without an address') has derivative meanings of anonymous, unknown, lost. Throughout the novel, the word resonates with the sense of one's inability to find oneself as well as whom no one else can find: he is both lost to himself and the world.

** Samjhauta Express is the name of the train started between Pakistan and India following the historic Simla Agreement. Literally, *samjhauta* means compromise.

ಯು. ಆರ್. ಅನಂತ ಮೂರ್ತಿ

ಸೂರ್ಯನ ಕುದುರೆ

ಹದಿನಾಲ್ಕು ವರ್ಷಗಳ ನಂತರ ಪೇಟೆಯಲ್ಲಿ ನನಗೆ ಪ್ರತ್ಯಕ್ಷನಾದ ಹಡೆ ವೆಂಕಟನನ್ನು ಕುರಿತು- ಅವನ ನಿಜವಾದ ಹೆಸರು ವೆಂಕಟಕೃಷ್ಣ ಜೋಯಿಸ – ಇದನ್ನು ಬರೆಯುತ್ತಿರುವೆ. ಊರುಬಿಟ್ಟು ಹೋಗಿದ್ದ ನನ್ನ ಗುರುತು ಅವನಿಗೆ ಹತ್ತದಿದ್ದರೂ ಅವನನ್ನು ನಾನು ಮರೆಯುವುದು ಸಾಧ್ಯವೆ? ಭ್ರೂಮಧ್ಯ ಕುಂಕುಮವಿಟ್ಟು, ಕಮಾನು ಕ್ರಾಪು ಬಿಟ್ಟು, ಅಲ್ಲಿ ಇಲ್ಲಿ ಉದುರಿದ ಹಲ್ಲುಗಳಿಂದಾಗಿ ಆರತಿಯಂತಿದ್ದ ದವಡೆಗಳನ್ನು ತೆರೆದು ತೋರಿಸುತ್ತ ನಗುವ ಬಾಯಿಯ ನನ್ನ ಬಾಲ್ಯದ ಸಖ.

ಮಾರ್ಕ್ಸ್ ಹೇಳುವ ವಿಲೇಜ್ ಈಡಿಯಸಿಯ ಇಂಥವರಿಂದಾಗಿಯೇ ಈ ದೇಶ ಏನೂ ಬದಲಾಗದೆ... ಇತ್ಯಾದಿ ಇತ್ಯಾದಿ ಅಂದುಕೊಂಡೆ: ಜಡತ್ವದ ಪರಮ ಸ್ಥಿತಿಯಲ್ಲಿ ಬದುಕುತ್ತಿರುವವರನ್ನೆಲ್ಲ ಸಂಕೇತಿಸುವಂತೆ ವೆಂಕಟ ನನಗೆ ಕಂಡ. ಈ ದೇಶ ಎಂದೂ ಬದಲಾಗುವುದೇ ಇಲ್ಲವೇನೋ ಎಂದು ಈಚೀಚೆಗೆ ಗೆಳೆಯರ ಜೊತೆ ಮಾತನಾಡುವಾಗ ಕಳವಳಪಡುವ ನಾನು ನನ್ನ ಧೋರಣೆಯನ್ನು ಆದಷ್ಟು ಸೀರಿಯಸ್ಸಾಗಿ ವೆಂಕಟನಲ್ಲಿ ನಿವೇದಿಸಿಕೊಳ್ಳಲು ಪ್ರಯತ್ನಿಸಿದೆ. ಅವನೇನು ಕಿವಿಗೊಡುವ ಆಸಾಮಿಯೇ?

‘‘ಮಳೆಯೇ ಬಂದಿಲ್ಲೊ,

ಮುಂದಿನ ಡಿಸೆಂಬರಿನಲ್ಲಿ ಮಾವಿಗೆ ಹೂವು ಕಚ್ಚಿ ಕೊಳ್ಳುವುದೋ ನೋಡಬೇಕೋ,

U.R. ANANTHA MURTHY

EIN PFERD FÜR DIE SONNE

[Auszüge aus der Kurzgeschichte]

Ich schreibe dies über den Nichtsnutz Venkata – sein richtiger Name ist Venkata Krishna Joisa –, der nach vierzehn Jahren eines Tages auf dem Marktplatz plötzlich vor mir auftauchte. Er erkannte mich nicht, ich hatte das Dorf verlassen und war weggezogen, aber wie konnte ich ihn je vergessen? Da stand er also, mein Kumpel aus der Schulzeit, einen Kumkumklecks zwischen den Augenbrauen, sein Kopf ein rasierter Halbmond, mit einem Mund, der beim Lachen offenstand und dem hier und da ein Zahn entfallen war, und einem Unterkiefer, der sich im Kreise drehte wie ein Arti-Teller. Wie konnte ich so einen Venkata vergessen?
[...]
Ich wurde nachdenklich, die dörfliche Verblödung, von der Marx sprach, die der Grund dafür ist, daß dieses Land rückständig bleibt, und so weiter - Venkata schien mir alles zu symbolisieren, was in einem Zustand der Trägheit verharrt. Ich versuchte so ernsthaft wie möglich, Venkata meine

U.R. ANANTHA MURTHY

A HORSE FOR THE SUN*

[Extracts of the short story]

I am writing this about Good-for nothing Venkata – his real name is Venkata Krishna Joisa – who suddenly appeared before me one day in the market place after fourteen years. He didn't recognise me, I had left the village and gone away, but how could I possibly forget him? There he stood, my boyhood chum, a spot of *kumkum* between his eyebrows, his head a shaven crescent, an open-mouthed laugh with teeth fallen off here and there, and a jaw that moved round and round like an *arati* platter. How can I forget such a Venkata?
[...]
I began to think: the village idiocy, that Marx spoke of, which is the cause of this country remaining backward... and so on, Venkata seemed to symbolise everything for me that lived in a state of inertia. I tried as seriously as possible to expound to Venkata my anxieties about

ಹೋದವರ್ಷ ಒಂದು ಮಿಡಿಯೂ ಹತ್ತಲಿಲ್ಲೋ,

ನೋಡು ಆ ಮರದ ತುಂಬ ಗಿಣಿಗಳು ಹಿಂಡುಕಟ್ಟಿ ಬರುವುದುಂಟೊ,

ಅದು ನವಿಲಿನ ಗುಡ್ಡವೊ, ಅಲ್ಲೊಂದು ಗುಹೆಯುಂಟೊ, ಮಕ್ಕಳಿಗೆ ಮದುವೆಯಾದದ್ದೇ ನಾನಲ್ಲಿ ಹೋಗಿ ಇದ್ದು ಬಿಡುವೆನೊ,

ಎಷ್ಟು ಚಂದ ಅಲ್ಲಿಂದ ಸುತ್ತ ನೋಡಲಿಕ್ಕೆ ಅಂತೀಯ? ಪೆನ್‌ಶನನ್ನು ಹೆಂಡತಿಗೆ ಕೊಟ್ಟುಬಿಡುವೆ - ಆಮೇಲೆ ಅಲ್ಲಿದ್ದುಬಿಡುವೆನೊ,''

ಇತ್ಯಾದಿ ವಟಗುಟ್ಟುತ್ತಲೇ ನನ್ನನ್ನು ಕೇಳಿಸಿಕೊಂಡ, ಈ ಬಗೆಯ ವೆಂಕಟನ ಪ್ರತಿಕ್ರಿಯೆಗಳ ನಡುವೆ ನಾನು:

''ರಾಜಕೀಯವೆಂದರೆ ಏನು?

ಜೀವಂತಿಕೆಯ ಲಕ್ಷಣ ಬದಲಾವಣೆ,

ಯಾವ ದಿಕ್ಕಿನಲ್ಲಿ ಬದಲಾವಣೆ? ಉಳ್ಳವರ ದಿಕ್ಕಲ್ಲೋ? ಇರದವರ ದಿಕ್ಕಲ್ಲೋ? ಇದನ್ನು ಮಾಡಲು ಯಾಕೆ ಹಠದ ಅಗತ್ಯವುಂಟು?

ನಮ್ಮ ಆಸೆ ಆಕಾಂಕ್ಷೆಗಳಿಗೆ ತಕ್ಕಂತೆ ಪ್ರಕೃತಿಯನ್ನೂ, ಉಳಿದ ಜನರನ್ನೂ ಬದಲಾಯಿಸಬೇಕೆಂಬ ಹಠವೇ ಎಲ್ಲ ರಾಜಕೀಯದ ಮೂಲದಲ್ಲಿರುವುದು, ವಿಜ್ಞಾನದ ಮೂಲದಲ್ಲಿರುವುದು,

ಧಾರ್ಮಿಕ ಕ್ರಿಯೆಗಳ ಮೂಲದಲ್ಲೂ ಇರುವುದು,

ಅದೂ ಕೂಡ ರಾಜಕಾರಣವೇ - ಶಾಶ್ವತದಲ್ಲಿ ನಡೆಯುವ ರಾಜಕಾರಣ...

ನಿನ್ನ ಹೆಂಡತಿ ನಿನ್ನ ಮಕ್ಕಳು ನೀನು ಯಾವುದನ್ನು ಸರಿಯೆಂದು ತಿಳಿದಿದ್ದಿಯೋ ಆ ದಿಕ್ಕಲ್ಲಿ ನಡೆಯಬೇಕೆಂದು ನೀನು ಇಷ್ಟಪಡುವುದಿಲ್ಲವೆ? ಇರುವುದು ಇದ್ದಂತೆಯೇ ಇರಲಿ ಎಂಬುದೂ ಕೂಡ ರಾಜಕೀಯವೇ,

Besorgnisse über den Stillstand in diesem Land darzulegen, die ich in letzter Zeit mit meinen Freunden geteilt hatte. Aber er ist nicht der Typ, der zuhört.

"Keine Rede von Regen ... Mal sehen, ob der Mangobaum überhaupt blüht im Dezember ...Voriges Jahr lieferte er nicht einen einzigen Mangokeim zum Einlegen ... Sieh mal da, auf dem Baum: Schwärme von Papageien! ... Da ist der Peackock Hill, dort ist eine Höhle: da will ich leben, sobald die Kinder verheiratet sind. ... Hast Du eine Ahnung, wie schön von dort aus alles ringsherum aussieht. ... Meine Rente geb ich meiner Frau - und dann bleib ich dort."

So plapperte er den ganzen Weg, aber auch, was ich sagte, drang zu ihm durch. In den Pausen zwischen Venkatas verschiedenen Entgegnungen sagte ich:

"Politik ist nichts anderes als die Veränderung der Lebensqualität ... Aber Veränderung in welcher Richtung? Hin zu denen, die haben? Oder zu den Habenichtsen? Aber wozu braucht man Entschlossenheit, um sie zu bewirken? ... Die Entschlossenheit, die Natur und die übrige Welt zu verändern, um sie unseren Zielen und Wünschen anzupassen, ist die Grundlage aller Politik. Sie ist auch die Grundlage der Wissenschaft. Sie ist die Wurzel aller religiösen Handlungen. Auch das ist Politik - die Politik des Ewigen ... Möchtest Du nicht, daß deine Frau und Kinder so leben sollten, wie du's für richtig hältst? Zu sagen, daß sich die Dinge nicht ändern sollten, sondern weitergehen wie bisher, ist auch Politik ... Weißt du warum? Veränderung ist der natürliche Gang der Dinge. Ein paar versuchen, ihn zu ihrem eigenen Vorteil aufzuhalten, aber das funktioniert nicht lange ... Alles zerbricht, explodiert, nichts bleibt sich gleich. Deshalb müssen wir uns weiter um eine Ordnung bemühen, die wir für richtig halten. "

Alles das gab ich von mir, während ich weiterging.

"Woraufs ankommt, ist, womit jeder geboren wird."

the stagnation in this country that I had been sharing of late with my friends. But is he the kind who would listen?

"No rains at all.

"Should see this coming December whether the mango tree will blossom at all.

"Last year it didn't yield a single bud-mango for pickles.

"Look, flocks of parrots come to that tree.

"There is Peacock Hill, there's a cave, I'll go live there the moment my children are married...

"Do you know how beautiful everything around looks from there? I'll give my pension to my wife - and then I'll stay there."

He blabbered like this all along the way, yet he heard me through. In the spaces between Venkata's various responses, I said:

"What is politics but changing the quality of life?

"But then, change in which direction? In that of the haves? Or the have-nots? But why does one need determination to bring it about?

"The determination to change nature and the rest of the world to suit our goals and desires, is the foundation of all politics. It is also the foundation of science.

"It is the root of all religious acts. That too is politics - the politics of the eternal...

"Don't you wish that your wife and children should live in the way you think is right? To say that things should not change but go on the way it is, is also politics.

ಯಾಕೆ ಗೊತ್ತ? ಬದಲಾಗೋದು ಪ್ರಕೃತಿಯ ಲಕ್ಷಣ. ಅದನ್ನ ಕೆಲವರು ತಮ್ಮ ಹಿತಕ್ಕಾಗಿ ತಡೆಯೋಕೆ ಪ್ರಯತ್ನಿಸುತ್ತಾರೆ, ಅದು ಹೆಚ್ಚು ಕಾಲ ನಡೆಯಲ್ಲ.

ಎಲ್ಲ ಬಿರಿಯತ್ತೆ, ಸಿಡಿಯತ್ತೆ, ಯಾವುದೂ ಇರುವಂತೇನೊ ಇರಲ್ಲ, ಆದ್ದರಿಂದಲೇನೇ ಒಂದು ನಮಗೆ ಸರೀಂತ ಕಂಡ ಸುವ್ಯವಸ್ಥೆಗಾಗಿ ಪ್ರಯತ್ನಿಸ್ತಾನೇ ಇರಬೇಕು''–

ಹೀಗೆಲ್ಲ ಹೇಳುತ್ತ ನಡೆದೆ.

''ಎಲ್ಲ ಅವರವರ ಜಾಯಮಾನ.''

ಹೀಗೆಂದು ವೆಂಕಟ ಚೀಲವನ್ನು ಕೆಳಗಿಟ್ಟು ಕೈಮುಗಿದು ಆಕಾಶ ನೋಡ್ತ:

''ನಿಮ್ಮಂಥ ಧೀರರಿಗೆ ನಮೋನ್ನಮಃ ಈ ಹಡೇ ವೆಂಕಟನನ್ನ ನಿಮ್ಮ ಪೈಕಿಯವರು ಕ್ಷಮಿಸಿ ಬಿಡಲಿ. ಧೀರರಿಗೆ ತಲೆ ಬಿಸಿಯಾದಾಗ ನನ್ನಂಥವನ ಆಭ್ಯಂಜನದ ಸೇವೆ ಬೇಕೇ ಬೇಕಲ್ಲ.'' ಎಂದು ಬಾಗಿ ತನ್ನೆದುರೊಂದು ತಲೆಯಿದೆಯೆಂದು ನಟಿಸುತ್ತ ಅದನ್ನು ರಪರಪನೆ ತಿಕ್ಕಿದ.

ಈ ತಾಡನ ಕ್ರಿಯೆಯ ನಂತರದ ವಿಧಿಗಳು ನಾನಾ ಬಗೆಯ ಕಂಪನಗಳನ್ನು ಉಂಟುಮಾಡುವ ಉದ್ದೇಶ ಹೊಂದಿದ್ದವು. ವೆಂಕಟನ ಏದುಸಿರಿನ ಮೃದುವಾಗಿ ಕಂಪಿಸುವ ಮಾತುಗಳ ರನ್ನಿಂಗ್ ಕಾಮೆಂಟರಿ ಸಹಿತ ಈ ಕಂಪನಾಕ್ರಿಯೆ ನಡೆದಿತ್ತು. ದೂರದಲ್ಲಿ ನನ್ನ ಬೆನ್ನಿಗಿದ್ದ ಬೆಂಕಿಯಿಂದ ನನ್ನ ಹಿಂಭಾಗ ಕಾದಿತ್ತು. ಈಗ ವೆಂಕಟ ಪ್ರದಕ್ಷಣೆ ಸುತ್ತುತ್ತ ನನ್ನ ತಲೆಯ ಮೇಲೆ ಬೇರೆ ಬೇರೆ ಭಾಗಗಳನ್ನು ಬೆರಳುಗಳ ವೈವಿಧ್ಯಮಯ ಸಂಯೋಜನೆಗಳಿಂದ ಕಚಗುಳಿಯಿಡುತ್ತ. ಚಿವುಟುತ್ತ, ಹಿಂಜುತ್ತ, ಮಿಡಿಯುತ್ತ, ಸವರತ್ತು, ಕೆರೆಯುತ್ತ, ನೂಕುತ್ತ, ಎಳೆಯುತ್ತ ಎಣ್ಣೆಯಿಂದ ಪೂಜಿಸಿದ. ''ಈಗ ನಿನ್ನ ತಲೆಯೇ ನನ್ನ ಜೊತೆ ಮಾತಾಡ್ತಿದೆ''– ಎಂದು ತನ್ನ ತಲೆಗೆ ಸುತ್ತಿದ್ದ ಪಾಣೆಪಂಚೆಯಿಂದ ಬೆವರೊರಸಿಕೊಂಡು ಷಟ್ಚಕ್ರಗಳನ್ನು ಎಬ್ಬಿಸುವ ತೈಲಮರ್ಧನದ ಪೂಜೆಯ ಎರಡನೇ ಹಂತಕ್ಕೆ

Während er das sagte, stellte Venkata seine Tasche hin, legte die Hände zusammen und betete:

"Ich verneige mich, ich verneige mich vor Helden wie dir. Leute wie du mögen diesem Clown Venkata vergeben. Aber wenn euer Kopf so richtig angeheizt ist, dann braucht ihr bestimmt die Dienste von einem wie ich, der euch ein Ölbad verpaßt", und er tat, als massierte er mit Bravour einen imaginären Kopf vor sich.

[...]

"Ich habe gerade mit deinem Kopf gesprochen", sagte er, wischte sich den Schweiß mit dem Handtuch ab und machte sich bereit für die zweite Stufe des Ölmassagen-Ritus. Während ich mich allmählich fragte, ob er zwanzig oder hundert Finger besaß, veränderte sich auch der Rhythmus und Klang seiner fortlaufenden Kommentare entsprechend und nahm die Form eines mantra-ähnlichen Singsangs an. Das klang folgendermaßen:

"Ananthu, Ananthu, du bist jetzt in den Wald eingetreten. In den Wald eingetreten... in den Wald, Baum, Baum, Baum... auf dem Baum... ein Papagei, ein Papagei. Grüner Papagei... zwischen den Blättern, ein grüner, grüner Papagei... ein grüner Papagei mit krummem Schnabel, im krummen Schnabel, im krummen Schnabel eine rote Frucht, rote, rote Frucht...

Es ist kühl unten, am kühlen Ort ein Busch. Vom Busch ein Duft, ein Duft... 's ist wie eine gelbgetönte Kedigeblume. Sieh... sieh... sieh durch den Riß, wie sie sich spaltet - sieh... langes, rauhes, dorniges, grünes Blatt, im Grün weiches Gelb... sanftes Gelb, duftiges, duftiges Gelb... pulvriges, pulvriges Gelb... schlüpfriges Gelb... geheimnisvolles Gelb...

Geh weiter, geh leise... geh sachte, sachte und sieh... dies ist Basari, dies ist Brotfrucht, dies

"Do you know why? To change is the way of nature. Some try to stop it for their benefit, but that doesn't work for long.

"Everything cracks, explodes, nothing remains the same. That is why we have to keep striving towards an order that we think is right."

I walked on, saying these things.

"What counts is what each one is born with."

Saying this, Venkata put the bag down, joined his hands, looked up at the sky and prayed:

"I bow, I bow to heroes like you. Let people like you forgive this Clown Venkata. But then when your head is all heated up, you will certainly need the services of someone like me to give you an oil bath," and he pretended to massage briskly an imaginary head in front of him.

[...]

"I was now talking to your head," he said and wiped off his sweat with the towel and readied himself to commence the second stage of the oil worship. As I wondered whether he had twenty fingers or a hundred, his running commentary appropriately changed its rhythm and melody and took the form of a *mantra*-like chant. It went like this.

"Ananthu, Ananthu, you have now entered the forest. Entered the forest... in the forest, tree, tree, tree... on the tree... a parrot, a parrot. Green parrot... between the leaves, a green, green parrot... a green parrot with a hooked beak, in the hooked beak, in the hooked beak a red fruit, red, red, fruit..."

ಉದ್ಯುಕ್ತನಾದ. ಅವನಿಗಿದ್ದದ್ದು ಇಪ್ಪತ್ತು ಬೆರಳೊ, ನೂರಾರೊ ಎಂದು ನನಗಚ್ಚರಿಯಾಗುತ್ತಿದ್ದಂತೆ ಅವನ ರನ್ನಿಂಗ್ ಕಾಮೆಂಟರಿ ಮಂತ್ರದ ಉದ್ದೀಪನವನ್ನು ತನ್ನ ಲಯಬದ್ಧ ರಾಗದಲ್ಲಿ ಅಗತ್ಯಕ್ಕನುಗುಣವಾಗಿ ಬದಲಾಗುತ್ತ ಪಡೆದುಕೊಂಡಿತು–ಈ ಪರಿಯಲ್ಲಿ:

"ಅನಂತು ಅನಂತು ಇದೀಗ ಕಾಡುಹೊಕ್ಕಿ, ಕಾಡುಹೊಕ್ಕಿ... ಕಾಡಲ್ಲಿ ಮರ, ಮರ, ಮರ... ಮರದ ಮೇಲೆ ಗಿಣಿ, ಗಿಣಿ, ಹಸಿರು ಗಿಣಿ... ಎಲೆಗಳು ನಡುವೆ ಹಸಿರು ಹಸಿರು ಗಿಣಿ... ಹಸಿರು ಗಿಣಿಗೆ ಬಾಗಿದ ಕೊಕ್ಕು. ಬಾಗಿದ ಕೊಕ್ಕಲ್ಲಿ ಕೆಂಪು ಹಣ್ಣು, ಕೆಂಪು, ಕೆಂಪು, ಹಣ್ಣು...

ಕೆಳಗೆ ತಂಪು, ತಂಪು. ತಂಪಿನಲ್ಲೊಂದು ಮೊಟ್ಟು. ಮೊಟ್ಟೆನಿಂದ ಘಮಘಮ... ಅದು ಹಳದಿ ಬಣ್ಣದ ಕೇದಿಗೆ. ನೋಡು... ನೋಡು... ಸಂದಿಂದ ನೋಡು. ಹೇಗೆ ಬಿರೀತಿದೆ–ನೋಡು... ಒರಟಾದ ಉದ್ದನೋಯ ಮುಳ್ಳಂಚಿನ ಹಸಿರೆಲೆ, ಹಸಿರಿನ ಒಳಗೆ ಮೃದುವಾದ ಹಳದಿ... ನುಣುಪಾದ ಹಳದಿ, ಘಮಘಮ ಹಳದಿ...ಪುಡಿ ಪುಡಿ ಹಳದಿ...ಜಾರೋ ಹಳದಿ...ಗುಟ್ಟಾದ ಹಳದಿ...

ಮುಂದೆ ನಡಿ ಮೆತ್ತಗೆ ನಡಿ...ಮೆಲ್ಲ ಮೆಲ್ಲ ನಡೀತ ನೋಡು...

ಇದು ಬಸರಿ, ಇದು ಹಲಸು, ಇದು ನಂದಿ, ಇದು ಮುತ್ತುಗ, ಇದು ಮಾವು, ಇದು ಆಲ, ಇದು ರಂಜ, ಆಲದ ಬೀಳು ನೋಡು, ಬೀಳಿನ ತುದಿ ನೋಡು... ತುದೀಲಿ ಅದಕ್ಕೆ ಊಗುರಿದೆ... ಇದು ಖುಷಿಯೋ–ಜಡೆ ಬಿಟ್ಟ ಖುಷಿ...

ಇಲ್ಲೆಲ್ಲ ಆಕಾಶ ಚೂರು ಚೂರಾದ ನೀಲಿ. ಹಣುಕೋ ನೀಲಿ, ಕೆಣಕೋ ನೀಲಿ, ಕಿರಿಕಿರಿ ನೀಲಿ, ಪಿರಿಪಿರಿ ನೀಲಿ. ಮುಂದೆ ನಡಿ. ಮೆತ್ತಗೆ ನಡಿ. ಮುಂದೆ ನಡಿ... ನಿಲ್ಲು... ಈಗ ಬಯಲು. ಬಯಲೋ ಬಯಲು. ಬಟ್ಟಂಬಯಲು, ನೋಡು...

ಎದುರೊಂದು ಪುಟ್ಟ ಗಿಡ. ಗಿಡದ ಮೇಲೊಂದು ಎಲೆ, ಎಲೆ ಮೇಲೊಂದು ಚಂಗನೆ ನೆಗೀತಿದೆ. ಚಂಗನೆ ನೇಗೀತಿದೆ...ಪುಟೀತಿದೆ....ಹೀಗೇ...ಹೀಗೆ ಯಾವತ್ತೋ ಒಂದು ದಿನ ನೀನು ಸ್ಕೂಲಿಗೆ ಬರ್‍ತಿದ್ದಾಗ ಅದು ನೆಗೆದಿತ್ತು–ಅಲ್ವ? ನೀನು ಚೀಲಾನ್ನ ಬಿಸಾಕಿ ನೋಡ್ತಾ ನಿಂತಿ, ನೋಡ್ತಾ ನಿಂತಿ. ನೋಡ್ತಾನೇ...

ಸೂರ್ಯನ ಕುದುರೇನ ನೋಡ್ತಾ ನಿಂತಿ. ಅದರ ಡೊಂಕು ಕಾಲನ್ನು ನೋಡ್ತಾ ನಿಂತಿ. ಅದರ ಡುಬ್ಬು ಬೆನ್ನನ್ನು ನೋಡ್ತಾ

Nandi, dies Muthaga, dies Banyan, dies Ranja. Sieh dir die Wurzel des Banyanbaums an... sieh dir das Ende der Wurzel an... sie hat Nägel an den Enden... Dies ist ein Weiser, ein Weiser mit verflochtenem Haar...

Überall hier ist der Himmel zersplittert, blau zersplittert. Lauerndes Blau, aufreizendes Blau. Schmerzendes Blau, stechendes Blau. Geh weiter. Geh weiter... halt... jetzt offener Raum. Offener offener Raum, weit offener Raum, sieh...

Vor dir eine winzige Pflanze. An der Pflanze ein Blatt, auf dem Blatt ist etwas, das springt und hüpft. Springt und hüpft, springt und hüpft... zerspringt, so wie hier.

... so wie hier sprang's eines Tages, vor langer langer Zeit, als du aus der Schule kamst - nicht? Du warfst deine Tasche weg, bliebst stehen und sahst zu. Standst und sahst zu. Sahst zu...

Du standst und sahst dem Sonnenpferd zu. Du standst und sahst seinen gekrümmten Beinen zu. Du standst und sahst seinem buckligen Rücken zu. Du standst und sahst seinen kreisenden Fühlern zu. Hier, dann dort. Hier, dann dort. Dort. Dort... ohoho, dann hier...

Winziges Pferd, winzigkleines Pferd...Du standst und sahst zu und fragtest dich, wie die Sonne auf seinem Rücken reiten mag...

O wie die Sonne reitet auf dem Grün - sie ist der Reiter... dies das winzige Pferdchen. Winzigkleines grünes Pferd. Pferd, das leichthin springt und fliegt: Auf seinem buckligen Rücken saß leicht die große Sonne, saß sanft, saß leicht, saß ungesehn, saß blitzend zwischen den Rissen...

Sieh, wo sie blitzt. Sie blitzt auf dem Dach. Sie blitzt auf dem Grün. Sie blitzt in der Pupille des Auges, sie blitzt am Rand der Wolke. Sie donnert und rollt. Sie gleitet im Wasser. Sie gleitet fällt zersplittert. Sie war ganz, doch nun zerbricht sie in tausend Splitter. Sie wird Schatten, sie wird

"It's cool below, cool, in the cool place a bush. From the bush a fragrance, a fragrance... it's a yellow-hued *kedige*. Look.... look... look through the crack, how it is splitting - look... long, rough, thorny, green leaf, inside the green soft yellow... gentle yellow, fragrant, fragrant yellow... powdery, powdery yellow... slippery yellow... mysterious yellow..."

"Walk on, gently walk... walk softly, softly and look... this is *basari*, this is jack fruit, this *nandi*, this *muthaga*, this banyan, this *ranja*. Look at the root of the banyan... look at the tip of the roots... it has nails at the tips... This is a sage, a sage with matted hair..."

"All over here the sky is splintered, splintered blue. Lurking blue, provoking blue. Irritating blue, exasperating blue. Walk on. Walk on... stop... now an open space. An open open space, a wide open space, look..."

"In front of you a tiny plant. On the plant a leaf, on the leaf something is springing and leaping. Springing and leaping, springing and leaping... bursting... like this."

"... like this one day, long long ago, as you were coming from school it sprang - didn't it? You threw away your bag and stood watching. Stood watching. Watching..."

"You stood watching the sun's horse. You stood watching its crooked legs. You stood watching his humped back. You stood watching his whirling whiskers. Here, then there. Here, then there. There. There... ohohoh then here..."

"Tiny horse, teeny horse... You stood watching wondering how the sun rides on its back..."

"On the green, oh how the sun rides - he's the rider... this the little horse. Teeny green horse. Horse who springs lightly and flies. On its humped back the big sun lightly sat, gently

ನಿಂತಿ. ಅತ್ತ, ಮತ್ತಿತ್ತ, ಅತ್ತ, ಮತ್ತಿತ್ತ, ಅತ್ತ, ಅತ್ತ... ಅರರೆ ಮತ್ತಿತ್ತ...

ಪುಟ್ಟ ಕುದುರೆ, ಪುಟಾಣಿ ಕುದುರೆ...ಹೇಗೆ ಸೂರ್ಯ ಅದರ ಬೆನ್ನ ಮೇಲೆ ಸವಾರಿ ಮಾಡ್ತಾನಲ್ಲಾಂತಾ ನೋಡ್ತಾ ನಿಂತಿ...

ಹಸಿರಿನ ಮೇಲೆ ಸೂರ್ಯ ಸವಾರಿ ಮಾಡ್ತಾನೋ-ಸರದಾರ ಅವ... ಇದು ಪುಟ್ಟ ಕುದುರೆ. ಹಸೀರು ಬಣ್ಣದ ಪುಟಾಣಿ ಕುದುರೆ. ಚಂಗನೆ ಹಗುರಾಗಿ ಹಾರೋ ಕುದುರೆ. ಅದರ ಡುಬ್ಬು ಬೆನ್ನಿನ ಮೇಲೆ ದೊಡ್ಡ ಸೂರ್ಯ ಈಟೀಟು ಕೊತ, ಈಟೀಟು ಕೂತ, ಹಗುರಾಗಿ ಕೂತ, ಕಾರಣದಂತೆ ಕೂತ, ಸಂದೀಲಿ ಮಿಂಚುತಾ ಕೂತ...

ಎಲ್ಲಿ ಎಲ್ಲಿ ಮಿಂಚುತಾನೆ ನೋಡು. ಚುಂಚದಲ್ಲಿ ಮಿಂಚುತಾನೆ. ಹಸಿರಿನ ಮೇಲೆ ಮಿಂಚುತಾನೆ, ಕಣ್ಣು ಪಾಪೇಲಿ ಮಿಂಚುತಾನೆ, ಮೋಡದ ಅಂಚಿಂದ ಮಿಂಚುತಾನೆ. ಬುಡು ಬುಡೂ ಉರುಳುತಾನೆ. ಹರಿಯೋ ನೀರಲ್ಲಿ ಜಾರುತಾನೆ. ಜಾರಿಬಿದ್ದು ಒಡೀತಾನೆ. ಇಡಿ ಇದ್ದವನ್ನು ಬಿಡಿ ಬಿಡಿಯಾಗುತ್ತಾನೆ. ನೆರಳಾಗ್ತಾನೆ. ಬಣ್ಣವಾಗ್ತಾನೆ. ಕತ್ತಲಾಗ್ತಾನೆ. ಉಷೆಯಾಗ್ತಾನೆ. ಸುರೀತಾನೆ...

ನೋಡು ಈಗ ಬರೀ ಬಯಲು. ಬಟ್ಟಂಬಯಲು. ಮೇಲೆ ಸುರೀತಿರೋ ಸೂರ್ಯ. ಅವನ್ನ ಹಗುರಾಗಿ ಹೊತ್ಕೊಂಡು ನೆಗೀತ, ನೆಗೀತ ಇರೋದು ಬಯಲಲ್ಲಿ ಇದೊಂದು ಸೂರ್ಯನ ಕುದುರೆ ಮಾತ್ರ. ಜೀನಿಲ್ಲದ ಅದರ ಜರ್ಬು ನೋಡು. ಅಂಕೂ ಡೊಂಕೂ ಕಾಲು ನೋಡು... ಸೆಟುಕೊಂಡು ಇರೋ ಬಾಲ ನೋಡು... ದೇಶ ಹುಡುಕೋ ಮೀಸೆ ನೋಡು.

ಎಲೇಂದ ಎಲೇಗೆ ನೆಗೀತ ಇದೆ. ಇಡೀ ನೋಡು, ಬಿಡಿಬಿಡಿಯಾಗಿ ನೋಡು. ಹಸಿರಿನ ರಾಶೀಲಿ ಕೆನೆಯಾದ ಹಸಿರು. ಕಣ್ಣೂ ಹಸಿರು. ಹೇಳ್ತಿದೆ ಕೇಳು. ಸೂರ್ಯನ ಕುದುರೆ ಹೇಳ್ತಿದೆ ಕೇಳು:

ನಾನೇನು ಕುದುರೆ, ನೀನ್ಯಾವ ಮನುಷ್ಯ. ನಾನೂ ನೀನೂ ಅದಲೂ ಬದಲೂ.

ಅನಂತಣ್ಣ, ಅನಂತಣ್ಣ, ಚಂಗನೆ ಹಾರೋ ಅನಂತಣ್ಣ. ಸೂರ್ಯನ್ನ ಹೊರೋ ಅನಂತಣ್ಣ.

ಈಗ ಬಿಡ್ತು, ಬಿಡ್ತು ಬಿಡ್ತು, ಸಿಟ್ಟು ಬಿಡ್ತು, ಸಿಡುಕು ಬಿಡ್ತು. ಗರ್ವ ಬಿಡ್ತು. ರಾವು ಬಿಡ್ತು. ದುಡ್ಡಿನ ಮೇಲಿನ ಮೋಹ ಬಿಡ್ತು. ಹೆಸರಿನ ಮೇಲಿನ ಜರ್ಬು ಬಿಡ್ತು. ಎಲ್ಲಾ ಬಿಡ್ತು. ಎಲ್ಲಾ ಬಿಡ್ತು...

Farbe, sie wird Nacht, sie wird Licht. Sie gleitet, sie schimmert...

Sieh nun, offener Raum. Weit offener Raum. Obendrüber ergießt sich die Sonne. Und in all diesem offenen Raum ist nur dieses Sonnenpferd: leicht trägt es die Sonne auf dem Rücken und springt und hüpft und springt und hüpft herum. Sieh seinen ungeschirrten Rücken, seinen ungezügelten Stolz. Sieh seine gekrümmten Beine... sieh seinen aufgerichteten Schwanz... Sieh seine Fühler die Welt erkunden.

Er springt von Blatt zu Blatt. Sieh es ganz. Sieh's Stück für Stück. Sahniges Grün auf gehäuftem Grün. Selbst die Augen sind grün. Hör, was es zu sagen hat. Hör, was das Sonnenpferd zu sagen hat.

Was für ein Pferd bin ich, was für ein Mensch bist du. Du bist ich, und ich bin du.

Ananthanna, Ananthanna, springender, hüpfender Ananthanna. Ananthanna trägt die Sonne auf seinem Rücken.

Jetzt ist's weg. Weg weg weg. Ärger ist weg. Hochmut weg. Wut ist weg. Feuer weg. Geldgier weg. Eitelkeit weg. Alles ist weg.

Aller böser Zauber ist weg - Vaterzauber, Mutterzauber, Ministerzauber, Magierzauber, Hurenzauber, Witwenzauber, Grabeszauber, Zauber des Mutterleibs, alter Zauber, gebrochener Zauber, Zauber aller Bücher, die du gelesen hast - er ist weg weg weg. Aller böser Zauber ist weg.

Nur das Sonnenpferd bleibt. Du bist das Pferd, du bist das Pferd..."

[...]

Als ich im Garten ein Geräusch hörte, stand ich auf und ging draußen nachsehen - es hörte sich an, wie wenn jemand Bäume fällt. "Wer ist das?" sagte ich und begann die Stufen hinabzusteigen. "Wenn du näher kommst, leg ich dich um", rief Subba mit erhobenem Messer in der diesigen

sat, sat lightly, sat unseen, sat flashing between the cracks..."

"Look where he flashes. He flashes on the roof. He flashes on the green. He flashes in the pupil of the eye, he flashes in the fringe of the cloud. He thunders and rolls. He glides in the water. He glides, falls and shatters. He was whole but now he breaks into a thousand splinters. He becomes the shadow, he becomes the hue, he becomes the night, he becomes the light. He glides, he shimmers..."

"Look, now an open space. A wide open space. Up above, the sun pouring down. And in all this open space, there's only this sun's horse, lightly carrying the sun on his back and springing and leaping and springing and leaping around. Look at his unharnessed back, his unbridled pride. Look at his crooked legs... Look at his erect tail... Look at how his whiskers explore the world."

"It's leaping from leaf to leaf. Look at it whole. Look at it piece by piece. Cream of green on a pile of green. Even the eyes are green. Listen to what the sun's horse has to say."

"What kind of horse am I, what kind of a man are you. You are me and I am you."

"Ananthanna, Ananthanna, springing leaping Ananthanna. Ananthanna carrying the sun on his back."

"Now it's gone. It's gone, it's gone, it's gone. Anger's gone, arrogance's gone. Fury's gone. Fire's gone. Love of money's gone. Pride of name's gone. Everything's gone.

All the evil spells have gone - father's spell, mother's spell, minister's spell, magician's spell, whore's spell, widow's spell, tomb's spell, womb's spell, old spell, broken spell, spell of all the

ಅಪ್ಪನ ದೃಷ್ಟಿ ಅಮ್ಮನ ದೃಷ್ಟಿ ಮಂತ್ರಿ ದೃಷ್ಟಿ ತಂತ್ರಿ ದೃಷ್ಟಿ ಸೂಳೇ ದೃಷ್ಟಿ ರಂಡೇ ದೃಷ್ಟಿ ಮುಂಡೇ ದೃಷ್ಟಿ ಸುಡುಗಾಡು ದೃಷ್ಟಿ ಯೋನಿ ದೃಷ್ಟಿ ಓಣಿ ದೃಷ್ಟಿ ಹರಕಲು ದೃಷ್ಟಿ ಮುರುಕಲು ದೃಷ್ಟಿ ಓದೋ ಎಲ್ಲಾ ಪುಸ್ತಕದ ದೃಷ್ಟಿ ಬಿಡ್ತು ಬಿಡ್ತು ದೃಷ್ಟಿ ಬಿಡ್ತು.

ಉಳಿದದ್ದೊಂದೇ ಸೂರ್ಯನ ಕುದುರೆ. ನೀನೇ ಕುದುರೆ ನೀನೇ ಕುದುರೆ...''

[...]

ತೋಟದಲ್ಲಿ ಏನೋ ಸದ್ದಾಗುತ್ತಿದೆಯೆಂದು ನಾನು ಹೊರಗೆದ್ದು ಹೋದರೆ, ಅದು ಮರವನ್ನು ಕಡಿಯುವ ಶಬ್ದ. 'ಯಾರು' ಎನ್ನುತ್ತ ಇನ್ನೇನು ನಾನು ಮೆಟ್ಟಲಿಳಿಯಬೇಕು – ಆಗ ಸುಬ್ಬ ಕತ್ತಿಯನ್ನೆತ್ತಿ ''ಹತ್ರ ಬಂದ್ರೆ ಕಡಿದುಬಿಡ್ತೀನಿ'' ಎಂದು ಮಸಕು ಮಸಕು ಬೆಳಕಲ್ಲಿ ಕೂಗಿದ. ನಾನು ಕದಲದೆ ನಿಂತೆ. ಉಷಸ್ಸಿನ ಮಂದ ಬೆಳಕಲ್ಲಿ ಪಾರಿಜಾತ ಮರವನ್ನು ಹಲ್ಲು ಕಚ್ಚಿ ಕಡಿಯುತ್ತಿದ್ದ ಅವನು ಕೆದರಿದ ಕೂದಲಲ್ಲಿ ನನಗೆ ರಾಕ್ಷಸನಂತೆಯೇ ಕಂಡ. ಮೃದುವಾದ ಕಾಂಡದ ಹೂವಿನ ಗಿಡಗಳನ್ನೆಲ್ಲ ಅವನು ಈಗಾಗಲೇ ನೆಲಸಮ ಮಾಡಿದ್ದ. ಒರಟಾದ, ವಕ್ರವಾದ, ಪಾರಿಜಾತದ ಮರ ಮಾತ್ರ ಸುಬ್ಬನ ಕತ್ತಿಯ ಏಟಿನ ಗುರಿ ತಪ್ಪಿಸುತ್ತ ಇನ್ನೂ ನಿಂತಿತ್ತು. ನನ್ನ ಹಿಂದೆ ಬಂದ ವೆಂಕಟ ಸುಬ್ಬನಿದ್ದಲ್ಲಿಗೆ ಓಡಿಹೋದ. ಸುಬ್ಬ ಅಪ್ಪನನ್ನು ಕಡಿಯಲೆಂದು ಹೇಗೆ ಕತ್ತಿ ಎತ್ತಿದನೆಂದರೆ, 'ಅಮ್ಮ ತಾಯಿ' ಎನ್ನುತ್ತ ವೆಂಕಟ ಚಂಗನೆ ಪಕ್ಕಕ್ಕೆ ಹಾರಿ, ಹಿಂದೆಯೋಡಿ ಬಂದ. ನಾನು ತಡೆದರೂ ಕೇಳದೆ ರುಕ್ಕು ನನ್ನ ತೆಕೆಯಲ್ಲಿ ಒದರಾಡಿದಳು. ''ಕಡಿದು ಬಿಡೋ ಕಡಿದು ಬಿಡು. ನನ್ನನ್ನು ಕಡಿದು ಹಾಕಿಬಿಡು. ನನ್ನ ಹೊಟ್ಟೇಲೇ ಹುಟ್ಟಿದ ವಿಷಾನ್ನ ನಾನೇ ಕುಡಿದು ಸತ್ತುಬಿಡ್ತೀನಿ'' ಎನ್ನುತ್ತ ತಾಯಿ ಕೊಸರಿಕೊಂಡು ಮಕ್ಕಳು ತಡೆದರೂ ಕೇಳದೆ ಸುಬ್ಬನ ಎದುರು ಓಡಿಹೋಗಿ ನಿಂತಳು. ''ಬೇಡ, ಬೇಡ. ನನ್ನ ಕೆಣಕಬೇಡ, ನಿನ್ನ ತಲೆ ಕಡಿದು ಬಿಡ್ತೀನಿ'' ಎಂದು ಸುಬ್ಬ ಕತ್ತಿಯನ್ನೆತ್ತಿದ. ನಾವೆಲ್ಲರೂ ಕಣ್ಣು ಮುಚ್ಚಿ ನಿಂತುಬಿಟ್ಟೆವು. ನಾನು ಭಯದಿಂದ ಕಣ್ಣು ತೆರೆದಾಗ, ಸುಬ್ಬ ಶಪಿಸುತ್ತ, ಕತ್ತಿ ಹಿಡಿದು ಕೈಬೀಸಿಕೊಂಡು ಉಣುಗೋಲು ದಾಟಿ ಹೊರಗೆ ಹೋಗುತ್ತಿದ್ದ. ಬಿರಬಿರನೆ ನಡೆಯುತ್ತ ಎದುರಿನ ಪೇಟೆಗೆ ಹೋಗುವ ದಾರಿಯಲ್ಲಿ ಕಣ್ಮರೆಯಾದ. ಕಣ್ಣು

Dunkelheit. Ich erstarrte. Im trüben Morgenlicht hackte Subba den Parijathabaum um, mit zusammengebissenen Zähnen und fliegenden Haaren. Er sah wie ein Dämon aus. Alle zarteren blühenden Pflanzen hatte er schon umgemäht. Nur der knorrige und verwachsene Parijathabaum widerstand den Hieben seiner Sichel und stand noch an seinem Platz. Venkata, der hinter mir herkam, rannte zu Subba hin. Als Subba das Messer hob, um seinen Vater niederzustechen, sprang Venkata mit dem Schrei "Amma!" zur Seite und kam zurückgerannt. Obwohl ich versuchte, Rukku, die neben mir stand, zurückzuhalten, brach es aus ihr heraus: "Stich mich nieder, stich mich nieder. Zerstückel mich. Ich will das Gift trinken, das aus meinem Schoß stammt, und sterben." Sie riß sich von ihren Töchtern los, die versucht hatten, sie festzuhalten, und stellte sich vor Subba. "Bleib weg, bleib weg. Reiz mich nicht. Ich schlag dir den Schädel kaputt", brüllte Subba und hob das Messer. Alle standen wir still, mit geschlossenen Augen. Als ich verängstigt die Augen öffnete, war Subba über die Steige geklettert und entfernte sich mit dem Messer in der Hand, fluchend. Mit eiligen Schritten verschwand er in der Straße, die zum Marktplatz führte. Rukku stand unbeweglich und hatte die Augen geschlossen, als erwartete sie zu hören, wie das Messer herunterfiel. Venkata zog sie an der Hand und nahm sie mit hinein. Als die Schwestern sahen, wie Ganga beim Anblick ihres verwüsteten Gartens weinte, weinten sie mit. Ich saß benommen auf der Lehmbank. In mir waren keine Trostworte mehr übrig. Ich meinte, Venkata müßte durch alles, was geschehen war, gebrochen sein. Aber am Morgen erwartete mich eine Überraschung.

Ganz gleich, wer stirbt, ganz gleich, wie lieb und teuer einem die Person - das Leben mit seiner alltäglichen Routine geht weiter, nicht wahr? Sogar in Venkatas Haus, das aussah, als hätte es einen Tod in der Familie gegeben, bereitete Shakuntala den Morgenkaffee. Ich bürstete mir die Zähne mit Reisschalenasche. Venkata beendete sein Bad und setzte sich hin, um die

books you've read, it's gone, it's gone, it's gone. All the evil spells are gone.
Only the sun's horse remains. You are the horse, you are the horse..."

[...]

Hearing some noise in the garden I got up and went out to see - it was the sound of trees being felled. "Who's it?" I said and started to go down the steps. "If you come near, I'll chop you down," cried out Subba with a knife raised, in the haze of darkness. I froze. In the dim light of day break, Subba was hacking down the *parijatha* tree with his teeth clenched and hair flying. He looked like a demon. All the softer flowering plants had already been felled by him. Only the knotted and twisted *parijatha* tree withstood the strokes of his sickle and still stood in its place. Venkata who came behind me ran up to Subba. When Subba raised the knife to hack down his father, Venkata sprang to the side crying "*Amma*, mother!" and came running back. Although I tried to restrain her, Rukku blurted out by my side. "Cut me down, cut me down. Hack me. I'll drink the poison that was born in my womb and die." She broke free of her daughters who were trying to hold her back and ran and stood in front of Subba. "Don't, don't. Don't provoke me. I'll split your head open," cried out Subba raising the knife. All of us stood still with our eyes closed. When I fearfully opened my eyes, Subba had crossed the stile and was walking away with the knife in his hand, cursing. Walking swiftly, he disappeared down the road that led to the market place. Rukku stood still with her eyes closed, as if waiting for the knife to fall. Venkata dragged her by her hand and took her in. Seeing Ganga weep at the sight of her ravaged garden, her sisters wept with her. I sat stunned

ಮುಚ್ಚಿ ನಿಂತಿದ್ದ ರುಕ್ಕು ಕತ್ತಿ ಬೀಳುವುದಕ್ಕೆ ಕಾದು ಹಾಗೇ ನಿಂತಿದ್ದಳು. ವೆಂಕಟ ಅವಳ ಕೈ ಹಿಡಿದು ತಳ್ಳುತ್ತ ಒಳಗೆ ಕರಕೊಂಡು ಹೋದ. ಗಂಗೆ ನಿರ್ನಾಮವಾದ ತನ್ನ ತೋಟ ನೋಡುತ್ತ ಅಳುವುದನ್ನು ಕಂಡು ಇಬ್ಬರು ಅಕ್ಕಂದಿರೂ ಅತ್ತರು. ನಾನು ಮಣ್ಣಿನ ಚಿಟ್ಟೆ ಮೇಲೆ ಕಂಗಾಲಾಗಿ ಕೂತಿದ್ದೆ. ನನ್ನಲ್ಲಿ ಯಾವ ಸಾಂತ್ವನದ ಮಾತುಗಳೂ ಉಳಿದಿರಲಿಲ್ಲ. ಆದರೆ ವೆಂಕಟ ಇದರಿಂದೆಲ್ಲ ಜರ್ಜರಿತನಾಗಿ ಬಿಡಬಹುದೆಂದು ತಿಳಿದ ನನಗೆ ಇನ್ನೊಂದು ಆಶ್ಚರ್ಯಕಾದಿತ್ತು. ಬೆಳಗಾವ ಮೇಲೆ.

ಎಷ್ಟು ಹತ್ತಿರದ ಯಾರೇ ಸಾಯಲ್ಲಿ, ನಿತ್ಯದ ವಿಧಿಗಳೆಲ್ಲಿ ಹೇಗೂ ನಡೆದುಕೊಂಡು ಹೋಗುತ್ತವೆ. ಅಲ್ಲವೇ? ಯಾರೋ ಸತ್ತಂತೆ ಅನ್ನಿಸುತ್ತಿದ್ದ ವೆಂಕಟನ ಮನೆಯಲ್ಲೂ ಬೆಳಿಗ್ಗೆ, ಶಕುಂತಳ ಕಾಫಿ ಮಾಡಿದಳು; ನಾನು ಉಮಿಕರಿಯಲ್ಲಿ ಹಲ್ಲುಜ್ಜಿದೆ; ವೆಂಕಟ ಬೇಗ ಸ್ನಾನ ಮುಗಿಸಿ ಹೊಳೆ ಬದಿಯ ದೇವಸ್ಥಾನದ ಪೂಜೆಗೆಂದು ಗಂಧ ತೇಯುತ್ತ ಕೂತ. ರುಕ್ಕು ಹಾಸಿಗೆ ಹಿಡಿದಿದ್ದಳು. ದನ ಕಾಯುವವ ಬಂದಾಗ ಗೌರಿ ಬೇಗಬೇಗನೆ ದನಗಳ ಹಾಲು ಕರೆದು ಕೊಟ್ಟಿಗೆಯಿಂದ ಅವನ್ನು ಅಟ್ಟಿದಳು. ವೆಂಕಟನ ಒಳಗೆ ಏನೋ ಸತ್ತಿದೆಯೆಂದು ನನಗೆ ಅನ್ನಿಸಿದ್ದರಿಂದ ಅವನಿಗೆ ಕಣ್ಣು ಕೊಡದಂತೆ ನಾನು ಹೊರಚಿಟ್ಟೆಯ ಮೇಲೆ ಕೂತೆ.

ಆದರೆ ಹಾಳುಬಿದ್ದ ತೋಟ ನೋಡಲಾರದೆ, ಮನೆಯನ್ನು ಬಳಸಿ ಹೋಗಿ ಹಿತ್ತಲಿನಲ್ಲಿದ್ದ ದಾಳಿಂಬೆ ಗಿಡದಡಿ ನಿಂತೆ. ಬೇಲಿಯ ಬಳಿ ವೆಂಕಟ ಕೌಪೀನವುಟ್ಟು, ಡೊಂಕು ಕಾಲಲ್ಲಿ ಸೊಟ್ಟಗೆ ನಿಂತಿದ್ದ. 'ಅರೆ ವೆಂಕಟ, ಹಿತ್ತಲಿನ ಬೇಲಿ ಹತ್ತಿರ ಅಷ್ಟು ತತ್ಪರನಾಗಿ ನಿಂತು ಏನು ಮಾಡುತ್ತಿದ್ದಾನೆ ಇವ' ಎಂದು ನನಗೆ ಆಶ್ಚರ್ಯವಾಯಿತು. ಸ್ನಾನ ಸಂಧ್ಯಾವಂದನೆಗಳಾದ ಮೇಲೆ ಚೊಂಬು ತಗೊಂಡು ಬಹಿರ್ದೆಶೆಗೆ ಹೋಗಿರುವುದು ಸಾಧ್ಯವಿಲ್ಲ; ಕಿವಿಯ ಮೇಲೆ ಜನಿವಾರ ಹಾಕಿಕೊಂಡಿಲ್ಲ. ತಾನು ಇಲ್ಲ ಎನ್ನಿಸುವಂತೆ ಚೂರೂ ಹಂದಿದೆ ನಿಂತಿದ್ದ. ನಾನು ಅವನ್ನನ್ನೇ ನೋಡುತ್ತ ನಿಂತಲ್ಲೇ ನಿಂತೆ.

ರತ್ನಗಂಧಿಯ ಬೇಲಿ, ಅದರ ಎದುರು ನಿಶ್ಚಲನಾದ, ತನ್ಮಯನಾದ, ಬರಿ ಮೈಯಲ್ಲಿ ವಕ್ರವಾಗಿ ನಿಂತ ವೆಂಕಟ. ಎದುರಿನ ಹಸಿರು ಬೇಲಿ ಬಿಟ್ಟರೆ ಮತ್ತೇನೂ ಕಾಣದು. ನಾನು ಮೆತ್ತಗೆ ಸದ್ದು ಮಾಡದಂತೆ ಅವನತ್ತ ಚಲಿಸಿದೆ. ಅವನ ಬೆನ್ನ ಹಿಂದೆ ನಿಂತೆ.

ಆದರೂ ವೆಂಕಟನಿಗೆ ನನ್ನ ಧ್ಯಾಸವಿಲ್ಲ. ಅರೆ, ಎಂದು ಕುತೂಹಲದಿಂದ ನಾನೂ ರತ್ನಗಂಧಿಯ ಬೇಲಿಯನ್ನು ದಿಟ್ಟಸಿದೆ. ಅಲ್ಲಲ್ಲಿ ಹಳದಿಯ ಗೊಂಚಲು ಗೊಂಚಲು ಹೂವುಗಳು, ಹಸಿರೆಲೆಗಳು. ಎಲೆ ಎಲೆಯನ್ನೂ ನೋಡಿದೆ. ಅವನ ಕಣ್ಣುಗಳ ಗುರಿ

Sandelholzpaste für die Morgenandacht im Tempel am Flußufer zu mahlen. Rukku lag auf dem Bett. Als der Kuhhirte kam, um die Kühe zu weiden, melkte Gowri die Kühe schnell und ließ sie gehen. Ich meinte, irgendetwas mußte in Venkata gestorben sein, und vermied es, ihm in die Augen zu sehen. So saß ich also draußen auf der Bank. Weil ich aber den Anblick des verwüsteten Gartens nicht ertragen konnte, ging ich um das Haus herum in den hinteren Hof und stellte mich unter den Granatapfelbaum.

Venkata stand am Zaun, ziemlich schlaff auf seinen krummen Beinen. Er hatte nur ein Lendentuch um. Ich war überrascht: Menschenskinder, Venkata, was treibt er hier bloß, steht da am Zaun und scheint ganz mit sich selbst beschäftigt zu sein. Er konnte nicht hinausgegangen sein, um sich zu erleichtern: er hatte seine Waschungen und Morgengebete schon hinter sich; seine heilige Schnur war nicht mehr ums Ohr geschlungen. Er stand völlig bewegungslos, meiner Gegenwart nicht gewahr. Ich stand und sah ihm zu. Vor einem Rathnagandizaun stand Venkata, gebeugt, mit bloßem Oberkörper, bewegungslos und völlig versunken. Außer dem hohen grünen Zaun vor ihm war nichts zu sehen. Ich ging ganz behutsam zu ihm hin, gab keinen Laut von mir. Ich stellte mich hinter ihn. Er bemerkte mich noch immer nicht. Mein Gott, dachte ich und sah mir neugierig den Rathnagandizaun an. Hier und dort gelbe Blumenbüschel. Neugierig zu erfahren, worauf sein Blick gerichtet sein könnte, musterte ich alles genau, was mir in die Augen fiel. Dann sah ich's: ein Sonnenpferd. Als ich sah, mit welcher Hingerissenheit mein unschuldiger Freund dieses Insekt mit seinen hochgestellten, gekrümmten Beinen, seinem leichtgewichtigen Körper, seiner grünen, geometrischen, winkligen Ashtavakra-Form beobachtete, fand ich das einen Augenblick lang komisch. Aber nur einen Augenblick lang. Das Sonnenpferd sprang hoch, und als es sprang, da sprang Venkatas angespannt folgender Kopf mit seinen gestutzten Haaren voller

on the mud bench. There were no words of solace left in me. I thought that Venkata would be broken by all that had happened. But a surprise awaited me that morning.

No matter who dies, no matter how dear the person, life's daily routines go on, don't they? Even in Venkata's house, which looked as if there had been a death in the familiy, Shakuntala prepared the morning coffee. I brushed my teeth with ash of the paddy husk. Venkata finished his bath and sat grinding the sandal paste for the morning worship at the temple by the riverside. Rukku lay in bed. When the cow herd came to graze the cows, Gowri quickly milked the cows and sent them away. I thought something must have died inside Venkata and did not want to meet his eyes. So I sat on the bench outside. But unable to bear the sight of the ravaged garden I went round the house to the backyard and stood under the pomegranate tree.

Venkata was standing by the fence, quite limp, on his bandy legs. He was wearing only a loin cloth. I was surprised: *Arre*, Venkata, what's he doing here, standing by the fence and looking so engrossed? He couldn't have gone out to relieve himself; he had already finished his ablutions and morning prayers; his sacred thread was not twined around his ear. He stood absolutely motionless, unaware of my presence. I stood watching him. In front of a *rathnagandi* fence stood Venkata, crooked, bare bodied, motionless and totally entranced. Except for the tall green fence in front of him nothing else was visible.. I softly walked up to him, not making a sound. I stood behind him. Yet he was not aware of me. *Arre*, I thought and curiously

ಯಾವುದಿರಬಹುದೆಂದು, ಕುತೂಹಲದಿಂದ ನನ್ನ ದೃಷ್ಟಿಯ ಅವಧಿಯಲ್ಲಿದ್ದುದನ್ನೆಲ್ಲ ಸೂಕ್ಷ್ಮವಾಗಿ ನೋಡುತ್ತ ಹೋದೆ. ಕಾಣಿಸಿದ್ದು : ಒಂದು ಸೂರ್ಯನ ಕುದುರೆ.

ನನ್ನ ಈ ನಿರುಪದ್ರವಿ ಗೆಳೆಯ ಆ ಉಬ್ಬಿದ ಡೊಂಕುಕಾಲಿನ, ಹಗುರಾದ ದೇಹದ, ದಟ್ಟ ಹಸಿರಿನ, ಜಾಮಿತಿಯ ಕೋನಗಳಂತೆ ಅಷ್ಟಾವಕ್ರ ರೂಪದ ಕೀಟವನ್ನು ಬೆರಗಾಗಿ ನೋಡುವುದು ಕಂಡು ನನಗೆ ಕ್ಷಣ ಮೋಜೆನಿಸಿತು. ಕ್ಷಣ ಮಾತ್ರ. ಸೂರ್ಯನ ಕುದುರೆ ಡೊಂಕು ಕಾಲನ್ನೊತ್ತಿ ಚಿಮ್ಮಿದ್ದು, ಅದು ಚಿಮ್ಮುತ್ತಿದ್ದಂತೆಯೇ ತದೇಕ ಮಗ್ನನಾದ ವೆಂಕಟನೂ ತಿರುಗಿ, ನನ್ನ ನೋಡಿ ಅದೆಷ್ಟು ಮುಗ್ಧ ಮಂದಹಾಸದಲ್ಲಿ ''ಸೂರ್ಯನ ಕುದುರೆ'' ಎಂದ. ಸೂರ್ಯನ ಕುದುರೆಯನ್ನು ಕಂಡ ಅವನ ಬೆರಗಿನ ಕಣ್ಣುಗಳಲ್ಲಿ ನನ್ನ ಕಣ್ಣೂ ನೆಟ್ಟು, ಬಾಯಿ ತೆರೆಯಿತು:

''ಸೂರ್ಯನ ಕುದುರೆ'' – ಎಂದೆ.

[...]

Einfühlung mit. Ich fühlte mich glücklich. Venkata drehte sich um, sah mich an und sagte in ganz unschuldigem Entzücken: "Das Sonnenpferd." Meine Augen hingen an seinen verzückten Augen, die das Sonnenpferd gesehen hatten, und mein Mund öffnete sich: "Das Sonnenpferd", sagte ich.

O

(Tr. from English by Lothar Lutze)

looked at the *rathnagandi* fence. Bunches of yellow flowers, here and there. Green leaves. I examined them, leaf by leaf. Curious as to what his gaze was aimed at, I closely scrutinised everything that fell within my view. Then I saw it: a sun's horse. Seeing this innocent friend of mine watch with such rapture this insect with its raised crooked legs, a light body, a green geometrical angular *ashtavakra* form, I was amused for a moment. But only for a moment. The sun's horse sprang; and as it sprang, Venkata's intent head with its crop of hair sprang with it in sympathy. I felt happy. Venkata turned around and, looking at me, said with such innocent ecstasy: "The sun's horse." My eyes looked into those wonder-struck eyes of his that had seen the sun's horse and my mouth fell open: "The sun's horse" I said.

O

(Tr. from Kannada by Manu Shetty and A.K. Ramanujan)

* The sun's horse (or a horse for the sun) is a translation of the common Kannada name for a grasshopper (*Suryana Kudure*).

सत्येन कुमार

झरना

[कहानी *आयाम* का एक अंश]

एक धुन होती है जिन्दगी···किसी साज पर बजती हुई धुन···बिलकुल जैसे तुम बजाते हो इस माउथ आर्गन पर···समझे ? और उसके साथ ही खनकती हुई वह हँसी बहुत ऊँचाई से किसी चट्टान पर गिरते झरने की तरह बिलकुल बिखर-बिखर जाती थी···और वह सपना भी बिलकुल उसी तरह बिखरकर वहीं खत्म हो जाता था।

रात-भर बस यही एक सपना था, जो रह-रहकर हर बार एक ही तरह से खत्म होकर शुरू हो जाता था। बार-बार वही हँसी। पिछली रात का बस वह उतना-सा टुकड़ा--चाँदनी और उसमें बेखबर सोये हुए जंगल की साँसों से महकते हुए वक्त का वह टुकड़ा, जिसमें देर तक मैं उस चट्टान पर बैठा माउथ आर्गन पर--'मून-रिवर' बजाता रहा था और सीमाजी मेरी गोद में सिर टिकाए हुए लेटी उसे सुनती रही थीं···।

···नीचे घाटी में हम दोनों चलते-चलते बहुत दूर निकल गए थे। मुझे तो बिलकुल ही पता नहीं चला था कि हम लोग कितनी दूर तक बह आए थे। आसमान से, नीचे घाटी में बरसती हुई उस चाँदनी में। सीमाजी, बस, बातें करती रही थीं

Satyen KUMAR

WASSERFALL

[Auszug aus einer dreiteiligen Kurzgeschichte mit dem Titel *Ayam* (Dimension)]

" Weißt du, das Leben ist eine Melodie, eine Melodie auf einem Instrument, so wie du sie auf deiner Mundharmonika spielst!" Dem folgte ihr helles Lachen, das wie ein Wasserfall von großer Höhe herabfiel und auf einem Felsen zerstäubte .... und auch dieser Traum ging wieder zuende.

Der Traum hatte eine Nacht lang gedauert, und wiederholte sich nun immer wieder von neuem. Immer wieder dieses Lachen. Nur dieses kleine Stück war von der letzten Nacht geblieben: Mondlicht und darin ein Stück Zeit, duftend vom friedlich schlafenden Atem des Waldes, in dem ich auf einem Felsen saß und auf der Mundharmonika 'Moon River' spielte. Sima hatte ihren Kopf auf meinen Schoß gebettet und hörte zu. -

Wir waren weit gelaufen auf unserem Spaziergang. Unmerklich waren wir so immer tiefer in das mondbeschienene Tal vorgedrungen. Sima redete in einem fort, nur unterbrochen von ihrem typischen, aufreizenden Lachen, und der Weg unter unseren Füßen schien uns von selbst

---

Satyen KUMAR

WATERFALL

[An excerpt from a three part short story entitled *Ayam* (The Dimension)]

"Life is a melody as though played on some musical instrument – almost like the way you're playing this harmonica! Can you understand me?" And her ringing laughter shattered like a waterfall on a rock ... and the dream also shattered the same way, every time.

The dream that lasted the night, starting all over again – every time it ended. And that laughter echoed endlessly through the night, fragrant with the breaths of the jungle, asleep unawares of the maddening moonlight. I had been playing *Moon River* on the harmonica, sitting on that rock for God knows how long. And Seemaji, lying with her head in my lap, had been quietly listening.

We had walked up the jungle path far into the valley. I had not even realised how far, in that moonlight pouring from the sky. Seemaji had been chattering away

और बीच-बीच में अपने खास ढंग से मुझे छेड़कर हँसती रही थीं, और जंगल के बीच बिछी वह पगडण्डी अपने आप ही हमारे पैरों के नीचे से गुजरती गई थी। एकाएक फिर सोयी हुई रात की खामोशी में एक अजीब-सी आवाज न जाने कब उभर आयी थी। ऊँचाई से गिरते हुए पानी के शोर की मद्धिम, उलझी-उलझी-सी साँसें। तब मुझे खयाल आया था कि बात करते-करते सीमाजी काफी पहले चुप हो गयी थीं और मेरा हाथ पकड़े चुपचाप चल रही थीं। और उसके साथ ही वही फीलिंग मुझे फिर हुई थी—बिलकुल वही फीलिंग—जैसे ढेर सारा गुलाबी रंग आसपास फैल गया है, और मेरे भीतर कहीं किसी ने एक कमान को बिलकुल खींच लिया है, उस गुलाबी धुँधलके को कहीं से बेधने के लिए···

"अरे···ये तो झरना आ गया। माई गुडनेस···कितनी दूर आ गए हम लोग ! और वही चमचमाती हुई, चाँदी की-सी झनकार !"

उस हँसी से चौंककर पास ही किसी परिन्दे ने अपने पर फड़फड़ाए। भीतर की वह कमान किसी ने फिर ढीली कर ली।

मैं चुपचाप उनकी तरफ देखकर मुस्कराया था। सामने, घाटी के दूसरी तरफ झरना गिर रहा था। पिघली हुई चाँदी।

वे अपने हाथ छुड़ाकर आगे बिछी चट्टानों पर चढ़ गयी थीं,—ऐ ऐ···इधर आओ, यहाँ बैठेंगे···

घाटी के इस तरफ, काफी आगे की तरफ निकली हुई चट्टान के बिलकुल आखिरी सिरे पर हम दोनों बैठ गए। झरना अब पूरी तरह दिखलाई दे रहा था। घाटी में बहुत नीचे शायद किसी बड़ी-सी चट्टान पर गिरता हुआ वह बेहिसाब पानी और सबकुछ भूलकर उससे बुरी तरह से चिपटी हुई चाँदनी। चट्टान से टकराकर बिखरता, उफनता और मचलता हुआ पानी, जिसे फिर चाँदनी अपनी बौछारों से ढक लेती थी। और उस धुँधलके से कुछ दूर हटकर जब दोनों बाहर निकलते थे, तो थकान से चूर, एक-दूसरे में घुले-हुए-से। फिर कुछ दूर जाकर दोनों एक नदी में बहने लगते थे। गहरी नींद में बेखबर,

davonzutragen. Langsam wurde in der Stille der schlafenden Nacht ein eigenartiges Geräusch hörbar: der verhaltenene, stoßartige Atem eines von großer Höhe herunterrauschenden Wasserfalls. Erst da wurde mir bewußt, daß Sima schon seit längerem verstummt war, sie hatte meine Hand ergriffen und lief still neben mir her. Ein Gefühl überkam mich, als färbe sich ringsum mich her alles rosa, und in mir spannte sich ein Bogen, der darauf drängte, in diesen rosa Nebel um mich hinauszuschnellen.

"Wir sind ja schon am Wasserfall, wie kann das sein? Wie lange sind wir denn schon unterwegs?"

Von ihrem Lachen aufgescheucht flog in der Nähe ein Vogel auf. Der Bogen in mir entspannte sich wieder. Vor uns am Ende des Tals lag schimmernd der Wasserfall wie flüssiges Silber. Sie machte sich von mir los, und begann auf die Felsen gegenüber zu klettern. Sie rief mich herauf. Auf dem letzten Vorsprung des Felsens, der über das Tal ragte, setzten wir uns nieder. Von dort ließ sich der Wasserfall ganz überblicken: Unermeßliche Wassermassen, die auf den Felsen niederfielen, und das Mondlicht, das sich wie benommen daran festgeklammert hielt. Das Wasser schlug in einer schäumenden Gischt auf dem Felsen auf und zerstäubte im Mondlicht, welches es bereitwillig wieder umfing. Und als beides, Wasser und Licht, aus dem Sprühnebel wieder auftauchten, waren sie ineinander verschmolzen, versunken in ihrer Erschöpfung, und flossen ein Stück weiter in einem friedlichen Bach zusammen weiter, in tiefem, bewußtlosen Schlummer. Vollkommen sorglos.

Sima schwieg noch immer. Eine seltsame Nervosität befiel mich, nicht eigentlich Nervosität, ein ganz besonderes Gefühl. Bis jetzt hatte Sima sich immer mit mir unterhalten, wenn wir zusammen waren, sei es bei uns zu Hause oder inmitten anderer Leute. Aufgrund ihrer mitteilsamen

non-stop, teasing me in her good-humoured manner. Suddenly a strange sound disturbed the silence of the sleeping jungle: the tangled breaths of a stream falling from high above. It was only then that I realised that Seemaji, her hand in mine, had stopped talking quite a while ago. And it was that which had precipitated that strange feeling in me – as if I were engulfed by an endless mist of pink, as if someone across that mist had stretched a bow taut inside me.

"My goodness! How far have we come! Look, that's the waterfall there!" And that dazzling laughter again.

Her laughter startled a bird in the trees. The bow within went slack and I smiled at her. In front of us, on the other side of the valley was the waterfall. The molten silver. She ran towards a rock and climbed onto it. "Aye! Come, let's sit here!"

We sat on the edge of the rock, jutting out over the valley. We had a full view of the waterfall now. The torrent of water splattering over the huge rock, far below, foaming white, held in an unabashed embrace by the misty moonlight. Still in each other's arms they disappeared behind yet another rock, emerging at last further down exhausted and spent. Beyond, the river lay languid, unmindful of her body.

Seemaji was quiet. I started feeling a little nervous, for she was by nature a talkative person. It was mainly because she was an extrovert that we had become so friendly in such a short time. She had been with us just a couple of weeks as a

आड़ी-तिरछी-सी लेटी एक नदी। बिलकुल केयर-लैस-सी।

सीमाजी चुप थीं। एक अजीब-सी घबराहट मुझे होने लगी थी। घबराहट नहीं, बल्कि कुछ और···ए स्ट्रेंज फीलिंग। अभी तक ऐसा होता आया था कि सीमाजी मेरे साथ या घर पर और लोगों के बीच भी हमेशा बातें करती थीं। बल्कि उनके इतना एक्स्ट्रोवर्ट होने की वजह से ही न सिर्फ हम दोनों की ही काफी पटने लगी थी, बल्कि घर पर भी दस-बारह दिनों में ही वे हरेक से बेहद घुल-मिल गई थीं। मम्मी-पापा से लेकर छोटी-सी सिम्मू तक, हर किसी के साथ वे घण्टों बातचीत करती रहती थीं। लेकिन अब जैसे मुझे पता चल गया था कि वे एकदम चुप भी हो सकती थीं। और मैं नहीं चाहता था कि वे चुप हो जाएँ। चुप हो जाने पर सबकुछ कितना बदल जाता है। एक आवाज का पुल क्या टूट जाता है, लगता है, जैसे दूसरे आदमी या दूसरी चीज के बारे में हम कुछ जानते ही नहीं हैं। और एकाएक किसी के चुप हो जाने से तो और भी ज्यादा उलझन होती है न ? लगता है, जैसे कोई बात कहीं पर या तो गलत हो गयी है, या कोई गलत या अजीब-सी बात होनेवाली है···पता नहीं, क्या बात थी, लेकिन उस वक्त उनके चुप हो जाने से मुझे एक अजीब-सा तनाव महसूस हो रहा था। लेकिन वे काफी देर तक उसी तरह खामोश बैठी रही थीं।

बहुत देर बाद अचानक जैसे, उन्होंने अपने आपसे कहा था—झरना भी···हमेशा बहता रहता है न ! और फिर जैसे अपनी ही आवाज से चौंककर उन्होंने मेरी तरफ देखा था। कुछ क्षणों तक वे एक अजीब-से ढंग से मुझे देखती रही थीं।

फिर एकाएक वही हँसी फूट पड़ी थी और वे सरककर मेरे बिलकुल पास आ गईं—मालूम है, इस वक्त तुम काफी बड़े लग रहे हो। आई मीन, मोर दैन योर एज, यू नो, और फिर हँसते हुए उन्होंने मेरे बालों को अपने हाथ से बिलकुल बिखरा दिया।

मैं अपने हाथ से अपने बाल ठीक करने लगा। वे उसी तरह मुस्कराती हुई मुझे देखती रहीं और जब मैंने अपने बाल

Art hatten nicht nur wir beide uns bald angefreundet, auch alle andern bei uns zu Haus waren schnell mit ihr warm geworden. Von den Eltern bis zur kleinen Simmu konnte sie sich stundenlang mit jedem unterhalten. Erst jetzt hatte ich gemerkt, daß sie auch vollkommen still sein konnte. Alles veränderte sich durch dieses Schweigen. Wenn die Brücke der Stimme versagt, scheint es plötzlich, als wüßten wir überhaupt nichts über die andere Person. Was kann es Verwirrenderes geben, als wenn das Gegenüber plötzlich in Schweigen verfällt? Man denkt darüber nach, ob man irgendetwas Falsches gesagt oder getan hat, oder erwartet etwas gänzlich Unvorhergesehenes. Eine seltsame Spannung hatte von mir Besitz ergriffen.

Nach geraumer Zeit sagte sie plötzlich, wie zu sich selbst: "... dieser Wasserfall, unendlich rauscht der so..." Sie sah mich plötzlich an, als sei sie über ihre eigene Stimme erschrocken. Ein eigenartiger Ausdruck stand in ihrem Gesicht. Dann rückte sie ganz nahe an mich heran. "Weißt du, daß du schon richtig erwachsen aussiehst? Ich meine, viel älter, als du eigentlich bist!" Lachend zerzauste sie mir die Haare.

Ich fuhr mir glättend mit den Händen über den Kopf, und sie sah mir dabei amüsiert zu, dann brachte sie erneut meine Haare durcheinander: "Aus dir wird mal ein schöner Mann werden später!" Diesmal ließ ich meine Haare wie sie waren. Wie sie näher zu mir rückte, vermischte sich die mondhelle Nacht um uns her und unser Atem, schwer wie die Wucht des Wasserfalls, zu einem mir ganz unbekannten Duft. Auch das zarte Parfum, das immer von ihr ausströmte, kam mir jetzt irgendwie schwerer und beinahe träge vor. Eine seltsames Konglomerat von Gerüchen.

"Weißt du, das bei dir schon viele Dinge genau wie bei einem Erwachsenen sind? Zum Beispiel, daß du deine Haare jetzt so gelassen hast! Oder als ich gerade so still da saß und du ganz ruhig geblieben bist. Selbst wenn da ein richtiger Erwachsener gesessen hätte, wäre

guest of my elder sister but already everyone at home, right from my parents to little Simmu, my niece, had taken to her. She would spend hours talking to them. But that she can become so quiet was a discovery to me. I did not at all want her to be quiet. Becoming quiet changes everything. With the bridge of speech gone, we feel stranded. It is worse if someone falls suddenly silent. It feels as if some fateful thing is going to happen. Her silence filled me with a strange tension. But she just sat there, lost in herself.

After a long while, her lips moved as if she were talking to herself – "Isn't it strange that a waterfall always keeps flowing!" Then, as if startled by her own voice, she turned to look at me. Suddenly then that ringing laughter gushed forth from her lips, and she moved closer." You know what, you are looking kind of grown up. I mean, more than your age." And she ruffled my hair teasingly.

I tried to rearrange my hair while she looked on, amused. When I had finished, she ruffled them yet again, more mischievously and laughed: "You will be a handsome man someday!" I gave up trying to rearrange my hair. Her close proximity. The sharpness of the scent of the moonlight, the rhythm of the panting breaths of the waterfall had all changed. Even the perfume Blue Grass which she wore felt heavy and lazy.

"Tell you what, you have many things common with the grown-ups", she said, with a smile. "Like ... you didn't mind your hair being ruffled this time. Or when I was

ठीक कर लिए, तो उन्होंने फिर उन्हें बिखरा दिया। वही हँसी—यू विल बी अ वेरी हैंडसम मैन, सम डे !

इस बार मैंने अपने बाल उसी तरह रहने दिए। उनके पास आ जाने से मुझे अपने चारों तरफ फैली हुई चाँदनी रात और झरने की तेजी से उठती-बैठती साँसों की मिली-जुली-सी महक, एकाएक बदली हुई-सी महसूस होने लगी थी। बल्कि 'ब्लू ग्रास' की वह भीनी-सी महक, जो हमेशा उनके पास से आती थी, वह भी इस वक्त मुझे कुछ ज्यादा भारी, अलसायी-सी महसूस हो रही थी। कुछ अजीब ही थी वह खुशबू।

—मालूम है, तुममें बहुत-सी बातें अब भी बिलकुल बड़ों जैसी हैं। उन्होंने उसी तरह से मुझे देखते हुए कहा था—जैसे देखो, इस बार तुमने अपने बाल ठीक नहीं किए। वह मुस्कराहट फिर उनके चेहरे पर छा गई थी—या अभी, मैं जब वहाँ बैठी हुई थी, चुपचाप। तो तुम भी बिलकुल चुपचाप बैठे रहे थे। बल्कि इस वक्त कोई बड़ा आदमी होता तो, शायद वह भी चुप न बैठ पाता। इट्स सो फनी रिअली···जब लोग बड़े हो जाते हैं, बस बातें करना क्या आ जाता है, समझते हैं कि हर जगह कुछ-न-कुछ कहना जरूरी है। चाहे खुशी का मौका हो, चाहे गम का, कुछ-न-कुछ बोलेंगे जरूर। समझते हैं, जैसे सब चीज़ें बोलने से हल हो जाती हैं···यू नो, दे जस्ट कांट कीप शट···नैवर··· मैंने पहली बार महसूस किया था कि बात करते वक्त उनका चेहरा बदल जाता था।

कुछ देर के लिए वे चुप होकर नीचे घाटी की तरफ देखती रही थीं। और उसके बाद अचानक फिर खिलखिलाकर हँस पड़ी थीं—तुम भी सोचते होंगे कि मैं कितनी उल्टी-सीधी बातें करती हूँ न। भला, अपने आप ही मैं, खुद कितनी बातें करती रहती हूँ। यू नो, आई नो आई एम अ चेटर बॉक्स और फिर भी दूसरे लोगों को मैं बुरा-भला कहती हूँ। इट्स सो सिली···द लाइफ। ऐंट इट ?

उनकी हँसी देखकर मैं भी मुस्करा पड़ा।

er bestimmt nicht so still geblieben. Wirklich komisch, wenn Leute älter werden, meinen sie, bei jeder Gelegenheit müsse unbedingt irgendetwas geredet werden. Ob es ein freudiger Anlass ist oder ein trauriger, irgendetwas müssen sie immer sagen. Als ob sich durchs Reden alle Dinge lösen ließen. Sie können einfach nicht den Mund halten!"
Ich bemerkte zum ersten Mal, wie sich ihr Gesicht beim Reden veränderte.
Sie starrte wieder schweigend ins Tal hinunter. Dann lachte sie plötzlich auf: "Du mußt auch denken, was ich für einen Unsinn daherrede. Ich rede ja selbst ununterbrochen. Ich weiß, was für eine Plaudertasche ich selber bin und maße mir ein Urteil über andere Leute an! Schon komisch, das alles, oder?"

Ich mußte lächeln. Nach einer Weile fing sie an, eine Melodie zu summen. Dann packte sie mich plötzlich an der Schulter und fragte: "He, warum spielst du nicht auf deiner Mundharmonika! Du bist ja dumm, warum hast du nicht darangedacht?"
"Jetzt?" fragte ich leise.
"Wann sonst? Komm, stell dich nicht so an!"
"Von mir aus ... " Ich zog langsam die Mundharmonika aus der Tasche. Ohne groß nachzudenken spielte ich von selbst 'Moon River'. Diese Melodie gefiel ihr sehr gut und sie hatte sie mir in den letzten Tagen immer wieder vorgesungen. Ich wußte gar nicht, wie gut ich das Lied auf der Mundharmonika spielen konnte, als ob jemand anderes am Werk sei. Nach einer Weile legte sie sich ganz vorsichtig neben mich. Sie suchte nach einer Stütze für ihren Kopf und bettete ihn schließlich ganz sacht auf meinen Schoß.
Einen Moment dachte, jetzt würde der gespannte Bogen in mir zerspringen, als zöge jemand mit aller Gewalt daran. Vielleicht begann ich deswegen mit dem zweiten Teil des Stückes, in

sitting there silently, you also kept quiet! Even a grown up man might not have done that. It's so funny really. Most grown-ups think its imperative to say something everytime and everywhere. Whether they are at a party or a funeral. As if saying something is the answer to all things. You know, they just can't keep shut... never!" I observed that she looked transformed when she was talking.

She turned her gaze down into the valley. Then suddenly she burst out laughing. "You must think I've gone crazy! Being so talkative myself yet criticising others for being talkative! Well, well, I know that I'm a chatterbox, yet I must complain! Silly, isn't it? But so is life." Her laughter brought a smile to my face.

She started humming to herself. After a while she turned round and placed her hand on my shoulder, saying impatiently: "Aren't you playing the harmonica for me? My...my, aren't you being stupid?" "Now?" I asked incertainly. "When else? Oh come on now. Don't put on airs, young man!" She insisted, shaking my shoulders playfully. "Okay." I smiled, and took out the harmonica from my pocket.

Without a thought I started playing *Moon River*. It was her favourite melody. I do not know how long I kept playing it. Also, I had no idea I could play it so well on a harmonica. It seemed as if somebody else was playing it. Or maybe it was just the restless breaths of moonlight borne aloft on the breeze.

She lay down near me, trying to find a comfortable spot for her head. And then, she reached up and let it rest on my lap. For a moment I felt as if that bow inside

कुछ देर हम फिर चुपचाप बैठे रहे। उन्होंने धीरे-धीरे कुछ गुनगुनाना शुरू कर दिया था, जिसे फिर कुछ क्षणों बाद अचानक छोड़कर उन्होंने मेरे कन्धे पर हाथ रखते हुए कहा, "अरे··· तुम अपना माउथ ऑर्गन नहीं सुनाओगे ! माई, माई···कितने बुद्धू हो जी तुम···उसे बजाते क्यों नहीं हो !"

"अभी ?" मैंने धीरे-से पूछा।

"और कब··· ? ओह, कम ऑन नाउ··· नखरे मत करो जी।" उन्होंने मचलते हुए मेरे कंधे को हिलाया।

"ओके···," मैंने धीरे-से मुस्कराकर कहा और जेब से माउथ ऑर्गन निकाल लिया।

बिना कुछ सोचे अपने आप ही मैं 'मून-रिवर' बजाने लगा था। यह धुन उन्हें बहुत अच्छी लगती थी और पिछले दिनों कई बार उन्होंने मुझसे कह-कहकर इसे सुना था।

कितनी देर तक फिर मैं वही धुन बजाता रहा था। मुझे खुद पता नहीं था कि मैं उसे माउथ ऑर्गन पर इतनी अच्छी तरह बजा सकता था। लगा था, जैसे कोई और बजा रहा था। या शायद खुद चाँदनी और हवा की साँसें ही जैसे एक-दूसरे में घुल गई थीं और वह धुन बनकर बहती रही थीं।

कुछ देर बाद वे आहिस्ता-से, वहीं मेरे पास ही लेट गई थीं। कुछ क्षणों तक वे अपना सिर ठीक से टिकाने की कोशिश करती रही थीं। और उसके बाद···धीरे-से उसी तरह सरककर उन्होंने अपना सिर मेरी गोद में रख लिया था।

एक क्षण के लिए मुझे लगा था, जैसे भीतर कहीं वह कमान बिलकुल टूट जाएगी। किसी ने उसे इस बार इतनी जोर से खींच लिया था कि मैं घबरा उठा था। शायद इसीलिए फिर यह हुआ था कि मैंने उस थीम का अगला हिस्सा बजाना शुरू कर दिया था, जिसमें धीमे-धीमे बहती हुई नदी के सोफ्ट नोट्स एकाएक तेज हो जाते हैं, अजीब तरह से उलझे और मचलते हुए वे तेज, हाई म्युजिकल नोट्स, जो नदी के एकाएक काफी ऊँचाई से गिरने को कैप्चर करते हैं···

dem die weichen Töne des plätschernden Baches plötzlich anschwellen, aufgewühlte, erregte hohe Töne, die von großer Höhe niederfallendes Wasser widerspiegeln ...
Ich weiß nicht, wie lange sie das Thema weitersummte. Mir war, als stiege der Bach von unten langsam empor, hinauf bis auf unseren Felsen, wo ich saß, ihren Kopf auf meinem Schoß... Wer weiß wie lange diese Töne, das Wasser des Baches und darin geschmolzen das Mondlicht über uns hinwegströmten.

Ich setzte die Mundharmonika plötzlich ab. Sie hatte ihren Kopf zur Seite an meine Brust gedreht und blickte mich an. Ich hatte ihre seltsam schweren Atemzüge nur kurze Zeit ertragen können, dann hörte ich auf zu spielen. Sie blieb genauso liegen. "Das Leben ist eine Melodie, eine Melodie auf irgendeinem Instrument", sagte sie, während sie sich aufrichtete, dann lachte sie und sah mich still und eindringlich an.
"Verstehst du denn auch, was ich sage, oder nickst du einfach so mit dem Kopf?" sagte sie in amüsiertem Ton.
"Einfach so", antwortete ich. Wir mußten beide lachen.
Dann fragte sie mich mit einer seltsamen Leere in ihrer Stimme, als hätte sich ihr Lachen plötzlich erschöpft: "Warum hast du dann aufgehört zu spielen?"

In dem Moment sah ich ihr zum allerersten Mal direkt in die Augen. Die mondhelle Landschaft um uns spiegelte sich darin, und in ihnen stand noch die Frage, auf die ich keine Antwort gegeben hatte. Dann verbanden sich unsere Blicke, wie zwei lange, dunkle Tunnel, und dann... nicht nur wurde das Summen immer stärker, das sich durch den Tunnel einen Weg in mein Inneres bahnte, es erschien mir auch, als hätte jemand die Tür am Ende dieses Tunnels aufgestoßen, der sich inmitten eines Meeres in weiter Ferne öffnete. Sie beugte sich zu mir

me would snap. It had been pulled so taut that I was filled with dread. Perhaps that was why I started playing the next part of the melody which was full of high and strong notes that captured the change of pace of the river, when she is about to yield to a waterfall. The soft, lazy notes of the river flowing quietly suddenly giving way to the high and feverish cadence of a waterfall of immense height.

I do not know for how long that melody kept echoing in that sleeping wilderness then. In fact, it felt as if the river flowing below in the valley had pulled herself up. Higher than the rock on which I sat with Seemaji's head in my lap ...No one knows how long we remained submerged in those waters fragrant with moonlight, heavy with the notes.

Suddenly then I stopped playing the harmonica. She turned over on her side and her mouth came to lie somewhat below my chest. Only a few of those warm, almost steaming hot breaths were all I could take. "Life is a kind of melody ...", she said, sitting up, "played on a musical instrument," she laughed, her eyes on me. "Do you understand what it means," she asked, an amused smile on her lips, "or is it that you just keep nodding like that?" "Maybe," I smiled back at her. "Then why did you stop playing?" she asked in a small voice, drained of all laughter.

For a brief moment I looked straight into her eyes reflecting the moonlit wilderness echoing with her unanswered question. Our eyes, locked to each other's, were dark tunnels filling with that echo. Someone, it seemed, had thrown open the gate of that tunnel, the one that gave on to the sea. The sea was mad, foaming and roaring. It was impossible

पता नहीं, कब तक फिर वह थीम वहाँ गूँजती रही थी। बल्कि लगा था, जैसे नीचे बहती हुई वह नदी फिर आहिस्ता-आहिस्ता ऊपर उठ आई थी। उस चट्टान से भी ऊपर जिस पर मैं बैठा हुआ था और मेरी गोद में सिर टिकाए वे लेटी हुई थीं···न जाने कब तक वे सारे स्वर, नदी का वह पानी और उसमें घुली हुई महकती-सी वह चाँदनी हम लोगों के ऊपर से बहती रही थी।

मैंने ही फिर एकाएक माउथ ऑर्गन बजाना बन्द कर दिया था। उन्होंने लेटे-लेटे अचानक दायीं तरफ करवट ली थी और उनका चेहरा मेरे सीने के नीचे कहीं बिलकुल सट गया था। वो अजीब गर्म-गर्म-सी कुछ ही साँसें मैं बर्दाश्त कर पाया था और उसके बाद रुक गया था। लेकिन वे उसके बाद भी काफी देर तक उसी तरह लेटी रही थीं।

"एक धुन होती है जिन्दगी···" अचानक फिर उन्होंने उठकर बैठते हुए कहा था—किसी साज पर बज रही धुन। हँसते-हँसते फिर वे एकदम चुप कर एकटक मेरी तरफ देखने लगी थीं।

"तुम्हें मेरी बातें समझ में भी आती हैं···" कुछ क्षणों बाद उन्होंने उसी एम्यूज्ड-सी टोन में पूछा था, "या यूँ ही गर्दन हिलाते रहते हो।"

"यूँ ही···" मैंने मुस्कराकर कहा था।

और हम दोनों हँस पड़े थे।

कुछ देर बाद उनके भीतर की वह सारी हँसी जैसे कहीं बह गई थी और उसके पीछे छूट गई उस बेहद खाली आवाज में उन्होंने अचानक मुझसे पूछा था—तुमने माउथ ऑर्गन बजाना बन्द क्यों कर दिया ?

एक क्षण के लिए फिर पहली बार मैंने उनकी आँखों में देखा था। बिलकुल सीधे। दूर तक सिर्फ चाँदनी से ढकी हुई वीरानी की तरह, वे आँखें बिलकुल खाली थीं और उनका वह सवाल उनमें गूँज रहा था, जिसका मैंने कोई जवाब नहीं दिया था। न जाने फिर कब और कैसे, एकाएक हम दोनों की आँखें बिलकुल जुड़ गई थीं। दो लम्बी, अँधेरी सुरंगों की तरह और उसके बाद···न सिर्फ वह गूँज फिर और भी तेज होकर उन सुरंगों के जरिए मेरे भीतर उतरती गई थी, बल्कि लगा था, जैसे किसी ने उस सुरंग का वह दूसरा दरवाज़ा खोल दिया था, जो बहुत दूर किसी समुद्र के बीचोंबीच जाकर निकलता था। चाँदनी की शरारत और छेड़ से उफनते हुए, तूफानी समुद्र के बीचोंबीच मेरी तरफ झुकते हुए उन्होंने धीरे-से कुछ कहा था। पता नहीं क्या···मुझे बस इतना याद है कि उनका चेहरा मेरे बिलकुल पास आ गया था। वह अजीब-सी खुशबू फिर एकाएक उस सुरंग में तेज समुद्री हवा की तरह बहने लगी थी और उसके पीछे-पीछे भागती हुई, मचलती और उफनती लहरों का वह भयानक शोर। लगा था, जैसे हम दोनों एक-दूसरे में बेतरह उलझे हुए, घाटी में नीचेवाली उस चट्टान पर लेटे हुए हैं जिसके ऊपर वह झरना गिरकर टूट रहा था।

[...]

in diesem schäumenden, im Licht glitzernden, aufgewühlten Meer, aber ich kann mich nicht mehr an das erinnern, was sie sagte, nur daß ihr Gesicht ganz nah dem meinen kam. Gleichzeitig wehte ein seltsamer Duft zu mir her wie eine starke Brise, überrollt vom gewaltigen Lärm der anbrausenden Brandung. Es war, als lägen wir ineinanderverschlungen dort unten auf dem Felsen, auf dem der Wasserfall in tausend Tropfen zersprühte.
[...]

(Tr. from Hindi by Barbara Lotz)

to listen to anything then, not even to what she was trying to say. I only remember that her face held close to mine. A strange fragrance rose on the sea wind, chased by the maddening roar of high waves, as we lay, our bodies entangled, on that rock on which fell that waterfall shattering itself.
[...]

(Tr. fom Hindi by the author)

उदय प्रकाश

छप्पन तोले का करधन

[कहानी का एक अंश]

वह छप्पन तोले का करधन दादाजी लेकर आए थे। दादाजी हमारे घर की कहानी के नायक थे। उन्होंने सारे संसार की यात्रा की थी और बड़े-बड़े कारनामे किए थे। मुझे लगता पूरी दुनिया उनके बारे में जानती होगी। उनकी एक धुँधली-सी तस्वीर अम्माँ की कोठरी में लटकी हुई थी। वह अकेली तस्वीर थी जो नमी और समय के असर से काँच के साथ चिपककर धीरे-धीरे गल रही थी। दादाजी के सिर पर मराठी पगड़ी थी, जाँघों में बन्दूक टिकी हुई थी और बड़ी-बड़ी मूँछें थीं।

लालटेन की रोशनी में जब भी सोने के करधन का जिक्र होता, दादाजी की भी कहानी शुरू हो जाती। अम्माँ बतातीं कि दादा को चिड़ियाँ पालने का बड़ा शौक था। गाँव के तालाब की हर बत्तख से उनकी पहचान थी और दादा हर बत्तख को उसके अलग नाम से बुलाते थे। कई को वे अपने साथ अपने घर ले आते। फिर तो सारे घर में बत्तखें ही बत्तखें होतीं। हर जगह। बड़ी आफत होती।

Uday PRAKASH

DER GOLDENE GÜRTEL

[Auszug aus der Kurzgeschichte]

Den Gürtel, der sechsundfünfzig Tola wog, hatte Großvater mitgebracht. Großvater war der Held in der Geschichte unseres Hauses. Er hatte die ganze Erde bereist und gewaltige Taten vollbracht. Ich meinte, die ganze Welt müßte von ihm wissen. Sein verblaßtes Bild hing in Mutters Raum. Es war das einzige Bild von ihm; der Feuchtigkeit und der Zeit ausgesetzt, klebte es an einem Stück Glas und moderte vor sich hin. Großvater trug einen Marathenturban, zwischen den Schenkeln klemmte ein Gewehr, und er trug einen gewaltigen Schnurrbart.

Immer wenn im Schein der Petroleumlampe die Rede auf den goldenen Gürtel kam, begann auch Großvaters Geschichte. Die Mutter erzählte, daß es Großvaters Lieblingsbeschäftigung war, Vögel zu halten. Jede Ente auf dem Dorfsee kannte er, und jede rief er bei ihrem eigenen Namen. Manchmal brachte er welche mit nach Hause. Dann wimmelte das ganze Haus von Enten. Überall Enten. Eine richtige Heimsuchung war das. Großvater war ständig auf dem laufenden,

---

Uday PRAKASH

THE GOLDEN WAISTCHAIN

[Extract from the short story]

That golden waistchain of fifty-six tolas Grandfather had brought. Grandfather was the hero of the story of our house. He had travelled over the entire world and accomplished amazing feats. It seemed to me the whole world must have known about him. A faded photo of him hung in Mother's room. It was the only photograph in the house; it was stuck to the glass, and the humidity and the effects of time were slowly destroying it. Grandfather wore a Marathi turban, a gun was held between his legs, and he had a huge moustache.

In the light of the lantern, whenever the golden waistchain was mentioned, Grandfather's story was always begun. Mother would explain how much Grandfather liked to raise birds. He knew every duck in the village pond and called each one by its own name. Many of them he brought to the house. Then the entire house was full of ducks. Ducks everywhere! What

दादा को पता रहता था कि जंगल के किस पेड़ की किस डाल पर कौन-सी चिड़िया के बच्चे कितने बड़े हो गए हैं। वे सिर्फ बत्तखों से ही नहीं, कौओं और बैलों से भी बातचीत कर सकते थे। वे कई बार चींटियों से पूछकर बिल्लल सही-सही बता देते कि पानी बरसेगा या नहीं।

गाँव के उसी तालाब में, जिसमें दादा की सारी बत्तखें, पनडुब्बियाँ, चाहे, मटावर, टिटहरी, बगुले और जाने कौन-कौन-सी चिड़ियाँ रहती थीं, अँग्रेज अफसर अपनी गोरी मेम के साथ आकर बारह बोर के छर्रे से बत्तखों को मार कर ले जाता था। दादा कभी-कभी उदास होकर तालाब से लौटते और बुदबुदाते—"आज गोरे ने मोहन, सावंत और दूजी को मार डाला।"

अम्माँ बताती हैं कि एक शाम दादा आँगन में खाट पर लेटे हुए चुपचाप आकाश में अभी-अभी उभरते हरनगरा, ध्रुव और शुकवा तारों को देख रहे थे कि अचानक शाम का नारंगी-नीला आसमान चिड़ियों से भर गया। सारे संसार की चिड़ियाँ वहाँ आकाश में पागल होकर चीख रही थीं। दादा के पैर पर एक जलमुर्गाबी गिरी। वह खून से तर थी, सारे शरीर में छर्रे थे और गर्दन आधी कट चुकी थी। दादा ने अपनी बन्दूक की नाल साफ की, उसमें कारतूस भरे, सिर पर पगड़ी रखी और तालाब की तरफ चले गए।

इसके बाद कहते हैं, दादा ने तालाब की दूसरी मेड़ पर खड़े होकर अँग्रेज़ अफसर से कहा कि इस तालाब में चिड़ियाँ मारना जुर्म है। सारी चिड़ियाँ मेरी घरेलू और पालतू हैं और तुम आज के बाद से शिकार खेलने के लिए इस तालाब में मत आना। उस दिन अँग्रेज़ अफसर अकेला था, इसलिए वह चुपचाप अपनी मेम के साथ चला गया। लेकिन दूसरे दिन दादा के सारे खेत कुर्क कर लिए गए, जानवर

welcher Vogel auf einem bestimmten Zweig eines bestimmten Baumes im Wald Junge hatte und wie alt sie gerade waren. Nicht nur mit Enten, auch mit Krähen und Ochsen konnte er sich unterhalten. Ein paar Mal sagte er, nachdem er Ameisen befragt hatte, ganz genau voraus, ob es regnen würde oder nicht.

Zu diesem Dorfsee, auf dem Großvaters Enten, Fischreiher, Perl- und Moorhühner, Zwergsteißfüße, Wasserläufer und was sonst noch alles für Vögel lebten, kam häufig ein englischer Beamter mit seiner weißen Frau, schoß mit seiner Schrotbüchse Enten und nahm sie mit. Manchmal kam Großvater ganz bedrückt vom See zurück und murmelte: "Heute hat der Weiße den Mohan, den Sawant und die Duji umgebracht."

Mutter erzählt, wie eines Abends Großvater im Hof auf der Bettstelle lag und schweigend zusah, wie am Himmel gerade der Große Bär, der Polarstern und die Venus auftauchten, als plötzlich der orange-blaue Abendhimmel von Vögeln bevölkert war. Die Vögel der ganzen Erde, außer Rand und Band geraten, schrien dort am Himmel. Dem Großvater fiel eine Krickente vor die Füße. Sie war blutgetränkt, im ganzen Körper steckten Schrotkugeln, und ihr Hals war halb durchgetrennt. Großvater reinigte den Lauf seines Gewehrs, lud es mit Patronen, band sich den Turban um und begab sich zum See.

Danach, heißt es, stellte sich Großvater auf die gegenüberliegende Uferböschung und ließ den englischen Beamten wissen, daß es kriminell sei, an diesem See Vögel zu schießen. Alle Vögel habe er in seinem Haus großgezogen, der Engländer solle sich mit seiner Büchse fortan also nicht mehr hier sehen lassen. An jenem Tag war der englische Beamte allein, deshalb zog er sich mit seiner Frau zurück, ohne ein Wort zu sagen. Aber am Tag darauf wurden dem Großvater alle Felder beschlagnahmt, das Vieh vertrieben und unser Dorf zum Rebellendorf erklärt.

a problem! Grandfather always knew which bird nested on which branch of which tree and how big its young were. Not only ducks, he could also talk with crows and oxen. A number of times he talked with the ants, and he could always tell from them whether or not it would rain.

In that same pond where all Grandfather's ducks, coots, waterhens, lapwings, herons and who knows how many other kinds of birds lived, the Angrez Officer would come with his fair Mem Saheb and shoot ducks with his twelve-gauge shotgun. Sometimes Grandfather would return from his pond in despair and mutter, "Today the whiteman murdered Mohan, Saawant and Doojee."

Mother explained that one evening Grandfather was lying quietly on his cot in the courtyard, looking up at the Big Dipper, the North Star and Venus, which were then rising, when birds suddenly filled the bluish-orange sky. Birds from all over had gone crazy and were screeching through the air. A waterhen fell on Grandfather's foot. She was covered in blood, her body was full of buck shot, and her neck was half slit. Grandfather cleaned out the bore of his gun, filled it with bullets, put on his turban and headed for the pond.

Then they say that Grandfather stood on the other shore of the pond and told the Angrez Officer it was a crime to kill the birds of that pond. They're all my pets and domestic fowl, Grandfather said, so don't come here again for hunting. That day the Angrez Officer was hunting alone, so he left silently with his Mem Saheb. But the next day all Grandfather's fields were confiscated, his cattle were led away, and our village was declared a rebel village.

हाँक ले जाए गए और हमारे गाँव को बागी गाँव घोषित कर दिया गया।

अब अँग्रेज़ अफसर हर रोज़ शाम को आता, तालाब में बारह बोर के छर्रों से चिड़ियों को मारता। दादा आँगन की खाट में लेटकर चुपचाप देखते कि आकाश चिड़ियों से भर गया है, लहूलुहान मुर्गाबियाँ, घायल बत्तखें, चीखती हुई टिटहरियाँ और डरे हुए बगुले। अम्माँ बतातीं कि जिस रोज़ उस अँग्रेज़ अफसर ने गुस्से में पागल होकर धाँय-धाँय तालाब की बत्तखों पर बन्दूक दागी थी, वह वही दिन था जब पंजाब के जलियाँवाला बाग में गोली चली थी।

एक दिन दादा ने फिर अपनी बन्दूक साफ की और तालाब की दूसरी मेड़ पर लगे आम के पेड़ की डाल पर पत्तों के पीछे बैठे गए। अँग्रेज़ अफसर अपनी मेम और कारिंदों के साथ आया था। वह सामने की मेड़ पर आम की डाल पर बने मचान पर बैठा था। दादा ने चिल्लाकर दूसरी मेड़ से आवाज़ दी–"आज से सब बंद लाट साहेब, मैं तालाब का मालिक और चिड़ियों का मालिक, तुम्हें हुक्म देता हूँ..." लेकिन दादा तो आम के पेड़ में छिपे हुए थे। न उन्हें अँग्रेज़ अफसर देख पाया न उसके कारिंदे। सबने समझा उनके भीतर का डर बोल रहा है। अँग्रेज़ को गुस्सा भी आया। अँग्रेज़ उस वक्त सारे हिन्दुस्तान के राजा थे और यहाँ एक बत्तख मारने पर दादा की आवाज खिलाफत में उठ रही थी।

अँग्रेज़ अफसर ने मचान से जल मुर्गाबियों के झुंड पर निशाना लगाया–धाँय, बन्दूक चली और कारिंदों ने देखा कि पूरा आसमान चीखती हुई चिड़ियों से भर गया। लेकिन तभी उन्होंने देखा कि इस बार ऊपर से मरी हुई मुर्गाबियाँ नहीं गिरीं, गिरी अँग्रेज़ अफसर की लाश।

दरअसल दो बन्दूकों के घोड़े एक साथ दबे थे। दादा परली वाली मेड़ के नीचे उतरे, अपनी बन्दूक

Von jetzt an kam der englische Beamte täglich gegen Abend an den See und schoß Vögel mit seiner Schrotbüchse. Großvater lag auf der Bettstelle im Hof und sah schweigend zu, wie Vögel den Himmel verfinsterten: verletzte, blutüberströmte Enten, schreiende Wasserläufer, verängstigte Fischreiher. Mutter erzählte, daß der Tag, an dem der englische Beamte, toll vor Wut, sein Gewehr auf die Enten auf dem See abfeuerte, auch der Tag war, an dem im Panjab die Schüsse von Jaliyanwala Bagh fielen.

Eines Tages reinigte Großvater wieder sein Gewehr und setzte sich, hinter Laub versteckt, auf einen Ast eines Mangobaums am anderen Ufer. Der englische Beamte war mit seiner Frau und seinen Leuten gekommen. Er saß auf einem Hochsitz, der auf einem Mangobaum am diesseitigen Ufer angebracht war. Großvaters Stimme scholl von drüben herüber: "Schluß damit, Lord Saheb, ein für allemal! Ich bin der Herr des Sees und der Herr der Vögel, ich befehle es dir ..." Großvater war im Mangobaum versteckt, so konnten ihn weder der englische Beamte noch seine Leute sehen. Alle meinten, in ihnen spräche die Angst. Der Engländer wurde wütend. Die Engländer waren damals Herrscher über ganz Hindustan, und hier war einer, der wegen einer getöteten Ente laut dagegen aufbegehrte.

Der englische Beamte zielte von seinem Hochsitz auf einen Schwarm Krickenten - peng, ging das Gewehr los, und die Leute sahen, wie der ganze Himmel von schreienden Vögeln wimmelte. Aber dann sahen sie, daß diesmal nicht tote Krickenten herabfielen - was fiel, war die Leiche des englischen Beamten.

Es waren nämlich zwei Gewehre gleichzeitig losgegangen. Großvater stieg von der Uferböschung drüben herab und reinigte den Lauf seines Gewehrs, dann sah er zu den Vögeln hin und lächelte, winkte und machte sich davon. Danach, berichtete Mutter, war Großvater

Now the Angrez Officer came to the pond every evening and hunted the birds with his twelve-gauge shotgun. Grandfather lay quietly on his cot in the courtyard and watched the sky fill with birds - bloody guinea hens, wounded ducks, screaming lapwings and frightened herons. Mother said that the day the Angrez Officer went mad with anger and started firing off his shotgun at the pond's ducks was the same day that shots were fired in Jallianwala Bagh in Punjab.

One day Grandfather again cleaned his gun, went to the other side of the pond, climbed a mango tree and hid among its leaves. The Angrez Officer arrived with his Mem Saheb and subordinates. He took his position on a platform built in a mango tree. From the other side Grandfather hollered out to him, "From now on it's all over, Lat Saheb! I am the Malik of this pond and of these birds, and I order you..." But in the mango tree Grandfather was invisible. Neither the Officer nor his subordinates could see him. They all supposed it was just their inner fear talking. The Officer became angry. At that time the English ruled over all of Hindustan, and here Grandfather's voice rose up against him for hunting ducks!

From his platform the Angrez Officer aimed at a flock of waterhen; bang! his gun went off, and his subordinates saw the whole sky fill with screaming birds. But then they saw come tumbling out of the sky not a dead bird but the dead body of the Angrez Officer.

Actually, two triggers had been pulled at exactly the same time. Grandfather came down the high bank on the other side of the pond, cleaned the bore of his gun, looked at the birds and smiled, and then he waved his hand and disappeared. Mother said that for twenty-five

की नाल का धुआँ साफ किया, चिड़ियों की ओर देखकर मुस्कराए, फिर हाथ हिलाया और फरार हो गए। अम्माँ बतलाती हैं कि फिर पच्चीस साल तक दादा का कहीं पता ही नहीं चला। कोई कहता वे साधू हो गए हैं, कोई कहता डाकू। ज़मीन सारी कुर्क हो गयी थी। खाने के लाले पड़े थे। दादी घर में अकेली तीनों बच्चों, यानी पिताजी, चाचा और बुआ को पालती रहीं। उस जमाने में दादा के बारे में हज़ारों किस्से घर-घर चलते कि दादा जर्मनी गए, फिर रूस गए। समुद्र में तैरकर अँग्रेजों के जहाज के पेंदे में छेद कर दिया। ट्रेन में डकैती डाली। कोई कहता कि मुठभेड़ में उन्हें मार डाला गया, फाँसी दे दी गई, कैंसर से मर गए।

लेकिन दादा पच्चीसवें साल, बृहस्पतिवार की शाम, कार्तिक के महीने में, दीपावली के ठीक एक दिन पहले लौट आए। वे बिल्कुल बूढ़े और दुबले हो गए थे। चेहरे पर सफेद दाढ़ी थी, सिर गंजा हो गया था। और कहते हैं, दीवाली की रात उन्होंने दादी को छप्पन तोले का करधन दिया था। सोने का।

उसी साल आजादी मिली थी, उसी साल दादा लौटे थे, लेकिन उसी साल वे बीमार हो गए थे। कहते हैं, दादा जब मजबूत थे तो एक बार वे चलती हुई रेल के इंजन को रोककर उसे ठेलते हुए डेढ़ मील तक पीछे ले गए थे, लेकिन आज़ादी के बाद उनसे अपना टट्टीवाला लोटा भी नहीं उठता था। उन्हें दमा था और वे हाँफते रहते थे। तब तक पिताजी, चाचा और बुआ खूब बड़े हो गए थे। बुआ कहती हैं कि जिस साल से आज़ादी मिली उस साल से वे सारे लोग बीमार हो-होकर मरने लगे थे, जिन्होंने अँग्रेजों से लड़ाई लड़ी थी। दादा भी उसी साल मर गए। आखिरी दिनों में उनके मुँह पर

fünfundzwanzig Jahre spurlos verschwunden. Einer behauptete, er sei Asket, ein anderer, er sei ein Räuber geworden. Sein ganzes Land hatte man beschlagnahmt. Die Familie hatte nichts zu brechen und zu beißen. Großmutter zog ganz allein drei Kinder groß; meinen Vater, den Onkel und die Tante. Damals gingen unzählige Geschichten über Großvater von Haus zu Haus: Er sei nach Deutschland gegangen, hieß es, und dann nach Rußland. Er sei durchs Meer geschwommen und habe in den Boden eines englischen Schiffes ein Loch gebohrt. Er habe einen Zug ausgeraubt. Weiter hieß es, er sei in einer tätlichen Auseinandersetzung zu Tode gekommen, habe am Galgen geendet, sei an Krebs gestorben.

Aber fünfundzwanzig Jahre danach, an einem Donnerstagabend im Spätherbstmonat Kartik, kehrte Großvater zurück, gerade am Tag vor Diwali. Ganz alt und dürr war er geworden. Er hatte einen weißen Bart und einen kahlen Kopf. Und man erzählt sich, er habe in der Diwalinacht Großmutter den Gürtel gegeben, der sechsundfünfzig Tola wog. Und aus Gold war.

In ein und demselben Jahr waren wir unabhängig geworden und war Großvater zurückgekehrt, im selben Jahr aber war er auch krank geworden. Man behauptet von Großvater, daß er, als er noch bei Kräften war, einmal die Lokomotive eines fahrenden Zuges angehalten und anderthalb Meilen zurückgeschoben hatte; aber als wir unabhängig waren, konnte er nicht einmal das Wassertöpfchen aus Messing hochheben, mit dem er seine Notdurft verrichten ging. Er hatte Asthma und keuchte in einem fort. Inzwischen waren mein Vater, der Onkel und die Tante erwachsen geworden. Die Tante meint, seit dem Jahr, in dem wir unabhängig geworden waren, seien alle die, die den Kampf gegen die Engländer ausgefochten hatten, einer nach dem anderen krank geworden und gestorben. Auch Großvater starb in jenem Jahr. In seinen letzten Tagen hatte sich auf seinem alten Gesicht, das klebte wie ein Zuckerklumpen, ein Fliegenschwarm

years after that no one knew where Grandfather was. Some said he became a sadhoo, others a dakoo. All our land was confiscated. Food became hard to get. Alone in the house Dadi raised the three children - Father, Uncle and Jasidih wallee Auntie. During that time thousands of stories about Grandfather spread from house to house. Grandfather went to Germany, then to Russia. He swam the Ocean and drilled holes in the hulls of English vessels. He became a train robber. Some said he was killed in a fist fight, he was hung, or he died of cancer.

But after twenty-five years, on a Thursday evening, in the month of Kartik, just one day before Divali, Grandfather returned. He had become very old and thin. He had a white beard, his head was bald. And people say that on the night of Divali he gave Dadi a waistchain weighing fifty-six tolas. Pure gold.

India got her freedom the same year Grandfather returned, but from then on he was ill. They say that when Grandfather was strong, he once stopped a moving train engine all by himself and pushed it back a mile and a half; but after Independence he couldn't even lift the lota he filled with water when he went out to defecate. He had tuberculosis and was always short of breath. By then Father, Uncle and Jasidih wallee Auntie themselves had grown up. Jasidih wallee Auntie said that the year Independence came, all the people who fought the British got sick and started dying. Grandfather, too, died that same year. During his last days flies covered his face, which was greasy like a ball of brown sugar. He, too, started looking like an old vulture, and he forgot the language of the birds. The day he returned home, he went to his pond, but none of the ducks there recognized him. All the old ducks had died,

ढेर सारी मक्खियाँ बैठी रहती थीं और दादा का बूढ़ा चेहरा गुड़ के ढेले की तरह चिपचिपाता रहता था। दादा भी बूढ़े गिद्ध की तरह लगते थे और वे चिड़ियों की भाषा भूल गए थे। जिस दिन वे घर लौटे थे, उसी दिन वे तालाब गए थे, लेकिन वहाँ किसी भी बत्तख ने उनको नहीं पहचाना था। सारी पुरानी बत्तखें खत्म हो चुकी थीं और उनकी नई पीढ़ी के लिए दादा बिल्कुल अजनबी थे। वे भीतर से टूट गए थे। 'सब बदल गया'–सिर्फ इतना उन्होंने कहा था। उनका टट्टीवाला पीतल का लोटा अब भी हमारे घर की अटारी में था, जिसे मैं नहीं उठा पाता था।
[...]

niedergelassen. Großvater sah aus wie ein alter Geier, doch die Sprache der Vögel hatte er vergessen. An dem Tag, an dem er heimgekehrt war, war er an den See gegangen, aber dort hatte ihn nicht eine einzige Ente erkannt. Alle alten Enten waren längst tot, und für ihre Nachkommen war Großvater ein Fremder. Daran war er innerlich zerbrochen. "Alles ist anders geworden" - das war alles, was er noch gesagt hatte. Sein Messingtöpfchen stand immer noch in unserm Haus in der Dachkammer; ich war zu schwach, es hochzuheben.
[...]

(Translated from Hindi by Lothar Lutze)

and for this new generation Grandfather was a complete stranger. He was crushed. All he said was, "Everything's changed." In our upstairs storage room was his brass lota he used for cleaning himself after defecating, and I couldn't even lift it.
[...]

(Translated from Hindi by R.A. Hueckstedt)

कृष्णा सोब्ती

मित्रो मरजानी

[*मित्रो मरजानी* उपन्यास का एक अंश]

भिड़ा किवाड़ खुला तो गुरुदास देखते के देखते रह गए।

मँझली बहू नंगे सिर बैठी चारपाई पर हिन-हन हँसती थी और बड़ा लड़का बनवारी छाती पर हाथ कसे खड़ा-खड़ा दाँत पीसता था।

गुरुदास गरजे—सरदारी लाल। तेरे होश ठिकाने हैं ? बहू से कह कपड़ा करे !

बाघ की झपट से सरदारी लाल घरवाली की ओर झपटा कि कड़ी मूठ से बनवारी ने बीच ही में रोक दिया।

गुस्से के मारे गुरुदास थर-थर काँपने लगे—तेरे नालायकों को तो बाद में समझूँगा, धनवन्ती, पर यह कह कि उघड़े माथे इन जल्लादों में बैठी तुम्हारी बहू क्या करती है ?

Krishna SOBTI

MITRO MARJANI

[Auszug aus dem Roman *"Mitro Marjani"* ('Verflixte Mitro')]

[Im gemeinsamen Haushalt leben neben den Eltern Gurudas und Dhanavanti deren drei Söhne mit ihren Frauen. Die Schwiegertöchter werden, nach der Rangfolge der Söhne als die 'Älteste' (Suhag, Frau von Banwarilal), die 'Mittlere' (Mitro oder Sumitra, Frau von Sardarilal) und die 'Jüngste' (Phulan, Frau von Gulzarilal) angesprochen. In der Nacht kommt es zum Streit zwischen Sardarilal und Mitro; Banwarilal und Suhag schreiten ein, Suhag holt schließlich die Schwiegereltern zu Hilfe.]

Als die Tür aufsprang, blieb Gurudas wie vom Donner gerührt stehen. Ohne Schleier saß die mittlere Schwiegertochter auf dem Bett und lachte herausfordernd. Der älteste Sohn Banwarilal stand zähneknirschend vor ihr, die Hände an die Brust gepresst. Gurudas polterte los: "Bist du noch ganz bei Trost, Sardarilal? Sag deiner Frau, sie soll sofort den Schleier überziehen!" Sardarilal wollte sich wie ein Raubtier auf seine Frau stürzen, doch sein Bruder hielt ihn zurück. Zornbebend wandte sich Gurudas an seine Frau: "Dhanavanti, um deine nutzlose Brut kümmere ich mich später, aber erklär mir mal, was deine Schwiegertochter hier unverschleiert zwischen

---

Krishna SOBTI

MITRO MARJANI

[Extract from the novel *Mitro Marjani* ('Wretched Mitro')]

When the door, hitherto ajar, was thrown open, Gurudas couldn't take his eyes away from what he saw. Manjhali was sitting on a cot with her head uncovered and was laughing shamelessly and his eldest son Banawari was standing, his hands on his chest, gnashing his teeth. Gurudas shouted, "Sardari Lal, are you in your senses? Ask your wife to cover her head!" Sardari Lal sprang towards his wife like a leopard but Banawari held him off with a firm hand. Gurudas shook with rage - "I'll deal with these unworthy sons of yours later, Dhanawanti, but first tell me what your bahu is doing here, sitting among these wretches, without a cloth over her head."
The eldest son looked at his mother in helpless abject humility and with a gesture of his hand, said, "Amma, don't provoke her to speak, don't. If Bapu gets a single blast of her tongue, this household will not see the morning light."

बड़े बेटे ने बड़ी आजिजी से माँ की ओर देखा और हाथ से रोककर कहा—कुछ न कहलवाओ, अम्मा, इससे, कुछ न कहलवाओ ! इसके बोल एक बन्द भी बापू ने सुन लिया तो इस घर में सवेरा न होगा !

आँखें चमका दीं—अरी मेरी सयानी जिठानी, तुम क्या जानो यह किस्से प्रीति-प्यार के !

बनवारी से सुना नहीं गया। भाई का हाथ पकड़ बाहर खींचते हुए कहा—मँझली को अपने कमरे में सुला ले, सुहाग।

दोनों भाइयों ने जा साथवाले कमरे का किवाड़ भिड़ाया तो—हरे राम ! हरे राम, बनवारी लाल, ऐसा भी क्या अंधेर ? सुनने को जो तुम्हारे बापू नहीं सुन सकते, उसे सुनने को मैं अभागिन ही क्या ज़िन्दा हूँ ?

बड़ी बहू ने सास की मिन्नत की—अम्मा, बापू को कमरे में लौटा ले चलो। यह नहले-दहले उनके बस के नहीं !

धनवन्ती ने पति की बाँह थाम ली तो गुरुदास ने सिर हिला-हिला कहा—यह कलजुग है, कलजुग ! आँख का पानी उतर गया तो फिर क्या घर-घराने की इज्जत और क्या लोक-मरजाद ?

सास-ससुर को समझा-बुझा सुहाग बाहर आई तो किवाड़ में से दोनों भाइयों को गुमसुम खड़े देख सहम गई।

अन्दर जा मित्रो से कहा—मित्रो बहन, काहे का झंझट-बखेड़ा है ? देवर जो कहता है वह मान ।

मँझली ने पहले सरदारी की ओर देखा फिर बनवारी की ओर मँझली माथे पर हाथ मार हँसी—बुरे माथेवाले ! मर्द जन होते तो या चटखारे ले-ले मुझे चाटते या फिर शेर की तरह कच्चा चबा डालते !

den Kerlen zu suchen hat!"
Der älteste Sohn sagte beschämt und hilflos zu seiner Mutter: "Paß auf, daß sie ja kein Wort mehr sagt, kein einziges Wort! Wenn Vater nur einen Ton von ihrem frechen Geschwätz hört, erlebt dies Haus den nächsten Morgen nicht mehr!"
"Hare Ram, Hare Ram, Banwarilal, was für eine Ungerechtigkeit! Was dein Vater schon nicht ertragen kann, das soll ich Unglückliche mir anhören? Bin ich dazu am Leben?"
"Bring Vater zurück in sein Zimmer, Mutter, dieses Hickhack ist einfach zuviel für ihn", bat Suhag.
Als Dhanawanti ihren Mann hinausführte, murmelte er nur noch kopfschüttelnd: "Das ist das Ende, das ist das Kaliyuga! Wenn sich solche Unverschämtheiten erst durchsetzen, braucht man keinen Gedanken mehr an Ehre und Ruf der Familie zu verschwenden."
Als Suhag aus dem Zimmer kam, wo sie versucht hatte, die Schwiegereltern zu beruhigen, erschrak sie beim Anblick der grimmig schweigenden Brüder an der Tür. Sie ging zu Mitro hinein und sagte zu ihr: "Mußt du denn immer so ein Theater machen? Hör doch auf das, was dir dein Mann sagt!"
Mit einem Funkeln in den Augen wandte sich Mitro an die Schwägerin: "Oh, meine ehrwürdige ältere Schwägerin! Kannst du auch schon mitreden in diesen Liebesgeschichten!" Banwarilal hatte genug. Er zog seinen Bruder am Arm fort und sagte zu seiner Frau: "Suhag, laß die Mittlere heute bei dir im Zimmer schlafen."
Mitro sah erst Sardarilal an, dann Banvarilal und schlug sich dann an die Stirn: "Ach, ihr armen Wichte! Wärt ihr richtige Männer, hättet ihr euch entweder genüßlich über mich hergemacht, oder mich nach Strich und Faden verprügelt!"

The two brothers went to the adjoining room and closed its door when their mother said :
"Hare Ram! Hare Ram! Banawari Lal, what kind of justice is this? Why should I be alive to hear what your father cannot bear to hear? Why should I be so unfortunate?"
The eldest daughter-in-law entreated her mother-in-law: "Amma, take Bapu to his room. These bouts of crudity are not for him."
When Dhanawanti caught hold of her husband's arm, Gurudas said, shaking his head again and again, "This is Kaliyuga, Kaliyuga! If one loses one's sense of shame, one ceases to bother about the family honour and tradition."
When Suhag returned after placating and calming down her in-laws, she saw the two brothers standing silent and sullen in the doorway. She became anxious. Going in, she told Mitro, "Mitro sister, why have you created this row? Do what your man tells you to do."
With a glint in her eyes, Mitro turned towards Banawaris's wife:
"Arri, my wise Jethani, what do you know of these matters of love and heart?"
Banawari couldn't stand it anymore. Dragging his brother out by the hand, he said to his own wife, "Take Manjhali along and let her sleep in your room, Suhag."
Manjhali first looked towards Sardari and then, with a glint in her eyes, towards Banawari. Then striking her forehead, she laughed, "You are indeed unfortunate! If you had been manly enough, you would either have licked me all over with relish or like a lion devoured me raw."
Suhag did not look towards her. She pulled out a cot, spread the bedding and placing a quilt on it, said, "Sister Mitro, it's getting very late in the night. Now put aside all your worries and

सुहाग ने देवरानी की ओर ताका नहीं। खटिया खींच बिछाई और लिहाफ़ डालकर बोली—बहन मित्रो, घनी रात गई। अब चिन्ता-जंजाल छोड़ तनिक आराम कर लो।

मित्रो ने ओंठ बिचकाए—चिन्ता-जंजाल किसको ? मैं तो चिन्ता करनेवाली के पेट ही नहीं पड़ी।

छिः-छिः सुनकर सुहाग के कान जलने लगे। मित्रो उठ खटिया के पास आई। पहले लिहाफ़ उठाया, खेस टटोला, फिर उलट-पलट सिरहाना टटोल बोली—जिठानी, तुम्हारे देवर-सा बगलोल कोई और दूजा न होगा। न दुःख-सुख, न प्रीति-प्यार, न जलन-प्यास···बस आए दिन धौल-धप्पा···लानत-मलामत !

एकाएक आँखों में कोई मद उतर आया। खींच गले की ओढ़नी उतारी। कुरता, फिर सलवार उतार परे फेंक दी और हँस-हँस बोली—बनवारी कहता है, मित्रो तेरी देह क्या निरा शीरा है शी-रा ! उस नास-होने से कहती हूँ···

—अरे, इसी शीरे में तेरी जान को डंक मारते सर्पों की फौजें पलती हैं !

नई बहू का चेहरा काला-स्याह पड़ गया, कानों पर हाथ रख कहा—हाथ जोड़ती हूँ, देवरानी, मेरे सिर पाप न चढ़ा !

मँझली फटाक बिछौने पर सीधी लेट गई। ऊपर कुछ ओढ़ा नहीं। देख सुहाग के बदन सुइयाँ चुभने लगीं। इस कुलबोरन की तरह जनानी को हया न हो तो नित-नित जूठी होती औरत की देह निरे पाप का घट है।

रजाई खींच मुँह-सिर लपेट लिया।

मित्रो ने आवाज़ दी—टुक आँखें खोल, इधर तो निरख जिठानी !

Suhag konnte ihre Schwägerin nicht ansehen. Sie zog ein Bettgestell hervor und breitete Bettzeug und Steppdecke aus. "Komm, Mitro, es ist schon mitten in der Nacht. Vergiß deinen Kummer und die ganze Aufregung und leg dich schlafen!"
Mitro verzog spöttisch den Mund. "Was meinst du mit Kummer? Ich wüßte nicht, woher ich das haben sollte, meine Mutter war jedenfalls kein Kind von Traurigkeit!"
"Pfui, hör auf!" Suhag brannten die Ohren vor Scham.
Mitro ging zu ihrem Bett und schlug die Decke zurück. Sie klopfte die Unterlage zurecht und schüttelte das Kissen auf. "Weißt du, Suhag, du kannst dir keine größere Tranfunzel als deinen Schwager vorstellen. Er kennt weder Ärger noch Freude, keine Gefühle, keine Zärtlichkeit, kein Feuer, kein Verlangen, – nur jeden Tag Streit und Schläge, Prügel und Dresche, das ist alles!"
Plötzlich bekamen ihre Augen einen leidenschaftlichen Ausdruck. Sie nahm ihren Schal vom Hals, zog dann Kurta und Salwar aus und warf alle Kleider lachend von sich. "Banwari hat immer zu mir gesagt: 'Mitro, dein Körper ist wie süßer Syrup, der reinste Zucker!' Und ich hab dem Gauner geantwortet: 'Paß nur auf, in diesem süßen Syrup winden sich tausend Schlangen, die nur drauf warten, dich zu beißen!'"
Suhag, die Frischvermählte, wurde aschfahl im Gesicht. Sie hielt sich die Ohren zu und sagte: "Ich bitte dich, Schwägerin, häuf keine Sünde über mich."
Mitro ließ sich aufs Bett fallen. Sie deckte sich nicht einmal zu. Suhag war ihr Anblick unerträglich. 'Frauen wie sie sind ein Schandfleck ihrer Familie. Ihr Körper wird benutzt und immer schmutziger, bis er nur noch aus Sünde besteht', dachte sie und zog sich die Decke über den Kopf. Mitro rief: "Mach nur kurz die Augen auf und guck mal hierher!"

botherations and rest a bit."
Mitro pursed her lips – "Who is worried or bothered? Not me at least. I wasn't born to one ever given to worrying."
Chi ... Chi... Hearing this, Suhag got red in the ears. Mitro got up and came close to the cot. First, she lifted the quilt, fumbled with the khes, and then picking up the pilllow and turning it up and down, she said, "Jethani, I don't think there is anyone as naive as your devar. No sharing of joys and sorrows, no show of affection and love, no sign of desire and intimacy ... only beating and thrashing, day after day ... abuses and scolding!"
All of a sudden, something crazy came upon her. She pulled off the *odhni* from around her neck. Took off her *kurta,* then removed her *salwar* and threw it away and laughing, said, "Banawari says, Mitro, your body is all *sheera* and I tell that rascal: 'Arre, in this *sheera* lurk hordes of snakes ready to sting you!"
The badi bahu's face darkened. She looked aghast. Covering her ears with her hands, she said, "I beseech you, Devarani, don't heap sins on my head!"
Manjhali stretched out on her back on the bed – bare all the way from head to foot. Seeing her, Suhag was on pins and needles. A women like her without any sense of shame is no friend of the family, and her body is only a receptacle of sin.
She pulled up her quilt, and covered her head and face.
Mitro called out – "Open your eyes, look this side, elder sister."
Suhag scolded her, "These brothers have very sharp ears, ri. Supposing they heard?" Mitro remained

नई ने मुँह ढँके-ढँके झिड़की दी—इन भाइयों के कान बड़े पतले हैं, री ! सुन लेंगे तो···

मित्रो लेटी-लेटी इतराई—सुन लें, इससे क्या डरती हूँ ?—फिर जिठानी से कहा—बहनेली, इतनी-सी बात मेरी रख लो। बस !

सुहाग ने खीजकर एक बार आँख खोल दी।

सिर उठाया—क्या है, री ?

मँझली लेटी-लेटी उठ बैठी। हाथों से छातियाँ ढँक मग्न हो कहा—सच कहना, जिठानी सुहागवन्ती, क्या ऐसी छातियाँ किसी और की भी हैं ?···

सुहाग का तन-बदन फुँकने लगा। बिछौना छोड़ पास आई और अपने माथे पर दोहत्थी मार बोली—फिटक जोगी, मरे पीछे पता भी न पाएगी कि कभी तू जीती भी थी ! दिन-रात घुलती इस औरत की देह पर तुझे इतना गुमान ? अरी, लानत तुझ पर ! घर-घर तेरे-जैसी काली-मकाली औरतें हैं। उनके भी तुझ-जैसे ही दो-दो हाथ हैं, पाँव हैं, आँखें हैं और यही तुझ-जैसी दो छातियाँ ! क्या तू ही अनोखी इस जून पड़ी है ?

मँझली ने निर्लज्जता से बाँहें फैला दीं—मैं सदके-बलिहारी ! अपने जेठ की सती-सावधी नार पर ! जिठानी मेरे जेठ से कह रखना जब तक मित्रो के पास यह इलाही ताकत है मित्रो मरती नहीं।

भले स्वभाववाली बनवारी की बहू एकाएक रणचण्डी बन आई। कड़ककर कहा—चुप री धर्म-पिट्टी ! उठकर कपड़े पहन, नहीं तो मुझसे बुरा कोई न होगा !

जिठानी का गुस्सा देख मित्रो ने हँसते-हँसते लीड़े पहर लिए तो सिर हिला-हिला सुहाग जैसे अपने से ही

Unter der Decke wisperte Suhag zurück: "He, wenn das die Brüder hören, die haben gute Ohren!"
"Na und wenn schon, laß sie doch!" sagte Mitro aufsässig. "Guck nur einmal, ja?"
Widerwillig öffnete Suhag die Augen. "Was ist denn?"
Mitro setzte sich auf. Mit beiden Händen umfaßte sie ihre Brüste und sagte ganz stolz: "Sag mal ehrlich, liebe Schwägerin Suhagwanti, kennst du jemand, der so schöne Brüste hat wie ich?"
Suhag fühlte flammende Hitze in sich aufsteigen. Sie sprang aus dem Bett, ging zu Mitro hinüber und schlug sich an die Stirn. "Schande über dich, wenn du irgendwann stirbst, weißt du nicht mal mehr, daß du je gelebt hast! Was bildest du dir eigentlich auf deinen Körper ein, meinst du, der ist unvergänglich? Du solltest dich schämen! In jedem Haus gibt es Weiber wie dich, in allen Schattierungen! Die haben alle genau wie du zwei Hände, Füße, Augen und zwei Brüste! Was glaubst du eigentlich, was an dir so besonderes ist?"
Schamlos streckte Mitro ihre Arme aus. "Ich bin dir zutiefst ergeben, oh tugendhaftes Weib meines Schwagers! Suhag, du kannst deinem Mann sagen, solange in Mitro noch diese Kraft steckt, denkt sie gar nicht ans Sterben!"
Jetzt wurde die sanftmütige und geduldige Frau von Banwarilal zur rasenden Kriegsgöttin Kali. Sie kreischte: "Halt jetzt den Mund, du Schlampe! Steh sofort auf und zieh dir was an, sonst wirst du mich kennenlernen!"
Als sie ihre Schwägerin so aufgebracht sah, zog sich Mitro lachend etwas über, während Suhag nur vor sich hinmurmelte: "Was für eine Schande, eine Schwiegertochter, die feierlich in der Sänfte ins Haus getragen wurde, führt sich dermaßen auf! Oh große Göttin des Lichtes,

lying and warbled vainly – "So what? Let'm hear, I'm not afraid." Then addressing her jethani, she said, "My dear sister, don't refuse this little request of mine. That's all." Irritated, Suhag opened her eyes, just once. She raised her head – "What's it, ri?" Manjhali sat up. Cupping her breasts in her hands, she said blithely – "Tell me, Jethani Suhagwati, does anyone else possess breasts like these?"
Suhag was afire all over. Leaving her bed, she came close and beating her forehead, said, "Damn you, after you die, you won't even know that you had ever lived! You're priding yourself so much on this woman's body which is wearing out day and night? Arri, you should hang your head in shame! Every house has women like you, dark and fair. They also have hands, feet, eyes and two breasts like yours! What's so unique about you?"
Manjhali stretched out her arms shamelessly – "I bow and offer my good wishes to you, O pure and devoted wife of my jeth! Jethani, tell my jeth that as long as Mitro possesses this gift of God, she will not die."
Banawari's good-natured wife suddenly got transformed into fury incarnate. She snapped at her sternly, "Shut up, you immoral woman! Get up and put on your clothes. Otherwise you will find me ranged against you no end."
Seeing her jethani's angry mood, Mitro put on her clothes with a smile while Suhag kept muttering to herself as it were, "What a sinful thing to have taken place! That a daughter-in-law of the family, brought in ceremoniously in a palanquin, should behave like this! O Goddess of lights! Protect the honour, the name of this house!"
Then opening her eyes wide, she said to Mitro, "Devrani, it's a pity that you escaped the hands of

कहती चली—ऐसा पाप-वरत गया कि डोले में लाई, परणायी बहू के ये हाल-हीले ! हे जोतोंवाली देवी ! इस घर की इज्जत-पत रखना ।

फिर आँखें फैला मित्रो से कहा—देवरानी, तेरी किस्मत बुरी थी जो तू आज इन भाइयों के हाथों बच निकली। मर-खप जाती तो तू इस जंजाल से छूटती और वे भी सुरखरू हो जाते । फिर ठुड्डी पर हाथ रख बुरे मुँह पूछा—सच-सच कह, देवरानी, तू इस राह-कुराह कैसे पड़ी ?

मित्रो झिझकी—हिचकिचाई नहीं। पड़े-पड़े कहा—सात नदियों की तारू, तवे-सी काली मेरी माँ, और मैं गोरी चिट्टी उसकी कोख पड़ी। कहती है इलाके के बड़भागी तहसीलदार की मुँहादरा है मित्रो। अब तुम्हीं बताओ, जिठानी तुम-जैसा सत-बल कहाँ से पाऊँ-लाऊँ ? देवर तुम्हारा मेरा रोग नहीं पहचानता। …बहुत हुआ हफ्ते-पखवारे…और मेरी इस देह में इतनी प्यास है, इतनी प्यास कि मछली-सी तड़पती हूँ।

सुहाग फटी-फटी आँखों देवरानी को ऐसे तकती रही कि पहली बार देखा हो, कि नाक-नक्शा ध्यान में न आता हो, सिर हिला फीके गले कहा—देवरानी, इन भले लोगों को भुलवा दे तुम्हारी माँ ने अच्छा नहीं किया, तब एकाएक मुँह तमतमा आया—देवरानी बहू-बेटियों के लिए तो घर-गृहस्थी की रीति ही लच्छमन की लीक। जाने-अनजाने फलांगी नहीं कि…

मित्रो ने कानों पर हाथ दे आँखें नचाईं—ठोंक-पीट मुझे अपने सबक दोगी तो मैं भी मुंडी हिला लूँगी, जिठानी, पर जो हौंस इस तन व्यापी है…

सुहाग से सुना नहीं गया तो हाथ से टोक दिया—बस, देवरानी !

beschütze die Ehre dieses Hauses!" Dann sah sie Mitro mit weitgeöffneten Augen an. "Weißt du, eigentlich war es dein Pech, daß du heute den Händen der Brüder entwischt bist. Wenn sie dich erledigt hätten, wärst du wenigstens diesem ganzen Unglück hier entkommen, und die beiden hätten auch eine Sorge weniger." Sie stützte ihr Kinn auf und sagte mißtrauisch: "Sag mal ehrlich, wie bist du eigentlich so auf die schiefe Bahn geraten?"

Mitro war dadurch keineswegs in Verlegenheit zu bringen. Im Liegen erwiderte sie: "Meine Mutter ist ja mit allen Wassern gewaschen, selbst war sie schwarz wie eine Chapattipfanne und dann hat sie so ein Schneeweißchen wie mich zur Welt gebracht! Sie sagt immer: 'Kommt meine Mitro nicht ganz nach unserem ehrenwerten Tehsildar?' Jetzt sag selbst, Schwägerin, woher soll ich wohl Anstand und Benehmen gelernt haben? Und dein Schwager Sardari kapiert einfach nicht, was mir fehlt. Wenn's hochkommt, einmal die Woche oder alle vierzehn Tage..., und in mir steckt so ein Verlangen, ich zappel wie ein Fisch auf dem Trockenen..."

Mit aufgerissenen Augen starrte Suhag Mitro an, als sähe sie sie das erste Mal, als hätte sie Mühe, in ihr ihre Schwägerin wiederzuerkennen. Dann sagte sie mit schwacher Stimme: "Mitro, deine Mutter hätte diese ahnungslosen Leute hier nicht so hinters Licht führen dürfen." Und, mit mehr Nachdruck: "Wir Töchter und Schwiegertöchter müssen uns doch nach den Regeln des Hauses richten, und wer sich darüber hinwegsetzt, absichtlich oder nicht, der..."

Mitro hielt sich die Ohren zu und verdrehte die Augen. "Wenn du mir jetzt deinen Sermon aufzwingen mußt, nicke ich natürlich brav zu allem! Und trotzdem, in mir kocht eine Leidenschaft..."

Suhag war das unerträglich und sie gab ihr einen Stoß: "Schluß jetzt, Mitro!"

Mitro legte sich aufs Kissen, schloß die Augen und redete sich gut zu: 'Mitro Rani, sollen sich die andern doch ärgern! Der Schöpfer, der dich auf die Welt geschickt hat, dein Glück

those brothers today. If you had died, you'd have been free of all hassles and they, too, would've felt relieved."

And then, placing her hand on her chin, she asked wryly, "Tell me truly, Devarani, how did you happen to fall into such disreputable ways?"

Mitro didn't flinch, didn't hesitate a bit. Lying as she was, she said, "Black like a tawa is my mother, who has been through the experience of the world, and she gave birth to a fair white daughter that's me. She says Mitro takes after the blessed Tehsildar of the area. Now tell me, Jethani, how can I boast of moral purity like yours? Your devar doesn't understand my ailment ... At the most, once in a week or a fortnight... and this body of mine feels so parched, so thirsty that I keep tossing about like a fish out of water!"

Suhag remained staring at her devarani with eyes wide open as though she was looking at her for the first time, as if she couldn't recollect her features. Then, shaking her head, she said in a faint voice, "Devarani, it wasn't right for your mother to deceive these good people." Getting worked up suddenly, she added, "Devarani, for daughters and daughters-in-law, it's best to stay within the family bounds."

Touching her ears, Mitro fluttered her eyelashes and said, "If you give me lessons to set me right, I'll no doubt nod my head, Jethani, but this fire that is raging all inside me..." Suhag couldn't bear to hear further, and she stopped her with a gesture of her hand – "Enough, Devarani!" Mitro rested her head on the pillow and closing her eyes, pretended to console herself – "Mitro Rani. Not for you to worry. The Creator who has shaped you and sent you to this earth to have your fill of the

मित्रो ने सिरहाने पर सिर रखा और आँखें मींच अपने को समझाया—मित्रो रानी ! चिन्ता-फिकर तेरे बैरियों को ! जिस घड़नेवाले ने तुझे घड़ दुनिया का सुख लूटने को भेजा है, वही जहान का वाली तेरी फिकर भी करेगा !

बन्द आँखों में बनारसी का यार नयामत थानेदार दीख पड़ा। ऊँचा-लम्बा, मुच्छल। पहले पास खड़ा-खड़ा हँसता रहा फिर कड़ककर कहा—अरी ओ सुभान कौर ! उठकर बैठ ! देखती नहीं कौन आया है !

—मेरी तरफ से काला चोर आया है। जरा जर के नयामत राय, यह तेरा थाना नहीं, मेरी चौकी है !

नयामत ने बाँह बढ़ा ओढ़नी खींच ली।

—बस···बस···बहुत हुआ। पड़ी रहेगी और चौकी लुट जाएगी।

मित्रो ने खुश हो बाँहें फैला दीं—वाह रे कमज़ात बिल्ले, मलाई देख मुँह मारने आया है !

रजाई परे जा गिरी तो सुहाग ने घुड़की दी—ख्याली घोड़े न दौड़ा, देवरानी, सीधी तरह सो जा। अबकी हिलते देखूँगी तो···

मित्रो कुलबुलाई । जी तो हुआ, जिठानी से कहे, जिसे भड़वे की सूरत-मूरत मेरे तन-मन बसी है उस पर तेरा क्या जोर ? पर सोचा, जिठानी मेरी जरूर धर्म-सतवाली है। नहीं तो क्योंकर जान लेती कि मैं पड़ी-पड़ी नियामत से जवाब-सवाल करती हूँ !

मित्रो ने भिनसरे आँख खोली तो जिठानी के बदले सास को पास बैठे देख रात की सारी कथा-वार्ता याद हो आई। चमककर बाँहें फैलाईं, अलसाई-सी अँगड़ाई ली और सास को ऐसे घूरा जैसे आँख-ही-आँख में हँस-हँस कहती हो, सासु जी, जवानी कहीं से माँगकर तो नहीं लाई।

zu suchen, der wird sich auch weiterhin um dich kümmern!'
Vor ihren geschlossenen Augen tauchte das Bild des Polizeiinspektors Nayamat wieder auf, ein Bekannter von Banarasi: Groß und stattlich, schwarzer Schnurrbart. Erst hatte er nur lachend neben ihr gestanden, sie dann aber schließlich angepöbelt: "Na, gnädigstes Fräulein, wie wäre es, wenn du dich erhebst? Du weißt wohl nicht, wer vor dir steht!"
"Von mir aus kann es der schwarze Mann persönlich sein! Hör zu, mein bester Nayamat, das hier ist nicht deine Polizeistation, das ist mein Revier!"
Nayamat hatte die Hand ausgestreckt und ihr den Schal weggezogen. "Genug jetzt, das reicht! Bleib nur liegen, und du kannst einen Überfall auf dein Revier erleben!"
Vergnügt hatte sie sich geräkelt : "Na sieh mal an, der räudige Kater! Sieht das Sahnetöpfchen und muß gleich die Schnauze reintunken!"
Ihre Bettdecke geriet ins Rutschen und Suhag schimpfte: "He, gib dich nicht mit Hirngespinsten ab! Leg dich ordentlich hin und schlaf! Wenn ich dich noch einmal herumwälzen sehe ..."
Mitro schmollte. Am liebsten hätte sie zu Suhag gesagt: 'Was machst du denn, wenn dir das Gesicht von einem Mann nicht mehr aus dem Kopf geht?' Dann dachte sie: 'Meine Schwägerin hat wirklich überirdische Gaben! Wie hätte sie sonst ahnen können, daß ich mich hier insgeheim mit Nayamat abgebe?'

Als Mitro morgens die Augen öffnete, saß statt ihrer Schwägerin die Schwiegermutter an ihrem Bett, und ihr fiel die ganze Geschichte der vorigen Nacht wieder ein. Sie räkelte sich genüßlich, mit einem Ausdruck wie: 'Tja Mutter, alles echt an mir, nichts geborgt oder gestohlen!' Sie verdrehte die Augen und sagte herausfordernd: "Was machst du denn hier in aller Herrgottsfrühe?

pleasures of this world, that verysame Lord of the universe will surely provide for your needs."
With eyes closed, she visualized Banarasi's friend Nyamat Thanedar. A tall, moustachioed fellow! At first, he stood besides her, smiling and then shouted in a voice full of authority – "Arri, blessed wench! Sit up! Can't you see who has come?"
"As far as I'm concerned, a black burglar has come. Have patience, Nyamat Rai, this is not your police station, this is my post!"
Nyamat extended his arm and pulled away her odhni and said, "Enough, enough...I don't want to hear anything. If you remain lying, your post will be plundered!" Mitro was delighted and opened her arms -"Hai re! What a cheeky tomcat you are! On seeing cream, you've come to lick it!"
When her quilt slipped off and fell aside, Suhag rebuked her – "Don't you go riding imaginary horses, Devarani, go to sleep like decent folks. If I find you moving in bed, I..."
Mitro whimpered a bit. She felt like telling her jethani – Look, how do you escape someone who has captivated you.. body and soul? But then she thought – My jethani is surely a virtuous woman with divine powers, otherwise she couldn't have divined that I was arguing with Nyamat.

Next morning when Mitro woke up, she found that instead of her jethani, it was her mother-in-law who sat beside her. She remembered all that had transpired the previous night. Brightening up, she spread her arms, yawned a bit languorously, and stared at her mother-in-law as though saying smilingly and teasingly with her eyes: 'Sasooji, this youth of mine isn't something I've borrowed or begged from somewhere."

आँखें मटका ढिठाई से कहा—मुँह अँधेरे यहाँ कैसे, माँ जी ? मित्रो बिचारी अगले जहान तो नहीं चली कि उसका दीवा-बत्ती करवाने आई हो ?

धनवन्ती कई छिन बहू की ओर तकती रही, फिर सिर हिला बोली—बेटी, मुझ कर्म-जली के ऐसे भाग कहाँ ? इज़्ज़तमान से तेरा साईं तुझे भू पर उतारता तो मैं भी अपनी समित्रारानी को दिल खोलकर रोती, पर फूटी किस्मत मेरी, वह दिहाड़ा मुझे देखना न बँधा था।

—दिन-दहाड़े अभी बहुतेरे आएँगे, माँ जी, सारी चिन्ता-सोग आज ही न निपटा लो।

चौके से सुहाग की हाँक सुन धनवन्ती उठ बैठी और जाते-जाते माथे पर हाथ मार बोली—लख लानत है, बीबी मुझे, जिसने तुम्हारी माँ से माथा लगाया !

मित्रो कुछ कहने जाती थी कि द्वार पर जेठ की ऊँची परछाईं देख ठिठक गई। कल रात की बात याद कर मसखरी से छोटा-सा घूँघट निकाल बोली—जेठ जी, अपनी जिठानी के तुल तो मैं कहाँ पर एक नजर इधर भी⋯

सुना-अनसुना कर बनवारी लाल परत गए कि सुहाग ने आ देवरानी से कहा—तावली-तावली नहा-धो आयी, मँझली। छोटी का जी अच्छा नहीं। मैं घर-अँगना बुहार लेती हूँ, तुम चौके की सँभाल लो।

—मैं मर गई। जिठानी ! यह पापड़गिरों की फूलाँ आए दिन स्वांग रचती है। खाने को दिन में चार दोने मिठाई और रात आधा सेर पक्के दूध में जलेबियाँ !

सुहाग ने सिर हिलाया—न⋯न⋯देवरानी, उसे झूठा दोष न दे, उसका तन ठीक नहीं।

Ist Mitro vielleicht gestorben, daß du die letzten Riten an ihr vollziehen mußt?"
Dhanavanti sah sie einen Moment lang an, dann schüttelte sie den Kopf: "Nein Mitro, wie könnte ich Unselige vom Schicksal wohl so belohnt werden! Wenn dein Mann dich tatsächlich mit allen Ehren aufgebahrt hätte, wahrhaftig, auch ich würde um meine Sumitra Rani weinen, aber es ist mir nicht vergönnt, diesen Tag zu erleben..."
"Es wird noch eine Menge solcher Gelegenheiten geben, Mutter, heb deinen Kummer auf für später..."
Dhanavanti hörte Suhag aus der Küche rufen, deshalb stand sie auf und und schlug sich an die Stirn: "Verflucht sei ich, daß ich mich mit deiner Mutter eingelassen habe!"
Mitro wollte ihr gerade eine passende Antwort geben, als sie den Schatten ihres älteren Schwagers an der Tür bemerkte und sich zurückhielt. In Erinnerung an die Vorfälle in der Nacht zupfte sie ihren Schal ein winziges Stück tiefer ins Gesicht und sagte spitzbübisch: "Na, ich kann es natürlich nicht mit meiner Schwägerin aufnehmen, aber vielleicht riskierst du trotzdem mal einen Blick?" Banwari wandte sich ab, als habe er nichts gehört, und Suhag kam herein. "Mitro, ich habe mich beeilt mit meinem Bad. Die Jüngste fühlt sich nicht wohl. Ich wische die Böden drinnen und im Hof, kümmer du dich um die Küche!"
"Das darf doch wohl nicht wahr sein! Diese Phulan aus der Familie von Papad-Produzenten hat doch ständig eine neue Krankheit auf Lager! Aber wenn's ans Essen geht, verdrückt sie pro Tag vier Schachteln Süßigkeiten und nachts noch ein halbes Kilo Jalebis mit Milch!"
Suhag schüttelte den Kopf: "Nein, nein, du darfst sie nicht ungerecht beschuldigen. Sie hat eben eine empfindliche Gesundheit!"
Mitro rollte die Augen. "Heute knacken ihre Knochen, morgen zerspringt ihr die Stirn, dann

Rolling her eyes, she said stubbornly: "How come, you here, so early in the morning, Maaji? Poor Mitro isn't going to leave for the other world that you've come to preside over her obsequies."
Dhanawanti kept looking at her daughter-in-law for several moments. Then shaking her head, she said, "Beti, I'm not so fortunate as to be able to do that. If your husband had placed your corpse on the ground with honours due to a wife, then certainly I too would have cried my heart out for my Sumitra Rani, but it was my misfortune that I was not destined to see that day."
"Maaji, there'll be many such occasions yet, so you needn't be done with all the worrying and mourning today itself..." Hearing Suhag calling from the kitchen, Dhanawanti got up and, while leaving, she struck her forehead and said, "A million curses on me for making your mother our kin."
Mitro was about to say something but, noticing the tall shadow of her jeth at the door, she checked herself. Remembering what had transpired the previous evening, she pulled down her veil a little over her forehead and said good-humouredly – "Jethji, I am just no match to my jethani in looks but cast a glance towards me also ..."

Ignoring what he had heard, Banawari Lal went back, but Suhag came in and said to her devarani, "I have come after having a quick bath, Manjhali. The chhoti bahu isn't well. I'll sweep the floors. You take charge of the kitchen."
"Curse on me, Jethani! This Phoolan of paapad-makers keeps feigning illness every other day. She consumes four donas of sweets during the day and half a kilo of boiled milk with jalebis each night!"
Suhag shook her head – "No, no, Devarani, don't blame her falsely, she's really not feeling well!"

मँझली ने आँखें नचाईं—आज हड्डी टूटती है, आज माथा फटता है, आज कमर दुखती है, आज दिल छिपता है...

सुहाग ने टोका। फूलावन्ती को आज सच ही दन्दल पड़ी है, देवरानी। देह उसकी काठ-सी अकड़ी पड़ी है।

—लाडो को क्या दिन चढ़े हैं ! फूलावन्ती का तन ठीक रहे तो, बहन मेरी, वह पापड़गिरों की लड़की कैसी ? मुटियार तो पक्की, ऐसे-ऐसे पापड़ बेल ले कि मर्द को पता न पाने दे कब कपड़ों से होती है।

सुहाग का जी तो हुआ खुलकर हँस ले, पर गम्भीर बनी रही। पुचकारकर कहा—उठ, मेरी बहना, जल्दी नहा-धो आ।

मित्रो ऐसे उत्साह से उठी कि सोलहवाँ लगा हो। आँगन में घरवाले को देखा तो और भी इतराई।

—मैं अभी मरी नहीं हूँ, चन्न जी, जिन्दा हूँ।

जवाब में सरदारी ने कसे-कसाए तेवर दिखा दिए तो लापरवाही से बाँह हिला, मुँह चिढ़ा कहा—मेरी भी बोलेगी बला !

और नहान-घर में जा घुसी।

नहा-धो आई तो जिठानी चौके में बैठी पराठे सेंकती थी। सासरानी लड़कों के संग बापू के कमरे में बैठी कोई खिचड़ी पकाती थी।

उमंग में चलती-डोलती मित्रो फूलावन्ती के कमरे में आई तो देवरानी की बेहोशी टूट चुकी थी। पास बैठा

tut der Bauch weh oder das Herz macht schlapp..."
Suhag unterbrach sie: "Phulavanti hat wirklich einen Anfall, ihr Körper ist verkrampft und steif wie ein Brett!"

"Als ob unser Liebling schwanger wäre! Wenn der mal nichts fehlt, dann stimmt was nicht, dann kann sie nicht die Phulan aus der Papad-Sippe sein! Das ist doch ein richtiges Luder, die tischt ihrem Mann ein Papad nach dem andern auf, solange bis der nicht mal mehr weiß, ob sie ihre Regel hat oder nicht!"
Suhag mußte sich das Lachen verbeißen. "Los, ab ins Bad, Mitro!" Mitro schwang sich aus dem Bett wie eine Sechzehnjährige. Als sie im Hof ihren Mann sah, tänzelte sie vor ihm auf und ab und rief ihm zu: "Ich bin noch am Leben, mein Süßer, und wie!" Als Sardarilal nur finster zurücksah, winkte sie abfällig und zog einen Flunsch: "Schon gut, ich sag ja nichts mehr." Dann verschwand sie im Bad.

Als sie herauskam, saß ihre ältere Schwägerin bereits in der Küche und war mit dem Backen von Parathas beschäftigt. Ihre Schwiegermutter und die beiden älteren Söhne saßen beim Vater im Zimmer und hielten Kriegsrat. Übermütig spähte sie in Phulavantis Zimmer, und stellte fest, daß sich ihre Schwägerin inzwischen von ihrer Bewußtlosigkeit erholt hatte. Schwager Gulzari saß neben seiner Frau und massierte ihre Hände. Ihr Lachen verbergend, begrüßte sie Phulan nach außenhin mit einem mitfühlenden Kuß und sagte: "Ach du Ärmste! In deinem zarten Alter solche schlimmen Krankheiten! Diese gräßlichen Anfälle saugen dir noch das letzte Blut aus den Adern!"
Phulan warf ihrem Mann einen vorwurfsvollen Blick zu und ließ kraftlos ihren Arm sinken.

Manjhali rolled her eyes – "One day it's her bones aching, another day her forehead splitting, then one day her waist is paining and some day it's her heart sinking..." Suhag stopped her – "Today Phoolawanti has really got a fit of hysteria, Devarani. She is lying stiff like a piece of timber."
"Is that darling pregnant? That daughter of the paapad-makers wouldn't be true to her lineage if she remained in good health, my sister. She is bloody cunning and capable of putting on ruses so that her man wouldn't even know when she has her periods."
Suhag was tickled into open laughter, but remained sedate. She said endearingly, "Get up, my sister, go and come back after having a quick bath!"
Mitro got up enthusiastically like one who has just entered her sixteenth year. Seeing her husband in the courtyard, she swaggered some more. "I'm not dead yet, love. I'm still alive!"

When in response, Sardari maintained a solemn hard expression, she teased him by flaunting her arm carelessly and putting on a taunting expression on her face – "As if I care! I'm also not going to talk to you!" And she went and got into the bathroom.
When she returned after her bath, she found her jethani making parathas in the kitchen. And her mother-in-law was in Bapu's room with her sons, hatching some conspiracy. Sallying forth with abandon, when Mitro entered Phoolawanti's room, her devarani had regained consciousness. Mitro's devar Gulzari Lal was sitting beside her, rubbing Phoolan's palms. Manjhali had a secret laugh. Outwardly she released a kissing sound with her lips and said: "Haye, Haye! Phoolawanti, t a range of ailments to have at such a tender age! These wretched fits suck up all blood from

देवर गुलजारी लाल फूलाँ के हाथों की तालियाँ झसता था।

मँझली दिल में हँसी। ऊपर से देवरानी को चुमकारकर कहा—हाय-आय ! फूलावन्ती, इस कच्ची उम्र तू कैसे-कैसे रोग लगा बैठी ? यह बेहोशी नास-होनी तो देह का सारा रक्त चूस लेती है !

फूलाँ ने उलाहने से गुलजारी की ओर देखा और निढाल-सी बाँह फैला कहा—बहन कोई सुने भी ! कह-कह हार गई। मुझमें हिम्मत-आँगस नहीं, पर घरवाले तो समझें मैं मचल मार लेटी हूँ। कैसे बताऊँ कि मेरी जान को धड़की का रोग लगा है।

—धड़की ?···क्या कहती हो, देवरानी ? यह तो नामुराद राज-रोग है ! फिर देवर की ओर देखा—गुलजारी लाल, काम-धन्धा छोड़ मेरी देवरानी की दवा-दारू करा, नहीं तो बाँकी नार हाथ से गँवा लेगा।

भौजाई सीख देती है कि बोली मारती है गुलजारी लाल कुछ समझा नहीं। बिट-बिट तकता चला।

फूलाँ ने लेटे-लेटे गबरू पर तीर फेंका मेरे मरने-जीने की किसी को क्या परवाह ?

मित्रो ने पास आ फूलाँ की छाती पर हाथ रखा और सिर हिला बोली—गज़ब है, देवर, गज़ब ! बेचारी का कलेजा क्या धड़कता है आसमानी उछलता है ! फड़क···फड़क···

गुलजारी का चेहरा 'फक्क' रह गया। घिघियाते-से पूछा—डरवाली बात तो नहीं, भौजाई ?

—डरवाली ? गुलजारी लाल, इस धड़कन से कोई बचता है ! यह जान-लेवा बीमारी तो प्राण लेकर ही रहती है ! फूलाँ रानी को मोती मुरब्बे खिला, देवर, और इलाज़ करवा इसका हकीम नादिरशाह से ।

गुलजारी ने हाथ बढ़ा फूलाँ की बाँह छूई कि बेचारी हुड़क-हुड़क रोने लगी—इस रोग से मैं नहीं बचती !

"Ach Schwester, als ob das einen interessiert! Auf mich hört ja keiner! Ich bin völlig schwach und elend, und alle hier meinen nur, ich spiele krank! Wie soll ich ihnen erklären, daß mein Herz rast wie bei hohem Blutdruck?"
"Herzrasen? Bist du dir sicher, Schwägerin? Das ist eine ganz gefährliche und komplizierte Krankheit! Gulzari, laß deine Arbeit liegen und kümmere dich um eine Behandlung für meine Schwägerin, sonst ist es womöglich mit einem Schlag vorbei mit ihr!"
Gulzarilal starrte sie an, nicht ganz sicher, ob ihr Rat ernst gemeint war oder sie sich über ihn lustig machte.
Phulan nutzte sein Zögern sogleich für einen Seitenhieb auf ihren Mann: "Wen kümmert es denn hier schon, ob ich lebe oder sterbe!"
Mitro trat zu ihr, legte ihr die Hand auf die Brust und fühlte den Herzschlag. "Unglaublich, Schwager, unfaßbar! Ihr Herz klopft ja wirklich, als würde es gleich zum Himmel springen! Phrak..Phrak..Phrak...!"
Gulzari wurde leichenblass. Verängstigt fragte er: "Es ist doch nichts Ernstes, oder?"
"Ernst? Dieses Herzrasen überlebt kein Mensch, Gulzarilal! Diese Krankheit führt unweigerlich zum Tod! Phulan soll sich das beste Perlenpräparat verschreiben lassen, und laß sie von niemand anderem als Doktor Nadirshah behandeln!"
Gulzari legte seine Hände auf Phulans Arm, die daraufhin in lautes Schluchzen ausbrach: "Das werde ich nicht überleben, ich weiß es! Laßt sofort ein paar Ärzte kommen!"
Mitro sah sich das eine Weile an, dann zwinkerte sie ihrem Schwager zu und klatschte in die Hände: "Hochachtung, Phulan, guter Auftritt! Gulzari, dein Schätzchen hier hat weder Herzrasen noch Schmerzen noch Schwächeanfälle! Sie ist einfach ein ganz raffiniertes Stück! Wenn du

the body!" Phoolan looked accusingly towards Gulzari and allowing her arm to drop lifelessly she said, "Sister, nobody believes me. I've been telling them again and again I've no strength left in me, but my people here think I'm only pretending. How do I tell them how my heart pounds and throbs?"
"Your heartbeat, is it? What are you saying, Devarani? This is a raj-rog, the disease of the royalty!" Then, looking towards her devar, she said, "Gulzari Lal, leave aside all work and get her properly treated, otherwise you'll lose this lovely bride."
Gulzari Lal couldn't make out whether his sister-in-law was tendering a piece of advice or only mocking. He kept looking fixedly. Phoolan, still lying in bed, shot a taunt at him: "Who cares whether I live or die!" Mitro got closer to her and placed her hand on her chest and shaking her head, said, "Amazing, Devar, it's fantastic! That poor thing's heart is thumping so fast! Flying up to the sky ...phadak...phadak...."
Gulzari turned pale. In consternation he whimpered, "I hope this isn't anything serious, bhauji."
"What do you know? It's deadly, Gulzari Lal, this type of heartbeat doesn't spare anyone. This death-dealing disease parts only with one's very last breath! Give her pearl-fortified jams to eat, Devar, and let Hakim Nadirshah treat her!"
Gulzari stretched his hand to touch Phoolan's arm when she broke into sobs — "I'm not going to survive this disease! Arre, call some vaidya, some hakim!"
At first, Mitro kept standing, looking on, and then winking to her devar, she clapped her hands "Phoolan Rani, you're really good at it, I admit. I give you marks for it." And to Gulzari, "Gulzari,

अरे, कोई वैद्य-हकीम बुलाओ।

मित्रो पहले खड़ी-खड़ी देखती रही, फिर देवर को आँख मार हाथ से ताली बजा दी—मान गई, फूलाँ रानी, मान गई। गुलजारी, तेरी इस बन्नो को न धड़की है, न कोई दर्द, न कमज़ोरी। यह तो गले-गले गहरे चरित्र है। गुलजारी देवर, तुम मिट्टी के माधो बने रहे तो एक दिन तुम्हारी अकल-बुद्धि सब चुरा ले जाएगी यह चोट्टी।

घायल शेरनी-सी फूलाँ गला फाड़-फाड़ दहाड़ने लगी—जो मेरे रोग-बीमारी झूठ माने उसके अपने नैन-प्राण दुखें ! दर्द-पीर से कालजा फटे !

मँझली ने घुड़की दी—चुप, री फूलाँ ! यह झूठ-मूठ के रोग छोड़, मर्द का बच्चा जन !

नहले-दहले ख़त्म होते न देख धनवन्ती अन्दर आई। तेवर चढ़ा बहुओं को घूरा और लड़के को उलाहना दे बोली—बेटा, पास बैठाल इन दोनों की कलह-कलत्र सुन रहा है ? मँझली तो जबान-छुट है, तू ही अपनी को समझा !

गुलजारी ने बेबसी से सिर हिला तत्ते-जले कहा—फूलाँ का दोष हो तो उसे कुछ कहूँ। जब भौजाई आप ही मुँह लगे, आप ही गले पड़े तो···

मँझली ओंठों को मरोर दे हँस दी।

—वाह रे निन्दक ! गुलजारी लाल, मैं तो समझी थी औरत क साथ ढुक तू अब मर्द बन गया होगा···

धनवन्ती ने बीच में ही डपट दिया, चुप कर, बहू, कंजरोंवाले फक्कड़ न तोल ! जबान काबू में रख !

मँझली ने आँखों-ही-आँखों में देवर को बेपर्द कर दिया और सिर हिला बोली—काका गुलजारी, माँ की इतनी-सी

dich weiterhin von der zum Narren halten läßt, hat sie dir bald noch das letzte bißchen Verstand geraubt!"
Wie eine verwundete Tigerin heulte Phulan auf und brüllte: "Wer sich über meine Krankheit lustig macht, der soll selbst jämmerlich verrecken! Dem wünsch ich die Beulenpest an den Hals!"
Mitro fuhr dazwischen: "Komm, hör doch auf mit deinen ewigen Krankengeschichten! Sieh lieber zu, daß du einen Sohn zustandebringst!"
Als Dhanavanti hörte, daß das Gezeter kein Ende nahm, kam sie herein. Sie runzelte die Stirn, sah ihre Schwiegertöchter streng an und sagte verächtlich zu Gulzari: "Und du hockst daneben und läßt dir das Theater gefallen? Die Mittlere hat nun mal ein loses Mundwerk, aber deine eigene Frau kannst du doch wenigstens unter Kontrolle halten!"
Gulzari schüttelte kraftlos den Kopf und sagte geschlagen: "Wenn Phulan schuld wäre, hätte ich schon was gesagt. Die da hat doch angefangen, die hat doch..."
Mitro schürzte höhnisch die Lippen: "Bravo, du Petze! Ich dachte eigentlich, aus dir wär ein Mann geworden, seit du mit einer Frau schläfst!"
Dhanavanti brauste auf: "Halt den Mund, Mitro, rede nicht wie eine hergelaufene Hure, paß auf, was du sagst!"
Mit einem vernichtenden Blick entlarvte Mitro ihren Schwager: "Komm, mein kleiner Gulzari, hab keine Angst, Mama hat ja nur ein bißchen geschimpft! Du bist doch schon groß und stark, läßt dich Phulavanti etwa nicht..."

"Pfui, Schluß damit!" Dhanavanti fühlte tausend Nadeln in sich. "Geh mir aus den Augen,

this darling wife of yours has no ailment, neither blood pressure, nor pain, nor weakness. This is sheer pretence, neckdeep feigning. Gulzari Devar, if you don't look sharp, she will soon rob you of all your intelligence."
Phoolan, like a wounded lioness, started roaring, "May anyone who doubts me be racked with unspeakable pain! May their hearts be rent asunder!" Manjhali snarled at her – "Shut up, ri Phoolan! Cast aside these false ailments and start making a male baby!"
Seeing no end of the squabble, Dhanawanti came into the room. Furrowing her forehead, she frowned at the two daughters-in-law and said accusingly, "Beta, you're listening to these squabbles sitting beside them? Manjhali is tongue-loose, but you can at least restrain your wife."
Gulzari showed his helplessness by shaking his head and said in a bitter tone, "I can stop Phoolan if she is at fault. But when bhaujai herself starts an argument, comes meddling in our affairs, then..."
Manjhali twisted her lips and smiled –
"Wah re, fault-finder! Gulzari Lal, I'd thought that having been with a woman, you would've turned into a man..."
Dhanawanti cut her short. "Stop it, bahu, don't dole out such words as prostitutes use. Keep your tongue under control!" Manjhali exposed her devar's feebleness with her looks and shaking her head, said, "Child Gulzari, you've been frightened by a mere growl from your mother? By now you are fully developed, aren't you Gulzari? Does Phoolawanti reject...?"
Chi...Chi...Dhanawanti's whole body bristled with thorns, as it were.
"Get lost, bahu, away from my sight!" and Dhanawanti covered her eyes with her hands. Mitro got

घुड़की से डर गया ? तू तो चोखा गबरू जवान है, फूलावन्ती क्या तेरे संग···

छि···छिः···धनवन्ती के बदन पर काँटे उग आए।

—मेरी आँखों से दूर हो, बहू ! —और धनवन्ती ने आँखों पर हाथ रख लिया।

मित्रो अंगुल-भर और ऊँची हो आई। सास को आँखें न खोलते देख कहा—खोल लो, माँ जी, आँखें खोल लो ! घुड़की सुन क्या मैं यहाँ से टल जाऊँगी ?

[...]

Mitro!" Sie schlug die Hände vors Gesicht.
Mitro reckte sich noch ein bißchen höher. Als die Schwiegermutter die Hände nicht von den Augen nahm, sagte sie: "Guck her, Mutter, mach die Augen auf! Ich verschwinde nicht einfach auf Befehl!"
[...]

(*Tr. from Hindi by Barbara Lotz*)

Kurta und *Salwar*: Langes Hemd mit weiten Hosen, zusammen mit einem leichten Schal (*Odhni*) eine typische Frauenbekleidung in Nordindien.
Chapattis, Rotis, Parathas: Frische Fladenbrote, trocken oder auch mit Füllung in Fett gebacken.
Papads: Hauchdünn ausgerollte Fladen aus Linsenmehl, in Fett knusprig fritiert.
Jalebis: In Öl ausgebackene Süßigkeit.
Tehsildar: Steuereintreiber eines Distrikts (*Tehsil*).

even more defiant. Seeing that her mother-in-law had not removed her hand from her eyes, she said, "Open your eyes Maaji, open them! Do you think you can send my away by a mere scowl?"
[...]

(*Tr. from Hindi by Shivanath and Jaidev*)

Manjhli : Lit. "The middle one". There are three *bahus*, daughters-in-law in the household. Manjhali (Mitro or Sumitra) occupies the second place in the hierarchy, i.e. between Suhag, who in age is the youngest of the three but is the *badi*, seniormost bahu by virtue of being married to the eldest of the three sons, and Phoolan, the *chhoti*, juniormost bahu.
Jethani : Wife of the *Jeth*, the 'higher' brother-in-law.
Devarani : Wife of the *Devar*, the 'lower' brother-in-law.
Saas : Mother-in-law.
Bhaujai : Brother's wife.
Beta, Beti : Son, daughter.
Khes : Thick, coarse bed-sheet
Salwar : A loose legwear used by women; goes with the *kurta*, a long shirt, and the *odhni*, a light shawl.
Sheera : The semi-liquid concentrated state of sugarcane juice prior to the formation of jaggery.
Tawa : Utterly black iron skillet used for making rotis.
Rotis, Paranthas : Bread-cakes, plain or with fillings.
Paapad : Thin crisp cakes made of pulse and spices.
Dona : Small containers made of leaves.
Tehsildar : Sub-collector of revenue.
Thanedar : Superintendent of a police station.
Jalebi : Sweet dish.
Vaidya : Ayurvedic doctor; *Hakim*: Doctor.

कृष्ण बलदेव वैद

अँधेरे की आत्मा

[कहानी]

मेरे मकान में एक छोटी-सी कोठरी है जिसमें उम्र-भर की सँभाली और भूली हुई बेकार चीजों के अलावा अँधेरा भरा रहता है—उम्र-भर का सँभाला और भूला हुआ बेकार अँधेरा भी, हर रोज़ में से फूटनेवाला बेकार अँधेरा भी। उस कोठरी के दरवाज़े की लकड़ी को जगह-जगह से अँधेरे और समय ने खा लिया है। इसीलिए शायद वह हमेशा थोड़ा-सा खुला रहता है, कुछ इस तरह से कि मुझे लगता है जैसे वह कोठरी एक साथ अँधेरे को उगल भी रही हो, निगल भी। कोठरी का बल्ब बरसों से जला पड़ा है। आज से कुछ बरस पहले तक उसे बदलने का खयाल आया करता था, फिर उस खयाल से खौफ़ आने लगा, अब यह बात ठीक ही लगती है कि अँधेरे की कोठरी का बल्ब जला हुआ हो। आज से कुछ बरस पहले तक मैं कभी-कभी उस कोठरी में घुसकर अँधेरे में ही वहाँ सँभाली और भूली पड़ी चीज़ों को उलटता-पलटता रहता था, इधर-उधर करता रहता था, मोमबत्ती की

Krishna Baldev VAID

DIE SEELE DER DUNKELHEIT

[Kurzgeschichte]

In meinem Haus gibt es eine kleine Abstellkammer, in der sich außer dem Gerümpel, das dort im Laufe eines Lebens angehäuft und vergessen wurde, Dunkelheit angesammelt hat, im Laufe eines Lebens angehäufte und vergessene Dunkelheit, wie sie jeder Tag abwirft. Hier und da ist die Holztür zu dieser Kammer bereits angefressen von Zeit und Dunkelheit, deswegen steht sie vielleicht immer einen Spalt offen, als ob die Kammer in gewisser Weise die Dunkelheit gleichzeitig ausspeien und einsaugen wolle. Die Glühbirne in der Kammer ist schon seit Jahren kaputt. Bis vor wenigen Jahren noch spielte ich hin und wieder mit dem Gedanken, sie auszutauschen, dann wurde mir der Gedanke plötzlich unheimlich, und jetzt ist es mir im Grunde recht, daß die Glühbirne in der Kammer nicht funktioniert. Bis vor wenigen Jahren noch ging ich auch öfters in die Kammer, um in dem dort angehäuften und vergessenen Gerümpel herumzustöbern, es immer wieder umzuschichten, einige der Dinge im flackernden Kerzenlicht

---

Krishna Baldev VAID

THE SOUL OF DARKNESS

[Short story]

There is a narrow dungeon in my house. It is cluttered with all kinds of junk I have saved all my life and forgotten about. And it is also cluttered with darkness – the useless darkness I have saved all my life and forgotten about, as well as the useless darkness that oozes out of every day that passes. The door of this dungeon has been eaten at several places by time and darkness. That is why, perhaps, it stands always ajar in a way that suggests to me that the dungeon emits darkness and swallows it simultaneously. The light bulb in the dungeon burnt out years ago. Until a few years ago, I used to play with the idea of changing the bulb, but never got round to doing it because of my fear of darkness. Then, gradually, it started seeming proper to me that the light bulb in the dungeon should remain burnt out forever. Until a few years

लड़खड़ाती हुई लौ में उनमें से कुछ चीज़ों को यूँ घूरा करता था जैसे वही मेरे जीवन की वीरानी और जड़ता का कारण हो, उन्हें उठाकर बाहर कहीं फेंक आने के फीके इरादे बाँधा करता था, और आखिर मोमबत्ती को फूँक मारकर उसकी गंध को सूँघता हुआ कोठरी को अँधेरे और बेकार चीज़ों के हवाले कर बाहर आ जाता था। फिर धीरे-धीरे यह हिमाक़त भी छूट गई। अब उस कोठरी में घुसने के खयाल से खौफ़ आने लगा है। कभी-कभी बाहर से ही कोई नई बेकार चीज उस कोठरी में यूँ फेंक देता हूँ जैसे कोई अंदर पड़े अँधेरे को पत्थर मार रहा हो। आज से कुछ बरस पहले तक कभी-कभी मुँह अँधेरे उस कोठरी में नंगा जा बैठता था—आँखें मूँदकर, आसन जमाकर, ध्यान मुद्रा में, जैसे कोई अँधेरे में अँधेरे की पूजा कर रहा हो। महसूस होता था जैसे अँधेरे की आत्मा से तादात्म्य स्थापित हो रहा हो। लेकिन साथ ही यह भी महसूस होता था कि ऐसा कुछ भी नहीं हो रहा, कि उस अँधेरे के कारण अस्थायी-सी सुरक्षा का अनुभव हो रहा था। फिर धीरे-धीरे वह आसन भी छूट गया। अब कभी-कभी सुबह की सैर को निकलने से पहले कोठरी के कुछ खुले दरवाजे पर यूँ ठिठक जाता हूँ जैसे कोई किसी दोराहे पर। उस क्षणिक ठिठकन के दौरान कई काली उमंगें मन में उछलती हैं। उनके साथ खेलता-सा हुआ सैर को निकल जाता हूँ।

आज सुबह भी यही करना चाहिए था, लेकिन आज न जाने किस मैली मौज में था कि सैर के बजाए मैंने उस कोठरी में भरे पड़े अँधेरे को चुन लिया। बरसों पहले की तरह कोठरी में पड़ी बेकार चीज़ों को उलटने-पलटने या अँधेरे में आसन जमाकर बैठ जाने के बजाए अपनी छड़ी से उन चीज़ों को और अँधेरे को एक साथ यूँ कौंचना शुरू कर दिया जैसे कोई किसी लाश या बला या साँप को तैश दिला रहा हो। कुछ देर तक कुछ नहीं हुआ तो मेरा हौसला बढ़ गया। मैंने उस छोटी-सी घड़ी से उम्र-भर की सँभाली और भूली हुई बेकार चीज़ों और

anzustarren, als läge in ihnen die Erklärung für die Leere und Abgestumpftheit meines Lebens verborgen, – immer mal wieder faßte ich den halbherzigen Entschluß, all diese Dinge wegzuwerfen, blies aber schließlich doch immer die Kerze aus und überließ die Kammer dem Kerzenrauch, der Dunkelheit und den darin angehäuften und vergessenen Dingen. Allmählich gab ich diesen Unsinn ganz auf. Heute jagt mir der bloße Gedanke, die Kammer zu betreten, schon Angst ein. Manchmal werfe ich achtlos irgendein neues Stück hinein, als wolle ich die Dunkelheit damit steinigen. Bis vor wenigen Jahren noch ging ich vor Tagesanbruch nackt in die Kammer, setzte mich mit gekreuzten Beinen nieder und meditierte mit geschlossenen Augen. Als hielte einer im Dunkeln eine Andacht für die Dunkelheit. Ich hatte dabei die Empfindung, als verschmelze meine Seele mit der Seele der Dunkelheit. Gleichzeitig empfand ich Zweifel an der Möglichkeit einer solchen Verschmelzung, und glaubte, daß die Dunkelheit mir nur ein vorübergehendes Gefühl der Sicherheit verschaffte. Dann allmählich gab ich auch diese Angewohnheit auf. Jetzt bleibe ich manchmal einen Moment zögernd an der offenen Kammertür stehen, bevor ich zu meinem Morgenspaziergang aufbreche, wie an einem Kreuzweg. Während dieses kurzen Moments werde ich von dunklen, erregenden Sehnsüchten befallen. Von ihnen lasse ich mich auf meinem Morgenspaziergang begleiten.

Heute morgen war ich wie gewohnt dabei, aus dem Haus zu gehen, aber ich weiß nicht, welcher Teufel mich ritt, – ich wandte mich stattdessen der in der Kammer angehäuften Dunkelheit zu. Doch statt wie früher im Gerümpel zu stöbern oder mich in Meditationshaltung zu versenken, begann ich mit meinem Stock in der Dunkelheit herumzustochern, so wie man einen toten Körper, einen bösen Geist oder eine Schlange auf Reste von Lebendigkeit überprüft. Als es ruhig blieb, wurde ich mutiger. Ich hieb mit meinem Stock auf das seit Jahren unnütz herumliegende Gerümpel

ago, I used to squeeze into the dungeon, every now and then, and potter around – in a manner of speaking – arranging and disarranging the long-forgotten junk, staring at some selected items in the staggering glow of a candle. Until a few years ago, I used to make feeble resolutions about throwing everything out into the street. Then, gradually, I got rid of this foolish habit. Now the very thought of entering that dungeon fills me with consternation. Every now and then I throw some new piece of junk into it with a fury that would suggest I am delivering a blow to the darkness stored inside. Until a few years ago, on some selected days, I used to enter the dungeon before the crack of dawn and somehow sit down, naked, my eyes closed, my body motionless in a yogic posture, like a man praying in the dark to the dark. I felt as if I was on the verge of establishing an ineffable .rapport with the darkness stored in the dungeon. I also felt as if I was on the verge of doing nothing of the sort, that all that had happened was that I had managed to snatch a false sense of security from that darkness. Then, gradually, I dropped this stupid practice. These days, sometimes, just as I am about to step out for my morning stroll, I stop short in front of the dungeon door, that always stands ajar, like a man seized by uncertainty at a forked path. During that brief seizure, I am assailed by many dark and beautiful longings. I keep playing with them during my morning stroll.

उम्रभर के सँभाले और भूले हुए बेकार अँधेरे को पीटना शुरू कर दिया—पैंतरे बदल-बदलकर, नाच-नाचकर, किसी कुशल तलवारबाज की, भौंडी नकल-सी उतारते हुए। कुछ देर और कुछ नहीं हुआ, लेकिन फिर अचानक किसी ने वह छड़ी मेरे हाथ से छीन ली, और उसी से मुझे इतना पीटा, इतना पीटा कि मेरी जगह कोई और होता तो वहीं ढेर हो गया होता। मैं बेहोश भी नहीं हुआ। अब एक अस्पताल में पड़ा उन चोटों को भोग रहा हूँ—बार-बार, आनंदविभोर।

○

und auf die seit Jahren unnütz herumliegende Dunkelheit ein, wie ein Wilder tanzend und die Kampfpositionen eines Fechters imitierend. Eine Weile blieb alles still, – dann riß mir plötzlich jemand meinen Stock aus der Hand und verprügelte mich mit solchem Ingrimm, daß jeder andere an meiner Stelle zusammengebrochen wäre. Ich verlor aber nicht einmal das Bewußtsein. Jetzt liege ich im Krankenbett, spüre meinen Verwundungen nach und empfinde dabei, wieder und wieder, ein sonderbares Wonnegefühl.

O

(*Tr. from Hindi by Barbara Lotz*)

This morning also, I was seized by incertainty wrapped in dark and beautiful longings as I stopped short before the dungeon door. I should have overcome the seizure, as I always do, and moved out of the house for my morning stroll, but I pushed the dungeon door open and stepped in. Instead of arranging or disarranging the barely visible junk or stripping myself naked and sitting down somehow in a prayer-like posture, I started prodding the darkness with my walking-stick in a manner that would suggest I was provoking a corpse or a demon or a serpent into life. Soon I was almost dancing in furious ecstasy in that narrow space even as I beat that darkness and that junk I had saved all my life and forgotten. I made fancy fencing passes, parodying a master swordsman with my little walking-stick. For a while nothing happened. Then, suddenly, an invisible hand snatched my stick and started giving me a thrashing the likes of which I never got even in my naughty childhood. Anyone else in my place would have been finished; I didn't even lose consciousness. I am lying now in a nursing home, recovering from those blows, experiencing them again and again with perverse pleasure.

O

(*Tr. from Hindi by the author*)

निर्मल वर्मा

लन्दन की एक रात

[कहानी का एक अंश]

वह गर्मियों की एक खुली और नरम रात थी···एक विराट, बनैले जन्तु की तरह ख़ामोश···जो दिन-भर की थकान के बाद अपनी माँद में समूची देह फैलाकर सो गया हो।

पसीना सूख रहा था। मैंने भरपूर साँस ली एक बार···दो बार···हल्का-सा पछतावा होता है···मैं ह्विस्की छोड़कर चला आया था···इस समय यदि वह मेरी देह के भीतर होती···मैं फिर साँस खींचता हूँ···काश, मैं एक सिगरेट पी सकता ! ···मैं बड़ी सड़क छोड़कर एक सँकरी लेन में चला आया हूँ।··· अक्सर गलियों के नुक्कड़ पर सिगरेटों की ऑटोमशीनें लगी रहती हैं···

—हियर ही इज़···द सन ऑफ़ ए बिच !

मैं रुक जाता हूँ···न, यह डर नहीं है। मैं बहुत शान्त हूँ···तिर्फ़ एक ठण्डी-सी चीज़ मेरी रीढ़ की हड्डी पर फ़िसल रही

Nirmal VERMA

EINE NACHT IN LONDON

[Auszug aus der Kurzgeschichte]

Es war eine offene und milde Sommernacht, still wie ein riesiges wildes Tier, das nach einem ermüdenden Tag in seiner Höhle eingeschlafen ist, alle viere von sich gestreckt.

Der Schweiß trocknete langsam. Ich atmete tief ein, einmal, zweimal. Ein leises Bedauern regt sich: Ich habe den Whisky stehen lassen. Wenn ich den jetzt in meinem Leib hätte! Ich hole wieder Atem. Mein Gott, wenn ich jetzt eine rauchen könnte! Ich habe die Hauptstraße hinter mir gelassen und bin in eine enge Gasse geraten. Oft hängen am Ausgang solcher Gassen Zigarettenautomaten.

"Here he is, the son of a bitch!"

Ich halte an. Nein, das ist keine Angst. Ich bin ganz ruhig. Nur etwas Kaltes gleitet meine Wirbelsäule entlang, ganz unbeteiligt: eine glitschige Eidechse.

Da sind sie -- die Schatten an der Wand rücken vor.

Nirmal VERMA

A NIGHT IN LONDON

[Extract from the short story]

It was a soft, open summer night, quiet, like a huge wild beast lying snugly warm in its lair.

The sweat was drying up. I heaved a full sigh... once... twice. There was a nagging sense of regret... I had foregone the whisky... I wished I had it inside me at this moment. Once again I took a deep breath. If only I could have smoked a cigarette! ... Crossing a wide road – I was out into a narrow street... Usually there are automachines for cigarettes at street corners.

"Here he is! The son of a bitch!"

I stopped short... No, it was not fear. I was quite calm... only, there was something cold sliding down my spine...

They were there... shadows clinging to the wall moved forward.

"Hold him!" There was a shriek - and my whole body was suddenly twisted backwards.

है—एक गिलगिली छिपकली की तरह तटस्थ।

वे वहाँ थे···दीवार से सटी छायाएँ आगे सरकती हैं।

—होल्ड हिम !—एक फटी-सी चीख ···और मैं अचानक पीछे मुड़ गया हूँ···एक सरसराती-सी हवा मेरी बगलों के बीच से निकल जाती है।

गॉडेम्ड निगर···

वेट, जस्ट वेट···

वह पीछे से आया था—मुझे पता भी नहीं चला कि मेरा सिर पीछे की ओर मुड़ता गया है···एक क्षण और···और मैं दो हिस्सों में बँट जाऊँगा···

काश, मैं उसके चेहरे को देख पाता ?···

हाथ है, जो नम है···मैं अपनी कनपटियों में सरसराता खून सुन सकता था। मैं थोड़ा-सा हिलता हूँ···और कुछ आगे की तरफ़ घिसट आता हूँ। वह भी मेरे संग घिसट आता है—यह कोई अन्य व्यक्ति है, इसने सिर्फ़ मेरे हाथ जकड़ रखे थे।

एक क्षण के लिए मुझे गहरा आश्चर्य होता है—यह क्या मेरी देह है, जो इस तरह थरथरा रही है ?

—यू शिटिंग स्वाइन !

मैं एक झटके से अपने को खींचता हूँ···लेकिन मेरे बाल···मेरे बाल उसके हाथों में फँस गए हैं—उसकी नंगी बाँह मेरे मुँह के सामने हिलती हैं···और अनायास मैं अपने दाँत उसमें गड़ा देता हूँ···ओह, लीव इट, बगर !···एक टूटती-सी साँस···वह मुझे हिलाता है एक बार, दो बार—और हर बार मैं शराबी-सा उसकी बाँह पर झूल जाता हूँ।

—लीव हिम एलोन, यू सन ऑव ए ह्वाइट ह्वोर !

"Hold him!" Ein zerrissener Schrei - und ich habe mich plötzlich umgedreht. Rechts und links zischt ein Luftstrom an mir vorbei.

"Goddamned nigger!"

"Wait, just wait."

Er war von hinten gekommen. Ich hatte nicht einmal bemerkt, daß sich mein Kopf immer weiter nach hinten gedreht hat. Noch einen Augenblick, und ich würde in zwei Teile auseinanderfallen.

Wenn ich bloß sein Gesicht sehen könnnte!

Da ist eine Hand, die ist feucht. Ich kann das Blut in meinen Schläfen rauschen hören. Ich bewege mich kaum merklich und rücke ein Stück weiter. Er rückt mit mir weiter – es ist jemand anderes, er hat nur meine Hände fest im Griff.

Einen Augenblick bin ich ganz betroffen - ist das wirklich mein eigener Körper, der so zittert?

"You shitting swine!"

Mit einem Ruck suche ich mich zu befreien, aber meine Haare – meine Haare haben sich in seinen Händen verfangen. Sein bloßer Arm bewegt sich vor meinem Gesicht, und plötzlich sch e ich meine Zähne hinein. "Oh, leave it, bugger!" Sein stockender Atem - er schüttelt mich einmal, zweimal, und jedesmal schaukle ich an seinem Arm wie ein Betrunkener.

"Leave him alone, you son of a white whore!"

Ist das Willys Stimme? Ich versuche aus aller Kraft zu schreien, aber außer einem furchteinflößenden Geröchel bringe ich keinen Laut hervor. Und dann kommt es mir mit einem Mal vor, als habe sich sein Griff gelockert. Ich kann mich aufrichten. Meine Augen öffnen sich. Ein blauer Strom von Dunkelheit fließt an mir vorbei, und dahinter schwimmen rote, grüne, rosa Flecken – ich

A whiff of breeze passed through my armpits.

"Goddamned nigger."

"Wait. Just wait."

He had come up from behind me. There was no time even to notice that my head was already drawn backward. Another moment and I would split into two.

I wished I could see his face!

There was the hand. I could hear the blood pounding at my temples. I stirred a little and crawled forward, dragging him along. But it was some other man - he had only my arms in his grip.

For a moment I was struck with astonishment. Is this my body quivering like this?

"You shitting swine!"

I tried to free myself with a jerk, but my hair... my hair was caught in his hands and I could see his hairy arm coming over my mouth... and suddenly I plunged my teeth into it... "Oh, let go, you bugger!" He shook me. Once, twice... but I clung to his arm, swaying as he tried to shake me off.

Was it Willie's voice? I tried to scream with all my strength... nothing but a terrible whirring sound came out.

Then suddenly I felt his grip slacken. I could now lift myself up. My eyes were wide open. Red, green and pink patches were floating in the horizon. It suddenly occurred to me that I had been there before, a long, long time ago. I was reviving all over.

क्या यह विली की आवाज़ है ? ···मैं पूरी शक्ति से चीखने की चेष्टा करता हूँ, किन्तु सिवाय एक भयावह घुर्र-घुर्र के मेरे मुँह से कोई भी स्वर नहीं निकल पाता।

और तब सहसा मुझे लगा, उसकी पकड़ ढीली पड़ गयी है···मैं अपने को उठा सकता हूँ। मेरी आँख खुलती है। अँधेरे का एक नीला दरिया मेरे सामने से गुज़र जाता है और उसके परे लाल, हरे, गुलाबी धब्बे तिरते जाते हैं—मैंने इन्हें कभी देखा है, मुद्दत पहले कभी देखा है, जैसे यह कोई पहचाना-सा दुःस्वप्न है, जिसे मैं दुहरा रहा हूँ···शुरू से अन्त तक।

मुझसे दो गज के फासले पर वह खड़ा था—गली की दीवार से सटा हुआ। एक क्षण के लिए विश्वास नहीं हो सका कि वह विली है, वही व्यक्ति जिसके संग कुछ देर पहले मैं लागर पी रहा था···

किन्तु क्या वह मुझे पहचान सकता है···

और वह ब्लोंड लड़की···और जार्ज···क्या वे स्मृति के घेरे से बाहर कहीं रात में डूब गए हैं···हमें यहाँ छोड़कर···जो इस क्षण खुद अपने को नहीं पहचान पाते ?

सिर्फ़ दो गज़···और बीच का अँधेरा।

भीड़, आधा चेहरा और एक लम्बा युवक, जो विली पर झुका है···विली की कमीज़ का कालर हाथ में पकड़कर वह उसे दीवार के पास घसीट लाता है—खटाक···खटाक···

वह स्कार्फ भूल जाता है···स्कार्फ जो उस लम्बे व्यक्ति ने गले में बाँध रखा है···रंगीन—उस पर गुलाब के फूल छपे हैं···

गुलाब के फूल और खून, जो विली के होंठों से फिसलता हुआ उसकी 'गोटी' तक बह आया है···

एक क्षण के झलमले में सब-कुछ उभर आया है···आवाज़ें, पसीना, लेन की खट्टी-सी गन्ध···और हँसी···

और तब वह आया था···एक ठिगना-सा व्यक्ति, जो अभी तक भीड़ के अँधेरे में छिपा था। उसकी घनी भौंहों के

habe sie irgendwann gesehen, vor längerer Zeit irgendwann gesehen, als wäre dies alles ein vertrauter Alptraum, durch den ich wieder hindurch muß, von Anfang bis Ende.

Nicht einmal zwei Meter von mir entfernt stand er, an eine Hauswand gelehnt. Einen Augenblick lag konnte ich einfach nicht glauben, daß dies Willy ist, der Mensch, mit dem ich kurz zuvor Lagerbier getrunken hatte.

Aber kann er mich überhaupt wiedererkennen?

Und das blonde Mädchen... und George... Haben Sie den Kreis unserer Erinnerung verlassen und sind irgendwo in der Nacht versunken, uns zurücklassend, die wir uns in diesem Augenblick selbst nicht wiederkennen?

Nicht einmal zwei Meter - und dazwischen die Dunkelheit.

Eine Menschenmenge, ein halbes Gesicht und ein hochgewachsener junger Mann, der sich über Willy beugt. Er packt Willys Hemdkragen mit der Hand und schleift ihn an die Wand. bumm. Bumm..bumm.

Der Schal bläht sich auf - der Schal, den der Lange um den Hals gewickelt hat, bunt, mit aufgedruckten Rosen.

Rosen - und Blut, das von Willys Lippen rinnt und seinen Spitzbart erreicht hat.

In einem Augenblick der Klarheit ist alles deutlich geworden: Stimmen, Schweiß, der säuerliche Geruch der Gasse - und Gelächter.

Und dann war er da: eine gedrungene Figur, die sich bisher im Dunkel der Menge versteckt hatte. Zwischen seinen dichten Brauen funkelten kleine, unruhige Augen. Die Brauen hingen ihm so lang und dicht über seine Augen, daß man glaubte, er habe sich eine Hundemaske übers Gesicht gezogen.

At a distance of two yards from me he was standing, stuck to the wall. For a moment I couldn't believe it was Willie, the man I had been drinking with only a while ago.

But, could he recognize me?

And that blonde... and George? ... had they all got lost or drowned in the night, beyond the pale of memory?

Only two yards, and the intervening darkness.

A mob, half a face, and a tall young man leaning over Willie... He seized Willie by his collar and dragged him to the other wall... Bang... Bang... The scarf puffed up... The colourful scarf the tall man had round his own neck... there were bright, red roses printed on it –

Roses... and blood, dripping from Willie's lips to his goatee.

In a flash, everything intermeshed - voices, perspiration, the acrid smell of the lane, the laughter.

The man appeared - a shortish man who had been hiding in the mob. His small, quick eyes shone under his thick dense and long, bushy eyebrows giving him a canine look. With very slow steps he was moving towards Willie.

"Where's your darling?" he lifted Willie's chin with a jerk.

"Speak, where is she?"

Each time he asked the question, he dashed Willie's head against the wall and each time Willie's body swayed like a drunkard's... And they were laughing.

"Kick him there!"

बीच छोटी अस्थिर आँखें चमक रही थीं···भौंहों के बाल इतने लम्बे और घने होकर उसकी आँखों पर झुक आए थे कि लगता था, जैसे उसने अपने चेहरे पर किसी कुत्ते का मॉस्क पहन रखा हो···

वह बहुत ही धीमे कदमों से विली की ओर बढ़ रहा था···

—कहाँ गयी तुम्हारी डार्लिंग ?—उसने झटके से विली की ठुड्डी को ऊपर उठा दिया।

—बोलो···कहाँ गयी ?

हर बार 'कहाँ गयी' कहते समय वह विली के सिर को दीवार पर धकेल देता था··· हर बार विली की देह एक शराबी की तरह झूम जाती थी।

—और वे हँस रहे थे···

—बैश हिम देयर !—दूसरे ने अपने···की ओर इशारा किया। खट-खट सिर के दीवार से टकराने की आवाज़। खट-खट मेरे दिल की पगली ज्वर-ग्रस्त धड़कन। पसीने और खून से लिथड़ी विली की कमीज़ और एक अनवरत, कभी न ख़त्म होनेवाली खट-खट और एक भुतैली-सी हँसी···

—बोलो, कहाँ गयी ? ···स्पीक ! स्पीक ! स्पीक! यू फिल्दी···हा-हा-हा···खट-खट-खट···

स्कार्फ में झूलते हुए रंगीन गुलाब के फूल ···

मुझे अब कुछ भी याद नहीं···सच पूछो, तो मुझे यही नहीं मालूम कि मैं स्वयं चिल्लाया था या कोई बाहर की चीख़ मुझे सहसा झिंझोड़ गयी थी। (नहीं···आज भी मैं विश्वास नहीं कर पाता कि वह भयावह चीख़ मेरे गले से निकली होगी) मुझे सिर्फ़ इतना-भर लगा था कि मेरी साँस···एक अन्धे चिमगादड़ की तरह मेरी छाती की दीवार से टकारती हुई बेतहाशा फड़फड़ाने लगी

Er ging mit ganz langsamen Schritten auf Willy zu.

"Wo ist sie denn geblieben, deine Braut?" Mit einem Ruck riß er Willys Kinn hoch.

"Sag schon, wo?"

Jedesmal wenn er 'wo' sagte, stieß er Willys Kopf an die Wand, und jedesmal schwankte Willys Körper wie der eines Betrunkenen.

Und sie lachten und lachten.

"Bash him there!" Jemand anderes zeigte auf seinen...

Bumm...bumm, stößt der Kopf an die Wand. Bumm... Bumm..., pocht mein Herz wie verrückt, wie im Fieber. Willys Hemd, von Schweiß und Blut getränkt, ein unablässiges, nie enden wollendes Bumm...bumm... und ein gespenstisches Gelächter.

"Sag endlich wo! Speak! Speak! Speak! You filthy..." Ha Ha Ha... bumm...bumm...bumm... Im Schal schaukeln die bunten Rosen.

Ich kann mich jetzt an überhaupt nichts mehr erinnern. Wirklich, ich weiß nicht einmal, ob ich selbst geschrien hatte oder mich plötzlich ein Schrei von draußen schüttelte. (Nein, auch heute kann ich nicht glauben, daß dieser Schrei aus meiner Kehle gekommen sein soll.) Es war mir nur vorgekommen, als wenn mein Atem wie eine blinde Fledermaus an meine Brustwand stieß und wild zu flattern begann. Und ich stieß die beiden Hände von meinem Hals, die mich eben noch gehalten hatten.

Nicht einmal zwei Meter - und dazwischen die Dunkelheit.

Ich bin an Willy herangetreten. Ich will ihm etwas sagen. Will ihn berühren. Ich habe das Gefühl, das ist sehr wichtig.

Dazwischen die Dunkelheit - und diese kalten Hände, und dann dieser Schrei.

Another man pointed to his crotch. Bang! Bang!

The sound of his head being pounded against the wall. Willie's shirt was spattered with sweat and blood. Bang, bang, incessant and endless... and weird laughter.

"Speak, where is she? ...Speak! Speak! Speak! You filthy ..." Ha-ha-ha... Bang, bang, bang... The colourful roses flowing down the scarf.

I can't recall anything now. As a matter of fact, I do not even know if it was I who cried out or whether it was somebody else's shriek which had shaken me so, (No, even today I can't believe that terrible shriek could have come out of my throat!) All I remember is my short rapid breath flitting desperately, like a bat, hitting the walls of my chest. With a wrench I freed my neck from the clutch that held me back.

Only two yards-and the darkness between us.

I leapt towards Willie. I wanted to tell him something. I wanted to touch him. It seemed to be of utmost importance then.

The intervening darkness ... and those cold hands, and that scream...

My head crashed against the invisible chin of the man who seized my arm as I fell forward. With his other hand, he clasped my face. My face rubbed against his shirt. "I'll teach you to run... you fucking bastard!" I was blindly beating the air with my legs, like an epileptic. It's no use, I thought, he won't let go of me – and then it seemed impossible to breathe. But I was breathing all right, each breath breaking the spell of its predecessor, coming up one after the other, and clinging to me, coming up in succession, no breath wanting to be

थी। और मैंने एक धक्के से उन दोनों हाथों को अपनी गर्दन से छुड़ा लिया, जिन्होंने अब तक मुझे रोक रखा था···

सिर्फ़ दो गज़···और बीच का अँधेरा।

मैं विली की तरफ़ बढ़ा था। मैं उससे कुछ कहना चाहता हूँ। उसे छूना चाहता हूँ। मुझे लगता है यह बहुत महत्त्वपूर्ण है।

बीच का अँधेरा—और वे ठण्डे हाथ और तब वह चीख़···

मेरा सिर उस अदृश्य व्यक्ति की ठुड्डी से टकराया था, जिसने मुझे बीच में पकड़ लिया था। दूसरे हाथ से उसने मेरा चेहरा भींच लिया··· मेरा मुँह उसकी कमीज़ पर घिसटता गया। आई विल टीच यू—हाउ टु रन···बास्टर्ड···न जाने क्यों, मैं अपनी टाँगों को बेतहाशा, मिरगी के मरीज़ की तरह, हवा में घुमाने लगा—कुछ नहीं होगा···मैंने सोचा···वह मुझे छोड़ेगा नहीं···और तब मुझे लगा, जैसे अब मैं साँस नहीं ले सकूँगा। किन्तु यह गलत था, हर दूसरी साँस पहली साँस की गिरफ्त से अपने को छुड़ाकर ऊपर आती थी और फिर मुझसे चिपक जाती थी और मैं सोचता था, यह आख़िरी है, लेकिन तीसरी साँस फिर छटपटाते हुए अपने को दूसरी साँस के पिंजरे से छुड़ा लेती थीं और मुझे आश्चर्य हुआ कि कोई भी साँस पीछे रहकर आख़िरी नहीं बनना चाहती···और तब एक भयंकर-सी खुशी ने मुझे अपने में लपेट लिया, जैसे मैं अब तक सिर्फ़ इस लमहे के लिए जी रहा था और अब वह आ गया है और आनेवाली घड़ियों में कोई भी ऐसी चीज़ नहीं होगी, जिसके मानी वही होंगे, जो पहले थे, कोई भी डर पहले जैसा डर नहीं होगा···मैं भूल गया था कि मैं अकेला हूँ···मैं सिर्फ़ यह जानता था कि वे मुझे अकेला नहीं छोड़ेंगे और मैं बच नहीं सकता और उस रात मुझे पहली बार लगा कि अकेला होना ही काफ़ी नहीं है···काफ़ी नहीं है क्योंकि वे हर जगह हैं और यह मैं जानता था, सिर्फ़ यह नहीं जानता था कि एक दिन वे मुझे पकड़ लेंगे···अब वह पहले-जैसा आकारहीन नहीं था।—वह डर। अब वह ठोस था और सीमित था—उतना ही बड़ा जितना मैं हूँ। हम दोनों अँधेरे में जानवरों की तरह साँस ले रहे थे और मुझे लगा, जैसे मैं आख़िर तक अपनी टाँगों को इसी हवा में घुमाता रहूँगा। आह डियर, हाऊ फ़नी इट इज···हाऊ फ़नी। कोई हँस रहा है—(क्या यह मैं हूँ ?) हँसी, जिसकी कोई आवाज़ नहीं। घूँसे···गालियाँ···और फिर वही हँसी !

[...]

Mein Kopf war mit dem Kinn der unsichtbaren Person zusammengestoßen, die mich eine Zeitlang festgehalten hatte. Mit der anderen Hand quetschte sie mein Gesicht. Mein Mund streifte an ihrem Hemd entlang. "I will teach you .... how to run .... bastard..." Keine Ahnung, warum ich anfing, meine Beine wie ein wildgewordener Epileptiker in der Luft herumzuwirbeln. Das bringt nichts, dachte ich, der läßt mich nicht los. Und dann kam es mir vor, als wenn ich jetzt nicht mehr atmen könnte. Aber das stimmte nicht; jeder zweite Atemzug löste sich aus der Umklammerung des ersten, stieg hoch und hielt sich an mir fest, und ich dachte, dies sei der letzte, aber der dritte Atemzug schüttelte sich dann wieder aus dem Käfig des zweiten frei, und ich staunte, wie sich jeder Atemzug weigerte, zurückzubleiben und der letzte zu werden. Und dann umfing mich eine beängstigende Freude, als hätte ich bisher nur für diesen Augenblick gelebt, und nun war er da, und in den kommenden Stunden würde nichts, aber auch gar nichts mehr seine frühere Bedeutung haben, keine Angst würde sein wie früher. Ich hatte ganz vergessen, daß ich allein war. Ich wollte nur wissen, ob sie mich allein lassen würden und ich alles überstehen würde; und in dieser Nacht spürte ich zum ersten Mal, daß Alleinsein nicht genug ist - nicht genug, weil sie überall sind, und ich hatte das gewußt. Nur das hatte ich nicht gewußt, daß sie mich eines Tages packen werden. Jetzt war sie nicht mehr gestaltlos wie früher, diese Angst. Jetzt war sie faßbar und fest umrissen, war nicht mehr größer als ich. Beide keuchten wir im Dunkeln wie wilde Tiere, und es kam mir vor, als würde ich meine Beine bis zum Ende in der Luft herumwirbeln. "Oh dear, how funny it is... how funny!" Jemand - bin ich das? - lacht ein Lachen, das keinen Ton hat. Faustschläge, Flüche - und wieder dieses Lachen. [...]

[Translated from Hindi by Lothar Lutze]

the last. And I was enveloped in an awful happiness as if this was the moment I had been longing for all my life and it had finally arrived and nothing in all the coming years would bear the same meaning to me – no fear the same as the one I had known in the past. I forgot that I was all alone. I knew only that they were not going to leave me alone, that it was impossible for me to escape. For the first time, I realized that night that it was not enough to be alone; not enough, for they were everywhere. And this I knew. But what I did not know was that they were sure to catch me one day. It was no longer amorphous - the fear, I mean. It was full - blooded and well defined, as large as myself. We were both breathing, like two distinct hearts in the dark, and it seemed that I would go on kicking my legs up in the air just like that... oh, dear! How funny it is! How funny! Someone's laughing (is it me?)... laughter which has no sound... blows... abuses and then the same laughter again. [...]

[Translated from Hindi by Girdhar Rathi)

कुमार अंबुज

॥ नए अपराधी ॥

इतनी निर्दोष इतनी परावलंबी होती हैं उनकी गलतियाँ
कि जीवन भर नहीं समझ पाते वे अपने अपराध
मसलन उनकी दाढ़ी कुछ अलग तरह की है
कि एक खास तरह का रंग नहीं आता उन्हें पसंद
कि उनके हँसने का तरीका
अच्छा नहीं लगा न्यायाधीश को
या यह कि उन्होंने एक चिट्ठी लिखी अपने दुःखों के बारे में
कि उनके विचार असहमति के हैं
और जीवित हैं उनके कुछ रिश्तेदार पड़ोस के देश में
जब सजा दी जा रही होती है
उन्हें तभी मालूम होता है कि वे अपराधी हैं

उन्हें नहीं पता
किस तरह बचा जाए इन अपराधों से
वे रोज़ सुबह उठते हैं
और अपने आपको हर रोज़
एक नए अपराध में शामिल पाते हैं।
○

Kumar AMBUJ

DIE NEUEN VERBRECHER

Erst während sie verurteilt werden
Wissen sie daß sie Verbrecher sind

Ihre Verbrechen sind so unschuldig und so fremdbestimmt
Daß sie ihr Leben lang ihre Verbrechen nicht verstehen
Ob sie zum Beispiel einen Bart tragen oder nicht
Oder daß ihnen Safranfarbenes vielleicht nicht liegt
Oder vielleicht hat ihre Art zu lachen
Dem Richter nicht gepaßt
Oder es leben Verwandte von ihnen in einem Nachbarland

Oder sie haben in einem Brief von ihren Sorgen geschrieben
Oder sie haben abweichende Gedanken
Oder sie haben gar keine Gedanken

Sie wissen nicht
Wie sie sich hüten können vor diesen Verbrechen
Stehen morgens auf
Und merken jeden Tag daß sie
In ein neues Verbrechen verwickelt sind.
❍

(Tr. from Hindi by Lothar Lutze)

NEO-CRIMINALS

Only when they are being sentenced
They come to know about their crimes

So innocent, so dependent on others are their wrongs
They can't comprehend them all their lives

For example, that their beards are somewhat different,
that they don't have a liking for a particular colour
That the way they laugh
did not go down well with the judge
Or that they wrote a letter about their sorrows
That their thoughts smack of dissent
That some of their kin are alive in a neighbouring country

They know not
how to escape these crimes
They wake up every morning
to find themselves
implicated in yet another crime.
❍

(Tr. from Hindi by Ashutosh Dubey)

॥ बिजली का खंबा ॥

लोहे के ऊपर हो गयी है जंग की वार्निश
वार्निश की पपड़ियाँ बताती हैं
खंबे की उम्र और इतिहास

जब नया था यह
चालीस वॉट की रोशनी में
नहीं समाता था फूला

इसके नीचे बैठकर बुआ ने बीने दाल-चावल
पिता ने पास किया हाईस्कूल
इसने बचाया कई लोगों को गिरने से
एक बूढ़े शराबी को दिया आठ बरस तक सहारा
बँधी रही इससे कई महीनों तक
रशीद मियाँ की बकरी
बच्चों ने मानकर गोल-पोस्ट इसे
सीखे हॉकी-फुटबॉल
नेताओं ने चिपकाये चुनावी-वायदे

हवाओं के साथ मौसम गिरते रहे इस पर
खड़ा हुआ फिर भी यह इस गली में
खोलता रहा अपनी उजली आँख
करता हुआ चौकीदारी

फिर उम्र बढ़ी
और गली में लोगों का यातायात
बल्ब पर धूल जमी रोशनी में आया पीलापन
कई बार बल्ब बने शरारती बच्चों के निशाने
रहा कई-कई रातों तक अँधेरे में
यह प्रकाश-स्तम्भ !

DER LICHTMAST

Auf dem Eisen hat sich eine Rostschicht gebildet
Die Risse darin verraten
Das Alter des Masts und seine Geschichte

Als er neu war
War er eitel Freude
Im Licht seiner vierzig Watt

Unter ihm saß die Tante und las den Reis und die Linsen
Bestand der Vater seine Highschoolprüfung
Ein paar Leute hat er vor dem Fallen bewahrt
Einen alten Säufer hat er acht Jahre gestützt
Ein paar Monate war an ihn angeseilt
Rashid Miyans Ziege
Die Kinder ernannten zum Torpfosten ihn
Als sie Hockey und Fußball lernten
Politiker beklebten ihn mit Wahlversprechen

Den Winden und dem Wetter ausgesetzt
Trotzte er ihnen in dieser Gasse
Hielt sein strahlendes Auge offen
Wache haltend

Mit seinem Alter wuchs
Der Verkehr in der Gasse
Auf der Birne sammelte Staub sich, das Licht vergilbte
Ein paarmal nahmen Straßenjungen die Birnen auf Korn
Und nächtelang lag im Dunklen
Dieser Lichtmast

Nach Monaten hat heute jemand an ihn
Ein Plakat mit einem Gedicht geklebt
Und nach Monaten hat er heute endlich
Eine neue Birne bekommen

THE ELECTRIC POLE

The iron is varnished with rust
The scales of paint
Indicate the age and history of the pole

When it was new
It burst with delight
In its 40-watt glow

My aunt separated pebbles and husk
From lentils and rice under it
My father passed his high school
Reading his books in its light
It saved many from falling
Gave succour to an old drunkard for eight years
For months Rashid Miyan's goat was tied to it
Children practised hockey-football
Taking it as goal-post
Leaders pasted election-promises on it

Seasons buffeted it like the winds
Yet it held to its place in this lane
Opening its bright eye
Standing guard

Then it aged
And people's traffic increased in the lane
A layer of dust settled on the yellowing bulb
which became the target of urchins several times
For many a night
The lighthouse stood in darkness

Today after many months
Someone has pasted a poster-poem on it
And after many months

आज महीनों बाद किसी ने इस पर
चिपकाया है एक पोस्टर कविता का
और महीनों बाद आज ही लगा है
इस पर नया बल्ब

खुश हुआ है बिजली का खंबा
जैसे किसी बूढ़े ने पहनी हो
बरसों बाद नयी अचकन
और ऐनक।

Da freut sich der Lichtmast
Wie ein alter Herr der nach Jahren
Einen neuen Gehrock trägt
Eine neue Brille.
❍

(*Tr. from Hindi by Lothar Lutze*)

Only today it has got a new bulb
The electric pole is happy
Like an old man wearing a new coat
After many years
And a new pair of spectacles.
❍

(*Tr. from Hindi by Vishnu Khare*)

॥ अकस्मात् एक दिन ॥

हम सिर्फ़ सोचते रहेंगे
लेकिन अकस्मात् एक दिन माँ आ जाएगी
विस्मय और पुलक से भर देगी एक सुबह
प्रकट होगी नए अचार और पापड़ में
खाना परोसेगी और वैसी ही ज़िद करेगी जो माँ कर सकती है
मेरी तरफ देखेगी और चिंतित हो जाएगी
वह देखेंगी उस काया का क्षय
जिसे निर्मित किया था उसी ने
मुझसे कुछ कहना चाहेगी लेकिन उसके पास बहुत कम शब्द होंगे
और वे भी दोहराए जा चुके होंगे कई बार
लेकिन वह उन्हीं से काम चलाना चाहेगी

मैं बचना चाहूँगा, बदल दूँगा बात

मैं बदल चुका होऊँगा इतना कि लज्जित हो सकूँ
फिर भी ढूँढ़ लेगी वह मुझमें पुराने पहचान-चिह्न
नष्ट होते हुए शरीर में खोज लेगी बचपन और किशोरावस्था
उसी में दुर्दिन और जीवटता
उसी में खोज लेगी वह मेरे बच्चों को जैसे उनमें खोजती है मुझे
मुसकरा देगी मूँछों में सफेद बाल देख कर
सहलाएगी सिर के आधे रह गए बालों को
वहाँ दोगुनी धूल और थकान देखकर खामोश रहेगी
अपने बारे में बताएगी सिर्फ़ इतना
कि बनवा लिया है नया चश्मा

UNERWARTET EINES TAGES

Wir denken nur darüber nach
doch irgendwann wird unerwartet Mutter kommen.
Mit Überraschung und mit Freude wird sie einen
Morgen füllen
In neuen Pickles und Gebäck wird sie sich
bekunden
wird Teller füllen und uns nötigen nach Mütter Art
mich ansehen mit sorgenvoller Miene
wird den Verfall des Körpers sehen
den sie selbst erschaffen hat
Sie wird mit etwas sagen wollen, doch nur ganz
wenig Worte finden
Auch diese werden oft gehörte sein
Doch wird sie sich darauf beschränken wollen.

Ich werde mich entziehen, ausweichen dem
Gespräch

Ich werde mich verändert haben. So sehr daß
ich beschämt sein könnte
doch das gerade läßt sie nach vertrauten Zügen
suchen
im welken Körper wird sie forschen nach
Kindheit, Jugendtagen
Nach schlechten Zeiten und nach großen Taten
in ihm wird sie nach meinen Kindern suchen,
genauso wie nach mir in ihnen
wird schmunzeln wenn sie graue Haare sieht im
Bart
die Hälfte meines Haares die noch auf dem Kopf
ist wird sie streicheln
das Zweifache an Müdigkeit und Staub darauf
wird sie verstummen lassen
Von sich wird sie nur soviel zu erzählen haben
daß sie sich eine neue Brille machen ließ.

MOTHER WILL ARRIVE

We'll only be thinking and
mother will arrive suddenly one day
Filling the morning with astonishment and thrill
She will manifest herself in fresh pickles and
papads
will serve me food and insist that I must have
little more
the way only mothers can do
She will look at me and be worried
She'll see the decline of the body
she had created herself
She would try to tell me something
but would have few words
Those too oft repeated
yet she would try to manage with them

Evasively, I'll change the topic

I would be changed enough to be ashamed
still, she would recognise old traces in me
and would find my childhood and adolescence
my lean days and perseverance
in my degenerating body
She'll discover my kids in me the way she
discovers me in them

She would smile
at the sight of grey in my moustache
she would caress my sparse hair
and remain silent at the doubled dust and fatigue
on my scalp
About herself she would say only this much
that she has got a new pair of spectacles made
Much life remains in a little time

थोड़े-से समय में बचा हुआ है ज्यादा जीवन
माँ जान चुकी है हमारे समय का धीरज
एक खाई में से निकल कर दूसरी खाई में गिरने की हमारी व्यस्तताएँ
वह विपत्तियों की सुरंग पार करके आई है
और कहती है ऐसा सबने किया है इसमें नया कुछ नहीं

हम सिर्फ़ सोचते रहेंगे
लेकिन अकस्मात् एक दिन माँ आ जाएगी
स्थगित करती हुई कुछ और समय के लिए
हमारे पश्चात्ताप !

○

So wenig Zeit und darin so viel Leben
Mutter hat schon den Gleichmut unserer Zeit
gelernt
kennt unser Beschäftigtsein um
aus einem Graben hochgekommen in den
nächsten abzustürzen
sie hat den Sumpf von Mißgeschicken hinter
sich gelassen
und sagt da muß man durch das war schon
immer so.

Wir denken nur darüber nach
Doch irgendwann wird unerwartet Mutter
kommen
und unsere Gewissensbisse noch verschieben
ein paar Tage.
❍

(Tr. from Hindi by Barbara Lotz)

She has come to know about the forbearance of
our time
Our being busy in falling from one abyss into
another
She herself has come a long way through the
tunnel of adversities
and says everyone does so there is nothing new
about it

We'll just be thinking
And suddenly one day she will arrive
putting off our repentances
for some more time.
❍

(Tr. from Hindi by Ashutosh Dubey)

शाइस्ता अनवर

॥ बचपन ॥

खूबसूरत झील का किनारा
आसपास बलखाती सड़क
रिमझिम-रिमझिम पानी
ऐसे में
बैठना झील के किनारे
अच्छा लगता है मुझे
बचपन से ही छूना पानी को
कंकर मार कर
घेरा बनाना पानी में
अच्छा लगता है मुझे
बचपन से ही

मेरा बचपन है मुझमें आज भी
मैं बचपन के किनारे बैठ कर
बचपन की झील में
घेरा बनाती हूँ
कंकर मार कर।

○

Shaista ANWAR

KINDHEIT

Anmutiges Seeufer
Angeschmiegter Uferweg
sanfter Nieselregen
So
Am Seeufer zu sitzen
Gefällt mir
Seit meiner Kindheit
Wasser berühren
Steine werfend
Kreise im Wasser ziehen
Gefällt mir
Seit meiner Kindheit.

Auch heute ist meine Kindheit in mir
Ich sitze am Ufer der Kindheit.
Im See der Kindheit
zieh' ich Kreise
Steine werfend.
❍

(*Tr. from Hindi by Petra Matusche*)

CHILDHOOD

Picturesque bank of the lake
The undulating path around
Drizzling rain
Amidst this
I love sitting by the lake
Touching the water
Since my childhood
I love making a ring in the water
With a pebble

My childhood still lingers in me
Sitting by the bank of my childhood
I make a ring
In the lake of my childhood.
❍

(*Tr. from Hindi by Vishnu Khare*)

॥ आदत ॥

भूख तो पहले भी लगती थी
अब भी लगती है
लेकिन पहले की भूख
और आज की भूख में अंतर है
पहले मैं हो जाती थी
भूख से व्याकुल
अब इंतजार करती हूँ
खाना मिलने का

भूखे गुज़ारने की
पीड़ा पहले भी होती थी
आज भी होती है
लेकिन पहले की पीड़ा
और आज की पीड़ा में अंतर है
पहले पीड़ा सही नहीं जाती थी
अब सह लेती हूँ

मैं अब इंतजार करना सीख गई हूँ
पीड़ा सहने की
आदत हो गई है।
❍

GEWOHNHEIT

Hunger hatte ich früher schon
habe ich auch heute.
Aber da ist ein Unterschied
zwischen dem Hunger von früher
und dem Hunger von heute.
Früher war ich verrückt vor Hunger
Heute warte ich
bis es Essen gibt.

Hunger leiden tat auch früher weh
schmerzt auch heute.
Aber da ist ein Unterschied
zwischen dem Schmerz von früher
und dem Schmerz von heute
Früher konnte ich den Schmerz nicht ertragen
Heute ertrage ich ihn.

Ich habe jetzt gelernt zu warten.
Schmerzen ertragen
ist jetzt Gewohnheit.
❍

(Tr. from Hindi by Barbara Lotz)

HABIT

I used to feel hunger before
I still get hungry
But there is a difference
Between the hunger of today and yesterday
Before I was tormented by hunger
Now I wait for food

I used to feel the pain
Of going hungry before
I feel it still
But there is a difference
Between the pain of today and yesterday
Before the pain was unbearable
Now I bear it

Now I have learnt to wait
Now I am used to pain.
❍

(Tr. from Hindi by Vishnu Khare)

॥ बाज़ार बहुत दूर है ॥

मुझे लगता है
बाज़ार मेरे घर से बहुत दूर है
जब भी कुछ काम होता है बाज़ार का
भेजा जाता है मेरे भाई को
जब भी मैं कुछ माँगती हूँ
माँ कहती है
जब बाज़ार जाएँगे पिता
तब उनसे मँगवा लेना

मुझे लगता है
बाज़ार मेरे घर से बहुत दूर है
मैं चाहती हूँ
बीच बाज़ार में हो मेरा घर
मैं बाज़ार के बीच
चलना चाहती हूँ
जैसे चलती हूँ घर में।

❍

DER BASAR IST GANZ SCHÖN WEIT WEG

Der Basar
Scheint ganz schön weit weg zu sein von zu Haus
Wenn irgendetwas zu erledigen ist im Basar
Wird mein Bruder geschickt
Wenn ich etwas brauche
Sagt die Mutter
Laß den Vater es holen
Wenn er zum Basar geht.

Der Basar
Scheint ganz schön weit weg zu sein von zu Haus
Ich möchte haben
Mitten im Basar unser Haus

Mitten im Basar möcht ich mich bewegen
Wie ich mich bewege zu Haus.
❍

(Tr. from Hindi by Lothar Lutze)

THE FAR-AWAY BAZAR

I feel
That the bazar is far away from my home
Whenever there is something to be done at the bazar
It is my brother who is sent
My mother says
When your father goes to the bazar
Ask him to bring it

I feel
That the bazar is far away from my home
I wish
My home to be in the centre of the bazar
I want
To walk in the bazar
As I walk in my home.
❍

(Tr. from Hindi by Vishnu Khare)

संजय चतुर्वेदी

॥ लुटेरे बनकर इतिहास ॥

पुल, अस्पताल, सड़कें और इमारतें
किसी न किसी हत्यारे के नाम पर मिली हैं इस शहर को
हर चीज़ पर लगे हैं पत्थर उनके नाम के
उनके आमाल का साया है बच्चों पर
उनकी तरह रक्खे गए हैं नाम नयी नस्ल के
वक़्त का हर बड़ा लुटेरा
अमर है इस शहर में
कभी जब खोदा जाएगा ये शहर
लुटेरे बनकर इतिहास
खा जाएँगे भविष्य को
कीड़ों की तरह
क़यामत के रोज़
जब मुर्दे उठकर खड़े हो जाएँगे
न जाने क्या होगा इस शहर में ?

○

Sanjay CHATURVEDI

DIE RÄUBER, GESCHICHTE GEWORDEN

Brücken und Straßen Krankenhäuser Bauwerke
Hat die Stadt bekommen im Namen
irgendwelcher Mörder
Überall hängen Steine mit ihrem Namen
Die Kinder sind von ihren Taten überschattet
Nach ihnen benennt man die neue Generation
Jeder Räuber der sich einen Namen machte zu
seiner Zeit
Ist unsterblich in dieser Stadt
Wird diese Stadt einst ausgegraben, werden
Räuber, Geschichte geworden
Die Zukunft auffressen
Wie Ungeziefer
Wenn am Jüngsten Tag
Die Toten auferstehen werden
Wer weiß was dann geschieht in dieser Stadt.
❍

(*Tr. from Hindi by Lothar Lutze*)

MARAUDERS BECOMING HISTORY

Bridges, hospitals, streets and buildings –
The city has them in one or the other murderer's
name
Every artefact bears a plaque with their names
the shade of their deeds falls on children
The new generation has been named after them
Every great marauder of his time
Is immortalised in this city
Sometime some day when it will be excavated
Marauders becoming history
Shall devour the future like termites
On the day of reckoning
When the dead will rise from their graves
What happenings will be witnessed in this city?
❍

(*Tr. from Hindi by Vishnu Khare*)

॥ पैसे के दाँत ॥

आदमी द्वार सताए जाने से
अधिक दारुण है पैसे द्वारा सताया जाना
सबसे क्रूर आदमी से अधिक क्रूर होता है वह
सबसे बड़ी फ़ौज भी नहीं होती उतनी असरदार
सबसे ताक़तवर दमनतंत्र भी नहीं
सर्वव्यापी होते हैं उसके दाँत

जब रात की परेड में मिकी माउस हिलाता है हाथ
अपने आँसू नहीं रोक पाते हैं भावातिरेक में वयस्क
लोग मार दिए जाते हैं सान-दिएगो की गलियों में
घर पहुँचने से पहले
फेंके जाते हैं नवजात शिशु
लॉस-एंजिलिस की सड़कों पर
और मुक्ति के नाम पर ठगी जाती हैं औरतें
जवानी की हर रात
जिन तक नहीं पहुँच पाए मिकी के सपने

जो सोते हैं बिना चादर, बिना खाए फुटपाथ पर लाखों
जिन पर गिरती है बिजली, बर्फ़ और बेशुमार अमीरी
जिन पर गिरता है बारहमाह का आदमख़ोर जाड़ा
जो मारे गए वियतनाम, कम्बोडिया में
जो मारे जा रहे हैं एल-साल्वादोर, निकारागुआ में
वे नहीं होंगे बेवर्ली हिल्स के बच्चे
वे नहीं होंगे बर्कले के प्रोफेसर
वे आए थे
वे आते हैं
एल्बामा, जॉर्जिया या डाउन-टाउन ग़रीबों से

DIE ZÄHNE DES GELDES

Grausamer als vom Menschen gequält zu
werden
Ist die Qual verursacht vom Geld
Brutaler als der brutalste Mensch ist es
Selbst die größte Armee ist so durchschlagend
nicht
Auch nicht die mächtigste Tyrannei
Allgegenwärtig sind seine Zähne

Wenn bei dem nächtlichen Festzug Mickey
Mouse winkt
Sind die Erwachsenen zu Tränen gerührt im
Gefühlsüberschwang
Menschen werden erschlagen in den Gassen
von San Diego
Noch eh sie ihre Wohnung erreichen
Weggeworfen werden die Neugebornen
Auf den Straßen von Los Angeles
Und im Namen der Freiheit werden Nacht für
Nacht
Die jungen Frauen betrogen
Die von Mickey nicht träumen

Die Hunderttausende die unbedeckt und hungrig
auf dem Fußweg schlafen
Gewitter Schnee maßlosem Reichtum
ausgesetzt
Das Jahr hindurch menschenfressender Kälte
ausgesetzt
Die erschlagen wurden in Vietnam in
Kambodscha
Die erschlagen werden in El Salvador in
Nicaragua
Das werden keine Kinder sein von Beverley Hills
Das werden keine Professoren sein von Berkeley
Sie kamen
Sie kommen

THE FANGS OF MONEY

More terrible than being tortured by man
Is being excruciated by money
It is crueller than the cruellest man
Even the largest army is not that effective
Not even the strongest oppressive regime
Money's fangs reach everywhere

When Mickey Mouse waves his hands in the
night carnival
And the adults cannot control their tears in a
surfeit of emotion
People get killed in the lanes of San Diego
Before they reach their homes
New-born babes are thrown out
On the streets of Los Angeles
And in every night of their youth
Women are betrayed in the name of liberation
Mickey's dreams failed to reach them

Those millions who sleep without cover, without
food on pavements
On whom falls lightning, snow and ceaseless
wealth
On whom falls the year-long carnivore winter
Who were killed in Vietnam, Cambodia
Who are being killed in El Salvador, Nicaragua
They will not be the children from Beverley
Hills
They will not be professors from Berkeley
They came
They come
From Alabama, Georgia, Downtown Poverty

भरे पेट वालों को भी गड़ते हैं उसके दाँत
ज़रा-सी हरकत होने पर
वे ठुके हैं सबकी आत्मा में कील की तरह

जब हम सोते हैं
उसके दाँत गड़ते हैं हमारे सपनों में
और मुँह में भर जाते हैं
डोनाल्ड डक के नुचे हुए पंख।

○

Aus Alabama Georgia oder der Armut von
  Downtown

Auch in die mit den vollen Bäuchen schlagen sich
  seine Zähne
Bei der geringsten Bewegung
Sind sie in aller Wesen gehämmert wie Nägel

Wenn wir schlafen
Schlagen sich seine Zähne in unsere Träume
Und es füllen den Mund
Die gerupften Flügel von Donald Duck.
❍

(Tr. from Hindi by Lothar Lutze)

Its fangs pierce those whose bellies are full
The least of movement
And they get hammered in every soul like nails

When we sleep
Its fangs pierce us in our dreams
And the mouth is full
Of plucked wings of Donald Duck.
❍

(Tr. from Hindi by Vishnu Khare)

दिलीप चित्रे

॥ आंधळ्याला दिसणारे देखावे ॥

आंधळ्याला दिसणारे देखावे
डोळसांची नजर तिथं पोचत नाही
कारण आंधळ्याची बघण्याची इच्छा
दृश्यांवर स्थिरावलेली नसतेच
दुपारच्या उन्हात रात्र किर्र होते
सूर्यास्तानंतर प्रकाश प्रखर होतो
सुन्नतेच्या पोळ्याभोवती
मधमाशा भणभणतात
हिवाळ्याच्या सुरवातीला
हजारो पाखरं उष्णतेच्या दिशेनं उडत जातात
तशा रक्ताच्या या टोकाकडून
त्या टोकाकडे झेपावत जाणातंया इच्छा
आंधळ्यांच्या निसर्गात
आंधळ्याला गुरुत्वाकर्षण दिसतं,
त्याला प्रत्येक चाहुलीची प्रतिमा दिसते,
त्याच्या त्वचेला दिसतो
जगाचा अनारंभ खरबरीत पृष्ठभाग,
आंधळ्यच्या तळहातात
देखावे उघडतात
स्त्रीपुरुषांसारखे
सलगपणे अलग
एकत्रपणे वेगळे
○

Dilip CHITRE

WAS DER BLINDE SIEHT

Was der Blinde sieht
erreicht das Auge der Sehenden nicht
Denn des Blinden Wille zu sehen
Ist nicht auf Szenen gerichtet
In der Nachmittagssonne vertieft sich die Nacht
Ist die Sonne gesunken verschärft sich das Licht
Um den Bienenstock des Schweigens
Summen Honigbienenschwärme
Am Winteranfang
Fliegen Vögel tausendfach der Wärme zu
Wie von einem Ende des Blutes
Zum andern Ende sich Wünsche schwingen
In der Welt der Blinden
Der Blinde sieht die Schwerkraft
Er sieht das Bild das jede Gegenwart anzeigt
Seine Haut sieht
Die uralte rauhe Oberfläche der Welt
In der Hand des Blinden
Tun sich Szenen auf
Wie Frau und Mann
Vereint entzweit
Gemeinsam verschieden.
O

(*Tr. from Marathi by Lothar Lutze*)

SIGHTS THE BLIND VIEW

Sights the blind view
The vision of the sighted does not reach there
Because the blind do not focus their desire to
see
Upon any scenes that can be viewed
There is a night that deepens in the afternoon
sun
There is a light that becomes strong after sunset
Around a hive that is void of any sound
There are bees humming
At the onset of winter
Thousands of birds go flying in the direction of
warmth
So from one Pole of blood to the other
There are flights of desire
In the nature of the blind.
The blind one can see gravity
At the slightest inkling of a movement the blind
one sees a whole image
The blind one's skin can see
The coarse primaeval surface of the world.
In the palms of the blind one's hand unfold
Vistas
Like man and woman
Separate yet coupled
Alone together.
O

(*Tr. from Marathi by Dilip Chitre*)

THE HOUSE OF MY CHILDHOOD

The house of my childhood stood empty
On a grey hill
All its furniture gone
Except my grandmother's grindstone
And the brass figurines of her gods

After the death of all birds
Bird-cries still fill the mind
After the city's erasure
A blur still peoples the air
In the colourless crack that comes before morning
In a place where nobody can sing
Words distribute their silence
Among intricately clustered glyphs

My grandmother's voice shivers on a bare branch
I toddle around the empty house
Spring and summer are both gone
Leaving an elderly infant
To explore the rooms of age
O

(English original)

DAS HAUS MEINER KINDHEIT

Das Haus meiner Kindheit stand leer
Auf einem grauen Hügel
Sein ganzes Mobiliar war weg
Bis auf Großmutters Mahlstein
Und die Messingfiguren ihrer Götter

Nach dem Tod aller Vögel
Erfüllen noch immer Vogelrufe die Gedanken
Nach dem Auslöschen der Stadt
Belebt noch immer ein Fleck die Luft
In dem farblosen Spalt der vorm Morgen kommt
An einem Ort an dem niemand singen kann
Verteilen Worte ihr Schweigen
Unter kompliziert gruppierten Glypten

Großmutters Stimme zittert auf einem kahlen Zweig
Ich watschle im leeren Haus herum
Frühling und Sommer sind vorbei
Ließen ein ältliches Kind zurück
Die Räume des Alters zu erkunden
❍

(*Tr. from English by Lother Lutze*)

॥ चवथा ब्रांडेनबुर्ग कॉंचेर्तो ॥

(1718?-1978!)

पारदर्शक काल्लोळच्या पक्ष्याभोवती
आकाश घडतं फडफडत्या पंखांचं
माझ्या अंतश्चक्षूची अतलस्पर्श्य विहीर
आकाशाचा पृष्ठभाग पांघरून निद्रिस्त होते

मरारीचा गज फिरतो आत पाण्याच्या
शांत तंतूंवर आकाशाच्या प्रतिबिंबाखाली
खोलवर, जिथं प्रकाश नव्हता अगोदर,
तिथं किरणांसारख्या श्रुती फुटतात

माझ्या कर्णपटलावर पसरतात पक्ष्यांचे थवे
थेबांसारखी फुटते तेजस्वी चिवचिव
पहाट किलबिलते अगणित रंग आणि छटा
वर येतं सूर्यबिंब वेल्हाळ, नवजात

मी परमेश्वरावर विश्वास ठेवलाही नसता
जर जाणवलं नसतं जागोजाग हें चैतन्याचं कारंजं
कोट्यावधी मुखांनी होणारा जिवंत उद्रेक
भाषेखाली फैलावणारी एक अनारंभ भाषा
○

VIERTES BRANDENBURGISCHES KONZERT

(1718?-1978!)

Durchsichtige Bewegung: Vogel um den
Sich ein Himmel aus flatternden Flügeln wölbt
Mein innres Auge wird zum bodenlosen Brunnen bedeckt
Sich mit der Himmelsfläche und schläft ein

Drinnen der Flug: Bogen der über die heiteren
Saiten des Wassers streicht unterm Abglanz des Himmels
Tief unten wo vorher kein Licht war
Erstrahlen die Intervalle

Über mein inneres Ohr breiten sich Vogelschwärme
Zwitschern blendet birst zu Tropfen
Morgenlicht trillert zahllose Farben und Töne
Auftaucht der Sonnenball: Kind, neugeboren

Ich hätte bestimmt nicht an Gott geglaubt hätt ich
Nicht gespürt überall diesen Ausbruch von Lichtfontänen
Die lebendige Flut aus Millionen Mündern
Eine ursprüngliche Sprache die unter der
Sprache sich ausdehnt.

❍

(*Tr. from English by Lothar Lutze*)

THE FOURTH BRANDENBURG CONCERTO

(1718?-1978!)

Around the bird of transparent tumult
A sky of fluttering wings is moulded
The bottomless well of my inner eye
Covers itself up with the sky and sleeps

The bow of the flight moves inside the water
Over serene strings under a mirrored sky
Deep down, where there was no light before,
There, like a radiance, microtones burst

Flocks of birds spread over the canvas of my hearing
A luminous tittering burst like dancing drops of water
Morning becomes a warbling of countless colours and tones
A newborn Sun comes up in its infant form

I would never have believed in the existence of God
Unless I had perceived this fountain of energy everywhere
Life springing and flowing out of millions of mouths
A primordial language spreading underneath all speech

❍

(*Tr. from Marathi by Dilip Chitre*)

मंगलेश डबराल

॥ पत्तों की मृत्यु ॥

कितने सारे पत्ते उड़कर आते हैं
चेहरे पर मेरे बचपन के पेड़ों से
एक झील अपनी लहरें
मुझ तक भेजती है
लहर की तरह काँपती है रात
और उस पर मैं चलता हूँ
चेहरे पर पत्तों की मृत्यु लिये हुए

चिड़ियाँ अपने हिस्से की आवाज़ें
कर चुकी हैं लोग जा चुके हैं
रोशनियाँ राख हो चुकी हैं
सड़क के दोनों ओर
घरों के दरवाज़े बंद हैं
मैं आवाज़ देता हूँ
और वह लौट आती है मेरे पास !

○

Mangalesh DABRAL

DER TOD DER BLÄTTER

Wieviel Blätter mir ins Gesicht fliegen
Von den Bäumen meiner Kindheit
Ein See schickt
Seine Wellen bis zu mir
Wie eine Welle zittert die Nacht
Und auf ihr geh ich
Den Tod der Blätter im Gesicht

Die Vögel haben längst zuende
Gesungen die Leute sind fort
Die Lichter zu Asche geworden
Auf beiden Seiten der Straße
Sind die Haustüren zu
Ich rufe
Und mein eigener Ruf kommt zurück.
❍

(Tr. from Hindi by Lothar Lutze)

THE DEATH OF LEAVES

The leaves that settle on my face
Fall from my childhood trees.
A lake sends me its waves, and,
Like a wave, the night quivers. I walk
On it, the death of leaves on my face.

The birds have made their sounds.
The place is empty. The lights
Are ash. The houses on either side
Of the road have locked front doors.
I call out and my voice rebounds.
❍

(Tr. from Hindi by Arvind Krishna Mehrotra)

॥ सपना ॥

मैं गिरा एकाएक
जैसे सपने से
जैसे चलते-चलते कोई गिरता है
सड़क पर अधबीच

यही मेरी त्वचा के गिरने का सपना था
अपनी आत्मा सहित
मुँह और रोंओं के गिरने का सपना
मेरी गृहस्थी गिरी मेरे साथ
जेब में रखी हुई चीज़ें
जिन्हें मैं बार-बार निकालकर
रखता था फिर जेब में

गिरते गए अब तक कमाए
तमाम मेरे अनुभव
रोने-धोने की आवाज़ें गिरीं साथ-साथ
किसी ने गिरा दिए
मेरे कपड़े भी
बारिश और हवा से दूर
गिरता रहा मैं धरती
और रसातल से दूर

गिरते हुए उसकी एक झलक
देखी मैंने
जो हँसते हुए मुझे गिरा रहा था
लगातार।

o

TRAUM

Ich fiel auf einmal
Wie aus einem Traum
Wie jemand im Laufen fällt
Mitten auf der Straße

Es war der Traum vom Fallen meiner Haut
Zusammen mit meiner Seele
Der Traum vom Fallen des Munds und der
Körperhaare
Mein Haushalt fiel mit mir
Die Dinge die ich in der Tasche trug
Und immer wieder herausnahm
Und wieder einsteckte

Es fielen alle meine
Bisher gemachten Erfahrungen
Alle Klagelaute fielen
Jemand ließ auch
Meine Kleider fallen
Fern von Regen und Wind
Ich fiel und fiel, fern
Von Erde und Unterwelt

Im Fallen fiel mein Blick
Flüchtig auf den
Der lachend mich fallen ließ
Unausgesetzt.
❍

(Tr. from Hindi by Lothar Lutze)

A DREAM

I fell all of a sudden
as if out of dream
as one trips and falls
on the street

It was a dream of my skin falling away
along with my soul
A dream of mouth and hair falling
my home fell along with me
Things I stuffed in my pocket
took out and
put back again

Moments fell relentless
all that I had been through
Down fell sounds of sobbing and weeping
Someone flung down
my clothing as well
Beyond wind and rain
I tumbled past earth
and the realm beneath

Still falling I saw
a flash
the one pushing me down laughing
and laughing
❍

(Tr. from Hindi by Christi Merrill)

॥ कुछ देर के लिए ॥

कुछ देर के लिए मैं कवि था
फटी-पुरानी कविताओं की मरम्मत करता हुआ
सोचता हुआ कविता की ज़रूरत किसे है
कुछ देर पिता था
अपने बच्चों के लिए
ज्यादा सरल शब्दों की खोज करता हुआ
कभी अपने पिता की नक़ल था
कभी सिर्फ़ अपने पुरखों की परछाईं
कुछ देर नौकर था सतर्क सहमा हुआ
बची रहे रोज़ी-रोटी कहता हुआ

कुछ देर मैंने अन्याय का विरोध किया
फिर उसे सहने की ताक़त जुटाता रहा
मैंने सोचा मैं इन शब्दों को नहीं लिखूँगा
जिनमे मेरी आत्मा नहीं है जो आततायियों के हैं
और जिनसे ख़ून जैसा टपकता है
कुछ देर मैं एक छोटे-से गड्ढे में गिरा रहा
यही मेरा मानवीय पतन था

मैंने देखा मैं बचा हुआ हूँ और साँस
ले रहा हूँ और मैं क्रूरता नहीं करता
बल्कि जो निर्भय होकर क्रूरता किए जाते हैं
उनके विरुद्ध मेरी घृणा बची हुई है यह काफ़ी है

बचे-खुचे समय के बारे में मेरा ख़याल था
मनुष्य को छह या सात घंटे सोना चाहिए
सुबह मैं जागा तो यह
एक जानी-पहचानी भयानक दुनिया में
फिर से जन्म लेना था
यह सोचा मैंने कुछ देर तक।

○

EINE WEILE

Eine Weile war ich Dichter
Der unfertige kaputte alte Zeilen reparierte
Und sich fragte wer eigentlich braucht ein Gedicht
Eine Weile war ich Vater
Der für seine Kinder
Nach einfacheren Worten suchte
Manchmal war ich ein Abklatsch meines Vaters
Manchmal nur der Schatten meiner Vorfahren
Eine Weile war ich Diener: behutsam, ängstlich,
Hoffend daß ihm sein täglich Brot erhalten bleibe

Eine Weile widerstand ich dem Unrecht
Dann sammelte ich Kraft es zu ertragen
Ich meinte ich sollte diese Worte nicht schreiben
In denen nicht meine Seele ist, die Worte der
    Gewalttäter
Aus denen so etwas wie Blut tropft
Eine Weile lag ich in einer kleinen Grube
Das war mein menschlicher Absturz
Ich sah ich hatte überlebt und atmete
Und beging keine Grausamkeit
Ja für die die sich erdreisteten
Weiter grausam zu sein hatte ich
Noch Zorn übrig
Das war genug

Was die übrige Zeit betrifft dachte ich
Der Mensch braucht bloß sechs, sieben Stunden
    Schlaf
Als früh ich erwachte mußt ich von neuem
In eine altbekannte Schreckenswelt
    hineingeboren werden
Darüber dacht ich eine ganze Weile nach.
❍

(*Tr. from Hindi by Lothar Lutze*)

FOR A WHILE

For a while I was a poet
Repairing my tattered old poems
Wondering who needs poetry
For a while I was a father
Searching for yet simpler words
For my children
Sometimes I was an imitation of my father
At times only a shadow of my ancestors
For a while a menial, anxious and petrified,
Praying for the safety of subsistence

For a while I opposed injustice
Before summoning up strength to bear it
I thought I shall not write words
Which do not have my soul and belong to the
    inquisitors
And ooze something resembling blood
For a while I remained fallen in a small pit
This was my human depravity
I found that I have remained
And breathe and am not cruel
But it is enough that I have repugnance left
For those who perpetrate cruelty fearlessly

About the remaining time my opinion was
That a man should sleep for six or seven hours
Waking up the next morning
Was like being reborn in a familiar horrifying
    world
So I thought for a while
❍

(*Tr. from Hindi by Vishnu Khare*)

॥ शहर ॥

मैंने शहर को देखा और मैं मुस्कराया

वहाँ कोई कैसे रह सकता है
यह जानने मैं गया
और वापस न आया।
○

DIE STADT

Ich betrachtete die Stadt und lächelte

Wie kann man hier bloß leben
wollte ich wissen als ich sie betrat
und kehrte nie zurück.
O

(Tr. from Hindi by Barbara Lotz)

CITY

I looked at the city
and smiled
and walked in
Who would ever want to live here
I wondered
and never went back.
O

(Tr. from Hindi by Girdhar Rathi)

অলোক্‌রঞ্জন দাসগুপ্তা

॥ ত্বরান্বিত ॥

চোখের উপর ঘটে চলেছে সব-কিছু এক
ঝড়ের বেগে। প্রেমিকারা উধর্ব শ্বাস
ছুটে চলছে-প্রেমিক যেন হাসপাতালে।
আজ সমস্ত অটোবানের ফলকগুলি
জলে উঠছে অন্ধকারের অভ্র আলোয়।
এসো আমরা অতর্কিতে গাড়ি থামিয়ে
পথের ধারে এক মুহূর্ত জিরিয়ে নিইঃ
কারা এভাবে পিকাসোর সেই পায়রাটাকে
ক্ষিপ্রহাতে জখম করে ফেলে গিয়েছে
পথের ধারে, ভালো হয়েছে, তাড়াতাড়িতে
মারতে গিয়ে পেরে ওঠেনিঃ পায়রাটাকে
বুকে জড়িয়ে এখুনি চলো রেড ক্রসের
ভ্রাম্যমাণ ইউনিটে ঐ অনতিদূরে,
কেননা আজ চিরদিনের শান্তিকেও
বাঁচাতে হলে তাড়াহুড়োয় সারাতে হবেঃ
হৃদয় আজ কেমন যেন ত্বরান্বিত
অটোবানের ফলক হয়ে জ্বলে উঠছে!

○

Alokeranjan DASGUPTA

HAST

Im Augenwinkel, kaum bemerkt, ist alles
sturmesschnell
vor sich gegangen. Außer Atem fahren
die Liebenden – als läge der Geliebte krank im
Hospital.
Die Schilder auf der Autobahn erglühen heute
allesamt im wolkigen Licht der Dunkelheit.
Komm, halten wir ganz unerwartet mal den
Wagen an
und dösen einen Augenblick am Straßenrand:
Wer hat Picassos Taube so verletzt
und hingestreckt mit schneller Hand
am Straßenrand? Und doch ein Glück, in seiner
Eile
hat er sie nicht töten können; fahren wir sogleich,
die Taube an der Brust, zum nächsten
mobilen Einsatztrupp des Roten Kreuzes;
denn heute muß es schnell gehen, selbst wenn's
gilt,
den Frieden aller Tage jetzt zu retten, fehlt die
Zeit:
Das Herz erglüht ganz seltsam heute
als Schild auf einer hastigen Autobahn.
❍

(Tr. from Bengali by Christian Weiss and Hans Harder with the author)

ACCELERATED

It is all happening before our eyes
at a furious pace. Women breathlessly
rushing along as if their lovers were in hospital...
Today all the roadsigns on the autobahn
are reflected in the mica-light radiance of
darkness.
Quite suddenly we slow down and draw in
to pause for a moment in a lay-by.
What are the people who, hurtling onwards,
struck down the peace-dove of Picasso, and
left it
maimed by the roadside. They intended to
kill it,
but luckily didn't succeed; we clasp
the dove to our breast, and take it at once
to the mobile Red Cross unit not far away.
For if we are to recover enduring peace
today we have to bring it instantaneous succour.
How strangely the heart now lightens and glows,
itself becoming the roadsign on the autobahn.
❍

(Tr. from Bengali by Roland Hindmarsh)

॥ গোধুলিময় একটি যুগল ॥

ক্ষতিপূরণ হয়ে এসেছে সূর্যাস্ত-
চলতে গিয়ে দাঁড়িয়ে পড়ি, একটু পরেই
চলতে থাকি, দ্বিধা ও গতি মিশে এখন
আরেকরকম ছন্দ জাগে, দেখতে পাচ্ছি
মাঠের মধ্যে পানের বরজ, তার পাশে এক
অদীক্ষিত পরিসরের নিচে কেমন
একটি যুবা তার নারীকে কথা বলছে;
মাথার উপর ভাঙা খিলান, যুবক তাকেই
মণ্ডলের অনন্য তাৎপর্য দিয়ে
কথা বলতে-বলতে মাথা নোয়াল আরু
পরক্ষণে নারীর সঙ্গে তাকিয়ে রয়
অনিশ্চিতের দিকে, ভাঙা খিলানটাতে
সূর্যাস্তের রশ্মি থেকে সমান্তরাল
থাম নেমেছে, একটি কিরণ ঐ যুগলের
শরীর থেকে আজকের এই দিনের কাপড়
খসিয়ে দিল, আরেক কিরণ পায়ের কাছে
গড়ল অগাধ সমুদ্র এক, ওরা দুজন
স্নান করতে ডুব দিতে যায়, আর তখুনি
যাপন-করা দিনের কাপড় পুঞ্জিত ঐ
ওদের দুয়ের গোড়ালিভর পরিত্যক্ত;
মূর্তি ওদের পূর্ণই প্রায়, তলায় শুধু
পাথর কিছু স্তূপীকৃত-অকৃতার্থ
ওদের আশীর্বাদ করেছেন, দাহ এবং
গাহনের মাঝখানে ওদের দাঁড়িয়ে থাকা।
○

EIN PAAR IN DER DÄMMERUNG

Als Entschädigung ist der Sonnenuntergang gekommen;
beim Gehen halte ich inne, kurz darauf gehe ich
weiter, Zögern und Bewegung vermischen sich jetzt
und wecken eine andere Art Rhythmus; ich kann
die Betelplantage auf dem Feld sehen, und daneben
auf einem nicht geweihten Feld redet
ein junger Mann mit seiner Gefährtin;
über seinem Kopf ein brüchiges Gewölbe, der junge Mann
hat ihm den eindeutigen Sinn eines Kreises gegeben;
er senkt den Kopf beim Reden und
blickt im nächsten Augenblick mit der Frau
in eine ungewisse Richtung. Durch das Gewölbe
haben die Strahlen des Sonnenuntergangs parallele
Säulen entstehen lassen, ein Strahl hat vom Körper
dieses Paares die Kleidung des Tages
abgestreift, ein anderer schuf zu ihren Füßen
ein bodenloses Meer, die beiden
tauchen ein zum Baden, und da
ist die Kleidung des verbrauchten Tages aufgehäuft
und bis zu ihrer beider Fersen abgelegt;
ihre Gestalt ist fast vollständig, nur unten
sind einige Steine aufgehäuft, der Erfolglose
segnet die beiden, sie stehen
zwischen Brennen und Baden.

❍

(Tr. from Bengali by Cnristian Weiss and Hans Harder with the author)

COUPLE CHARGED WITH DUSK

The setting sun will soon give compensation.
I pause, then go on walking; from hesitancy
and progression the measure now has changed.
In mid-terrain I see a dome of betel-leaves;
nearby in an unhallowed spot a young man
is talking with his girl.
To the broken arch above them he bows low
endowing it with mandala significance;
then looks on, in bewilderment, with her.
The slanting rays transmit to the cracked vault
a shaft of light. One sunbeam plucks away
the daily garments from the pair;
another makes an ocean at their feet.
They both plunge in; their discarded clothes
from the spent day lie gathered ankle-deep.
Their effigy's all but done; only a few
pieces of stone are missing from the base.
They stand, blessed in their unfulfilment,
between cremation and immersion.

❍

(Tr. from Bengali by Roland Hindmarsh)

॥ চিত্রিত আছো, নিসর্গ ॥

জলরঙে ধোওয়া জাপানি ছবিতে ছোট্ট একটা সেতু ঃ
প্রেমিকেরা পার হয়

দু'ধারে চৈতী চেরিগাছগুলি ফুল্ল খুশিতে জানায়
সামরিক অভিবাদন

রামধনু দিয়ে গড়া ঐ সেতু মজবুত, মসৃণ
প্রেমিকেরা পার হয়

চিত্রিত আছো নিসর্গ, বলো স্বেদাক্ত শ্রমিকেরা
কোন সাঁকো দিয়ে যাবে?
○

IN JAPANISCHEN WASSERFARBEN

Eine schmale Brücke für Liebespaare
Kirschblütenspalier in ordentlichen Reihen,
diese Regenbogenbrücke –
wie für Liebende geschaffen

Sag mir, gemalte Landschaft,
über welche Brücke sollten
verschwitzte Arbeiter gehen?
O

(Tr. from Bengali by Christian Weiss and Hans Harder with the author)

PAINTED NATURE

In a Japanese watercolour I see a small bridge
lovers are crossing over

saluted on either side by cherry blossom
in bright orderly rows

this bridge, made of a rainbow, is sound and
smooth
lovers may cross

tell me, you painted landscape, tell me please
which bridge sweaty workmen should use?
O

(Tr. from Bengali by Roland Hindmarsh)

॥ কাগজের গাড়ি ॥

মৃত শহরের মধ্যে শুধুমাত্র সাংবাদিকদের
গাড়ি চলে যায়-
কিছুই ঘটে না, তবু না-ঘটা দুর্ঘটনার জের
নিয়ে
সমাচার ইনিয়ে-বিনিয়ে
কফিন-ফিটনগাড়ি চলে যাচ্ছে। মরুময়তায়

নতুন কাগজ এক বেরিয়েছে
O

ZEITUNGSWAGEN

In der toten Stadt fährt allein der Wagen
der Journalisten;
nichts geschieht, doch aus Fetzen nicht
vorgefallener Unfälle
Neuigkeiten spinnend
rollt die Sargeskutsche voran. In der Ödnis
ist eine neue Zeitung herausgekommen.
❍

(*Tr. from Bengali by Christian Weiss and Hans Harder with the author*)

PAPER COACH

Only a coach carrying newsmen
passing through the dead city—
nothing has occurred. And yet,
speculating, manufacturing news
around some unhappened accident
a hearse draws by. Into this emptiness
a newspaper makes its appearance.
❍

(*Tr. from Bengali by Roland Hindmarsh*)

ندا فاضلی

سلیقہ

دیوتا ہے کوئی ہم میں
نہ فرشتہ کوئی
چھو کے مت دیکھنا
ہر رنگ بکھر جاتا ہے
ملنے جلنے کا سلیقہ ہے ضروری ورنہ
آدمی چند ملاقاتوں میں مر جاتا ہے

Nida FAZLI

DAS RICHTIGE BENEHMEN

Keiner von uns ist ein Gott
noch Engel.
Nur nicht berühren!
Zu leicht blättert die Farbe ab.
Wir müssen behutsam miteinander umgehen,
sonst
stirbt ein Mensch nach wenigen Begegnungen.
O

(Tr. from Urdu by Christina Oesterheld)

DISCIPLINE

No divinity amongst us
No blessed ones
Do not touch
Intimacy reveals cracks
Colours will drain away
Relationship demands discipline
Else a few meetings
And the person is dead.
O

(Tr. from Urdu by Priya Rajvansh)

نئی ڈائری کا ایک ورق

صرف کاغذ کے کلنڈر میں نیا دن بدلا
صرف لوہے میں بندھے وقت کا ڈائل گھوما
چابیوں والا کھلونا
چُپ چاپ
گھر کی دہلیز سے باہر آکر
دائرہ دائرہ
ناچا
جھُوما
تالیاں بجتی رہیں
قہقہے سجتے رہے
چوکڑی بھرتا ہوا دھوُپ ہرن
آخری بس کے سیہ پہیّے سے
ہانپتا کانپتا
ٹکرایا
گرا
ٹوٹ گیا
ایک دن اور کئی دن کی طرح روٹھ گیا
آج بھی وہی ہوا
جس کے ہونے کا بہت خدشہ تھا
آج بھی کچھ نہ ہوا

EINE SEITE IM NEUEN TAGEBUCH

Nur ein neues Blatt im Kalender,
nur ein Stück weiter gerückt der Zeiger
der in Eisen gefangenen Zeit.
Das mechanische Spielzeug
trat ganz still
über die Schwelle des Hauses.
Es tanzte
und wiegte sich
immer im Kreise.
Beifall ertönte,
Gelächter erschallte.
Wie eine Gazelle sprang die Sonne,
stieß zitternd und keuchend
gegen die schwarzen Räder des letzten Busses,
fiel
und zerbrach.
Ein Tag mehr wandte sich schmollend ab
wie so viele zuvor.
Auch heute geschah genau das,
was du befürchtet hattest:
Nichts geschah.
O

(Tr. from Urdu by Christina Oesterheld)

A PAGE FROM THE NEW DIARY

The day changed
Only on the calendar
The steel belted dial of time
Turned,
The clockwork-doll
Stepped beyond the threshold
Of its home
And danced in circles.
Hands clapped
Laughter crowned the scene
A playful sun-deer
Panted and trembled
Dashed into the black tyre
Of the last bus
Fell and went to pieces.
One more day
Turned away offended.
Exactly
What I had feared
Happened today
Today again
Nothing happened.
O

(Tr. from Urdu by Baidar Bakht and Leslie Lavigne)

راستے کی منطق

ابھی ابھی جو گیا ہے دھکیل کر تم کو
اسے بُرا نہ کہو
اپنے پیر مت روکو
جو چل سکو تو چلو
ورنہ راستہ چھوڑ دو!
تمھارے پیچھے بھی کچھ لوگ آرہے ہوں گے
دیا کی بھیک نہ مانگو
بڑھے چلو یونہی
اُبلتی بھیڑ کی لہریں ہیں تیز دھار بہت
یہاں کِسی کی کِسی سے نظر نہیں ملتی
نہ دوستی
نہ محبت
نہ فلسفہ کوئی
یہ راستہ ہے یہاں راستہ کی منطق ہے
تلاش سب کو ہے
موقع کی بات ہے ساری
کوئی پھسلتا ہے
کوئی پھلانگ جاتا ہے
جو آگے بڑھتا ہے دو چار کو گراتا ہے
ابھی ابھی جو گیا ہے دھکیل کر تم کو
اُسے بُرا نہ کہو

DAS GESETZ DER STRASSE

Schimpf nicht auf den,
der dich gerade zur Seite gedrängt hat.
Bleib nicht stehen!
Geh weiter, wenn du kannst,
sonst mach Platz für die anderen.
Hinter dir kommen sicher schon die nächsten.
Erwarte von ihnen kein Erbarmen,
geh einfach weiter.
Scharfkantig sind die Wogen der ausströmenden Menge.
Hier treffen sich keine Blicke,
keine Freundschaft,
keine Liebe,
keine Philosophie.
Dies ist die Straße, sie hat ihr eigenes Gesetz.
Nur die richtige Gelegenheit zählt.
Einer fällt,
ein anderer springt über ihn hinweg.
Wer nach vorn drängt, bringt ein paar andere zu Fall.
Schimpf nicht auf den,
der dich gerade zur Seite gedrängt hat.
❍

(Tr. from Urdu by Christina Oesterheld)

ON THE ROAD

He who has just pushed you aside
Curse him not
Don't stop your stride
If you can–keep moving
Or else quit the road
Others must be coming up behind you
Beg not for mercy
Keep moving
The current of the convulsing crowds
Has a speed too fast
Nobody looks at nobody here
No friendship
No love
No philosophy
Here only the road
Only the rules of the road
Everyone is in queue
Waiting
But 'tis all a game of chance
Some fall down
Some leap ahead
Whoever moves forward leaves a few crushed behind
He who has just pushed you aside
Curse him not.
❍

(Tr. from Urdu by Priya Rajvansh)

بس یونہی جیتے رہو

بس یونہی جیتے رہو
کچھ نہ کہو
صبح جب سو کے اُٹھو
گھر کے افراد کی گنتی کر لو
ٹانگ پر ٹانگ رکھے روز کا اخبار پڑھو
اس جگہ قحط پڑا
جنگ وہاں پر برسی
کتنے محفوظ ہو تم شکر کرو
ریڈیو کھول کے فلموں کے نئے گیت سنو
گھر سے جب نکلو تو
شام تک کے لیے ہونٹوں میں تبسّم سی لو
دونوں ہاتھوں میں مصافحے بھر لو
منہہ میں کچھ کھوکھلے، بے معنی سے جملے رکھ لو
مختلف ہاتھوں میں سکّوں کی طرح گھستے رہو
کچھ نہ کہو
اُجلی پوشاک
سماجی عزت
اور کیا چاہیے جینے کے لیے
روز مل جاتی ہے پینے کے لیے
بس یونہی جیتے رہو
کچھ نہ کہو

LEB EINFACH SO WEITER

Leb einfach so weiter
und halte den Mund.
Wenn du am Morgen aufstehst,
zähl die Häupter deiner Lieben,
leg die Beine übereinander und lies die Zeitung:
Hier eine Hungersnot
dort ein Krieg.
Sei froh, daß du in Sicherheit bist.
Schalte das Radio ein und hör dir die neuesten
Filmsongs an.
Wenn du das Haus verläßt,
laß deine Lippen bis zum Abend in einem Lächeln
erstarren.
Fülle beide Hände mit Händedrücken,
leg dir ein paar leere, nichtssagende Sätze
zurecht.
Laß dich von fremden Händen wie eine Münze
abgreifen.
Halte den Mund.
Ordentliche Kleidung,
ein guter Ruf,
Was brauchst du mehr zum Leben.
Kannst dich jeden Tag betrinken.
Leb einfach so weiter
und halte den Mund.
O

(Tr. from Urdu by Christina Oesterheld)

JUST KEEP ON LIVING

Just keep on living like this
Say nothing
When you get up in the morning
Take a headcount of the family
Slouch in the chair and read the paper
There was a famine there
And a war raged somewhere else
Be thankful that you are safe
Switch on the radio and listen to the new pop
songs
When you leave the house
Paste a smile on your face
Pack hand shakes in your hands
Keep a few meaningless phrases on your lips
Be passed through different hands like a coin
Say nothing
A white collar
Social respect
A few drinks every day
What else you need
Just keep on like this
Say nothing.
O

(Tr. from Urdu by Baidar Bakht and Leslie Lavigne)

गगन गिल

॥ मछली ॥

इस मछली के मस्तिष्क में
जल नहीं
आकाश भर गया है

पानी नहीं
उड़ने की लालसा
भर गई है
इस मछली की देह में

भरे समुद्र में वह
ख़ाली कर रही है स्वयं को
अनवरत सदियों से

छोटी-बड़ी मछलियों के
बीच से गुज़रती
चिंतन-मग्ना यह मछली
पूछती है खुद से—
समुद्र कहाँ गया
तुम्हारा ओ ?

तैरती हुई मछली
दोहराती है यह प्रश्न
जैसे प्रार्थना-मंत्र हो

जानती नहीं मछली
आकाश भर गया है
उसके मस्तिष्क में

कि कपाल-क्रिया उसकी
शुरू हो चुकी है
भीतर से
○

Gagan GILL

DER FISCH

Das Hirn dieses Fisches
füllt nicht Wasser
sondern Himmel

kein Wasser
die Sehnsucht zu fliegen
erfüllt
den Körper dieses Fisches

in den vollen Ozean
entleert er sich
seit unendlicher Zeit

treibend zwischen großen, kleinen Fischen
sinnt der Fisch
fragt sich -
wohin, sag selbst,
ist dein Ozean verschwunden?

der schwimmende Fisch
wiederholt die Frage
gebetsmühlenartig

der Fisch weiß nicht
daß sein Hirn
von Himmel erfüllt ist

daß das Ritual des Schädelbrechens
schon begonnen hat
von innen her
❍

(*Tr. from Hindi by Barbara Lotz*)

Kapal Kriya: Teil der Hindu-Riten bei der Kremation ist das Brechen des Schädels des Toten, um das Entweichen der Seele zu gewährleisten und sie so vor dem Zugriff böser Mächte zu schützen.

THE FISH

It's not water
But the sky
Which has filled the brain of this fish.

Not water,
A longing to fly,
Has filled the body of this fish.

She has been emptying herself
Into the sea
For centuries, endlessly.

Swimming past fish, large and small
Rapt in thought,
This fish asks herself,
Say, your sea, where has it gone?

Swimming, this fish
Repeats the question,
As if it were a prayer or *mantra.*

She doesn't know, this fish
That the sky has filled her brain
That the skull-breaking rites*
Have already begun
Within herself.
❍

(*Tr. from Hindi by J.P. Das, Madhu B. Joshi and Arlene Zide with the poet*)

* The skull of a dead person on the funeral pyre is cracked in order to allow the soul to escape.

॥ आधे सिर का दर्द - 2 ॥

कपाल के भीतर
टीला है एक
सूखे दुख का

कभी-कभी उसे भिगोने
चढ़ बैठती है
रक्त-नदी उस पर

लौटता है पुराना
आधे सिर कर दर्द

यह एक ज़िद है
देह और आत्मा में
आत्मा और उसका दुख
रचनेवाले में

अँधेरे हिस्से में पड़े
किसी फफोले को बिठाने की ज़िद

ईश्वर नहीं चाहता
उसकी माया में विघ्न हो

कि मनुष्य उससे छिपाकर
अपना दुख रखे
किसी संदूकची के नीचे

इसलिए ईश्वर
उफानता है रक्त-नदी

जैसे छूना हो
सूखे टीले के साथ-साथ
मनुष्य का रहस्य

अब यह मनुष्य पर है
कि वह ईश्वर की
उत्सुकता से
अनुकंपा से
कैसे बचकर रहे

○

MIGRÄNE - 2

Im Schädelinneren
liegt ein Häufchen
vertrockneten Leids

Manchmal,
es zu erweichen,
ergießt sich darüber
ein Blut-Strom

dann kehrt zurück
die alte Migräne

Ein zähes Ringen
zwischen Körper und Seele
zwischen Seele und Urheber
ihres Leids

die Blase dort im dunklen
Winkel aufzustechen

Der Herr duldet keine
Einmischung in Seiner Maya

daß der Mensch klammheimlich
sein Leid verberge vor Ihm
unter irgendeiner Kiste

Deswegen läßt der Herr
einen Blut-Strom aufbrausen

als wolle Er
zugleich mit dem trockenen Häufchen
das Geheimnis des Menschen anrühren

Jetzt liegt es am Menschen
wie er sich
vor der Neugier des Herrn
vor dem Mitleid des Herrn
in Sicherheit bringt
O

(Tr. from Hindi by Barbara Lotz)

MIGRAINE -2

There is a mound of dry grief
inside the skull
Sometimes the blood river swells
to dampen it
An old ache returns

This is an insistence
between body and soul
between soul and the creator of its grief
to puncture the blister
hidden in a corner

God doesn't want any meddling
In His Maya
When man keeps his grief a secret
under a suitcase
He swells the blood river
to touch this secret
as it were the dry mound

It is for man now
to save himself
from God's anxiety
from God's grace
O

(Tr. from Hindi by Nancy Postero with the poet)

॥ किसी दूसरे का प्रेम ॥

कभी-कभी किसी दूसरे का प्रेम भूल से कुछ देर के लिए हमारे जीवन में आ जाता था।

वह सड़क पर पायी ऐसी वस्तु होता, जो न हमारी होती, न हमने चुरायी होती। उसे अपने पास रख लेने का सम्मोहन भी कुछ देर बाद समाप्त हो जाता। अकसर कुछ समय बाद उसे ढूँढ़ता कोई आता और ले जाता। या वह खुद ही हमें अपने घर का पता बताता और हम उसे छोड़ आते। वह एक चमत्कार की तरह आता। चला जाता।

हम उससे उबरने के लिए किसी दूसरे प्रेम का इंतज़ार करते। और कभी-कभी तो अपना प्रेम ही किसी और के घर छोड़ आते।

❍

DIE LIEBE EINES ANDEREN

Manchmal gerät die Liebe eines anderen für eine Weile in unser Leben.

Sie kann wie etwas sein, was man auf der Straße findet, was uns weder gehört, noch jemandem gestohlen wurde. Die Versuchung, sie bei uns zu behalten, wird geringer nach einiger Zeit. Öfters kommt nach einer Weile jemand, sie zu suchen und nimmt sie mit. Oder sie sagt selbst, wohin sie gehört und wir liefern sie dort ab. Sie kommt wie ein Wunder. Und geht wieder.

Um darüber hinwegzukommen, warten wir auf die Liebe eines anderen. Und manchmal lassen wir selbst unsere Liebe im Haus eines anderen zurück.

❍

(Tr. from Hindi by Barbara Lotz)

SOMEBODY ELSE'S LOVE

Sometimes somebody else's love would drift into our lives.

It might be an object found on the road which wasn't ours and hadn't been stolen by us. The temptation to keep it would be over after a while.

Often, after a little while, someone would come looking for it and take it away. Or it would itself tell us where it belonged and we would go and drop it back where it came from. It would turn up miraculously and leave.

To get over it, we would wait for some other love. Sometimes, we would even leave our own love behind at somebody else's door.

❍

(Tr. from Hindi by Arlene Zide and the poet)

प्रमोद कौंसवाल

॥ दूकानें ॥

एक

सपना समाप्त
सुबह हुई आसमान में
उस्तुरा उठाकर
उसने पेड़ पर लटकाया आईना
एक भी आदमी ने आज
दाढ़ी नहीं बनवायी
नहीं कटवाये बाल

शाम को अपना ही चेहरा
आईने में थका देख
राम रहीम का नाम ले
लौटा घर
नाई की दूकान की
सच्चाई कुछ अलग
भाषा अजीब।

दो

मुट्ठियाँ तानकर
हाथ जोड़कर उसने अभी
सारी सब्ज़ियों को दिखायी धूप
सूरज को किया नमस्कार
पूरी इज्ज़त परमत के साथ
भगवान को किया याद
दिन भर अच्छी कमाई के लिए
माँगी दुआएँ

किस किसने सुनी उसकी
चार रुपए चार आने
हुआ असली लाभ
दिन भर धूप में सूख गयी सब्ज़ी को
वह एक मुसीबत की तरह
उठाता है एक साथ।

Pramod KAUNSWAL

LÄDEN

EINS

Ende des Traums
Am Himmel war Morgen
Er nahm das Rasiermesser
Und hängte den Spiegel an den Baum
Nicht einer ließ heut
Sich rasieren
Sich die Haare schneiden

Abends sah er sein eignes Gesicht
Müde im Spiegel
Mit Ram und Rahim auf den Lippen
Ging er nach Hause
Der Barbierladen hat
Seine besondere Wahrheit
Seine eigene Sprache.

(*Tr. from Hindi by Lothar Lutze*)

ZWEI

Die Fäuste angespannt
Die Hände zusammengelegt hat er
das Gemüse der Sonne dargeboten
Hat den Sonnengott gegrüßt
mit höchster Ehrerbietung
Hat Gott angerufen
für einen guten Tagesverdienst
hat er Gebete gesprochen.

Doch wer hat ihn gehört
vier Rupien vier Annas
das blieb unterm Strich
Das Gemüse welk von der Hitze des Tages
hievt er empor wie ein Verhängnis.

(*Tr. from Hindi by Barbara Lotz*)

SHOPS

ONE

End of dream
It is morning in the sky
Picking up the razor
He hangs the mirror on the tree-trunk
Nobody came for a shave
Nor a haircut

Looking at his own face
Tired in the mirror
He returned home
Uttering the names of Ram and Rahim
The reality of the barber's shop different
Language strange

TWO

Clenching his fists
Joining the palms together
He warmed the vegetables in the sunlight
Made obeisance to the Sun God
With total reverence and devotion
Remembered God
Seeking blessings for good earnings
During the day

Whosoever heard him
Four rupees four annas
Was the net profit
He lifts the withered vegetables under the harsh
sun
Like a calamity
Altogether

तीन

बहुत कमों को मालूम है
दिन खुला पहले कि दूकान
तीनों बेटों को बहुधा एक साथ लेकर
कोई खोलता है ताला
चीज़ों को चमकदार बनाता है दूसरा
तीसरा देखता है आज पूरे दिन के लिए
रेज़गारी की गुंजाइश

इन्सानियत ख़त्म होती जा रही है
माँगते हैं सब उधार
बेटों को बूढ़ों ने दी हिदायत
उन छोकरियों को मुँह न लगाएँ
उनको उधार देकर बैठ गया है भट्ठा
ग्राहक भी क्या हैं
बेटियों को भेजते हैं ख़रीदारी में
कोसता हूआ बूढ़ा सोचता है
बेटों की उदारता
और अपनी विवशता पर।

चार

चौंसठ साल की बुढ़िया का
शरीर उतर आया है
आँखों और पलकों पर
छा गया है धुँधलापन
हाथों और चेहरे पर झुर्रियाँ
आठ आना चार आना
रुपया दो रुपया
एक ही नज़र में पहचान लेती है
आते जाते कभी यह बुढ़िया
हमें देती है चने की थैलियाँ
भूख में खाए जाने वाले ठोस दाने
हम एक दिन खाते खाते
कर लेंगे चौंसठ पार
बुढ़िया ने पचास ग्राम की जगह
नहीं किया कभी उनचास
तौलते हुए नहीं काँपे
कभी उसके हाथ।

○

DREI

Ganz wenige wissen ob erst
Der Tag sich geöffnet hat oder der Laden
Meist kommt er mit allen drei Söhnen
Der eine schließt auf
Der zweite bringt die Waren zum Glänzen
Der dritte sieht zu daß heut für den ganzen Tag
Das Kleingeld reicht

Mit der Menschlichkeit geht es zuende
Alle wolln alles auf Pump
Den Jungen haben eingebläut die Alten
Sich nicht in die jungen Dinger zu vergaffen
Seit man denen auf Pump gibt ist der Ofen aus
Was sind das bloß für Kunden
Schicken ihre Töchter zum Einkaufen
Denkt der Alte und verwünscht
Die Freigebigkeit seiner Söhne
Und die eigene Hilflosigkeit.

(*Tr. from Hindi by Lothar Lutze*)

THREE

Very few know
Whether the day opens up first or the shop
Often with the accompanying three sons
One of them unlocks the shutters
The other polishes the wares
The third checks whether there are enough
loose coins for the day

This is humanity's last hour
Everybody seeks credit
The sons were admonished by the old man
Don't let the girls get familiar with you
Business gets ruined giving them credit
What kind of customers we have now
Sending their daughters for grocery
Cursing, the old man ruminates
On the generosity of sons
And his own constraints

VIER

Der Körper der vierundsechzigjährigen Alten
ist eingefallen
Augen und Lider überzieht
ein trüber Schleier
Runzeln auf Händen und Gesicht
acht Anna vier Anna
eine Rupie zwei Rupien
unterscheidet sie mit einem Blick
Die Alte gibt uns manchmal im Vorbeigehen
Tüten mit Rösterbsen
harte Körner gegen Hunger.
Knabbernd werden wir einmal
die vierundsechzig überschreiten
Die Alte hat uns nie
statt fünfzig neunundvierzig Gramm gegeben
nie haben ihre Hände
beim Wiegen gezittert.

❍

(*Tr. from Hindi by Barbara Lotz*)

FOUR

The body of the sixty-four year old hag
has run down
A rheuminess covers her eyes and lids
Wrinkles her hand
She recognises in one glance
Eight annas, four annas,
One rupee, two rupees
Sometimes, as we pass, the woman
Gives us little bags full of grams
The solid kern eaten in hunger
Eating them
One day we shall cross sixty-four
The old woman never weighed 49 instead of 50
grammes
Her hands never shook
When she weighed.

❍

(*Tr. from Hindi by Vishnu Khare*)

॥ गाँव के दो दिन ॥

कल गाँव में पूजा हुई
शंख बजा
सच्ची आस्थाओं के बीच
ईश्वर के नाम बजी घंटियाँ
ईश्वर के नाम झुकी गर्दनें
भ्रातृत्व की शपथ ली गयी
ख़त्म हुआ आपसी भेद
अर्पित हुए सुख के गीत

पानी के स्रोत पर आज
झगड़े कुछ लोग
कुछ ने किया हल्ला
खेत ख़लिहानों पर तड़के
कुछ कटे भागकर
कुछ ने बचाया अपने को
उन शराबियों से
कल की पूजा में
जो पुजारी थे।

O

ZWEI TAGE IM DORF

Gestern war Puja im Dorf Gott zu Ehren
Das Muschelhorn ertönte
inmitten aufrichtiger Gläubigkeit
zur Ehre Gottes erklangen Glocken
zur Ehre Gottes neigten sich Häupter
Schwüre der Brüderlichkeit wurden geleistet
Beendet war Zwietracht untereinander
Dargebracht wurden Hymnen der Freude

Heute entbrannte ein Streit
über den Zugang zur Wasserquelle
ein paar schlugen Krawall
in aller Frühe auf den Dreschplätzen
einige wurden hingemetzelt auf der Flucht
einige konnten sich retten
vor den Säufern
die gestern bei der Puja
die Vorbeter waren.
O

(Tr, from Hindi by Barbara Lotz)

TWO DAYS IN THE VILLAGE

There was worship in the village yesterday
Conch was blown
Amid true venerations
Bells were rung in the name of God
Necks were bent
Brotherhood was sworn
Differences were buried
Songs of happiness were proffered

Today some people
Quarrelled over the source of water
Some people created a disturbance
In fields and barns early in the morning
Some got mowed down while escaping
Some saved themselves
From the drunkards
who were the priests
In yesterday's worship
O

(Tr. from Hindi by Vishnu Khare)

विष्णु खरे

॥ दिल्ली में अपना फ़्लैट बनवा लेने के बाद एक आदमी सोचता है ॥

पिता होते तो उन्हें कौन-सा कमरा देता ?
उन्हें देता वह छोटा कमरा
जिसके साथ गुसलख़ाना भी लगा हुआ है
वे आज इकहत्तर बरस के होते
और हमेशा की तरह अब भी उन्हें
अपना निर्लिप्त अकेलापन चाहिए होता
लगातार सिगरेट पीना और स्वयं को
हिंदुस्तानी गेय तथा वाद्य शास्त्रीय संगीत का अभ्यासी व्याख्याकार समझना
उन्होंने अंत तक नहीं छोड़ा था सो आज क्या छोड़ते
इसलिए उनके लिए यही कमरा ठीक रहता
सिर्फ़ रेडियो और टेलीविज़न उनसे दूर रखने पड़ते

माँ होतीं तो उन्हें कौन-सा कमरा देता ?
माँ भी करीब सत्तर की होतीं
और दिनभर तो वे रसोई में या छत पर होतीं बहू के साथ
या एक कमरे से दूसरे कमरे में बच्चों के बीच
जो अगर उन्हें अकेला छोड़ते
तो रात में वे पिता के कमरे में
या उससे लगी हुई बालकनी में उनके पैताने कहीं लेट जातीं
अपनी वही स्थायी जगह तय कर रखी थी उन्होंने

बड़ी बुआ होतीं तो उन्हें कौन-सा कमरा देता ?
क्या वो होतीं तो अभी भी कुँआरी होतीं
और उसके साथ रहतीं ?
हाँ कुँआरी ही होतीं—जब वे मरी थीं तो ब्याहता होने की
उनकी आस कभी की चली गई थी
और अब अपने भाई के आसरे न रहतीं तो कहाँ रहतीं—
सो उन्हें देता वह वो वाला बैडरूम
जिसमें वह खुद अपनी पत्नी के साथ रहना चाहता है
वैसे माँ के साथ वे भी दिनभर इधर से उधर होती रहतीं

Vishnu KHARE

EINER, DER ES IN DELHI ZU EINER EIGENEN WOHNUNG GEBRACHT HAT DENKT NACH

Lebte Vater noch, welches Zimmer hätte er ihm dann gegeben?
Ihm hätte er das kleine Zimmer gegeben
Das mit dem eigenen Bad
Er wäre heute einundsiebzig
Und wie schon immer würde er jetzt noch
Abseits und allein sein
Kettenrauchen und sich
Als Interpret klassischer nordindischer
Vokal- und Instrumentalmusik sehen wollen
Davon hatte er bis zuletzt nicht gelassen—warum also heute
Deshalb wäre für ihn dieses Zimmer das richtige gewesen
Nur Radio und Fernsehen hätte man fernhalten
müssen von seiner Stimme und seiner Sitar

Lebte Mutter noch welches Zimmer hätte er ihr dann gegeben?
Mutter wäre auch an die siebzig gewesen
Und tagsüber in der Küche oder auf dem Dach mit der Schwiegertochter
Oder unterwegs aus einem Zimmer ins andre umringt von den Kindern
Und von ihnen allein gelassen
Hätte sie nachts sich in Vaters Zimmer
Oder auf den angrenzenden Balkon an sein Fußende gelegt
Das hatte sie sich zur ständigen Bleibe ausgesucht

Lebte die ältere Tante noch welches Zimmer hätte er ihr dann gegeben?
Wenn sie lebte wäre sie dann immer noch unverheiratet

HAVING BUILT A FLAT IN DELHI, A MIDDLE-AGED MAN RUMINATES

Which room would he have given to the father had he been living?
That small one with the bathroom attached
Babu, as he was called with fear and respect at home,
would be seventy-one today
And would require his aloof loneliness as always
He had abandoned neither his incessant smoking
Nor thinking of himself as a practising exponent
Of Hindustani vocal and instrumental classical music till the end
So why would he abandon them now
This would therefore be the only room good for him
Only the radio and the TV would have to be kept away from him

Which room for mother if she were also alive?
She too would be nearly seventy
And the whole day she would be with the daughter-in-law
Either in the kitchen or on the terrace
Or among the children from one room to another
And if at all left alone by them
She would lie down in father's room
Or in the adjoining narrow balcony by his feet
That was the permanent place she had chosen for herself

Which room would he give to the elder bua had she been living?
Would she still be unmarried and living with

घर की बड़ी औरतें मजबूरन ही
कुछ घंटों का आराम चाहती हैं

क्या छोटी बुआ होतीं तो वे भी अब तक कुँआरी होतीं ?
हाँ कुँआरी ही होतीं—जब बड़ी बहन अनब्याही चली गई
तो उन्हें ही कौन-सी साध रह गई थी सुहागिन होने की—
सो छोटी बुआ भी रह लेतीं बड़ी बुआ के साथ
जैसे मौत तक उनके साथ रहीं
जब जवानी में दोनों के बीच कोई कहा-सुनी नहीं हुई
तो अब क्या होती भाई-भौजाई बहू और नाती-नातिनों के बीच

इस तरह माता-पिता और बुआओं से और भर जाता घर
इस घर में और जीवित हो जाता एक घर बयालीस बरस पुराना
वह और उसकी पत्नी और बच्चे तब रहते
बचे हुए एक कमरे में
जिसमें बेटियों के लिए थोड़ी आड़ कर दी जाती
कितने प्राण आ जाते इन कमरों में चार और प्राणियों से

लेकिन वह जानता है कि हर आदमी का घर
अक्सर सिर्फ़ एक बार ही होता है जीवन में
और उसका जो घर था
वह चालीस बरसों और चार मौतों के पहले था
कई मजबूरियों और मेहरबानियों से बना है यह घर
और शायद बसा भी है
बहरहाल अब यह उसकी घरवाली और बच्चों का ज़्यादा है
अब इसका क्या कि वह इसमें अपने उस पुराने घर को बसा नहीं सकता
जिसके अलावा उसका न तो कोई घर था और न लग पाएगा

इसलिए वह सिर्फ़ बुला सकता है
पिता को माँ को छोटी बुआ बड़ी बुआ को
सिर्फ़ आवाज़ दे सकता है उस सारे बीते हुए को
पितृमोक्ष अमावस्या की तरह सिर्फ़ पुकार सकता है आओ आओ
यहाँ रहो इसे बसाओ
अभी यह सिर्फ़ एक मकान है एक शहर की चीज़ एक फ़्लैट
जिसमें ड्राइंग रूम डाइनिंग स्पेस बैडरूम किचन
वैसी अनबरती बेपहचानी ग़ैर चीज़ें हैं

und wohnte bei ihm?
Ja sicher was sonst–als sie starb hatte sie längst
Die Hoffnung auf eine glückliche Ehe aufgegeben
Und wenn sie jetzt nicht in der Obhut ihres
Bruders und seines Sohnes lebte wo dann
Also hätte er ihr das Schlafzimmer gegeben
In dem er selbst mit seiner Frau wohnen möchte
An und für sich wäre sie tagsüber mit der Mutter
auf Achse gewesen
Die älteren Frauen im Haus brauchen erst wenn
sie todmüde sind
Ein paar Stunden Ruhe

Lebte die jüngere Tante noch wäre sie dann
auch immer noch unverheiratet
Ja sicher was sonst–wenn die ältere Schwester
unverheiratet starb
Wie hätte sie dann den Wunsch hegen können
Frau und Mutter zu sein –
Also hätte die jüngere Tante mit der ältren
zusammengewohnt
Wie sie bis zu deren Tod zusammenwohnte mit
ihr
Wenn in jungen Jahren die beiden sich gut
vertrugen
Warum dann nicht jetzt mit dem Bruder und
seiner Frau den Enkeln und Enkelinnen
zusammen

So hätte das Haus sich mit Eltern und Tanten
noch mehr gefüllt
In diesem Haus wäre ein andres noch lebendiger
geworden das zweiundvierzig Jahre alt ist
Er und seine Frau und seine Kinder hätten dann
In dem übriggebliebenen Zimmer gewohnt
In dem man den Töchtern eine Ecke für sich
eingeräumt hätte
Wieviel Leben wäre in diese Zimmer gekommen
durch noch vier Lebewesen

Aber er weiß daß ein Mensch im Leben
Meistens nur ein Haus hat
Und sein Haus
Liegt vierzig Jahre und vier Tode zurück
Aus ein paar Verpflichtungen Vergünstigungen
und lebenslanger Verschuldung entstand

him
If she were alive?
Yes, she would be unmarried–when she died
she had lost all yearning to get married
And where shall she go except under her
brother's shelter
So he would give her the bedroom
He wishes to live in with his wife
As it is she would also accompany mother and
his wife from here to there
Senior women of the house require rest only
under duress

Had the younger bua been alive would she be
unmarried too?
Surely so–when the elder sister died unmarried
She too lost all desire for conjugal bliss–
Thus the younger bua would live with the elder
bua
The way she lived with her till death
When there were no recriminations between
the two in their youth
How could they be now
Living with Baboo and his sister-in-law Bhauji,
The daughter-in-law and the grandchildren?

This way the house would have been more
populated
With mother father and the two aunts
A house forty-two years old would become more
alive in this house
He and his wife would then live in the remaining
room
In which a partition would be created for the
daughters
How much life would come to these rooms
with four more souls

But he knows that the home of each man
Happens to be only once in his lifetime
And what was his home
Was before forty years and four deaths

आओ और इन्हें उस घर में बदलो जिसमें यह नहीं थीं
फिर भी सब था और तुम्हारे पास मैं रहता था
जिसके सपने अब भी मुझे आते हैं
कुछ ऐसा करो कि इस नए घर के सपने पुराने होकर दिखें
और उनमें मुझे दिखो
बाबू भौजी बड़ी बुआ छोटी बुआ तुम

○

dieses Haus
Und bleibt vielleicht auch bestehen
Obwohl es jetzt mehr seiner Frau und den Kindern gehört
Was liegt schon dran daß er darin sein altes Haus nicht unterbringen kann

Außer dem es für ihn kein Haus gab noch geben wird
Deshalb kann er den Vater die Mutter
Die jüngere Tante die ältere einladen nur
Kann all dies Vergangene anrufen nur
Wie zur Pitrimoksh Amavasya kann er nur rufen Kommt kommt
Bleibt hier richtet euch ein hier
Bis jetzt ist das nur ein Gebäude ein Ding in der Stadt eine Wohnung
In der lauter unbenutzte unbekannte fremdartige Dinge sind
Die sich Wohnzimmer Eßecke Schlafzimmer Küche nennen
Kommt und verwandelt sie in das Haus in dem sie alle nicht waren
Und doch alles war und ich zusammen wohnte mit euch
Von dem ich immer noch träume
Tut irgendetwas daß die Träume vom neuen Haus mir wie alte vorkommen
Und ihr darin vorkommt
Vater und Mutter und ihr Tanten ihr
○

(*Tr. from Hindi by Lothar Lutze*)

Pitrimoksh Amavasya: Neumondnacht, in der man Speisen für die Seelen der Vorfahren aufs Dach wirft; diese erscheinen in Gestalt von Krähen.

This home is built by many constraints and kindnesses
And is also populated
However it belongs more to his wife and children
What of it that he cannot populate his old home in it
Except which he neither has any home
Nor can consider another as one

Therefore he can only summon
Father mother and the two aunts
Can only call the entire bygone
Can only call out "come, come"
As to the birds on the ancestor's day of Pitramoksha
Live here populate it
This is now only a dwelling-place a thing of the city a flat
Which has unfamiliar unused things
Like drawing room dining space bed-room kitchen
Come and turn it into the home in which they were not
Yet there was everything and I with you
Of which I still dream
Do something that I may dream this house as that home
And see you in it
Baboo Bhauji elder Bua younger Bua you all
○

(*Tr. from Hindi by the poet*)

॥ सिंगल विकेट सीरीज़ ॥

मैंने अभी अभी फिर गार्ड लिया है
जूतों पैड दस्तानों हैल्मैट की कसावट को जाँचा है
सामने पिच को बैट से बराबर किया है
कुछ आश्वस्त कुछ व्यग्र
अब तक एकाध दफ़ा बीट हुआ हूँ
लेकिन अगली गेंद की प्रतीक्षा में हूँ

रोशनी के चार खंभों से सैकड़ों रोशनियाँ हो गई हैं स्टेडियम में
मैदान की हर चीज़ की परछाईं चौगुना करती हुईं
मैं भी अपने ही अक्स के कटपिट निशान वाले चार सायों के बीच
पाँचवाँ खड़ा हूँ
अजीब चुप्पी है दीर्घाओं में
क्या यह कोई ऐसा क्षण है जिसने सबकी साँसें रोकी हुई हैं

तभी दूसरे छोर से प्रकट होता है वह
अश्वारोही जैसा तेज़ फिर भी मानों चाँद पर चलता हुआ
काली सी पोशाक में जैसे कोई चोग़ा उड़ रहा हो पीछे
फेंकता है गेंद वह सिर झटककर
उसका पंजा झलकता है एक पल के लिए
कनपटी और जबड़े की रेखाएँ उभरती हैं
आँखें धँसी हुई इसलिए सिर्फ़ कालेय विवर दिखते हैं
उसके दाँत चमके थे एक बार देखा हुआ सा लगता है फिर भी
कौन है पोशीदा यह जिसका मुकाबला मैंने पहले कभी नहीं किया

लेकिन मेरे पैर सीसे के हो गए
मेरा बल्ला पत्थर का
कलेजा और हाथ सर्द होठ सूखे पपड़ियाए
और अपने पैरों के पीछे व सीने पर मैंने वह परिचित आवाज सुनी
जैसे हवा से दरवाज़ा खुलने पर लैबोरेटरी में
दीवार से काल्बुद खड़खड़ाया हो

KRICKET

Eben noch hab ich meine Stellung überprüft
Handschuhe Polster Helm und Schuhe
festgezurrt
Das Feld vor mir geebnet mit dem Schläger
Teils meiner Sache sicher teils verunsichert
Ein- zweimal hab den Ball ich schon verfehlt
Doch jetzt erwarte ich den nächsten Ball

Im Stadion die vier Lichtmasten sind Hunderte
von Lichtern jetzt geworden
Die jeden Schatten auf dem Feld vervierfachen
Auch ich steh zwischen den vier Schattenkreuzen
meiner eignen Silhouette
Als fünftes
Ein ungewohntes Schweigen herscht auf den
Tribünen
Ist das Augenblick der Art die aller Atem anhält?

Dann von der andern Seite erscheint Er
Wie ein Berittner schnell und doch wie einer der
den Mond begeht
In Schwarz gehüllt als flatterte ein Mantel hinter
ihm
Als er den Ball wirft zuckt er mit dem Kopf
Kurz schimmert seine Hand
Schläfe und Kiefer scheinen scharf umrissen
Die Augen sitzen tief in ihren schwarzen Höhlen
Die Zähne hab ich einmal funkeln sehen mein
ich, aber
Wer ist dieser Geheimnisvolle dem ich noch nie
entgegentrat?

Doch meine Beine sind aus Blei jetzt
Mein Schläger ist aus Stein
Das Herz die Hände feuchtkalt die Lippen trocken
rissig
Und hinter meinen Beinen an der Brust hör den

SINGLE-WICKET SERIES

I have just taken guard again
Have checked if my boots pads gloves and helmet
are securely fastened
Have just patted level the pitch in front with my
bat
A trifle confident a trifle anxious
I have been beaten once or twice so far
But I await the next ball to come.

From the four light-towers shine hundreds of
lights in the stadium
Multiplying by four the shadow of each object
Amidst the four-fold shadows of a crossed-out
sign
I too stand as my own shadow, a fifth
There's a strange stillness in the stands
What moment is this when everyone holds his
breath

Suddenly he appears from the other end
Like a horse-rider but loping as a moon-walker
In some dark outfit as if with a cape streaming
behind
He bowls with a jerk of the head
His grip flashing for a moment
The lines of his jaws and temple now picked out
Eyes sunken so that all one sees are black holes
His teeth flashed once, it's as if I have seen him
before
Who is this cloaked figure I've never faced before

But my feet have turned to lead
My bat to stone
My heart and hands grown cold my lips parched

ये यकायक बत्तियाँ किसने बुझा दीं
देखने वाले क्यों हो गए गूँगे
स्टेडियम में यह क्या सिर्फ़ हवा की साँय साँय है
अपने स्तंभित पथराएपन से मैं ही कैसे निकल आया बाहर
जैसे सारी पोशाक के ख़ोल से मुक्त हुआ हूँ
कि अपने तिरते हुए वेग में वह आ चुका होता है मेरे पास
कंधे पर महसूस करता हूँ मैं
उसकी ढाढस बँधाती मगर मज़बूत साग्रह पकड़
फिर अँधेरे में ही आख़िरकार उसके काले नक्श पहचानकर कहता हूँ
वैल बोल्ड सर
पिच मैदान बुझी बत्तियाँ अँधेरा स्टेडियम
सब जैसे नीचे होते जाते हैं तब तलक
फिर वह गेंद फेंकता रहता है मेरे हाथों में और मैं वापस उसे
जब हम ओझल होते चलते हैं
कहीं और किसी अगले दौर के एकल खेल के लिए
○

bekannten Laut ich
Wie wenn ein Windstoß im Labor die Tür aufreißt
Und das Skelett drin an die Mauer klirrt

Wer hat die Lampen plötzlich ausgeschaltet
Warum sind jetzt die Zuschauer stumm
Ist das im Stadion nur das Windgeheul
Wie hab ich mich gelöst aus Starre und Versteinerung
Als hätt ich aus der Schale meiner Kleider mich befreit
Da ist er schon bei mir mit seinem schwimmenden Schritt
Auf meiner Schulter spür ich
Seinen Griff der Mut macht doch nicht locker läßt
Dann endlich in der Dunkelheit erkenn ich sein finsteres Bild und sag
Well bowled sir
Spielfeld gelöschte Lampen dunkles Stadion
Scheinen inzwischen wegzusinken
Ein paarmal wirft er mir den Ball noch zu und ich werf ihn zurück
Dann gehen wir, verschwinden
Irgendwohin zu einem Einzelspiel in einer nächsten Runde.

o

(Tr. from Hindi by Lothar Lutze)

to flakes
Behind my feet and on my ribcage I hear
That familiar rattle
As when upon the wind pushing open the lab door
A skeleton knocks against the wall.

Who has suddenly switched off all the lights
Why have all the spectators gone mute
Is this just the wind howling through the stadium
How have I come out of my own petrified shock
As if I had been relieved of my whole armour
By now he has come floating through the air up close
I feel on my shoulder
His consoling but firm and insistent hand
Now making out his features still in the dark I say
Well bowled sir!
The pitch the extinguished lights the dark stadium
All seem to descend to some lower level meanwhile
He tosses the ball to me and I back to him
And so we gradually fade away from sight
For some other round of single-wicket somewhere else.

o

(Tr. from Hindi by Harish Trivedi)

ସିଲାଙ୍କାନ୍ତ ମହାପାତ୍ର

।। ସମୟ ବହିଯାଏନି ।।

ସମୟ ବହିଯାଏନି
ଲୋକମାନେ ବହିଯାଆନ୍ତି
ସଚରାଚର ପ୍ରାଣୀମାନେ ହିଁ ବହିଯାଆନ୍ତି ।।

ଖଇରିଆ କୋଟ୍ ପିନ୍ଧିଥିବା ମେଘ
ଦାଣ୍ଡ ପିଣ୍ଡାରେ କାନ୍ଥକୁ ଆଉଜି
ଆକାଶକୁ ଅନେଇ ବସିଥିବା ଚିତ୍ରପ୍ରତିମା
ବାପାଙ୍କୁ ବିଦାୟ, ବିଦାୟ କହି ବହିଯାଏ;
ତା' ପରଦିନ ବାପା ଆମକୁ ପଛକରି
ପଛେଇ ପଛେଇ ବହିଯାଆନ୍ତି ସେଇଆଡ଼େ
        ଦିଗ୍‌ବଳୟ ତଳକୁ
ବିଦାୟ ନେଉଥିବା ସୂର୍ଯ୍ୟଙ୍କ ସାଙ୍ଗରେ ।।

ବିଦାୟ ବିଦାୟ କହି ଝଡ଼ିପଡ଼େ ପତ୍ର
କାନ୍ଦୁଥିବା ଗଛକୁ ତହିଁ ଆରଦିନ
କାଠକଟାଳିଏ ହାଣି ନେଇ ଥାଆନ୍ତି
କୋଉଦିନୁ ଛିଡାହୋଇଥିବା ମାଟିଠୁ
ସେ ବିଦାୟ ନିଏ ।।

ଅଗ୍ନନକ ଦୁଶିଯାଏ
ଘର,ଘାଟ, ନଈ, ବଣ, ବିଲ, ପାଟ
ସ୍ତ୍ରୀ, ପୁଅ, ସାଙ୍ଗ ସାଥୀ
ଅକଳନ ସମୟର ଯେତେ ଚିତ୍ରପଟ
ବହିଯାଆନ୍ତି ଅନ୍ଧାର ଆଡ଼କୁ ।।

ସେ ଅନ୍ଧାର ତମ ଛାଇ
ତମକୁ ନିଶ୍ଚୟ ଜଣା
କାହିଁକି ଭାସିଯାଉଛୁ ଆମେ ସବୁ
        ଆଉ କୁଆଡ଼କୁ ।।

O

Sitakant MAHAPATRA

NICHT DIE ZEIT FLIESST

Nicht die Zeit fließt
Es fließen die Menschen
Alles was lebt fließt davon.

Die Wolke in ihrem dunkelroten Rock
Nimmt Abschied vom Vater
Der an die Terrassenwand gelehnt
Die Bögen und Bilder am Himmel mustert
Und fließt davon
Schon am Tag darauf
Dreht uns der Vater den Rücken zu
Und entfernt sich ganz langsam
Dorthin
Wo auch die Sonne jetzt Abschied nimmt
Unterm Horizont.

Abschied nehmen die fallenden Blätter
Den weinenden Baum fällen am Tag darauf
Die Waldarbeiter und bringen ihn fort
Er nimmt Abschied
Von der Erde auf der er
Wer weiß wie lang stand.

Auf einmal erscheinen
Haus, Ufer, Fluß, Steinplatte, Wildnis
Frau, Söhne, Freunde, Gefährten:
Alle Bilder aus einer unvorstellbaren Zeit
Fließen davon
Zur Dunkelheit hin.

Diese Dunkelheit ist Dein Schatten
Du wirst schon wissen
Warum und wohin
Wir alle fließen.
O

(Tr. from Hindi by Lothar Lutze)

TIME DOES NOT FLY

It is not time that flies.
It is men, all creatures
everywhere.

The cloud in a brown coat flies away
waving goodbye to my father
as he sits like a portrait,
his head propped against the wall
of the verandah of our house.

Next day, his back towards us,
father flies away and sinks
below the horizon
along with the sun.

Leaves fall
waving goodbye to the weeping tree.
And then the woodcutters come and fell the tree
and it waves goodbye
to the ancient soil
on which it stood.

Suddenly one sees
houses, rivers, forests, paddy fields
swamps, wife and children, friends, relatives
the endless images, crafted by time
everything rushing forward
into the darkness.

That darkness
is only your shadow.
Surely you should know
why we fly away, helpless,
and where.

(Tr. by the poet)

॥ ଧାଙ୍ଗଡ଼ାର ପ୍ରେମ ସଂଗୀତ ॥

ପାହାଡ଼ର ଗଡ଼ାଣିରେ
ତତେ ସ୍ନେହ ମାଗିଲି, ସ୍ୱପ୍ନ ମାଗିଲି ;
ସ୍ପର୍ଶ ମାଗିଲି, ଧୂଆ ତର ମାଗିଲି ;
କହିଲୁ, ଏଠି ପୋଡୁଗ୍ରଷର ହାଉଜାଉ ମଣିଷ
ଏଠି ନୁହେଁ ।।

ସଞ୍ଜ ଅନ୍ଧାରରେ
ମହୁଲ ଫୁଲ ବାସ୍ନାରେ ଅଥୟ ଗାଁ ମୁଣ୍ଡରେ
ତତେ ସ୍ନେହ ମାଗିଲି, ଦେହ ମାଗିଲି
ନୋହିଲେ କଥା ଦେ'କହିଲି,
କହିଲୁ, ଜୁଳୁଜୁଳିଆ ପୋକ ଓ ଏକୁଟିଆ ତାରାଙ୍କୁ
ମତେ ସବୁକାଳେ ଭାରି ଡ଼ର
ଏ ନକାଅଁନ ଜାଗାରୁ ପଳେଇ ଯିବା ଭଲ ।।

ଘନ ଅରଣ୍ୟରେ ନିଜ ଛାତିର ଦୁକୁଦୁକୁ ନିଜକୁ ଶୁଭୁଥିଲା
ତତେ ସ୍ନେହ ମାଗିଲି, ସ୍ପର୍ଶ ମାଗିଲି
କହିଲୁ, ଛି, ଏଠି ଏଇ ମଳିନ ଧୂସର ମାଟି
ଫୁଲପରି ଏ ଦେହ, ସୁନାପରି ମୋ ଆତ୍ମା
ମଉଳି ଯିବନି, ଧୂଳିଧୂସର ହୋଇଯିବନି !
ଏଠି ନୁହେଁ, ଏଠି ନୁହେଁ।।

ଝୋଲା କୂଳରେ କେହି ନ ଥିଲେ
ଏକୁଟିଆ ଚଢ଼େଇଟି ଯାହା ଗୀତ ବୋଲୁଥିଲା
ତତେ ସ୍ପର୍ଶ ମାଗିଲି, ଅନ୍ଧାର ମାଗିଲି
କହିଲୁ, ଝୋଲାପାଣିର ସ୍ୱଚ୍ଛ ଆଇନାରେ ଯେ ସବୁ ଦୁଶୁଚି
ଏଠି ନୁହେଁ, ଏଠି ନୁହେଁ।।

DHANGRAS LIEBESLIED

Am Berghang
Wollt ich Liebe von dir, einen Traum wollt ich
Wollte daß du mich anrührst, wollt ein
    Tabaksblatt;
Du hast gesagt: nicht hier
Hier auf den Feldern sind zuviel Leute.

Als der Abend dunkelte
Draußen vorm Dorf
Das trunken war vom Mahuablütenduft
Wollt ich Liebe von dir, wollt deinen Leib
Oder wenigstens ein Versprechen;
Du hast gesagt: vor dem Glühwurm, vor einem
    einsamen Stern
Fürcht ich mich immer
Komm, fliehen wir diesen verwunschenen Ort.

Im dichten Wald konnt in meiner Brust
Ich selbst das Pochen hören
Wollte Liebe von dir, wollte daß du mich anrührst;
Du hast gesagt: pfui, auf diesem schmutzigen
    Boden
Soll dieser blühende Körper, soll diese goldene
    Seele
Nicht verwelken
Nicht staubig werden.
Nicht hier, nicht hier.

Keine Seele war am Wasserfall
Nur ein Vogel sang sein Lied
Wollte daß du mich anrührst, wollte Dunkelheit;
Du hat gesagt: das Wasser, der klare Spiegel
Verrät alles.
Nicht hier, nicht hier.

Es schlief die ganze Erde
Es schliefen der Mond und die Sterne

DHANGDA'S LOVE SONG

On the hill's sloping ground
I asked you to give me love, dreams
a touch, tobacco leaves.
And you said: Here there are only
the harvesting men.
Not here.

In the twilight dark,
at the place where the village
now begins to be restless
with the scent of *mahula,*
I asked for your affection, your body;
or else, just give your word, I said.
And you said: I'm always afraid of
the fireflies and the lonely stars;
it is better that we leave this solitary place.

Inside the forest, when
the beating of the heart could be heard,
I asked for your love, your touch.
And you said: Oh no! here there is just
the pale grey earth. Wouldn't this
flower-like body, this pure
unblemished soul, turn earth-pale?
Not here, not here!

Beside the rivulet, there was no one,
just the lone bird that sang.
I asked for your touch, for darkness.
And you said: On the rivulet's clear mirror
everything is seen.
Not here, not here.

The whole world had dropped off to sleep,

ସାରା ପୃଥ୍ୱୀ ନିଦେଇ ଥିଲା
ଏମିତିକି ଜହ୍ନ ତାରା ବି
ତତେ ମୁଁ ସ୍ୱର୍ଶ ମାଗିଲି, ପ୍ରାଣ ମାଗିଲି
ଥୁରୁଥୁରୁ ମୋ ଆତ୍ମା ପାଇଁ
ତୋ ଦେହ ବସାରେ ଧାପେ ଜାଗା ମାଗିଲି
କହିଲୁ, ଅନ୍ଧାରରେ ବି ତମ ଆଖି ଆଇନାରେ
ସବୁ ଜଳ ଜଳ ଦିଶୁଚି
ଏବେ ନୁହେଁ, ଏବେ ନୁହେଁ।।

ଆଖି ଦୋଟି ତାଡ଼ି
ତେବେ ତୋତେ ପଦ୍ମଫୁଲ ପରି ଭେଟି ଦେଉଛି,ନେ,
ଏବେ ସ୍ୱର୍ଶ' ଦେ, ସ୍ନେହ ଦେ, ଅନ୍ଧାର ଦେ,
ନିକାଞ୍ଚନ ଆତ୍ମାକୁ ଆଶା ଦେ।।
O

Wollte daß du mich anrührst, wollte Leben
Für meine bibbernde Seele
Wollt ein Plätzchen im Nest deines Leibes;
Du hast gesagt: auch im Dunkeln spiegeln
Deine Augen alles ganz ganz klar.

Da hast du sie:
Beide Augen reiß ich heraus
Und mach sie dir zum Geschenk
Nun rühr mich an, hab mich lieb, gib mir
Dunkelheit
Laß meine einsame Seele
Unterschlüpfen bei dir.
O

(Tr. from Hindi by Lothar Lutze)

even the moon and the stars,
I asked for your touch, asked for life,
and for my helpless, shivering soul, begged for
a small place in the nest of your body.
And you said: Even in the dark, inside
your eye's mirror, everything is clearly seen.
Not now, not now.

Plucking out my eyes, I give them
to you, like a lotus gift. Take them.
And now give me the touch, the love, the dark,
give my lonely soul its much needed shelter.
O

(Tr. from Oriya by Shri Bibhu Padhi)

॥ ପବନ ॥

ପବନ କିଛି ଧରି ରଖେନି
ନିଜର କରେନି
ନିଜର କରିବାକୁ ଜାବୁଡ଼ି ଧରେନି ।।

ବାସ୍ ଛୁଇଁ ଛୁଇଁ ଗ୍ଲିଯାଏ
ତର ତର ବାଟୋଇ
ଯାହା କିଛି ସାମ୍ନାରେ ଆସିଲା :
ନାରୀର କୋମଳ ସ୍ତନ ; ଅଖଳା ହସ
ରୁକ୍ଷ ପଥର
ପୂତିଗନ୍ଧରେ ଫାଟି ପଡୁଥିବା ନର୍ଦ୍ଦମା
ହସ ହସ ଜହ୍ନ, ମହକୁଥିବା ଫୁଲ ।।

ଯେମିତି ଛୁଇଁ ଛୁଇଁ
ଗୁଣୁ ଗୁଣୁ ହୋଇ ମଧା ନୋଇଁ ଗ୍ଲିଯିବାଠୁଁ
ସରଳ କାମ ଏ ପୃଥିବୀରେ
ନାହିଁ କି କେଭେ ନ ଥିଲା ।।

ସବୁଠୁ ଅପ୍ରତ୍ୟାଶିତ ଜାଗାରେ
ତା' ସାଙ୍ଗରେ ଥରେ ଅଧେ ଭେଟ ହୋଇଛି :
ଦିନକର ଭୀଷଣ ଶୀତ ସଞ୍ଜରେ ସମୁଦ୍ର କୂଳ
କେହି କୋଉଠି ନ ଥାନ୍ତି
ନା ତୀର୍ଥଯାତ୍ରୀ, ନା ନୋଳିଆ, ଝାଲ ମୁଢ଼ିବାଲା
ସବୁ ଶୂନ୍‌ଶାନ, ସମୁଦ୍ର ଯାହା ଗର୍ଜୁଥାଏ
ସବୁ ଦିନ ପରି
ଆଉ ଛାତିରେ ଦୁଇହାତ ଜାକି

ଶୂନ୍ୟ ବେଳାଭୂଇଁରେ କାହାକୁ ଖୋଜିଲା ପରି
ସେ ଏକୁଟିଆଟି ବୁଲୁଥାଏ ।।

DER WIND

Der Wind hält nichts fest
Macht nichts sich zueigen
Hält nichts umklammert um sich's anzueignen.

Er berührt nur wenn er vorbeizieht
Der eilige Wanderer
Was ihm in den Weg kommt:
Die weiche Brust einer Frau,
Ein trugloses Lächeln
Die spitzen Steine
Die Abflußgräben berstend von Gestank
Den lachenden Mond, die duftenden Blumen.

Als wenn alles nur zu berühren
Und mit eingezogenem Kopf davonzusausen
Die einfachste Sache der Welt ist
Und schon immer war.

An ganz unerwarteten Orten
Bin ich ihm ein paarmal begegnet
an einem unwirtlichen Winterabend
Eines Tages am Meeresstrand
Niemand war zu sehen
Kein Pilger, kein Fischer, kein Bhelpuriverkäufer
Ringsum Öde, nur das Meer donnerte
Wie alle Tage
Und beide Hände in die Brust gegraben
Als suchte er jemand am leeren Strand
Irrte er einsam herum.

Und eines Tages lag tot am Straßenrand
Ein Bettlerkind
Wer weiß was er sich einbildete, was er erhoffte
Als er sich bückte und es streichelte
Als wenn allein dadurch das Kind
Sich die Augen reibend wieder aufstehen würde.

THE WIND

It holds on to nothing.
With a desire to possess
it grabs nothing.

A wayfarer in a hurry,
it just touches whatever comes before it
and then moves on:
soft pitchers of breasts, harsh stones
cherubic smiles, drains
choking with stench
and fragrant flowers.

As if there never was
nor will ever be
a task as simple as
walking away, one's head bent,
humming a tune.

A couple of times I have met him
in the most unexpected places.
A bitterly cold evening on the seashore
no one - fishermen, hawkers, pilgrims -
in sight
just the roaring sea, as on any other day
and there he was walking softly
arms clasped on the chest
as if looking for someone.

Another time
I saw him caressing gently the body
of a dead beggar boy beside the road -
perhaps he hoped
to wake him up again.

ଆଉ ଦିନେ ରାଜରାସ୍ତା କଡ଼ରେ
ଭିକାରୀ ଛୁଆଟେ ମରି ପଡ଼ିଥାଏ
କେଜାଣି କି ମୁହାଁସରେ ସେ ନଇଁପଡି
ତାକୁ ଆଉଁସି ଲାଗିଥାଏ
ଯେମିତି ସେତିକିରେ ସେ ପିଲାଟା
ଆଖିମଳି ଆଉ ଥରେ ଉଠି ବସିବ ।।
ଦେଖିଥିଲି ବାପାଙ୍କ ସହ
ତା'ର ଭରି ଭାବଦୋସ୍ତି ଥିଲା :
ବେଳେବେଳେ ମାଛି ଅନ୍ଧାରି ବାରଣ୍ଡାରେ
ବାପା ଦିଅଁ ଟିଏ ପରି ଏକା ଏକା ବସିଥିବାବେଳେ
ସେ ଆସି ବାରଣ୍ଡା କଡ଼ରେ
ଛିଡ଼ା ହୋଇ କ'ଣ ଗପୁଥାଏ;
ବିଛଣାରେ ପଡ଼ି ପଡ଼ି ବାପଙ୍କୁ ଚିଟା ଲାଗିଲେ
ଚୁପ୍ କରି ସେ ଦରଆଉଜା ଝର୍କା ବାଟେ ଆସି
କ'ଣ କ'ଣ ତାଙ୍କ କାନରେ କହିଦିଏ ।।

ଆଉ ସ୍ୱର୍ଗଦ୍ୱାରରେ ସେଦିନ
ତାଙ୍କ ଯୁଇ ଜଳିଲାବେଳକୁ
ଦେଖିଲି କୋଉଠୁ କେଜାଣି
ପାଗଳ ପରି ଧାଇଁ ଆସି
ସେ ହୁଦ୍ ହୁଦ୍ ସେଇ ନିଆଁ ଭିତରକୁ
ଧସେଇ ପଶିଗଲା
କେଜାଣି ତା' ମନରେ କ'ଣ
ଗୋପନ କଥାଟିଏ ଥିଲା!! ।।

Ich wußte daß er mit dem Vater
Eng befreundet war
Ab und zu in der Abenddämmerung
Wenn einem Standbild gleich der Vater
Allein auf der Terrasse sitzt
Stellt er sich an den Rand
Und redet über alles Mögliche;
Als der Vater auf dem Bett liegt
Mutlos geworden
Kommt er lautlos durchs halboffne Fenster
Und flüstert ihm
Wer weiß was ins Ohr.

An jenem Tag an der Verbrennungsstätte
Als Vaters Holzstoß brannte
Sah ich ihn irgendwoher
Wie ein Verrückter heranstürmen
Er fuhr in die flackernden Flammen
Wer weiß welches Geheimnis
Er mit sich nahm.
❍

(*Tr. from Hindi by Lothar Lutze*)

I knew of his great intimacy with my father:
sometime in the gathering dark
as he sat on the verandah
all alone like a lost deity,
he would quietly start a dialogue.

Some other time
he would stealthily enter through the window
and whisper something in his ear
as he lay on his sick bed.

By the sea at Puri
when father's body was on the pyre
and I lit it,
all of a sudden, from nowhere
it came running like a lunatic
and entered the leaping flames -
A secret intimacy
that he nursed for my father.
❍

(*Tr. from Oriya by Shri Bibhu Padhi*)

ਮੋਹਨਜੀਤ

1984

ਖਬਰ ਜੋ ਲਟਾਂ ਬਣ ਕੇ ਫੈਲ ਰਹੀ ਸੀ
ਉਹਦਾ ਇਕ ਚੰਗਿਆੜਾ ਮੇਰੇ ਵਿਹੜੇ 'ਚ ਵੀ ਡਿੱਗਾ
ਤੇ ਦੌਫ਼ੇਰੇ ਦੇ ਵਿਚ ਲਹਿ ਗਿਆ
ਤਦੇ ਉਹ ਆਈ ਹਫੀ ਹੋਈ, ਡਰੀ ਹੋਈ, ਸਹਿਮੀ, ਘਾਬਰੀ
ਤੇ ਕਹਿਣ ਲੱਗੀ : ਜਿਵੇਂ ਵੀ ਹੈ ਤੂੰ ਆਪਣੇ ਘਰ ਪਹੁੰਚ !
ਵਕਤ ਬੇਵਕਤ ਹੁੰਦਾ ਜਾ ਰਿਹਾ...

ਪਰ ਮੈਂ ਆਪਣੀ ਤਬੀਅਤ ਦਾ ਗ਼ੁਲਾਮ
ਸੋਚਿਆ—ਏਨਾ ਵੀ ਕੀ ਹੈ ? ਚੰਗਿਆੜਾ ਕਿਹੋ ਜਿਹਾ ਹੈ ?
ਤਦੇ ਉਹ ਫੇਰ ਆਈ ਹਫੀ ਹੋਈ, ਹੋਰ ਸਹਿਮੀ, ਹੋਰ ਹਿਰਖੀ
ਤੇ ਬੋਲੀ—ਅਜੇ ਵੀ ਇੱਥੇ ਏਂ ਤੂੰ ?
ਚੰਗਿਆੜਾ ਸੂਹਾ ਹੁੰਦਾ ਜਾ ਰਿਹਾ
ਤੂੰ ਇਥੋਂ ਕਿਉਂ ਨਹੀਂ ਜਾਂਦਾ ?
ਮੈਂ ਤੈਨੂੰ ਕਿਵੇਂ ਸਮਝਾਵਾਂ ?
ਭੀੜ ਸੰਘਣੀ ਹੁੰਦੀ ਜਾ ਰਹੀ ਹੈ...

ਘੁਸਰਮੁਸਰਾ ਸਫ਼ਰ ਤੂਫ਼ਾਨ ਤੋਂ ਪਹਿਲਾਂ ਵਾਲੀ ਚੁੱਪ
ਘਰ ਪੁੱਜਾ, ਲੱਗਾ, ਚੰਗਿਆੜਾ ਏਧਰ ਵੀ ਡਿੱਗਾ ਹੈ
ਜੋ ਸੰਧਿਆ ਹੋਣ ਤੀਕ ਮੱਚ ਪਿਆ ਸੀ
ਤੇ ਅਗਲੇ ਤੋਂ ਅਗਲਾ ਦਿਨ ਹਨੇਰੀ ਪੂਰੇ ਜ਼ੋਰਾਂ ਤੇ
ਲਹੂ ਦਾ ਰੰਗ ਆਪਣਾ ਹੀ ਵਰਣ ਭੁੱਲ ਬੈਠਾ....

ਬੰਦ ਕਮਰਾ
ਚਫ਼ੇਰੇ ਬਿਸੀਅਰ ਕਾਲੇ, ਕੰਧਾਂ ਨਾਲ ਬਸ ਠੂਹੇ ਹੀ ਠੂਹੇ
ਮੇਰੀ ਪਹਿਚਾਣ ਬਲਣ ਲੱਗੀ

ਮੈਂ ਆਪਣੇ ਬੇਟਿਆਂ ਦੇ ਲੰਮੇ ਕੇਸ ਵੇਖੇ
ਤੇ ਫਿਰ ਕੇਸਾਂ ਤੋਂ ਬਿਨਾਂ ਮੁਹਾਂਦਰੇ ਚਿਤਵੇ
ਮੈਂ ਜੂਏਬਾਜ਼ ਨਹੀਂ ਸਾ
ਫਿਰ ਵੀ ਆਪਣੀ ਪੰਚਾਲੀ ਨੂੰ ਨੰਗੀ ਨਹੁੰਦਰੀ ਹੋਈ ਵੇਖਿਆ...

Mohanjeet

1984

Eine Nachricht griff um sich wie Feuer
Ein Funke traf auch mich
setzte die Atmosphäre in Brand
als sie kam, außer Atem, bebend,
entsetzt, verstört
und sagte
Du mußt auf jeden Fall nach Hause
Die Zeit hat sich gegen uns gekehrt.

Ich verharrte in Trägheit
konnte alles nicht glauben
welcher Art Feuer konnte das sein?

als sie wiederkam, außer Atem, verstört,
von Entsetzen gepackt
und sagte
Du bist immer noch hier?
Die Funken schlagen immer höher!
hast du es nicht gehört?
Der Mob kommt draußen immer näher!

Die Heimfahrt wie betäubt
die Ruhe vor dem Sturm
zuhause schien es
auch hier waren schon Funken gefallen
die gegen Abend immer heißer glühten
vom einen Tag auf den anderen
wütete ein Feuersturm
Blut hat sich gegen eigenes Blut gekehrt.

Im Zimmer eingeriegelt
umgeben von schwarzen Vipern
die Wände voller Skorpione
die Glaubenszugehörigkeit ein brennender Makel

Das lange Haar
meiner Söhne

1984

The word was spreading like fire
A spark also fell in my lap
And engulfed the surroundings
Then she came - out of breath
horrified
apprehensive

and said:
Reach your home anyhow
Time is losing its identity
its contours

But I, slave of my mood
Thought - So what
What kind of spark it could be

Again she came - panting
more frightened
more anguished
And said: you are still here
The spark is getting more and more intense
flaring up
Why haven't you gone
Why don't you rush
The mob is approaching nearer

A grey distance
A silence that precedes the storm

Reaching home I
Felt the spark had fallen there also
And flared up in the evening
And the day after
The storm was in its full wrath
The blood had forgotten its own tribe

ਮੇਘ ਤਾ ਪਹਿਲਾ ਈ ਅੱਖਾ ਵਿਚ ਸਨ
ਤੇ ਫਿਰ ਇਕ ਕੰਧ ਉੱਭਰੀ
ਜਿਸ 'ਚ ਦੋ ਨਿੱਕੇ ਨਿੱਕੇ ਸੂਰਜੀ ਚਿਹਰੇ ਚਿਣੇ ਸਨ
ਮੈਂ ਇਕ ਮਾਂ ਨੂੰ ਠੰਡੇ ਬੁਰਜ ਦੇ ਵਿਚ ਬਰਫ਼ ਹੁੰਦੇ ਵੇਖਿਆ...

ਸੋਚਿਆ–ਇਤਿਹਾਸ ਸਿਰਫ਼ ਸੰਨ ਤੇ ਮਿਤੀਆਂ ਨਹੀਂ ਹੁੰਦਾ
ਇਤਿਹਾਸ ਹੋਣ ਤੇ ਜੀਣ ਦਾ ਵਿਉਹਾਰ ਵੀ ਹੈ
ਇਤਿਹਾਸ ਹੋਂਦਾ ਦਾ ਤਕਰਾਰ ਹੈ
ਤੇ ਹੋਂਦ–ਵਰਗ ਹੈ, ਵਰਣ ਹੈ, ਭੂਖੰਡ ਹੈ, ਪਹਿਚਾਨ ਹੈ
ਤੇ ਇਸ ਤੋਂ ਪਰ੍ਹੇ ਵੀ ਕੁਝ ਹੈ, ਵਰਕੇ ਤੇ ਲਿਖਿਆ ਕਾਵਿ ਦਾ ਬੋਲ

ਅੱਠ ਵਰ੍ਹੇ ਪਹਿਲਾ ਦੀ ਗੱਲ ਹੈ
ਉਹ ਮੇਰੇ ਕੋਲ ਆਈ
ਤੇ ਕਿਹਾ : ਵਕਤ, ਬੇਵਕਤ ਹੁੰਦਾ ਜਾ ਰਿਹਾ...
❍

ich seh es plötzlich vor mir
abgeschnitten
die Bärte abrasiert
ich bin nicht Yudhishthira der Würfelspieler
doch seh ich meine Draupadi bereits entehrt
und nackt
Der Schleier vor den Augen
läßt eine Wand erstehen
dahinter zwei kleine Gesichter eingemauert
die Mutter friert im kalten Turm zu Eis –

Ich dachte
Geschichte sind nicht nur Zahlen und Daten
Geschichte heißt auf seine eigne Art zu existieren
Geschichte ist Zusammenprall verschiedner
Existenzen
Und Existenz heißt Klasse, Kaste,
Glaube, Herkunft,

und vielleicht noch
ein paar Verse
auf einem Blatt.

Ein paar Jahre ist das her
als sie zu mir kam und sagte
Die Zeit hat sich gegen uns gekehrt.
❍

(*Tr. from Hindi by Barbara Lotz*)

Yudhishthira, der älteste der fünf Pandava Prinzen, verlor beim Würfelspiel gegen seinen Vetter Duryodhana zuerst sein Reich, dann die gemeinsame Gattin der Pandavas, Draupadi (auch Panchali). Episode aus dem Mahabharata.

Die beiden Söhne des zehnten Gurus der Sikhs, Guru Gobind Singh, wurden von den Moghulherrschern bei lebendigem Leib eingemauert, weil sie nicht zum Islam übertreten wollten. Die Mutter des Gurus wurde in einem Turm gefangengesetzt und erfror.

Closed room
vipers all around
scorpions on the walls
My identity was in flames

I saw my sons bearing long hair
I imagined my sons without hair
without beards

I was not a Yudhishthira*
But I saw my Panchali
Being stripped
Being molested
There were clouds in my eyes
From the depths of history arose a wall –
Two innocent faces entombed in it
I saw a mother freezing in a cold tower **

And I thought
History is not dates and eras
History is a way of life and living
History is the conflict between identities
And identity is - class
colour
geographical space
recognition

And beyond all this:
Is a verse written on a piece of paper
It is a song

Eight years have passed
Since she came to me
And said
Time is losing its identity
Time is losing its shape
❍

(*Tr. from Punjabi by Swaraj Bir and the poet*)

* The eldest of the five Pandava princes who gambled with his cousin Duryodhana and lost not only his kingdom, but his wife Panchali (Draupadi) as well. (From the Mahabharata).
** The reference is to the execution of the two sons of Guru Gobind Singh, the tenth Guru of the Sikhs, who were immured alive in a wall by the Moghul rulers for protesting against their conversion to Islam. The mother of the Guru was imprisoned in a cold tower and died subsequently.

॥ ਸੰਵਾਦ-ਚਿਤਰ ॥

1. ਤੇਰੇ ਮੇਰੇ ਵਿਚਕਾਰ
ਜੋ ਕੁਝ ਤੇ ਜਿੰਨਾ ਕੁਝ ਸਮਝਿਆ ਨਹੀਂ ਗਿਆ
ਉਸਨੂੰ ਉਸੇ ਤਰ੍ਹਾ ਰਹਿਣ ਦੇਣਾ ਚਾਹੁੰਦਾ ਹਾਂ
ਇਸ ਨੇੜਤਾ ਦੀ ਵੀ ਆਪਣੀ ਲੱਜਤ ਹੈ
ਇਸ 'ਜਿੰਨੇ ਕੁਝ' ਦੇ ਸਮਝੇ ਜਾਣ ਬਾਅਦ
ਜੋ ਕੁਝ ਹੋਏਗਾ
ਮੁਸ਼ਕਿਲ ਹੋਏਗਾ

ਆਪਣੀ ਹੁਣ ਦੀ ਮੁਸ਼ਕਿਲ ਸਾਂਹਵੇ
ਨਵੀਂ ਮੁਸ਼ਕਿਲ ਦੀ ਲੀਕ
ਕਿੰਨੀ ਓਪਰੀ ਹੋਵੇਗੀ
ਮੈਂ ਤਾ ਸਮਝਦਾ ਹਾ ਸ਼ਾਇਦ ਤੂੰ ਵੀ ਸਮਝਦਾ ਹੋਏਂ
ਤੇ ਜੇ ਇਹ ਠੀਕ ਹੈ
ਤਾਂ ਤੇਰੇ ਮੇਰੇ ਵਿਚਕਾਰ
ਜੋ ਕੁਝ ਤੇ ਜਿੰਨਾ ਕੁਝ ਸਮਝਿਆ ਨਹੀਂ ਗਿਆ
ਉਸਨੂੰ ਉਸੇ ਤਰ੍ਹਾਂ ਰਹਿਣ ਦੇਣਾ ਚਾਹੁੰਦਾ ਹਾਂ
○

GESPRÄCH

Alles was
zwischen dir und mir
nicht verstanden wurde
möcht ich genau so lassen wie es ist.
Es nah zu wissen hat seinen Reiz.
Alles was übrigbleibt,
wenn man das Alles versteht
sind Schwierigkeiten.

Vor unsern jetzigen Schwierigkeiten
wird eine Linie neuer Schwierigkeiten sich
erheben
fremd und unverständlich.
Ich weiß es - und vielleicht auch du,
wenn es dir recht ist:
Alles was
zwischen mir und dir nicht verstanden wurde
möcht ich genau so lassen wie es ist.
❍

(*Tr. from Hindi by Barbara Lotz*)

DIALOGUE

Between you and me
Whatever hasn't been understood
Let us not make it known
Let us keep it as it is
This closeness has its own pleasure
After knowing this 'whatever'
who knows what shall happen
It could be unbearable

After knowing the unsaid
Things will be so different
so unnatural
At least I do know that
And wish you would too
And, if so, then
Let us keep it as it is
That which hasn't been understood
Between you and me.
❍

(*Tr. from Punjabi by Swaraj Bir and the poet*)

कुँवर नारायण

॥ सरकस ॥

दर्शकों से खचाखच भरी हुई दुनिया में
पूरी ईमानदारी से
जोकर का पार्ट अदा करते
संतुलन बनाए रखना
सबसे बड़ा कमाल था।

पसीना पोंछो
मेकअप धो डालो
तुम पहले आदमी नहीं
जिस पर बिरादरी को नाज़ है
न तुम अन्तिम आदमी हो
जिसकी कामयाबियों पर
पेट भर हँसी आती।
O

Kunwar NARAYAN

ZIRKUS

In einer Welt voller Zuschauer
In aller Ehrlichkeit
Die Rolle des Clowns zu spielen
Und seinen Gleichmut zu bewahren
War deine größte Leistung.

Wisch dir den Schweiß ab
Wasch dir die Schminke ab
Du bist nicht der Erste
Auf den seine Leute sich was einbilden
Noch bist du der Letzte
Über dessen Erfolge
man sich die Hucke vollacht.
❍

(*Tr. from Hindi by Lothar Lutze*)

CIRCUS

In a world crammed with spectators,
balancing
while acting the clown's role
in good faith
was the greatest feat of all.

Wipe the sweat
wash off the make-up –
you are not the first man
to give the crowd a glow of pride;
nor yet the last
whose clever stunts induce
a bellyful of laughter.
❍

(*Tr. from Hindi by Rupert Snell*)

॥ अयोध्या, 1992 ॥

हे राम,
जीवन एक कटु यथार्थ है
और तुम एक महाकाव्य !
तुम्हारे बस की नहीं
उस अविवेक पर विजय
जिसके दस बीस नहीं
अब लाखों सिर–लाखों हाथ हैं,
और विभीषण भी अब
न जाने किसके साथ है।

इससे बड़ा क्या हो सकता है
हमारा दुर्भाग्य
एक विवादित
स्थल में सिमट कर
रह गया तुम्हारा साम्राज्य

अयोध्या इस समय तुम्हारी अयोध्या नहीं
योद्धाओं की लंका है,
'मानस' तुम्हारा 'चरित' नहीं
चुनाव का डंका है !

हे राम, कहाँ यह समय
कहाँ तुम्हारा त्रेता युग,
कहाँ तुम मर्यादा पुरुषोत्तम
और कहाँ यह नेता-युग !

सविनय निवेदन है प्रभु कि लौट जाओ
किसी पुराण–किसी धर्मग्रन्थ में
सकुशल सपत्नीक...
अबके जंगल वो जंगल नहीं
जिनमें घूमा करते थे वाल्मीकि !

○

AYODHYA 1992

He Ram
Das Leben ist eine rauhe Wirklichkeit
Und du bist ein episches Gedicht!
Du kriegst sie nicht klein
Diese Kopflosigkeit
Die jetzt nicht zehn oder zwanzig nein
Hunderttausende Köpfe und Hände reckt
Und wer weiß bei wem jetzt
Sich der Schreckens-Vibhishan versteckt.

Unserm Mißgeschick
Ist kein andres gleich
Auf einen umstrittenen Ort
Ist geschrumpft dein Reich

Ayodhya ist dein Ayodhya nicht mehr
Es ist Lanka mit seinen Horden
Der Manas, einstmals dein Lebenslauf
Ist zur Wahlwerbetrommel geworden.

He Ram, die Zeiten sind anders jetzt
Deine silberne Zeit ist verflossen
Wie fern von dir Mann aller Männer ist
Diese Zeit der Parteigenossen!

Sei höflichst gebeten Herr: geh zurück
In ein Purana, ein heiliges Buch
Wohlbehalten und wohlbeweibt
Die Wälder sind heut die Wälder nicht mehr
Durch die sich ein Valmiki treibt.

❍

(Tr. from Hindi by Lothar Lutze)

AYODHYA 1992

O Rama
life's a bitter reality
and you an epic ode.
your power's no match
for that unreason
which has not ten or twenty
but a thousand heads and hands;
and who now knows with whom
Vibhishan stands.

What greater misfortune than ours –
your empire shrinks,
contracts into a disputed site.

Ayodhya's your "unvanquished" realm no more
but a new Lanka battleground
and "Rama's Righteous Deeds"
the slogans that elections sound.

We humbly beg you,
go back now
to some Purana – to some sacred tome,
secure in wedded bliss;
our jungles are not those of days of yore
where roamed Valmiki.
No idyll this.

❍

(Tr. from Hindi by Rupert Snell)

॥ स्पष्टीकरण ॥

ग़लत से ग़लत वक़्त में भी
        सही से सही बात कही जा सकती है।
हम थोड़ी देर के लिए
        स्थगित कर सकते हैं युद्ध,
महत्व दे सकते हैं अपने भयभीत होने को,
        स्वीकार कर सकते हैं अपनी बदहवासी,
एक बार, कम से कम एक बार तो
        काँप सकते हैं हमारे हाथ,
हम चीख सकते हैं कि 'नहीं...
        ये सब पराये नहीं मेरे हैं,
        मैं इन्हें नहीं मार सकता,
        मैं युद्ध नहीं करूँगा...'

ऐसी विषम घड़ी में हमारे अन्तःकरण
        कम से कम एक बार तो
बना सकते हैं ईश्वर को साक्षी–
        माँग सकते हैं उससे भी स्पष्टीकरण...

○

KLARSTELLUNG

Auch zur falschesten Zeit
    Kann man die nackteste Wahrheit sagen.
Wir können eine Weile
    Den Krieg verschieben
Können unsere Ängste wichtig nehmen
    Können uns abfinden mit unserer
    Betroffenheit
Einmal, ein einziges Mal
    Können unsere Hände zittern
Können wir schreien: nein
    Das alles sind nicht Fremde, es sind Meine
    Ich kann sie nicht umbringen
    Ich führe keinen Krieg

In so einer schweren Stunde kann unser
    Gewissen
    Ein einziges Mal
Gott zum Zeugen machen
    Kann es auch von ihm
Klarstellung fordern.
❍

(Tr. from Hindi by Lothar Lutze)

CLARIF .CATION

At even the least opportune time
    the truest of things can be said.
For a little while
    we can defer war,
can give importance to our being afraid,
    accept our bewilderment;
once, at least once
    our hands can tremble,
we can cry out "No...
    these are not strangers but my dear ones;
    I cannot strike them down,
    I shall not wage war ..."

At such a critical moment
    once at least
we can call God to witness –
    can demand even of him
clarification.
❍

(Tr. from Hindi by Rupert Snell)

ਸੁਤਿੰਦਰ ਸਿੰਘ ਨੂਰ

॥ ਪਿਆਰ ਤੇ ਕਿਤਾਬ ॥

ਪਿਆਰ ਕਰਨ
ਤੇ ਕਿਤਾਬ ਪੜ੍ਹਣ ਵਿਚ
ਕੋਈ ਫ਼ਰਕ ਨਹੀਂ ਹੁੰਦਾ।

ਕੁਝ ਕਿਤਾਬਾਂ ਦਾ ਅਸੀਂ
ਮੁੱਖ ਪੰਨਾ ਦੇਖਦੇ ਹਾਂ
ਅੰਦਰੋਂ ਬੋਰ ਕਰਦੀਆਂ ਨੇ
ਪੰਨੇ ਪਰਤਦੇ ਹਾਂ ਤੇ ਰੱਖ ਦਿੰਦੇ ਹਾਂ।

ਕੁਝ ਕਿਤਾਬਾਂ ਅਸੀਂ
ਰੱਖਦੇ ਹਾਂ ਸਿਰ੍ਹਾਣੇ
ਅਚਾਨਕ ਜਦੋਂ ਜਾਗ ਆਉਂਦੀ ਹੈ
ਤਾਂ ਪੜ੍ਹਣ ਲਗਦੇ ਹਾਂ।

ਕੁਝ ਕਿਤਾਬਾਂ ਦਾ
ਸ਼ਬਦ ਸ਼ਬਦ ਪੜ੍ਹਦੇ ਹਾਂ
ਉਨ੍ਹਾਂ ਚਿਵ ਗੁਆਚ ਜਾਂਦੇ ਹਾਂ
ਬਾਰ ਬਾਰ ਪੜ੍ਹਦੇ ਹਾਂ
ਤੇ ਰੂਹ ਤਰ ਰਚਾ ਲੈਂਦੇ ਹਾਂ।

ਕੁਝ ਕਿਤਾਬਾਂ ਤੇ
ਰੰਗ ਬਰੰਗੇ ਨਿਸ਼ਾਨ ਲਾਉਂਦੇ ਹਾਂ
ਹਰੇਕ ਸਤਰ ਤੇ ਰਝਿਦੇ ਹਾਂ
ਤੇ ਕੁਝ ਕਿਤਾਬਾਂ ਦੇ
ਸੂਹਲ ਪੰਨਿਆਂ ਤੇ
ਨਿਸ਼ਾਨ ਆਉਣੋਂ ਵੀ ਤ੍ਰਹਿੰਦੇ ਹਾਂ।

ਪਿਆਰ ਕਰਨ
ਤੋ ਕਿਤਾਬ ਪੜ੍ਹਣ ਵਿਚ
ਕੋਈ ਫ਼ਰਕ ਨਹੀਂ ਹੁੰਦਾ।
o

Sutinder Singh NOOR

LIEBEN UND LESEN

Zwischen der Liebe
und dem Lesen eines Buches
besteht kein Unterschied.

An manchen Büchern fasziniert uns
nur die Titelseite
das Innere ist langweilig
wir blättern sie durch und legen sie weg

Andere Bücher legen wir
unters Kopfkissen
wenn wir nachts plötzlich wach werden
greifen wir gerne danach

Manche Bücher lesen wir
Wort für Wort
verlieren uns in ihnen
lesen sie von neuem
verinnerlichen sie

In manche Bücher kritzeln wir
mit bunten Stiften Kommentare
jede Zeile begeistert uns

Bei anderen Büchern
mit empfindlichen Seiten
schaudern wir schon beim Gedanken
sie zu beschmieren –

Kein Unterschied besteht
zwischen der Liebe
und dem Lesen eines Buches.

❍

(Tr. from Hindi by Barbara Lotz)

LOVE AND A BOOK

Making love
and reading a book
are not different.

Sometimes
we see only the title
we find the book tiresome
and we leave the book.

Some books
we keep under the pillow
we read them
when we awake suddenly.

Some books
we read word by word
absorbed so much that
we read them again and again
the words reach our soul.

Some books
we mark with coloured pencils
we love every line
but the pages of some books
that feel so tender
we fear to mark even a word.

Making love
and reading a book
are not different.

❍

(Tr. from Punjabi by the poet)

॥ ਏਨੀ ਵੀ ਉਡੀਕ ਨਾ ਕਰੋ ॥

ਏਨੀ ਵੀ ਉਡੀਕ ਨਾ ਕਰੋ
ਉਡੀਕ ਹੋਰ ਉਡੀਕ ਆਉਂਦੀ ਹੈ
ਤੇ ਬੰਦਾ ਉਡੀਕ ਦੀ ਜਕੜ ਵਿਚ
ਕੈਦ ਹੋ ਜਾਂਦਾ ਹੈ।

ਏਨਾ ਵੀ ਨਾ ਡਰੋ
ਕਿ ਡਰ ਤੁਹਾਡੇ ਅੰਦਰ
ਡਰ ਵਾਂਗ ਬਹਿ ਜਾਵੇ
ਤੁਸੀਂ ਡਰ ਤੋਂ ਵੀ ਭਿਆਨਕ ਹੋ ਜਾਉਂ
ਤੇ ਡਰ ਤੁਹਾਥੋਂ ਹੀ ਡਰਨ ਲਗ ਪਵੇ।

ਏਨਾ ਵੀ ਸੱਚ ਨਾ ਬੋਲੋ
ਕਿ ਸੱਚ ਸੱਚ ਨਾ ਰਹੇ
ਤੇ ਸੱਚ ਤੋਂ ਪਾਰ
ਬੋਲਣ ਲਈ ਕੁਝ ਨਾ ਬਚੇ।

ਵਕਤ ਅੱਗੇ ਏਨਾ ਵੀ ਨਾ ਝੁਕੋ
ਕਿ ਵਕਤ ਬਸ ਝੁਕਣ ਲਾ ਦੇਵੇ
ਆਦਮੀ ਝੁਕਦਾ ਚਲਾ ਜਾਏ
ਤੇ ਵਕਤ ਤੋਂ ਪਹਿਲਾਂ ਹੀ
ਦਫਨ ਹੋ ਜਾਏ।

ਚੰਗਾ ਹੈ ਘਰਾਂ ਚ ਵੱਸਣਾ
ਪਰ ਏਨੇ ਵੀ ਘਰਾਂ ਚ ਨਾ ਵੱਸ ਜਾਉ
ਕਿ ਵੱਸਣਾ ਹੀ ਘਰ ਚ ਘਰ ਕਰ ਜਾਵੇ
ਤੇ ਤੁਸੀਂ ਘਰਾਂ ਤੋਂ ਪਾਰ ਵਸਦੇ
ਘਰਾਂ ਨੂੰ ਭੁੱਲ ਜਾਉ।
O

WARTE NICHT SOLANGE

Warte nicht so lange
Warten schafft neues Warten
und der Mensch wird zum Sklaven
im Klammergriff des Wartens

Fürchte dich nicht so sehr
daß die Furcht sich in dir festsetzt
Werde furchterregender als die Furcht
und lehre sie vor dir das Fürchten

Sage nicht soviel Wahres
daß die Wahrheit nicht mehr Wahrheit bleibt
und es jenseits der Wahrheit
nichts mehr zu sagen gibt

Beuge dich nicht so sehr vor der Zeit
daß die Zeit dich gebeugt hält
und du gebrochen
vor deiner Zeit ins Grab gehst

Schön ist es ein Heim zu haben
doch hänge nicht so sehr daran
daß nur dein eigenes Heim dort heimisch ist
und du andere Heime, fern dem deinen
vergißt.
❍

(*Tr. from Hindi by Barbara Lotz*)

DON'T WAIT SO MUCH

Don't wait so much
wait makes more waiting
and the man becomes a slave
in the grip of wait.

Don't fear so much
fear will grip you like a fear
you will become more fearful
and fearsome to the fear.

Don't speak the truth so much
truth won't remain truth
and beyond the truth
nothing would remain to speak.

Don't yield so much before the time
time would make you yield more
you could become more yielding
and reach the grave before your time.

It is good to live in a home
but don't believe so much in home
the home would make you mere homely
you would forget the homes beyond your own.
❍

(*Tr. from Punjabi by the poet*)

॥ ਕਵਿਤਾ ਨੂੰ ਉੱਗਣ ਦਿਉ ਅਪਣੇ ਅੰਦਰ ॥

ਕਵਿਤਾ ਨੂੰ ਉੱਗਣ ਦਿਉ
ਅਪਦੇ ਅੰਦਰ
ਇਕ ਬਿਰਖ ਵਾਂਗ
ਤੇ ਬਿਰਖ ਨੂੰ ਗੱਲਾਂ ਕਰਨ ਦਿਉ
ਹਵਾ ਨਾਲ, ਧੁੱਪ ਨਾਲ
ਵਰ੍ਹਦੇ ਮੀਹਾਂ ਨਾਲ
ਤੂਫ਼ਾਨਾਂ ਨਾਲ
ਬਿਰਖ ਦੀਆਂ ਖੋੜਾਂ 'ਚ
ਪੰਛੀਆਂ ਨੂੰ ਗੁਆਚ ਜਾਣ ਦਿਉ
ਚੂਹ ਚੂਹ ਕਰਨ ਦਿਉ
ਤੇ ਆਲ੍ਹਣੇ ਪਾਉਣ ਦਿਉ।

ਕਵਿਤਾ ਨੂੰ ਉੱਗਣ ਦਿਉ
ਅਪਣੇ ਅੰਦਰ
ਇਕ ਖੁਦਰੌ ਫੁੱਲ ਵਾਂਗ
ਜੋ ਆਕਾਸ਼ ਵੱਲ ਦੇਖਦਾ
ਮਹਿਕਦਾ, ਵਿਗਸਦਾ
ਆਜ਼ਾਦ ਪੌਣਾਂ 'ਚ ਸਾਹ ਲੈਂਦਾ
ਕਿਸੇ ਦਾ ਮੁਹਤਾਜ ਨਹੀਂ ਹੁੰਦਾ
ਤੇ ਵੀਰਾਨ ਜੰਗਲਾਂ 'ਚ
ਮੀਲ੍ਹਾਂ ਪਰ੍ਹੇ ਜਾਂਦੇ
ਕਾਰਵਾਂ ਨੂੰ ਵੀ
ਹਾਕ ਮਾਰ ਲੈਂਦਾ ਹੈ।

ਕਵਿਤਾ ਨੂੰ ਉੱਗਣ ਦਿਉ
ਅਪਣੇ ਅੰਦਰ
ਸੂਰਜ ਵਾਂਗ
ਜੋ ਪਲਾਂ ਛਿਣਾਂ 'ਚ
ਵਣਾਂ-ਤ੍ਰਿਣਾਂ ਦਰਿਆਵਾਂ
ਸਮੁੰਦਰਾਂ ਤੇ ਫੈਲ ਜਾਂਦਾ ਹੈ
ਸੀਨੇ 'ਚ ਅਗਨ ਸਾਂਭੀ
ਬ੍ਰਹਿਮੰਡ ਨਾਲ ਗੱਲਾਂ ਕਰਦਾ
ਕਿਰਨ ਮਕਿਰਨੀਂ
ਅਰੋਕ ਤੁਰਿਆ ਜਾਂਦਾ ਹੈ।

ਕਵਿਤਾ ਨੂੰ ਉੱਗਣ ਦਿਉ
ਅਪਣੇ ਅੰਦਰ
ਚਾਨਣੀ ਰਾਤ ਵਾਂਗ
ਜਿਸਦੇ ਨਿਮ੍ਹੇ-ਨਿਮ੍ਹੇ ਸਰੋਦ ਵਿਚ
ਅਸੀਂ ਰੂਹ ਤੱਕ ਭਿਜ ਜਾਂਦੇ ਹਾਂ
ਦਿਸਹੱਦਿਆਂ ਤੱਕ ਫੈਲੀ
ਚੁੱਪ ਡੂੰਘੀ ਰਾਤ ਵਿਚ
ਗੋਰੀਆਂ ਰਿਸ਼ਮਾਂ ਦੇ ਜਾਮ
ਦਿਲ ਦੇ ਹਨੇਰੇ ਕੋਨਿਆਂ ਤੱਕ
ਡੀਕ ਜਾਂਦੇ ਹਾਂ।

ਕਵਿਤਾ ਨੂੰ ਉੱਗਣ ਦਿਉ
ਅਪਣੇ ਅੰਦਰ
ਬਿਰਖ ਵਾਂਗ
ਖੁਦਰੌ ਫੁੱਲ ਵਾਂਗ
ਸੂਰਜ ਵਾਂਗ
ਚਾਨਣੀ ਰਾਤ ਵਾਂਗ।
O

LASS GEDICHTE BLÜHN

Laß Gedichte blühn in dir
wie ein Baum blüht
und laß den Baum sprechen
mit dem Wind, der Sonne,
den Stürmen
Laß in den Höhlen des Baumes
die Vögel sich verlieren
laß sie zwitschern
und Nester bauen

Laß Gedichte blühn in dir
wie wilde Blumen
die zum Himmel schauen
die duften, sich entfalten,
in freien Lüften
die niemand dienen müssen
die mit ihrem Duft
Karavanen aus öden Ländern
in der Ferne herbeilocken

Laß Gedichte blühn in dir
wie das Sonnenlicht
das in einem Augenblick
zugleich bescheint den Wald
und Wiese, Fluß und Meere
das Feuer weckt im Gold
und seine Strahlen ausschickt
mit dem Kosmos Zwiesprache zu halten

Laß Gedichte blühn in dir
wie ein Baum blüht
wie wilde Blumen
wie die Sonne
wie Mondlicht bei Nacht.
❍

(Tr. from Hindi by Barbara Lotz)

LET POETRY GROW INSIDE YOU

Let poetry grow inside you
like a tree
let the tree have a dialogue with
air, sunshine
storms and rain
let the birds lost
in the hollows of a tree
chirp and
make the nests.

Let poetry grow inside you
like a wilful flower
which looks towards the sky
blooms, aromatises,
breathes in free air
and never becomes a slave
attracts caravans passing from miles away

Let poetry grow inside you
like a moonlit night
our soul is drenched
in the dim melody of light
in the silent deep night
which spreads towards the horizons
we drink the beauty of beams
and light the murky cores of heart.

Let poetry grow inside you
like a tree
like a wilful flower
like a sun
like a moonlit night.
❍

(Tr. from Punjabi by the poet)

ਸੁਰਜੀਤ ਪਾਤਰ

॥ ਇਕ ਪਸ਼ੂ-ਕਥਾ ॥

ਗੱਡੀ ਚੱਲੀ
ਗੱਡੀ ਦੇ ਵਿਚ ਸੀਟਾਂ ਮੱਲੀ
ਬੈਠੇ ਹੋਏ
ਕੁਝ ਸਨ ਲੇਲੇ
ਕੁਝ ਬਘਿਆੜ

ਗੱਡੀ ਲੰਘਦੀ ਗਈ ਸਟੇਸ਼ਨ
ਨਦੀਆਂ ਜੰਗਲ ਖੇਤ ਪਹਾੜ
ਨੱਗਰ ਖੇੜੇ ਸ਼ਹਿਰ ਉਜਾੜ

ਸੱਤ ਅੱਠ ਘੰਟੇ ਚੱਲਣ ਮਗਰੋਂ
ਕੀ ਤੱਕਿਆ ਡੱਬੇ ਵਿਚਕਾਰ
ਸਭ ਬਘਿਆੜ ਬਣ ਗਏ ਲੇਲੇ
ਸਭ ਲੇਲੇ ਬਣ ਗਏ ਬਘਿਆੜ

ਤੁਸੀ ਯਕੀਨ ਕਰੋ ਜਾਂ ਨਾ
ਇਹ ਸਭ ਅਪਣੇ ਦੇਸ਼ 'ਚ ਹੋਇਆ
ਤੇ ਬੰਦਿਆਂ ਦੇ ਭੇਸ 'ਚ ਹੋਇਆ
○

Surjeet PATAR

VOM PUNJAB NACH DELHI: EINE FABEL

Ein Zug fährt
auf den Bänken sitzen
ein paar Wölfe
ein paar Lämmer

Der Zug fliegt vorbei an Bahnhöfen
Flüssen, Wäldern, Bergen, Feldern,
Städten, Dörfern, Siedlung, Ödland –
Nach acht Stunden Reise: eine Verwandlung
Alle Wölfe wurden zu Lämmern
Alle Lämmer zu Wölfen.

Schwer zu glauben
daß all dies in unserm eigenen Land geschieht
und in der Verkleidung von Menschen.
❍

(*Tr. from Hindi by Barbara Lotz*)

AN ANIMAL TALE

The train started
The seats in it
were occupied
by some wolves and some lambs.

The train crossed stations
rivers, jungles, fields, mountains
hamlets, towns, cities and heaths

After the journey of seven, eight hours
What do I see in the train?
The wolves are transformed into lambs
and the lambs into wolves.

Believe it or not
all this happened
in our own land
and that too
in the guise of men.
❍

(*Tr. from Punjabi by Niranjan Tasneem*)

॥ ਪਰਦੇਸ ॥

ਮੈਂ ਦੋ ਤਿੰਨ ਪੈਰ ਹੀ ਤੁਰਦਾਂ
ਕਿ ਹੁਣ ਪਰਦੇਸ ਆ ਜਾਂਦਾ
ਮੇਰੇ ਲਾਏ ਹੋਏ ਰੁੱਖਾਂ ਦੇ ਸਾਏ
ਕਿੰਨੇ ਛੋਟੇ ਨੇ

O

AUSLAND

Ich geh nur ein paar Schritte
dann kommt schon das Ausland
Wie klein ist der Schatten
der von mir gepflanzten Bäume.
❍

(*Tr. from Hindi by Barbara Lotz*)

THE ALIEN LAND

I walk just two or three steps
and find myself in an alien land.
How small are the shadows
of the trees
planted by me.
❍

(*Tr. from Punjabi by Niranjan Tasneem*)

॥ ਦੋ ਰੁਖਾਂ ਦੀ ਗੁਫ਼ਤਗੂ ॥

ਮੇਰੀ ਸੂਲੀ ਬਣਾਓਗੇ
ਕਿ ਰਬਾਬ
ਜਨਾਬ
ਕਿ ਮੈਂ ਇਉਂ ਹੀ ਖੜੋਤਾ ਰਹਾਂ ਸਾਰੀ ਉਮਰ
ਕਰਦਾ ਰਹਾਂ ਪੱਤਿਆਂ 'ਤੇ
ਮੌਸਮਾਂ ਦਾ ਹਿਸਾਬ-ਕਿਤਾਬ
ਜਨਾਬ
ਕੋਈ ਜਵਾਬ

ਮੈਨੂੰ ਕੀ ਪਤਾ-ਮੈਨੂੰ ਕੀ ਭੇਤ
ਮੈਂ ਤਾਂ ਆਪ ਹਾਂ ਤੇਰੇ ਵਾਂਗ ਇਕ ਦਰਖ਼ਤ
ਤੂੰ ਇਉਂ ਕਰ
ਅੱਜ ਦੀ ਅਖ਼ਬਾਰ ਦੇਖ

ਅਖ਼ਬਾਰ ਵਿਚ ਕੁਝ ਨਹੀਂ
ਝੜੇ ਹੋਏ ਪੱਤੇ ਨੇ

ਫਿਰ ਕੋਈ ਕਿਤਾਬ ਦੇਖ

ਕਿਤਾਬਾਂ ਵਿਚ ਬੀਜ ਨੇ

ਤਾਂ ਫਿਰ ਸੋਚ

ਸੋਚ ਇਕ ਟੱਕ ਨੇ
ਦੰਦਾਂ ਦੇ ਨਿਸ਼ਾਨ ਨੇ
ਰਾਹੀਆਂ ਦੀ ਪੈੜ ਹੈ
ਜਾਂ ਮੇਰੀਆਂ ਨਹੁੰਦਰਾਂ
ਜਿਹੜੀਆਂ ਮੈਂ ਬਚਣ ਲਈ
ਧਰਤੀ ਦੀ ਹਿੱਕ ਵਿਚ ਖੋਭੀਆਂ

ZWEI BÄUME IM GESPRÄCH

Werden Sie aus mir ein Schafott bauen
oder eine Laute
mein Herr?
Soll ich mein Leben lang hier stehenbleiben
und Buch führen über Jahreszeiten
auf meinen Blättern?
Mein Herr,
eine Antwort?

Was weiß denn ich, was kümmert's mich?
Mir geht es gut, ich bin ein Baum wie Sie
wie wäre es wenn Sie
die Zeitung konsultieren?

In der Zeitung finde ich nichts
nur gefallene Blätter

Schauen Sie nach in einem Buch

In Büchern
stecken Samenkörner

Dann denken Sie nach

In Gedanken stecken Axthiebe
Zahnabdrücke
Fußspuren der Vorbeiziehenden
oder meine scharfen Nägel
die ich zu meinem Halt
in die Brust der Erde
geschlagen habe

Denken Sie nach
Weiter, weiter

Gedanken bergen Kerker
Gedanken bergen Schrecken

DIALOGUE BETWEEN TWO TREES

Would you construct
a scaffold
out of me
or a musical instrument, sir?
Or would I go on
standing like this
all through my life
counting and recounting seasons
on my leaves?
Tell me, sir.

What do I know
how can I discern?
I too am like you –
a tree.
Better you take the trouble of
reading today's newspaper

There is nothing in the newspaper
except fallen leaves.

Then consult some book

In the books
there is nothing except seeds

Then think

In the thoughts
there are axe-marks
the imprints of teeth
the footprints of wayfarers
or my pointed nails
which I have implanted

ਸੋਚ... ਸੋਚ... ਹੋਰ ਸੋਚ

ਸੋਚ ਵਿਚ ਕੈਦ ਹੈ
ਸੋਚ ਵਿਚ ਖ਼ੌਫ਼ ਹੈ
ਲਗਦਾ ਹੈ ਧਰਤੀ ਦੇ ਨਾਲ ਬੱਝਾ ਹੋਇਆ ਹਾਂ

ਜਾ ਫਿਰ ਟੁੱਟ ਜਾ

ਟੁੱਟ ਕੇ ਕੀ ਹੋਏਗਾ
ਰੁੱਖ ਨਹੀਂ ਤਾਂ ਰਾਖ ਸਹੀ
ਰਾਖ ਨਹੀਂ ਤਾਂ ਰੇਤੇ ਸਹੀ
ਰੇਤ ਨਹੀਂ ਤਾਂ ਭਾਫ਼ ਸਹੀ

ਚੰਗਾ ਫਿਰ ਚੁੱਪ ਕਰ

ਮੈਂ ਕਦੋ ਬੋਲਦਾਂ
ਇਹ ਤਾਂ ਮੇਰੇ ਪੱਤੇ ਨੇ
ਹਵਾ ਵਿਚ ਡੋਲਦੇ।
○

Ich bin doch an die Erde gebunden

Dann stürzen Sie um

Umstürzen, und was dann –
bleibt kein Baum
so doch Asche
wenn nicht Asche,
so doch Sand
wenn nicht Sand
so doch Rauch –

Dann geben Sie doch Ruhe

Ich sage ja nichts
es sind nur meine Blätter
die im Wind rascheln.
❍

(*Tr. from Hindi by Barbara Lotz*)

deep down
in the breast of the earth
for my survival

Think Think
Think more

There is imprisonment in thinking
fear and terror.
Seems as if I am bound
to earth.

Then go, fall apart

What would happen
if I fall apart
If not tree
I will be ash.
If not ash
I will be sand.
If not sand
I will be steam.

Then you keep mum

I am not speaking
these are my leaves
stirring in the wind.
❍

(*Tr. from Punjabi by Niranjan Tasneem*)

॥ ਕਵੀ ਸਾਹਿਬ ॥

ਮੈਂ ਪਹਿਲੀ ਸਤਰ ਲਿਖਦਾ ਹਾਂ
ਤੇ ਡਰ ਜਾਂਦਾ ਹਾਂ ਰਾਜੇ ਦੇ ਸਿਪਾਹੀਆਂ ਤੋਂ
ਸਤਰ ਨੂੰ ਕੱਟ ਦੇਂਦਾ ਹਾਂ

ਮੈਂ ਦੂਜੀ ਸਤਰ ਲਿਖਦਾ ਹਾਂ
ਤੇ ਡਰ ਜਾਨਾਂ ਗੁਰੀਲੇ ਬਾਗੀਆਂ ਕੋਲੋਂ
ਸਤਰ ਨੂੰ ਕੱਟ ਦੇਂਦਾ ਹਾਂ

ਮੈ ਅਪਣੀ ਜਾਨ ਦੀ ਖ਼ਾਤਰ
ਹਜ਼ਾਰਾਂ ਅਪਣੀਆਂ ਸਤਰਾਂ ਨੂੰ
ਏਦਾਂ ਕਤਲ ਕੀਤਾ ਹੈ

ਉਨ੍ਹਾਂ ਸਤਰਾਂ ਦੀਆਂ ਰੂਹਾਂ
ਮੇਰੇ ਅਕਸਰ ਚੁਫੇਰੇ ਫਿਰਦੀਆਂ ਹੀ ਰਹਿੰਦੀਆਂ ਨੇ
ਤੇ ਮੈਨੂੰ ਕਹਿੰਦੀਆਂ ਨੇ :
ਕਵੀ ਸਾਹਿਬ !
ਕਵੀ ਹੋ ਜਾਂ ਤੁਸੀ ਕਵਿਤਾ ਦੇ ਕਾਤਿਲ ਹੋ ?

ਸੁਣੇ ਮੁਨੀਸਫ਼ ਬੜੇ ਇਨਸਾਫ਼ ਦੇ ਕਾਤਿਲ
ਬੜੇ ਮਜ਼ਹਬ ਦੇ ਰਾਖੇ
ਆਪ ਮਜ਼ਹਬ ਦੀ ਮੁਕੱਦਮ ਆਤਮਾ ਨੂੰ
ਕਤਲ ਕਰਦੇ ਵੀ ਸੁਣੇ ਸਨ

ਸਿਰਫ਼ ਇਹ ਸੁਣਨਾ ਹੀ ਬਾਕੀ ਸੀ
ਤੇ ਇਹ ਵੀ ਸੁਣ ਲਿਆ ਹੈ
ਕਿ ਸਾਡੇ ਵਕਤ ਦੇ ਵਿਚ ਖ਼ੌਫ਼ ਦੇ ਮਾਰੇ
ਕਵੀ ਵੀ ਹੋ ਗਏ
ਕਵਿਤਾ ਦੇ ਹਤਿਆਰੇ !
○

HERR DICHTER

Ich schreibe die erste Zeile
und bekomme Angst vor den Soldaten des Königs
ich streiche die Zeile aus.

Ich schreibe eine andere Zeile
und bekomme Angst vor den Schergen der Rebellen
ich streiche die Zeile aus.

Mit Rücksicht auf mein Leben
habe ich so
tausende von Zeilen umgebracht.
Die Seelen dieser Zeilen
erscheinen manchmal vor mir
und fragen:

Was sind Sie eigentlich, Herr Dichter –
Dichter oder Mörder von Gedichten?
❍

(Tr. from Hindi by Barbara Lotz)

MR. POET

I write the first line
but recoil in fear of
the soldiers of the ruler
so I delete it.

I scribble another one
but the fear of
guerilla insurgents
unnerves me
so I delete it too.

In this manner
I have murdered
thousands of my lines
to save my skin

The ghosts
of the murdered lines
haunt me all the time
and often ask me –
Mr. Poet
are you a poet
or a slaughterer of poetry?
❍

(Tr. from Punjabi by Niranjan Tasneem)

भगवत रावत

॥ सच पूछो तो ॥

एक ऐसी जगह खोजता रहा जीवन भर
जहाँ बैठकर बेफिक्री से
लिख पाता एक नाम
और कोई यह न पूछता
यह किसका नाम है

हरदम चक्कर खाते चौबीसों घंटों में से
इतना सा समय चाहिए था मुझे
जिसे आसानी से छिपाकर रख लेता
अपनी जेब में
और कोई यह न पूछता
उसे मैंने कैसे किया खर्च

भाषा से पटी पड़ी दुनिया में
कुछ ऐसे शब्द चाहिए थे मुझे जिन्हें
किसी अबोध लड़की के हाथों
गोबर-लिपी ज़मीन पर
चौक की तरह पूर देता
और कोई यह न पूछता
इसका है क्या अर्थ

सच पूछो तो
इतने से कामों के लिए आया था पृथ्वी पर
और भागता रहा यहाँ से वहाँ
○

Bhagwat RAWAT

UM DIE WAHRHEIT ZU SAGEN

Ein Leben lang hab ich den Ort gesucht
wo ich mich sorglos niederlassen
und einen Namen schreiben kann
ohne daß einer fragt
wer das ist

Von vierundzwanzig Stunden in der Tretmühle
wollt ich nur soviel Zeit mir nehmen
daß ich sie schnell und ohne Aufsehen
in der Tasche verschwinden lassen kann
ohne daß einer später fragt
wie ich sie verbraucht habe

In einer Welt von Sprache überschwemmt
wollt ich nur ein paar Worte finden, die sich
zu glückverheißenden Mustern fügen
wie sie auf Lehmböden
von der leichten Hand unschuldiger Mädchen
gezeichnet werden
ohne daß einer fragt
was das bedeuten soll

Um die Wahrheit zu sagen,
das alles wollt ich tun auf Erden
und bin doch nur von hier nach dort gerannt.
❍

(Tr. from Hindi by Barbara Lotz)

IF YOU ASK ME THE TRUTH

All my life I kept looking for a place
where sitting carefree
I could have scribbled a name
without anybody asking
whose name it was

Out of the perennially spinning twenty-four hours
I needed just a wee bit of time
that I could have
easily pocketed
without anybody's demanding to know
how I spent it

In this world overstrewn with language
I craved for some such words
which I could fill in like
an auspicious pattern made by
an innocent girl on a
cowdung-pasted mud-floor
without anybody enquiring
what it meant

If you ask me the truth
I had descended on this earth just for these
but instead kept running from place to place.
❍

(Tr. from Hindi by R.K. Dixit)

॥ कचरा बीनने वाली लड़कियाँ ॥

आपने अपने शहरों में भी
ज़रूर देखी होंगी
कचरा बीनने वाली लड़कियाँ

मोहल्ले भर के कूड़े के ढेर पर
चौपायों सी चलती-फिरती
कचरे में अपने आप पैदा हो गई
नहीं लगतीं
ये कचरा बीनने वाली लड़कियाँ ?

जगह-जगह फटे
अपने कपड़ों जैसे टाट के बोरे में
भरती हैं वे बीन-बीन कर
हमारे आपके रद्द किए काग़ज़ के टुकड़े
टूटे-फूटे टीन और प्लास्टिक के डिब्बे

जब कोई छपा हुआ फोटू
या साबुत डिब्बा मिल जाता है उन्हें
तो वे रख देती हैं उसे अलग सँभालकर
और उस समय तो आप
उन्हें देख नहीं सकते जब वे
कचरे में से न जाने क्या उठाकर
चुपचाप मुँह में रख लेती हैं
अपने आस-पास
घूमते सुअरों के बीच कैसी लगती हैं
ये कचरा बीनने वाली लड़कियाँ ?

यह सवाल
समाजशास्त्र के कोर्स के बाहर का है

MÄDCHEN, DIE IM ABFALL WÜHLEN

Jeder kennt sie aus der eignen Stadt
die Mädchen, die im Abfall wühlen

Auf dem Müllhaufen vom ganzen Viertel
grasen sie wie die Viecher
sieht es nicht aus
als hätte der Abfall selbst
sie hervorgebracht
die Mädchen, die im Abfall wühlen?

Ihre Kleider zerlumpt und zerrissen
so wie die Jutesäcke in die
sie stopfen was sie aussortieren
Papierfetzen, von uns weggeworfen
zerbeulte Dosen und kaputte Plastikbecher

Fällt ihnen ein Hochglanzdruck
eine noch brauchbare Dose in die Hände
wird das sorgfältig weggesteckt,
aber man kann kaum zusehen wenn sie
Gott weiß was aus dem Abfall fischen
und es stillschweigend in den Mund stecken
Wie machen sie sich
inmitten der Schweineherde
die Mädchen, die im Abfall wühlen?

Die Frage
ist im Soziologiekurs nicht vorgesehen
eine Ästhetik für sie
noch nicht ausgearbeitet
In anspruchsvollen Fotobänden immerhin
sind sie die pikante Würze
die Mädchen, die im Abfall wühlen.

Ihre Haut überzieht sich
mit Schichten von Dreck
die Haare verfilzen

THE RAG-PICKING GIRLS

In your towns too
you must have come across
the rag-picking girls

On the garbage dump of the entire
neighbourhood
strolling like cattle
don't they seem to have been born
of their own
these rag-picking girls?

In their jute sacks
torn like their own tatters
they stuff pieces of paper
discarded and crossed out by us
and broken tins and plastic cans

Whenever they stumble upon
a printed photo or a container unbroken
they carefully put it aside
and you can't really
bear to look at them when
they quietly pick up who knows what
from the garbage
and put it in their mouth
How among the pigs roving round them
do they appear
these rag-picking girls?

The question
falls outside the courses in Sociology
and Aesthetics do not yet
exist for them
Yes, for an art photo session

और सौन्दर्यशास्त्र उनके लिए
अभी बना नहीं
हाँ, आजकल कलात्मक फोटोग्राफी के लिए
मसाला जरूर हो जाती हैं
ये कचरा बीनने वाली लड़कियाँ

अपनी त्वचा पर
कालिख की परतों पर परतें चढ़ाती
बालों को जटा-जूटों की तरह
फैलाती-बढ़ाती
बिना शरम-लिहाज़
शरीर को चाहे जहाँ खुजलाती
पसीने और पानी के छींटों से बनी
मैल की लकीरों वाले चेहरे पर
पीले दाँतों से
न जाने किसको मुँह चिढ़ाती
आठ-नौ बरस से
बीस-पच्चीस तक की उमर की
पता नहीं कब कैसे
किस कूड़े घर से
अपने पेट में
बच्चे तक उठा ले आती हैं
ये कचरा बीनने वाली लड़कियाँ

मर तो चुकी थीं सारी की सारी
चौरासी की गैस में
अब किससे पूछें
फिर कहाँ से उग आई हैं
ये कचरा बीनने वाली लड़कियाँ

किसी रजिस्टर में इनका नाम नहीं लिखा
ढूँढने पर भी इनके बाप का पता नहीं मिलता
इनका कहीं कोई भाई नहीं दिखता
यहाँ तक कि खुद ही
अपनी माँ होती हैं
ये कचरा बीनने वाली लड़कियाँ।

○

zur wilden Zottelmähne
ohne Hemmung ohne Scheu
wird da gekratzt wo's juckt
Schweiß und Wassertropfen
wie Schmutzrinnen im Gesicht
mit gelben Zähnen
ziehn sie Grimassen gegen irgendwen
kaum zu glauben wann und wie sie's schaffen
ab acht, neun Jahren
bis Mitte Zwanzig
von irgendeinem Abfallplatz
ein Kind sich aufzusammeln
im Bauch
die Mädchen, die im Abfall wühlen

Sie sind alle gestorben
im Gas von vierundachtzig
Jetzt frag dich
wie sind sie wieder aufgetaucht
die Mädchen, die im Abfall wühlen?

Keine Kartei führt ihren Namen
auch wenn man sucht erfährt man nie
den Namen ihrer Väter
kein Bruder in Sichtweite
bis dahin
daß sie ihre eignen Mütter sind,
die Mädchen, die im Abfall wühlen.
O

(*Tr. from Hindi by Barbara Lotz*)

they do become a spicy object
these rag-picking girls

Putting upon their skin
black dirt layer by layer
growing and spreading their tresses
like the matted hair of ascetics
scratching unabashed and uninhibited
their bodies anywhere at will
teasing who knows whom
with their yellow teeth their faces
marked with lines of grime
made by sweat and drops of water
of age groups of eight or nine
to twenty or twenty-five
no one knows
when how and from which garbage dump
they pick up even babies
in their wombs
these rag-picking girls

All of these did perish
in the Gas Tragedy of eighty-four
Who shall we ask know
from where once again
have cropped up
these rag-picking girls?

No registers have their names
their fathers are not traceable
howsoever you search for them
no brother of theirs is found anywhere
So much so that
They are their own mothers
these rag-picking girls.
O

(*Tr. from Hindi by R.K. Dixit*)

॥ इस शोर में ॥

यह जो शोर उठ रहा है
गैस-ट्रेजेडी के बादलों की तरह
रौंदता बच्चों-बूढ़ों को
इतिहास की अंधी गुफाओं से निकलकर
छाता हुआ
अखबारों के रंगीन पन्नों पर

किसी दिन जब कोई मरेगा इस शोर में
कोई कहेगा कि वह
कुछ देर पहले तक तो
बिलकुल ठीक था
कुछ नहीं हुआ था उसे
उसके बारे में किया गया
यह अंतिम वार्तालाप भी
खो जाएगा शोर में

उस दिन उसके घर के बाहर बज रहे होंगे
ढोल-नगाड़े
घर के अन्दर चल रही होगी टीवी पर
मारधाड़ वाली फिल्म फुल वाल्यूम पर

उस दिन कोई किसी को सुन नहीं रहा होगा
कोई किसी से मिल नहीं रहा होगा
कोई किसी को जान नहीं रहा होगा
उस दिन आसमान से कोई तारा नहीं टूटेगा
कहीं किसी का धीरज नहीं छूटेगा
सब होंगे अपने-अपने शोर में।

○

IN DIESEM LÄRM

Der Lärm der sich erhebt
genau wie die Wolken des Gasunglücks
betäubt er Jung und Alt
kriecht aus den dunklen Höhlen der Geschichte
senkt sich
über die Farbbeilage der Zeitungen

wenn eines Tages einer stirbt in diesem Lärm
wird jemand sagen daß
er bis vor kurzem noch
vollkommen gesund war
er gar nichts hatte
auch dieses letzte Gespräch über ihn
wird untergehen
im Lärm

An diesem Tag wird man die Trommeln schlagen
vor seinem Haus
und drinnen läuft auf voller Lautstärke
ein Actionfilm im Fernsehen

An diesem Tag wird keiner keinen hören
keiner keinen treffen
keiner keinen erkennen
kein Stern wird vom Himmel fallen
keiner wird die Geduld verlieren –
alle umgeben von ihrem eigenen Lärm.
❍

(Tr. from Hindi by Barbara Lotz)

IN THIS DIN

This din that's rising
like the clouds of the Gas Tragedy –
overrunning the young and the old
rolling out of the dark caverns of history –
spreads
over the colourful pages of newspapers

When some day someone dies
in this hubbub
someone will say
just a little while ago
he was alright
nothing had happened to him
Even this last exclamation about him
shall get lost in this clatter

That day outside his house
somebody would be beating
drums
inside the house would be running on the TV
a film full of violence on the highest pitch

That day no one would be listening to anyone
no one would be meeting anyone
no one would be knowing anyone
That day no star will shoot from the sky
no one's patience will be lost anywhere
All will be there in their own individual noises.
❍

(Tr. from Hindi by R.K. Dixit)

पद्मा सचदेव

॥ राजा के महल ॥

ये राजा के महल क्या आपके हैं ?
मैं घर से निकाली हूँ बेघर हूँ अब
मेरी बरसों में आँखों की ज्योति गयी
अंधी करके मुझे छोड़ गए थे जो
मेरे बागीचे से पौधा उखाड़ा था जो
उस पौधे को बौर भी पड़ा न था
मेरा साजन दूर भी गया न था
जिन्होंने काँपती टहनियाँ उखाड़ लीं

वो हँसुली दरातियाँ क्या आपकी हैं ?
ये राजा के महल क्या आपके हैं ?

मुँह में पड़ा ग्रास जो छीन गए
अनबना लहू जो चूस गए
हमारे कलपने तड़पने रोने का दिन
जिन शाहों के लिए मनहूस हुआ
हमारे काँपते हाथों को छड़ी से मार
हमारी आँखों के आगे न लुटिया रहने दी
जो झाड़ कर हमारे पिटार ले गए

उनकी लदी हुई छोड़िया क्या आपकी है ?
ये राजा के महल क्या आपके हैं ?

दीवारें ऊँची छूती आसमान सारा
महल तगड़े हैं माल खजाना भरा
ईंटें लाल रंग भरी भाती हमें
हमारे लहू की याद दिलाती हमें
हमारे कंधों से उतरे शहतीर यहाँ
बहे बदन से पसीने के नीर यहाँ
जिन्होंने धूप में जल कर ये दीवारें खड़ी कीं

Padma SACHDEVA

KÖNIGSPALÄSTE

Gehören sie euch, diese Königspaläste –
vertrieben wurde ich, bin heimatlos geworden
das Licht in meinen Augen erlosch vor Jahren
geblendet ließ man mich zurück
Das Pflänzchen riß man aus in meinem Garten
noch vor der Blüte
Mein Liebster war nicht weit
als sie die schwankenden Zweige brachen
    gehören sie euch, die Sicheln und
    Haumesser
    gehören sie euch, diese Königspaläste?

Den Bissen vom Mund weggeschnappt
Blut ausgesaugt, noch bevor es in den Adern
    kreiste
Die Tage des Klagens und Weinens
waren unsern Herrschern nur ein lästiges Übel
Auf unsere zitternden Hände fiel der Stock
vor unseren Augen räumten sie
das letzte Messing aus den Truhen
    gehören sie euch, die beladenen Pferde
    gehören sie euch, diese Königspaläste?

Hohe Mauern streben zum Himmel
umgeben wertvolle Schätze
Die roten Ziegelsteine kennen wir
sie erwecken Erinnerung an unser Blut
von unseren Schultern wurden die Balken
    geladen
Fundamente gewässert mit unserem Schweiß
Wir zogen die Mauern hoch in der Sonnenglut
    gehören sie euch, diese Bauwerke
    gehören sie euch, diese Königspaläste?

THE RAJA'S PALACES

Do these Raja's Palaces belong to you?
I am a wanderer without a home
My eyes lost their light years ago
They came, they plundered, they left me blind
Uprooted the little plant of my garden
Its sapling was yet to flower
My beloved had not yet gone very far
Before they severed the trembling branches
    Do the raping saw and sickle belong to
    you?
    Do the Raja's Palaces belong to you?

The morsel of food was snatched from our lips
The blood in the veins was sucked ere fully
    formed
The day of our sorrow, tears, our agony
Was just an unpleasant thing for our lords
The rained the lash on our trembling hands
And from under our eyes
Took the last brass from our homes
Emptying every box and iron trunk
    Do their loaded mares belong to you?
    Do the Raja's Palaces belong to you?

High walls kiss the sky
Entombed within are riches high
Bright red bricks are a lovely sight
Remind us of our blood and plight
Here the boulders
were unloaded from our shoulders
Here our sweat drenched the soil
These are the walls that rose from our toil
    Do these edifices now belong to you?
    Do these Raja's Palaces belong to you?

ये उनके महल क्या आपके हैं ?
ये राजा के महल क्या आपके हैं ?

बहरे कानों को तोप सुना गयी
मैं आज भी घंटा बजा गयी
मेरे चाँद के उगने की वेला हुई
कोई आहट न बाहिर गली में हुई
न ही पाँव ये दाड़ के लेने गए
पुकार साजन की मुझसे न सही गयी
आधी राह में घेर के ले गयी जो

वो लोहे हथकड़ियाँ क्या आपकी हैं ?
ये राजा के महल क्या आपके हैं ?

जिन्होंने हमारे लहू के दिये जला
रात काली को कर रखा है चाँद सा
हँसती चाँदनी चाँद गठबंधन थामे
हमें दूर से देखे मजाक करे
तारे मन में हमारे भी टूटते हैं
जब बम्ब आसमान पर छूटते हैं
बच्चे जिन्हें हैरान एकटक देखें

वो सुंदर दीवालियाँ आपकी हैं ?
ये राजा के महल क्या आपके हैं ?

जिन्हें खोद के खाद मिलाई हमने
जिनके मिट्टी के घरों की मैल भी पी
जिन्हें सींचा था धूप में पानी दे के
चाँद गुस्सा भी हुआ था सूखे मुँह पै
मन खिला था जिसमें अंकुर पाकर
हमारी दीवाली हुई थी बौर देखकर
आँखें बोली किसी का देख घूरजा

ये सुंदर क्यारियाँ क्या आपकी हैं ?
ये राजा के महल क्या आपके हैं ?

Auch heute haben meine tauben Ohren
die Kanone gehört
habe ich die Glocke geläutet
Zeit wird's für die Rückkehr des Liebsten
doch kein Laut in den öden Gassen
meine Schritte eilen ihm nicht mehr entgegen,
zur Begrüßung
sein Ruf hallt noch nach
wie sie ihn packten auf halbem Wege,
gefangennahmen
gehören sie euch, diese eisernen Ketten
gehören sie euch, diese Königspaläste?

Even today my deaf ears
Have heard the burst of the midday cannon
The hour of forced labour is over
'Tis time for my beloved to return
But there is not a sound in the lane
No longer my feet break into a run
To greet him walking down the lane
His voice echoes still in my ears
For me 'tis filled with fear and pain
Those that captured him midway
Do those chains belong to you?
Do the Raja's Palaces belong to you?

In ihren Öllämpchen
brennt unser Blut
erhellt ihre Nächte zum Lichterfest
Ihr Glanz grüßt uns spöttisch aus der Ferne
Auch unsere Seele zerspringt zu Sternenfunken
wenn ihr Feuerwerk zum Himmel steigt
und Kinderaugen staunend folgen
gehören euch diese Diwalifeste
gehören sie euch, diese Königspaläste?

In whose lamps
Our blood burns as oil
Turning the dark night
Into full moon light
These shining nights
Mock us from afar
It is the night of the Festival of Lights
Their crackers explode in the sky
Our hearts splinter into little stars
Our children gaze at the fireworks in wonder
Do these lovely Diwalis belong to you?
Do the Raja's Palaces belong to you?

Wir haben gepflügt und die Felder gedüngt
wir tranken, was aus der Erde sickerte
wir haben gewässert in sengender Glut
den Liebsten erzürnte mein verbranntes Gesicht
Beim Anblick der Sprossen ging unser Herz auf
und unser Diwali waren die Blüten
Wir fragen bei eurem finsteren Blick
gehören euch diese blühenden Felder
gehören sie euch, diese Königspaläste?

It is we who dug the pits and filled them with compost
It is we who drank the oozing out of the mud
It is we who irrigated the beds in the scorching heat
My beloved saw my dried face and was angry
The night of sapling brought joy to our hearts
When it came to flower, it was our festival of lights
But when we saw their growling eyes we asked
Do these lovely vegetations belong to you?
Do these Raja's Palaces belong to you?

जहाँ हक किसी का हो गया है
बचपन से ही कोई ले गया है
नैन जिसको देख के खिल उठे
जिसकी याद में दिन न रात रहे
जिसका नाम लेके छेड़ जाए सभी
जो बैठी है कोल करार किए

ये वो आत्माएँ क्या आपकी हैं ?
ये राजा के महल क्या आपके हैं ?
○

In der Jugend bereits durch Versprechen
gebunden
war ich dem Geliebten
wir hatten in Liebe zueinandergefunden
Sein Blick ließ meine Augen leuchten
nur um ihn kreisten meine Gedanken
die Freundinnen reizten mich mit seinem
Namen –
die hier jetzt warten, gebunden an heilige Eide
gehören sie euch, diese Seelen
gehören sie euch, diese Königspaläste?

o

(Tr. from Hindi by Barbara Lotz)

Das Lied reflektiert die blutigen Unruhen, die nach der Teilung Indiens 1947 ausbrachen und gewaltsame Übergriffe gegen die jeweilige Minderheit zur Folge hatten.

When I was young in years
I entrusted myself to my beloved
A loving exchange it was
That gave him all the rights
His thoughts lit up my days
And accompanied me into my nights
A fleeting glimpse was a thing of joy
His name a tool of banter for my friends
Those wedded in pledges loving and solemn
Do those souls belong to you?
Do these Raja's Palaces belong to you?

o

(Tr. from Dogri by Khushwant Singh)

॥ कबूतर ॥

शान्ति आहले चिट्टे कबूतर
सारे दे सारे गै बजुर्ग डोआरी गे न
हुन स्हाड़े कच्छ छड़े काले कबूतर न
जिन्दे म्याणे हुन्दे गै बिल्ली खाई जन्दी ऐ

अपनी नस्ल मुकदी दिक्खिऐ
कबूतर हुन बच्चे नी जम्म दे
बिल्ली दे डरै ने ओह
धरती कन्ने छोन्दे गै नेंई
गास्से च उड्डरदे रौहन्दे न
की जे ओह नी जानदे
गास्सै च वी इक मगोर होई शेदा ऐ
जेड़ा कुसै दिन बिल्ली बनिऐ
धरती गी निन्गली जाग

कबूतरें दे बचने दी कोई मेद नींऐ
होई सक्कै ताँ अक्खर बचाइयै रक्खो
अक्खरें च सम्हलोई दी रौहग
थुआड़ी जीन्दे रौहने गित्ते कीती दी कोशश
अक्खर गै थुअड़ी संस्कृति सम्बिऐ रखडग
पर बलगो सुनचै कबूतर केह अक्खा देन

केह गास्सै च उड्डरदे उड्डरदे अस बची जाग्गे
जाँ तुस अक्खर बचाई लैग्गेओ
ते जेकर अक्खर बची वी गै ताँ
उनेंगी कुन बाच्चग !
○

TAUBEN

All die weißen Friedenstauben
haben schon die Eltern freigelassen
was uns bleibt sind graue Tauben
Katzen fressen ihre Jungen

Wie sie ihre Jungen sterben sehen
stellen sie das Brüten ein
aus Angst vor Katzen
meiden sie den Boden
versuchen in der Luft zu bleiben
nicht wissend
daß ein Loch entstand im Himmel
das die Erde schlucken wird

Keine Hoffnung daß die Tauben überleben
Rette Worte, wenn du kannst
in den Worten wird bewahrt sein
dein Versuch zu überleben
Nur in Worten kann sich deine Welt erhalten

Warte was die Tauben sagen:
Werden wir am Himmel fliegend überleben
oder ihr, die Worte wahrend?
Und wenn Worte überleben
wer wird da sein sie zu lesen?
❍

(Tr. from Hindi by Barbara Lotz)

PIGEONS

White pigeons of peace, all of them
have been released by the elders
Now we're left with only grey pigeons
And their little ones are eaten up by cats

Seeing their progeny vanishing
Pigeons don't breed any more
Afraid of cats
They do not touch the ground even
They keep flying in the sky.
Because they do not know that
a hole has developed in the sky
which will swallow up the earth.

There is no hope for the survival of pigeons
Try to save words if you can
Words will preserve your efforts
to stay swing
Words alone will safekeep your culture

But wait! Hear what the pigeons are saying
Shall we be saved by flying in the sky?
Will you be able to preserve words?
And even if words do survive
Who'll read them?
❍

(Tr. from Dogri by Shivanath)

प्रयाग शुक्ल

॥ खंडहर होते एक महल को देखने के बाद ॥

पत्थर के सिंहों और बाघों की आँखों पर
जमी हुई काई।
जहाँ-तहाँ आई उग घास।
डीठ इस महल की
हो जैसे पथराई !

निकट नदी–
अभी नहीं बारिश की।
कहीं-कहीं पानी भर।
घूमती निगाह में
खुली चौड़ाई !

बरस-मास-दिन अनगिन
प्रहरों की छाया में
भीत खड़ी हो मानो
सहसा घबराई !

पेड़ हैं जरूर
हरे, नए-पुराने।
नूपुर सुर
थे कभी।

अब वे कथाएँ।

धुँधलाए दर्पण।
सन्नाटा चीरती–
चिड़िया उड़ आई
खुले किवाड़ों से
क्षण भर को
धूल भरी जागी
तसवीरें !

तो फिर
विदाई !
○

Prayag SHUKLA

BEIM ANBLICK EINES ZUR RUINE VERFALLENDEN PALASTES

Die Augen der Löwen und Tiger aus Stein
von Moos überzogen.
Dazwischen sprießt Gras.
Der Blick des Palastes selbst
scheint aus Stein zu sein.

Nahbei ein Fluß
nicht mehr gefüllt vom Regen
nur Tümpel hier und da.
Im schweifenden Blick
unendliche Weite.

Jahre-Monate-Tage ungezählt
im Schatten der Stundenwechsel
Mauern fahren auf
wie plötzlich aufgestöbert.

Umstanden von Bäumen
grüne, jung und alt
früher in diesen Räumen
Tanzglöckchenklang

jetzt nur Legenden.

Spiegel erblinden.
Das Schweigen zerreißt
durch offene Türen
fliegt ein Vogel herein –
eine Sekunde lang schrecken
die Ahnenbilder auf
unterm Staub.

Nun dann
Lebwohl!
❍

(Tr. from Hindi by Barbara Lotz)

ON VISITING A PALACE TURNING INTO A RUIN

Moss grown over the eyes
Of stone tigers and lions.
Grass sprouting here and there.
As if the Palace's sight
Had turned to stone.

River nearby
Run out of monsoon.
Just puddles here and there.
The eye roves
Over open scape.

In the shade of changing hours
Through countless years-months-days
The wall stands still
Frozen into panic.

Some trees stand green
Both old and young.
Once ankle-bells
had tinkled here.

Mirrors grown misty.
Piercing the stillness
A bird flies in
Through flung open doors
Awakening for a moment
Dusty portraits.

Well, then,
Farewell!
❍

(Tr. from Hindi by Harish Trivedi)

॥ यह लिख़ता हूँ ॥

जल्दी जल्दी सब गया बीत
आ गई उम्र उठ पड़ने की
ये वाहन ये सन्ध्या तारे
ये रोशनियाँ, ये पेड़-फूल
ये घर मकान दूकानें सब
सड़कें जिन पर सौ बार चला।
नदियाँ, ट्रेनें, चिड़ियाँ, फसलें
तन की सुगन्ध
मन की सुगन्ध
चीज़ें कितनी भूली बिसरीं
बाकी कितनी कुछ याद रहीं।

वे नावें कितनी दूर हुईं।

जो चित्रलिखित था वह पीछे
जो आगे है वह भी पीछे को
खिसक रहा,
पर अभी यहाँ मैं बैठा हूँ
यह लिखता हूँ,
यह जीवन है।
○

DAS SCHREIBE ICH

Wie schnell ging alles vorbei
das Alter ist gekommen abzutreten
Die Fahrzeuge, die Abendsterne,
die Lichter, die Blumen und Bäume
die Wohnstätten, Häuser, Geschäfte alle
die Straßen hundertmal beschritten.
Flüsse, Züge, Vögel, Jahreszeiten
Duft eines Körpers
Duft eines Geistes
Wieviele Dinge versäumt und vergessen
Wieviele flüchtige Erinnerungen

Wie weit entglitten diese Boote.

Was lebhaft vor uns stand liegt hinter uns.
Was vor uns liegt, auch das rückt in den Hintergrund allmählich
Doch hier wo ich sitze
das was ich schreibe
ist Leben.
❍

(Tr. from Hindi by Barbara Lotz)

THIS I WRITE

It's all gone, all too soon,
And it's time to get up and leave -
The vehicles and the evening stars
the lights, trees, the flowers
Houses, homes, the shopping arcades
And the paths I've traversed
Time and again.

Rivers, trains, sparrows, crops,
The body-fragrance
The mind-fragrance
Things so many I knew and forgot
And those that linger on in my thought.

And those boats - they have moved afar!

What was vivid is behind me.
What is ahead moves back.
Yet here, I sit, and
This I write:
It lives.
❍

(Tr. from Hindi by Girdhar Rathi)

॥ व्यंजन पकाने की विधियाँ ॥

[रघुवीर सहाय की स्मृति को समर्पित]

व्यंजन पकाने की विधियाँ कई हैं।
व्यंजन भी कई हैं।
स्वाद भी कई हैं ढेरों व्यंजनों के।
पर, व्यंजन, विधियों को
चकमा दे,
कब कैसे स्वाद को मधुर-तिक्त
करते हैं,
यही चमत्कार है।
चाहें तो हम इसे रहस्य भी कह लें।

हाथों का जस–
वह तो होता है।
उससे भी बड़ी चीज़ लेकिन
वह मन है, जो व्यंजन
पकाता है।
वह अदृश्य रहता है

स्वाद जो आता है जीभ पर
जान वह कैसे
पर लेता है–
किस मन से व्यंजन पकाया गया।

सामग्री–वह तो होनी होगी।
सामग्री बिन व्यंजन, यह तो
सुना नहीं।
हाँ, वह भी कैसे जुटाई गई,
यह महत्त्वपूर्ण है।

अन्त तब यही होगा
स्वाद का–
कैसे जुटाए गए
सामग्री मन व्यंजन विधियाँ।

○

ARTEN ZU KOCHEN

(IN ERINNERUNG AN RAGHUVIR SAHAY)

Es gibt verschiedene Arten zu kochen
Gerichte gibt es auch verschiedene
Und alle schmecken verschieden.
Ein Gericht mag aber oft die Arten
nicht preisgeben
welche wann und wie den Geschmack ins Süße
oder Bittre verkehrten,
das ist Zauberei.
Man könnte es auch Geheimnis nennen.

Fingerspitzengefühl–
das braucht es wohl.
Doch wichtiger als das
ist der Geist,
der hinter dem Gericht steht.
Er bleibt unsichtbar.

Der Geschmack auf der Zunge
er zeugt unbestimmbar
doch untrüglich
vom Geist in dem das Gericht entstand.

Zutaten - auch sie sind wichtig.
Ohne Zutaten zu kochen
ist noch niemand gelungen.
Doch wie man sie komponiert
ist allein entscheidend.

Und schließlich ergibt sich so
der Geschmack–
aus der Komposition von
Zutaten und Geist, Art und Gericht.
❍

(Tr. from Hindi by Barbara Lotz)

THE WAYS OF COOKING

(DEDICATED TO THE MEMORY OF RAGHUVIR SAHAY)

Several are the ways of cooking,
Several the dishes,
And several the tastes of dishes aplenty.
A dish may still dogde
The ways of cooking,
And turn it sweet or sour.
A miracle this?
We could even say it's a mystery.

The touch of the perfect cook, of course,
Does count. Though
Greater yet is the heart
That cooks.
And it's invisible.

The palate can make out
The way the heart lay
While the dish was cooked.

And, as for the ingredients,
They, too, count.
For whoever heard of a dish
Without them! Though
We must know how they are acquired.

The taste goes the way they are acquired.
That is: Ingredients,
The heart,
The dish,
And the Ways of Cooking.
❍

(Tr. from Hindi by Girdhar Rathi)

॥ दिल्ली में ॥

दिल्ली में भी कूकती हैं कोयल
झरते हैं पत्ते
चींटियाँ चढ़ती हैं पेड़ के तने पर
दिल्ली में।
दिल्ली में भी उड़ती हैं चिड़ियाँ
दिल्ली में भी दौड़ती हैं गिलहरियाँ।
आकाश दिल्ली में भी
हो जाता है लाल।

दिल्ली में भी उगते हैं तारे।
दिल्ली में भी उड़ती हैं
तितलियाँ।

हैं, हाँ, हैं—
ये सब भी
दिल्ली में।
○

IN DELHI

Auch in Delhi ruft der Kuckuck
fallen Blätter
krabbeln Ameisen den Stamm empor
in Delhi.
Sperlinge singen
auch in Delhi
Streifenhörnchen springen
auch in Delhi.
Auch der Himmel über Delhi
färbt sich rot.

Auch in Delhi gehn die Sterne auf.
Auch in Delhi fliegen
Schmetterlinge.

All das gibt es
ja, doch,
auch in Delhi.
❍

(*Tr. from Hindi by Barbara Lotz*)

IN DELHI

Even in Delhi
cuckoos call
Leaves fall
Ants crawl up the tree.

In Delhi, too
Sparrows fly
Squirrels hie
And red becomes the sky.

Even in Delhi
Rise the stars.
Even in Delhi
The butterfly darts.

These too,
Yes these too,
In Delhi.
❍

(*Tr. from Hindi by Girdhar Rathi*)

केदारनाथ सिंह

॥ कविता क्या है ॥

कविता क्या है
हाथ की तरफ़
उठा हुआ हाथ
देह की तरफ़

झुकी हुई आत्मा
मृत्यु की तरफ़
घूरती हुई आँखें
क्या है कविता

कोई हमला
हमले के बाद पैरों को खोजते
लहूलुहान जूते
नायक की चुप्पी

विदूषक की चीख़
बालों के गिरने पर
नाई की चिन्ता
एक पत्ती के टूटने पर

राष्ट्र का शोक
आख़िर क्या है
क्या है कविता
मैंने जब भी सोचा

मुझे रामचन्द्र शुक्ल की मूँछें याद आयीं
मूँछों में दबी बारीक-सी हँसी
हँसी के पीछे कविता का राज़
कविता के राज़ पर
हँसती हुई मूँछें !
○

Kedarnath SINGH

WAS IST EIN GEDICHT

Was ist ein Gedicht
Eine zur Hand
Erhobne Hand
Eine zum Leib
Geneigte Seele
Den Tod
Anstarrende Augen
Was ist ein Gedicht
Irgendein Angriff
Blutige Schuhe die
Nach dem Angriff die Füße suchen
Das Schweigen des Helden
Der Schrei des Narren
Die Besorgtheit des Barbiers
Wenn die Haare fallen
Die Staatstrauer
Wenn ein Blatt zerbricht
Was ist eigentlich
Was ist ein Gedicht
Immer wenn ich nachdachte darüber
Fiel mir Ramchandra Shuklas Schnurrbart ein
Sein in den Schnurrbart geklemmtes feines Lachen
Hinterm Lachen das Geheimnis eines Gedichts
Über dem Geheimnis eines Gedichts
Lachend der Schnurrbart!
○

(Tr. from Hindi by Lothar Lutze)

WHAT IS POETRY?

What is poetry?
A hand reaching
Towards a hand;
A soul bending
Towards a body;
Eyes staring
In death's direction.
What is poetry?
An attack;
After the attack
Bloodied shoes
Searching for feet.
A hero's silence;
A clown's scream;
A barber's anxiety
About hair loss;
A nation's grief
At a leaf falling.
What then is it,
What is poetry?
Whenever I have pondered this
I've thought of Ramchandra Shukla's moustaches
And a faint smile lurking in his moustaches:
Behind the smile the secret of poetry.
Moustaches smiling
At the secret of poetry!
○

(Tr. from Hindi by Rupert Snell)

॥ एक प्रेम-कविता को पढ़कर ॥

उस लम्बी प्रेम-कविता को पढ़ने के बाद
मैंने किताब बन्द कर दी
और पूछा—बत्तखें कहाँ हैं !
मुझे आश्चर्य हुआ दूर-दूर तक

वे कहीं नहीं थीं
यह कविता की तीसरी पंक्ति थी
या शायद पाँचवीं—जहाँ मुझे पहली बार लगा था
यहाँ बत्तखें हो सकती हैं।

मैंने उनके डैनों की छप्-छप् सुनी थी
यह मेरा भ्रम भी हो सकता है
वह स्त्री
न जाने कितनी देर से

कविता की बारहवीं पंक्ति में खड़ी थी
और बस का इंतजार कर रही थी
उसे कहाँ जाना है—कविता इसके बारे में
बिल्कुल चुप थी

सिर्फ एक हल्की-सी धूप
स्त्री के कंधों पर पड़ रही थी
कविता की सत्रहवीं पंक्ति से छनकर
स्त्री खुश थी

कम से कम उसके चेहरे पर ऐसा कुछ नहीं था
कि कविता की इक्कीसवीं पंक्ति तक जाते-जाते
वह अचानक गायब हो जाएगी
जैसे हर स्त्री हो जाती है

NACH DEM LESEN EINES LIEBESGEDICHTES

Nach dem Lesen jenes langen Liebesgedichts
Klappte ich das Buch zu
Und fragte: Wo bleiben die Enten!

Ich war erstaunt daß sie weit und breit
Nicht zu finden waren

Es war die dritte Zeile des Gedichts
Oder vielleicht die fünfte wo ich zum erstenmal
meinte
Hier könnten Enten sein

Ich hatte das Flappflapp ihrer Flügel gehört
Doch das kann ich mir auch eingebildet haben

Die Frau
Stand wer weiß wie lange
In der zwölften Zeile des Gedichts
Und wartete auf den Bus

Wohin sie mußte - das Gedicht
Verschwieg das völlig
Nur ein leichter Sonnenschein
Fiel auf die Schultern der Frau
Gefiltert durch die siebzehnte Zeile

Die Frau war vergnügt
Wenigstens deutete in ihrem Gesicht nichts an
Daß in der einundzwanzigsten Zeile des Gedichts
Sie plötzlich verschwinden wird
Wie jede Frau verschwindet

Wo die nächste Zeile begann
Standen Teakbäume
Die Bäume lösten im Gedicht
Eine eigenartige Panik aus

READING A LOVE POEM

After reading that long love poem
I closed the book
and asked - where are the ducks!

To my surprise they were nowhere at all,
not even far, far off.

It was in the poem's third line
or perhaps the fifth
where it first struck me
there could be ducks here.

I'd heard the clap and flapping of their wings
though I could have been mistaken

That woman
had been standing in line twelve of the poem
who knows how long
waiting for a bus.

Where she was going - the poem was silent
on this point;
just a gentle sunlight
was falling on the woman's shoulders
filtering through line seventeen.

The woman was happy;
at least nothing on her face said
that by the twenty-first line
she would disappear suddenly
as every woman does.

Where the next line began
teak trees stood;

जहाँ अगली पंक्ति शुरू होती थी
साखू के पेड़ वहीं खड़े थे
पेड़ कविता में एक अजीब-सी दहशत
पैदा कर रहे थे

हर अगली पंक्ति एक गहरी आशंका थी
हर अगली पंक्ति के बारे में
अगर मैं भूलता नहीं तो यह कविता की
उन्नीसवीं पंक्ति थी जहाँ स्त्री

आलू चीर रही थी
गोल और भूरे आलू चीरे जा रहे थे
कविता के अन्दर
और कविता ज्यादा चुप

ज्यादा ठोस होती जा रही थी
मेरा ख्याल है यह कटती हुई सब्जी की खुशबू थी
जो स्त्री को बचाए हुए थी
अगली अनेक पंक्तियों तक

बाईसवीं तक जाते-जाते मुझे लगा
कविता अपनी जगह बदल रही है
एक तेज गोली की तरह
स्त्री के कंधों से होती हुई

साखू के पेड़ों की ओर चली गई थी कविता
उसके आगे कोई पंक्ति नहीं थी
कोई शब्द नहीं था कविता में उसके आगे
सिर्फ़ स्त्री थी

सिर्फ़ उसके कंधे
उसकी पीठ
उसकी आवाज़—सिर्फ़ स्त्री थी
जो पूरी की पूरी

अब कविता के बाहर खड़ी थी
और कविता को ध्वस्त कर रही थी।
○

Jede nächste Zeile war ein bohrender Zweifel
an
Jeder nächsten Zeile

Wenn ich mich nicht irre war es die neunzehnte
Zeile des Gedichts wo die Frau
Kartoffeln kleinschnitt

Runde braune Kartoffeln wurden kleingeschnitten
Im Gedicht drin
Und das Gedicht wurde
Immer stiller immer bestimmter

Ich nehme an es war der Duft frisch geschnittnen
Gemüses
Der die Frau bewahrte
Die nächsten paar Zeilen hindurch

In der zweiundzwanzigsten schien mir
Das Gedicht seinen Platz zu wechseln
Wie ein schnelles Geschoß
War es über die Schultern der Frau
Zu den Teakbäumen hin verschwunden

Danach kam keine Zeile mehr
Kein Wort kam danach im Gedicht
Nur die Frau war da
Nur ihre Schultern
Ihr Rücken
Ihre Stimme - nur die Frau war da
Die jetzt ganz und gar
Außerhalb des Gedichts stand
Und das Gedicht zunichte machte.
❍

(*Tr. from Hindi by Lothar Lutze*)

the trees cast a strange dread
over the poem.

Each following line was a deep foreboding
about each following line.

If I'm not mistaken it was the
nineteenth line of the poem where the woman
was cutting up potatoes.

Round and brown potatoes were being cut
inside the poem
and the poem was growing more silent
more solid all the time.

In my opinion it was the smell of vegetables
being cut
that had preserved the woman
for the next several lines.

Reaching the twenty-second it seemed to me
the poem was shifting
flying like a bullet
past the woman's shoulders
towards the teak trees.

There were no more lines,
no word in the poem beyond that;
there was only the woman
only her shoulders
her back
her voice - only the woman
who now in her entirety
was standing outside the poem
and was breaking the poem apart.
❍

(*Tr. from Hindi by Rupert Snell*)

॥ बनारस ॥

इस शहर में बसन्त
अचानक आता है
जब आता है तो मैंने देखा है
लहरतारा या मड़वाडीह की तरफ़ से

उठता है धूल का एक बवंडर
और इस महान पुराने शहर की जीभ,
किरकिराने लगती है
जो है वह सुगबुगाता है

जो नहीं है वह फेंकने लगता है पचखियाँ
आदमी दशाश्वमेध पर जाता है
और पाता है घाट का आख़िरी पत्थर
कुछ और मुलायम हो गया है

सीढ़ियों पर बैठे बन्दरों की आँखों में
एक अजीब-सी नमी है
और एक अजीब-सी चमक से भर उठा है
भिखारियों के कटोरों का ख़ालीपन

तुमने कभी देखा है
ख़ाली कटोरों में बसन्त का उतरना !
यह शहर इसी तरह खुलता है
इसी तरह भरता

और ख़ाली होता है यह शहर
इसी तरह रोज़-रोज़ एक अनन्त शव
ले जाते हैं कंधे
अँधेरी गली से

चमकती हुई गंगा की तरफ़
इस शहर में धूल

BENARES

In dieser Stadt kommt der
Frühling ganz plötzlich
Wenn er kommt hab ich gesehen wie
Von Lahartara oder Mar Vadih her
Ein Staubwirbel aufsteigt
Und wie die Zunge dieser großen alten Stadt
Zu kribbeln anfängt

Was ist das regt und rührt sich
Was nicht ist sproßt und sprießt
Der Mensch geht ans Dashashwamedh
Und findet daß der letzte Stein des Ghats
Noch etwas weicher geworden ist
In den Augen der Affen die auf den Stufen sitzen
Ist eine seltsame Feuchte
Und mit einem seltsamen Glanz hat auf einmal
Sich die Leere der Bettelschalen gefüllt

Hast du jemals gesehen
Wie der Frühling sich in die leeren Schalen senkt!

So öffnet sich diese Stadt
So füllt sich
Und leert sich diese Stadt
So tragen Schultern Tag für Tag
Einen ewigen Leichnam
Aus einer dunklen Gasse
Zur schimmernden Ganga

In dieser Stadt fliegt
der Staub gemächlich
Gehen die Leute gemächlich

BANARAS

Spring comes to the city
suddenly
When it comes I've seen
dust storms kick up
in Lahartara or Maduvadih
leaving their grit
on the tongue of this great and ancient city

Whatever there is
becomes agitated
Whatever is not
starts to tremble
A man goes to Dashashwamedh Ghat
and finds the last step
smoother
There's a strange moisture
in the eyes of the monkeys sitting on the steps
A strange glow
in the emptiness of the beggar's bowls

Did you ever see
spring spilling out into empty bowls?
Like this the city unfolds
Like this it fills up
and is emptied
Like this day after day
endlessly
a corpse is borne along on shoulders
through dark alleys
toward the shimmering Ganga

In this city dust
rises in the air so slowly
So slowly the people walk

धीरे-धीरे उड़ती है
धीरे-धीरे चलते हैं लोग

धीरे-धीरे बजते हैं घंटे
शाम धीरे-धीरे होती है
यह धीरे-धीरे होना
धीरे-धीरे होने की एक सामूहिक लय

दृढ़ता से बाँधे है समूचे शहर को
इस तरह कि कुछ भी गिरता नहीं है
कि हिलता नहीं है कुछ भी
कि जो चीज़ जहाँ थी

वहीं पर रखी है
कि पानी वहीं है
कि वहीं पर बँधी है नाव
कि वहीं पर रखी है तुलसीदास की खड़ाऊँ

सैकड़ों बरस से
कभी सई-साँझ
बिना किसी सूचना के
घुस जाओ इस शहर में

कभी आरती के आलोक में,
इसे अचानक देखो
अद्‌भुत है इसकी बनावट
यह आधा जल में है

आधा मंत्र में
आधा फूल में है
आधा शव में
आधा नींद में है

आधा शंख में
अगर ध्यान से देखो
तो यह आधा है
और आधा नहीं है

Läuten die Glocken gemächlich
Kommt der Abend gemächlich

Dieses Gemächlichsein
mit seinem verhaltenen Rhythmus
Hält die ganze Stadt so fest zusammen
Daß nichts fällt
Daß nichts schwankt
Daß alles so bleibt
Wo es war
Daß das Wasser bleibt
Daß das Boot dort festgemacht bleibt
Daß die Holzsandale des Tulsidas bleibt
Wo sie seit Jahrhunderten war

Geh mal am Abend
unangekündigt
In diese Stadt hinein
Sieh mal im Artilicht sie
Unvorbereitet
Wie seltsam sie angelegt ist

Halb ist sie im Wasser
Halb in einem Mantra
Ist halb in einer Blume
Halb in einer Leiche
Ist halb im Schlaf
Halb in einer Muschel
Wenn man genau hinsieht
Ist sie halb
Und halb ist sie nicht

Was ist das steht
Ohne jede Säule
Was nicht ist stützen
Höhe Säulen aus Asche und Rauch
Säulen aus Feuer
Und Säulen aus Wasser
Aus Rauch
Aus Wohlgeruch
Säulen aus erhobnen Menschenhänden

so slowly temple bells sound
evening sets in so slowly

All there is
is
so slow
Slow existence is a collective rhythm
binding tight the city
so nothing ever falls away
nothing ever quakes
all that was
is
the water
an anchored boat
the sandals of saint Tulsidas
preserved in the temple for centuries

Enter this city any evening
unobtrusively
See it by the glow of votive lamps
Then you will discover
the splendour of its form
Half in water
Half in sacred chants
Half in flowers
Half in corpses
Half at rest
Half in the sound of the conch
Watch carefully
half is and
half is not

All there is
stands
without support
and all there is not
is supported by tall pillars of ash and light
pillars of fire
and pillars of water
of smoke
of scent
pillars of man's uplifted palms

जो है वह खड़ा है
बिना किसी स्तम्भ के
जो नहीं है उसे थामे हैं
राख और रोशनी के ऊँचे-ऊँचे स्तम्भ

आग के स्तम्भ
और पानी के स्तम्भ
धुएँ के
खुशबू के

आदमी के उठे हुए हाथों के स्तम्भ
किसी अलक्षित सूर्य को
देता हुआ अर्घ्य
शताब्दियों से इसी तरह

गंगा के जल में
अपनी एक टाँग पर खड़ा है यह शहर
अपनी दूसरी टाँग से
बिलकुल बेख़बर

❍

Einer unsichtbaren Sonne opfernd
Steht so seit Jahrhunderten
Im Wasser der Ganga
Diese Stadt auf einem Bein
Ohne sich um das zweite
Im geringsten zu kümmern.
O

(*Tr. from Hindi by Lothar Lutze*)

Offering water in homage
to the sun unseen
The town has stood for centuries this way
on one leg
in the Ganga's waters
unaware of its other leg.
O

(*Tr. from Hindi by Manohar Bandopadhyay, Christi Merrill & Daniel Weissbort*)

वरयाम सिंह

॥ कताब ॥

शुटके थी बैठी हुंदी
सोह एकू तीरे परंदे।
जासा इँहूदे नांई पछेणने आखर
टोल्हा का बी गौर्की तीहा सौह जाणुधा थी।
खोलनी त दूर तेसा छुहणे री बी
पौड़दी नीं थी हीमत कोही।

पर एकसा धियाड़ी
हीमत कौरी आठा साला रे शोहरु
तेसा खोलने री,
कताबा मीह्तर ज़ौह काईद थी
तीऊ गेना तीऊ ज़ाद कौरनी दीनी।

झंणण...ण...ण कौरु कताबा रै बोर्के
जाणना ठाणे रे खुली हुणे दुआर-शाणे,
धूड़ ऊड़ी कताबा का बौक्ता साही,
आछी खोलधै लागे कताबा रै आखर,
ओठ तीहारै चूकते लागे।

दू...र पता नीं कासा जुगा का
इंहदी लागी मीह्नी जेही छेड़,
कताबा सेटा लाई शोहरु आपणे कणेट
पर पटाखरा नीं तीऊ केह शुणू थी।

एक बोकों खौलू, तेऊका दूजौ, चीऊथौ,
चौणधा लागा शुणदा मीह्तर केह।
ज़रूर ईओ सौह गेन हुणा
चौघड़ूहंदा एक-सी जाघा बेशी बेशी।

शोहरुआ, कताबा नीं दे तीरे परंदे बेशी रोहणे
गेन लोड़ी हिलदा-चूकता रौहू
तीऊरी लोड़ी सभी सेटा पूजदी रौही छेड़...
○

Varyam SINGH

DAS BUCH

Schweigend stand es in der Ecke
still, wer weiß seit wieviel Jahren
Des Lesens nicht mächtig erschien es ihnen
Wie eine tonnenschwere Last
Niemand wagte es zu berühren
geschweige denn es aufzuschlagen.

Eines Tages
faßte ein Achtjähriger Mut
es zu öffnen
Das Wissen, das gefangen saß im Buch
zu befreien.

Ein Raunen fuhr durch die Blätter,
als ob bewehrte Türen aufgesprungen wären
Staub flog vom Buch auf, dick wie die Zeit
Die Buchstaben erwachten zum Leben
bewegten die Lippen

Von weitem, aus ferner Zeit
drang eine schwache Stimme
ans Ohr des Jungen fest ans Buch gepreßt,
Doch blieb sie unverständlich

Er schlug die zweite Seite auf, die dritte,
ein Stöhnen entrang sich dem Buch
es mußte vom Wissen stammen
das sich streckte, steif vom langen Sitzen

Laß das Buch nicht in der Ecke verstauben,
mein Sohn:
Wissen braucht Bewegung!
Nur dann vernimmt man seine Stimme.
❍

(*Tr. from Hindi by Barbara Lotz*)

BOOK

Silent it sat in the niche,
Silent, who knows, for how many ages!
Those unable to recognise even letters,
Heavy as a rock it felt to them.
Forget opening it, even to touch
It, not one would dare.

But, one day,
an eight year old boy took courage
To open it;
He tried to unlock the knowledge
Imprisoned within the book.

Srrrr, the pages of the book rustled,
As if the locks and doors of a jail had opened;
The dust rose from the book, as thick as time,
The letters began to open their eyes,
Their lips started to move.

From afar, who knows from what era,
Came a voice so faint;
The boy put his ear to the book,
Something could be heard, but not distinct.

Opened a page, then another, a third,
A moan he heard from inside the book.
Whatever be it, this is knowledge,
Stiff though through sitting at one place.

Son, don't let the book stay in the niche;
Knowledge should always be on the move
And its voice reach one and all.
❍

(*Tr. from Siraji [Himachali] and Hindi by GJV Prasad*)

॥ बोली ॥

ज़िंदगी हुंदा बोली री बी
जेहड़ी हुंदा आपू मंणशा री।

खांदे-पींदे मंणशारी
बोली हुंदा तीहू ज़ेही टंडी-तगड़ी।
गरीबा मंणशा री बोली
तीहू जेही हुंदा हेरनी बमार।

बौड़े मंणशा री बोली का
झौझकता बोली होछे मंणशा री।
बौड़े मंणशा री बोली
सारे हेरुधा सिधा प्रियाशा।
होछे मंणशा री बोली रै
मूंड हुंदा झड़ाखुते निहारै।

कोई आसा हीक, कोई आसा खरै,
कोई रोंहदा झूरी, कोई रोंहदा बशुआ ?
बौड़े मंणशा री बोली
एसा गला रा थोघे नीं हुंदा।
होछे मंणशा री बोली
सभी रै शुणधा खरै।

होछे मंणशा साही
तेसरा बी होऊ जीउणा काठा।
ज़ेहड़े तैंरै बौड़े मंणशा सुआरदा होछो मंणश
तेंढे तेरे बौड़ी री बोली सुआरदा होछे री बोली।
जेहड़े तेरे बौड़ो मंणश बिसुरता होछे, मंणशा
बौड़े री बोली बी पाऊंदा बिसरी होछे री बोली।

मेरी तू सराजा री बोलीऐ,
केह खोजू हां ताह
गला एखो बोली रै फीटणे री !
पता नीं पौहिले कूहण फीटता—बोली कि मंणश !

आहृद ईहदा मांहृ एहड़े मोके
रेड इंडियना परंदे जुल्मा री कथा,
इंका होर माया ज़ेही तहज़ीबा रा तिहास,
फीटणा तीहा रा बोली होंर मंणरो संघा।

मेरी गल ताह बुझणी आई—
खोज़ मांहृ लेड़े, मेरी सराज़ा री बोली ऐ !
○

SPRACHE

Sprachen haben ihr eigenes Leben
So wie die Leute die sie sprechen

Die Sprache der Wohlgenährten
ist wohlgestalt, gesund wie diese
Die der Armen
ist auch wie diese – kränkelnd, siech.

Über die Lippen reicher Leute
geht schwerlich die Sprache armer Menschen
Für die Sprache der Besseren
ist jeder Ort und jedes Ding voll Glanz
Die Sprache der Armen
schlägt sich ans Haupt im Dunkeln.

Wo bleibt das Herz, und wo das Leiden
wo bleibt die Liebe, wo pulsiert das Leben
Die Sprache der Reichen
weiß nichts davon
Die Sprache der Niedrigen
ist das Sprachrohr der gemeinen Sorgen

Nicht nur für die Armen, auch für ihre Sprache
wird Überleben immer schwerer
Wie die Höheren ihren Status durch die Niederen
bekommen
So gewinnt auch die Hochsprache durch die schwachen Sprachen Ansehen
Und wie die Reichen die Armen vergessen
vergißt auch ihre Sprache die Sprachlosen

Sag mir, meine Sprache Siraji,
wer stirbt zuerst:
Die Sprache oder die Leute die sie sprechen?
❍

(Tr. from Hindi by Barbara Lotz)

LANGUAGE

Languages too have their own life
Just as people themselves have.

The language of the well-fed
Is beautiful, healthy, just like them;
That of the poor
Is like them – unhealthy, sick.

From the rich people's tongue
Shies away the language of the poor;
To the language of the high,
Every place, every thing is bright;
The language of the poor
Keeps striking its head in the dark.

Where is the heart, where the suffering,
Where lives love, where does life trust–
The language of the rich
Doesn't feel any of this ...
The language of the low
Hears everybody's distress.

Like the poor, even their tongue
Finds life difficult now;
As the higher-up is made so by the lower
The greater tongue is so by the tongue of the
weak.
Just as the rich person forgets the poor,
Their language forgets that of the meek.

Tell me, the language of my Siraj,
What dies first in this world,
The language or those who speak it?
❍

(Tr. from Siraji and Hindi by GJV Prasad)

॥ ऊड़दी रौहे ॥

चेली आसा तू, त चेली रौह
ऊड़दी रौह तू मेरे सौर्गा मंज़े।
रांबड़ा भेटणा तो मौसम आपणी डिया वै,
पोकली जे भरै नीहचै वेशै मेरी शाणी परदै।

होरी रौ नांई, केलहो आसा हां तैरो पेड़,
तेरी तंगा आसा मेरी ईआ शाणी,
तर चूकते फियाखा साही चूकता मेरे पाच,
मांहबै एथरा बतेराह,
कि तू आपणै समझदा मेरे पेड़ा, मेरे सौगा।
खरी-डारी मंज़े रोंहदा भी
बोहू मौनदा हां तेरे सान
कि कधी नीं रौहू मेरौ सौर्ग बिणही चेली।
मौज़े संघा नडौर ऊड़दी रौही
बोहू नांई त एक चेली।

जेबा सारै होयै बिखरी हूंदे चेली रैं फ़ियाख,
सारै शुहणै डोरी हूंदी चेली रै बोल,
एक भी नीं होयै आपू सेटा शाददौ पेड़,
हां डांहदो आओ तेरी तंगां
आपणै सौर्गा सभी खतरै का दूर।

माड़ी-रांबड़ी जेहड़ी भी बागूरी न्हीं आणी होली तू
मैरै सौर्गा सेटा
मौजै संघा तू ऊड़ती रौह।
घौकली ज़े भरै बेशै तू मेरी शाणी परंधै,
धीजा डाहै
ज़ेभरे तंगा भी चाहली तू
तेरौ आपणौ रोहणौ
ईओ सोगे, ईओ पेड़...
○

FLIEG WEITER

Wenn du ein Vogel bist, so bleibe einer,
flieg weiterhin in meinem Himmel
Günstiges Wetter soll dich begleiten
Wenn du ermüdest ruh dich aus auf meinen Ästen.
Für niemand anders, nur für dich bin ich dein Baum
nur für dich sind meine Äste da.
Wie dein Flügelschlag meine Blätter streift
Genügt es mir zu wissen
daß du mich als deinen Baum annimmst.
Auch inmitten von Schwierigkeiten
bin ich dir zu Dank verpflichtet:
Daß mein Himmel niemals ohne Vögel war,
sie unbeschwert und furchtlos fliegen konnten –
wenn nicht viele, so doch einer, wenigstens

Wenn ringsumher die Vögel Federn lassen
von überall ihr Klagerufen dringt
und nicht ein einziger Baum sie zu sich ruft
hab ich, um deinetwillen,
meinen Himmel frei von Gefahr gehalten.

Ob gute oder schlechte Winde wehten
die dich hierher brachten:
flieg weiterhin in meinem Himmel
mit Freuden
wenn du ermüdest, such dir einen Ast
hab Vertrauen
so lange wie es dir gefällt
gehören dir allein
der Himmel und ich – der Baum.
❍

(*Tr. from Hindi by Barbara Lotz*)

KEEP FLYING

If a bird you are, remain one,
Keep flying in my sky.
You'll get lovely weather to fly in;
When tired sit on my branches.
I am not others', only yours I am the tree;
Only for you are my branches.
Like your beating wings move my leaves;
It is enough for me
That you think of me as your tree.
Even when surrounded by troubles,
I am beholden to you
That never has my sky been bereft of birds –
At ease, without fear, have flown
If not many, atleast one bird.

When fallen all around are feathers of birds,
All around can be heard the birds in fear,
And there be not one tree which calls to itself,
I have, for your sake,
Kept my sky clear of threat.

Good or bad be the wind
That has brought you flying here,
Keep flying in my sky
With pleasure;
When tired, sit on any branch.
Keep faith,
As long as you want
This will be your own,
This sky and this me–the tree.
❍

(*Tr. from Siraji and Hindi by GJV Prasad*)

नितिन नेमा 'सुबोध'

॥ वह औरत ॥

न जाने क्यों सोचना पड़ता है
औरत को
अपने पति का शहर से
सुरक्षित लौट आना
क्यों उठती है हर बार उसके मन में
एक ही बात
कि कहीं कोई
अनहोनी न घट जाए

शहर क्या है उस औरत के लिए
जो सिर्फ यही सोचती है
यह कभी नहीं सोचती वह
कि क्या लेकर लौटेगा उसका पति
शहर से।

○

Nitin Nema SUBODH

DIE FRAU DORT

Keiner weiß, warum Zweifel
Die Frau dort
Bedrängen, ob ihr Mann aus der Stadt
Sicher zurückkehrt.
Warum sorgt sie sich jedesmal
Nur um dies eine,
Ob nicht irgendwo
Etwas Schlimmes geschieht?

Stadt - was ist das für diese Frau,
Die nur an das eine denkt.
Niemals denkt sie an das,
Was ihr Mann mitbringen wird,
Wenn er zurückkehrt
Aus der Stadt.
❍

(Tr. from Hindi by Petra Matusche)

THAT WOMAN

Why does the woman have to think of
Her husband's safe return
From the city
Why only one misgiving arises
In her heart–
Lest something inauspicious should happen

What is the city to the woman
Who thinks of only this
Never thinks of
What will her husband bring from the city
With him
❍

(Tr. from Hindi by Vishnu Khare)

॥ सीताफल ॥

रामू रोज जाता है
अपनी माँ के साथ सीताफल बेचने
दिनभर की थकान के बाद
सीताफल के बदले में मिली
रोटी खाकर सो जाता है

पूछना चाहता हूँ मैं रामू से
कि किस तरह देखता रहता है
वह दिन भर
सीताफलों का बिकना
मैंने देखा नहीं उसे
सीताफल खाते।

○

SITAFRÜCHTE

Jeden Tag geht Ramu
mit seiner Mutter Sitafrüchte verkaufen
nach einem langen Tag voll Mühe
ißt er sein Brot, für Sitafrüchte eingehandelt
geht schlafen –

Fragen möchte ich Ramu
was er sich so denkt
den ganzen Tag
beim Sitafrucht-Verkaufen
Sitafrüchte essen
habe ich ihn nie gesehen.
❍

(Tr. from Hindi by Barbara Lotz)

CUSTARD APPLES

Ramu goes everyday
To sell custard apples with his mother
After the exhaustion of the whole day
He goes to sleep
Having eaten the bread
He earned from custard apples

I wish to ask Ramu
How he looks at the custard apples
Being sold the whole day
I have never seen him eat one
❍

(Tr. from Hindi by Vishnu Khare)

॥ बँटवारा ॥

आज जब घर में
फिर हुआ झगड़ा
और चाचा ने गुस्से में आकर
अलग रहने की कह दी बात
तो लगा कि ख़त्म हो गया
मेरा भविष्य का खज़ाना

कहाँ जाऊँगा मैं बँटवारे में
रात भर सोचता रहा
सुबह चाचा की होगी
या पापा की
शाम मेरी होगी
या सोनू की।

○

TRENNUNG

Als es heute wieder
Zu Hause Krach gab
Und der Onkel im Zorn
Von Trennung sprach
Schien am Ende zu sein was die Zukunft
Für mich auf Lager hatte

Wohin soll ich gehn wenn's zur Trennung kommt
Grübelte ich die Nacht hindurch
Wird der Morgen dem Onkel gehören
Oder dem Vater
Der Abend mir
oder Sonu.
❍

(Tr. from Hindi by Lothar Lutze)

PARTITION

Today when there was
Yet another quarrel in the house
And uncle declared in anger
That he would live separately
I felt that the coffers of my future
Were empty

Where would I be in partition
I thought the whole night
Will the morning belong to uncle
Or to Papa
Will the evening be mine
Or Sonu's
❍

(Tr. from Hindi by Vishnu Khare)

अशोक वाजपेयी

॥ देह की पुकार देह ही सुनता है ॥

न सुनती है हवा,
न पता चल पाता है धूप को–
अँधेरा रहता है, अन्यमनस्क,
और चीज़ें और दृश्य हमेशा की तरह
उद्वासीन–
देह की पुकार,
सुमुखि,
सुनती है
देह ही।
○

Ashok VAJPEYI

DEN RUF DES LEIBES HÖRT NUR DER LEIB

Nicht der Wind hört hin
Nicht die Sonne nimmt Kenntnis
Die Dunkelheit kümmert sich nicht
Und die Dinge und Bilder bleiben wie immer
Gleichgültig -
Den Ruf des Leibes
Meine Schöne
Hört nur
Der Leib.
❍

(Tr. from Hindi by Lothar Lutze)

A BODY IS HEARD BY A BODY

Not by wind
not by the sun
not by the weary dark
not by the indifferent
scenes and objects,
a body's call is
heard, my dear, only
by a body.
❍

(Tr. from Hindi by Krishna Baldev Vaid)

॥ सम्भावना ॥

शहर अब भी एक सम्भावना है
जाड़ों की एक दोपहर
एक व्यस्त सड़क पर
स्वेता के मित्र-हाथों को छूकर मैंने जाना—
मेरे हाथ ज़रा-सी देर बाद भूल गए
स्पर्श को
और हमेशा की तरह अकेले मेरे पास रह गए
ट्रैफिक सिगनल पर रुकी हुई भीड़ में
        कहीं नहीं था
मेरे शरीर के लिए कोई अर्थ,
कहीं नहीं थी वह शान्त निजी गरमी
जिसे मैं अपना प्रेम कह सकता—
एक हल्की-सी अप्रासंगिक हवा थी
जिसे झटका-सा देती हुई रुक गयी एक बस :
हैण्डेल पकड़ते अपने हाथों को
मैंने दुखी होकर देनी चाही अपनी करुणा
तो याद आए वे हाथ,
जो अभी थोड़ी देर पहले उनमें थे,
उनसे जुड़ा वह शरीर जो प्रतिफलित हो चुका है
एक और शरीर में,
और फिर मुझे मिल गए कुछ शब्द
जिन्हें मैं वहाँ रख सकता था
जहाँ पहले वे हाथ थे—
खिड़की के हवा के ठण्डे झोंके से सिहरते हुए
मेरे हृदय में हाथों के लिए
कविता के लिए
अब एक आशा थी

शहर अब भी एक सम्भावना है !
○

MÖGLICHKEIT

Die Stadt ist immer noch eine Möglichkeit
Als ich an einem Wintermittag
Auf einer belebten Straße
Swetas vertraute Hände berührte merkte ich's -
Meine Hände vergaßen nach kurzer Zeit
Die Berührung
Und blieben wie immer allein zurück
In der Menge an der Verkehrsampel war nirgends
Ein Sinn für meinen Körper
War nirgends die stille persönliche Wärme
Die ich meine Liebe hätte nennen können -
Ein leichter unbedeutender Wind ging der
Dem Bus einen Schubs gab als er hielt:
Meine Hände erfaßten den Griff
Ihnen wollte ich, traurig, mein Mitleid schenken
Da fielen mir jene Hände ein
Die eben noch in ihnen lagen
Und der Körper dazu der längst in einem andern
Körper
Sich widerspiegelt
Und dann fand ich ein paar Worte
Die ich dort hätte hinlegen können
Wo vorher jene Hände waren -
In meinem Herzen das im kalten Windstoß
Vom Fenster zitterte war für die Hände
War für ein Gedicht
Jetzt eine Hoffnung

Die Stadt ist immer noch eine Möglichkeit!
❍

(*Tr. from Hindi by Lothar Lutze*)

A POSSIBILITY

The city
is still a possibility -
a winternoon
as I touched the warmth of Sveta's friendly
hands
and realized ...
A little later my hands forgot
the touch and remained with me
lonely as ever.

At the crossroads
among the crowds waiting at the traffic signs
there was no meaning anywhere
for my body;
nowhere the quiet and intimate warmth
I could call my love, my very own.

A bus stopped
and jarred the slight breeze
out of place.
Unhappy, I tried giving over my kindness
to my hands
that held tight to the straps
at the thought of hands those hands
had just held and the body
of those hands
that has found meaning
in another body.
And then I found a few words
that I could put
where those hands had been.
Shivering in the draft from the window
there was now a hope in my heart
for my hands;
The city
is still a possibility.
❍

(*Tr. from Hindi by the poet*)

॥ तलाश ॥

उस अँधेरे रास्ते पर मुझे
दूसरी शताब्दी की एक बच्ची मिली
जो अपने घर पहुँचने की कोशिश में थी

वह रास्ता कुछ भूल-सा गयी थी,
पर उसे विश्वास था कि आगे जाकर
ठीक मोड़ आ जाएगा
और वह जल्दी ही घर पहुँच जाएगी
उसे डर सिर्फ़ यह था कि
उसके देर से पहुँचने के कारण
क्रोध से उसका छोटा भाई
उसकी पोथियाँ तहस-नहस न कर दे

वह कहाँ से आ रही थी
यह मैंने नहीं पूछा
दरअसल शुरू में तो मैंने उसे लक्ष्य ही नहीं किया
पता नहीं कब, मैंने पाया कि वह मेरे साथ है
उसका ख़याल था कि मुझे रास्ता मालूम है—
मैं उसे कैसे बताता कि मुझे भी रास्ते की तलाश है

आगे पेड़ के नीचे बाईसवीं शताब्दी का एक बूढ़ा
बैठा था—
और उसने बताया कि जहाँ हम जाना चाहते थे वहाँ
कई रास्ते जाते हैं
उसने यह भी कहा कि आगे अच्छी धूप होगी
और काफ़ी लोग मिलेंगे, बस्तियाँ भी

तब से हम चल रहे हैं—
बहुत देर से एक घर भी दिख रहा है,
जहाँ हम उम्मीद करते हैं कुछ गुड़-पानी मिलेगा

SUCHE

Auf jenem dunklen Weg traf ich
Ein Kind aus dem zweiten Jahrhundert
Das versuchte nach Hause zu kommen.

Die Kleine hatte sich wohl verlaufen
Aber sie glaubte fest daß ein Stückchen weiter
Die richtige Biegung kommt
Und sie bald nach Hause gelangt.
Sie fürchtete nur daß
Wenn sie zu spät kommt
Ihr kleiner Bruder im Zorn
Ihre Bücher zerreißen könnte.

Woher sie kam
Fragte ich nicht.
In Wirklichkeit hatt ich sie anfangs gar nicht
bemerkt.
Ich weiß nicht wann ich gespürt daß sie neben
mir war.
Sie dachte ich wüßte den Weg -
Wie sollt ich ihr erklären daß auch ich auf der
Suche war nach dem Weg.

Ein Stück weiter saß unter einem Baum ein
alter Mann
Aus dem zweiundzwanzigsten Jahrhundert
Und der meinte wohin wir wollten
Dort führten mehrere Wege hin.
Er sagte auch ein Stück weiter scheint schön
die Sonne
Und gibt's eine Menge Leute und Siedlungen
auch.

Seither gehen wir also -
Seit längerer Zeit ist auch ein Haus in Sicht
Wir hoffen, dort gibt's was zu essen und zu
trinken.

SEARCH

On that dark road, I
met this girl from the second century
trying to get back home.

She'd sort of lost her way
but she believed that just ahead
she'd find the right turning
and she'd soon be home.
She was only afraid
that if she arrived late
her little brother
would destroy her books in a fit of rage.

I didn't ask her
where she was coming from.
In fact, at first,
I didn't notice her at all.
I don't know when
I discovered
she was there alongside me.
She believed that I knew the way -
How could I tell her
that I too was looking for the way?

Up ahead, there under a tree
sat an old man from the twenty-second century.
He told us -
there were many roads that led where we want-
ed
to go.
He told us that
there'd be plenty of sunlight up ahead
and we'd come across
lots of people and bustees too.

उसके पार धूप भी दीखती है–
पर अपनी-अपनी उम्मीद लिये,
फ़िलहाल हम चल रहे हैं–
उस मोड़ की ओर,
उस घर की ओर,
    उस जल और धुप की ओर

○

Dahinter scheint auch die Sonne -
Aber jeder mit seiner Hoffnung
Gehn wir einstweilen
Jener Biegung entgegen
Dem Haus entgegen
Dem Wasser, dem Sonnenlicht.
❍

(*Tr. from Hindi by Lothar Lutze*)

We've been walking ever since ...
For quite some time,
a house has been visible too
where we hoped to get some jaggery and water*
We can also make out sunlight beyond it
but we go on for the time being, each in our own hope -
towards that turning
that house
that water
and that sunlight.
❍

(*Tr. from Hindi by Teji Grover and Arlene Zide*)

* In Bundelkhand, it is customary never to offer just water without also offering a lump of jaggery (brown sugar) to guests, as a mark of courtesy.

Part II

FROM GERMAN INTO INDIAN LANGUAGES AND ENGLISH

Jureck BECKER

NEW YORKER WOCHE

[Auszug]

I

New York fängt gut an, das Flugzeug muß 50 Minuten über Kennedy-Airport kreisen, weil keine Landebahn frei ist. Ich sehe aus dem Fenster und möchte gern ergriffen sein bei dem Gedanken. Das da unten ist also New York. Es ist Abend und regnerisch, ich weiß sofort, daß ich nie zuvor so viele Lampen auf einmal habe brennen sehen. Zu einem besonders hellen Strich denke ich mir das Wort Broadway. Nach zwanzig Minuten Kreisen ist das Licht nur noch das Licht. Nicht einmal mehr die Kinder schauen aus den Fenstern.

Mein Visum verrät mich als jemand, der nicht zur Einwanderung berechtigt ist. Der Paßbeamte studiert es lange. Dann fragt er mich, ob ich wirklich nicht hierzubleiben vorhabe. In seiner Stimme klingt unüberhörbar mit: Na los, sag schon, wir sind hier unter uns. Ich bin glücklich, weil ich ihn sofort verstehe. Ich lächle und schüttle den Kopf, er kann beruhigt sein, ich will nicht bleiben. Denke aber im nächsten Augenblick: Woher will ich das jetzt schon so genau wissen?

यूरेक बेकर

॥ न्यूयॉर्क के पाँच दिन ॥

[कुछ अंश]

न्यूयॉर्क की शुरूआत शानदार होती है—जहाज को केनेडी हवाई अड्डे के ऊपर पचास मिनट तक चक्कर लगाना पड़ता है क्योंकि कोई पट्टी खाली नहीं है। मैं खिड़की के बाहर देखता हूँ और इस विचार से रोमांचित होना चाहता हूँ : तो यह रहा नीचे न्यूयॉर्क। शाम है और बारिश-जैसा है, मुझे फौरन समझ में आ जाता है कि मैंने एक साथ इतनी सारी रोशनियाँ कभी जलते नहीं देखीं। एक खास तौर से जगमगाती पट्टी के लिए मैं ब्रॉडवे शब्द सोचता हूँ। बीस मिनट तक चक्कर काटने के बाद रोशनियाँ सिर्फ रोशनियाँ रह जाती हैं। बच्चे तक एक बार और खिड़कियों के बाहर नहीं देख रहे।

मेरा वीज़ा मुझे एक ऐसे व्यक्ति के रूप में उजागर करता है जिसे आव्रजन का अधिकार नहीं है। पासपोर्ट अधिकारी देर तक उसका अध्ययन करता है। फिर वह मुझसे पूछता है कि क्या मैं सचमुच यहाँ टिकना नहीं चाहता। उसके स्वर में यह साफ-साफ गूँजता है : बताओ यार, यह अपनी आपस की बात है। मैं खुश हूँ कि उसे फौरन समझ जाता हूँ। मैं मुस्कराता हूँ और इन्कार में सिर हिलाता हूँ, वह बेफिक्र रह सकता है, मैं यहाँ नहीं रहना चाहता। लेकिन अगले ही

Jurek BECKER

A WEEK IN NEW YORK

[Extracts]

I

New York starts great - the airplane has to circle over Kennedy Airport for fifty minutes because no runway is open. I look out of the window and would like to be stirred by the thought : So that's New York down there. It is evening and rainy, I know at once that I never before saw so many lights burning at one time. For one particularly bright strip I think of the word Broadway. After twenty minutes of circling the lights are only lights. Not even the children are looking out of the windows anymore.

My visa betrays me as someone who is not authorized to immigrate. The passport official studies it for a long time. Then he asks me whether I really don't intend to stay here. I can't miss hearing in his voice: come on, tell me, this is just between us. I'm glad because I understand him at once. I smile and shake my head, he can be reassured, I don't want to stay. But the next moment I think: How can I be so sure now of knowing that already.

Der Zollbeamte fragt mich, welche Schriften ich bei mir habe. Ich unterdrücke die Antwort, daß ihn das einen Dreck angeht, da ich es seit vielen Jahren von zuhause her gewohnt bin, diese Antwort zu unterdrücken. Ich sehe ihm an, daß er meinen Koffer untersuchen wird, egal was ich sage. Ich zeige ihm meine wenigen Manuskripte und denTalmud, den ich mir als Lektüre für Amerika vorgenommen habe. Sein Blick wird wohlwollend, wahrscheinlich ist er Jude.

II

Von Amerika-Kennern ist mir geraten worden, nie mehr als zwanzig Dollar bei mir zu tragen. Und sie jedem Räuber auf Verlangen sofort zu geben. Kühn aber halte ich 45 Dollar in der Tasche, und den Schlüssel zum Hotelsafe, in dem der Rest liegt, dazu mein Paß, auch ein Wertstück.

Das erste Problem, als ich am Morgen auf die Straße trete: Ich weiß nicht die Umrechnungsformel von Fahrenheit auf Celsius. Es ist kalt, doch ich weiß nicht, wie kalt. Ich weiß nicht, wie sehr ich zu frieren habe. Das ist nicht nur ein Witz. Ich vermute, daß man im gleichen Maße nach dem Thermometer friert, wie man etwa nach der Uhr hungrig wird. Eine Art Opportunismus der Empfindungen.

Ein zweiter mitgebrachter Rat: In New York mußt du laufen, laufen. Die Verwahrlosung der Stadt trifft mich nicht unvorbereitet. Dennoch habe ich das Gefühl, einen Rekord zu sehen: das Äußerste, was an Verwahrlosung rauszuholen ist. Daber meide ich schon die Wege, vor denen ich gewarnt worden bin. Ich stecke Münzen in eine Sammelbüchse, die mir hingehalten wird. Eine junge Frau lächelt unwiderstehlich. Ich habe keine Ahnung, für welchen Zweck sie sammelt. Zehn Minuten lang beobachte ich aus sicherer Entfernung, wer noch Geld spendet. Nicht einer.

In einer stillen Nebenstraße drehe ich mich ein paarmal um, doch niemand folgt mir. Die Feuerleitern an den Hausfassaden sind alte Bekannte, ich kenne sie, seit ich ins Kino gehe. Plötzlich

पल मैं सोचता हूँ : अभी से ही मुझ से यह सही सही जानने का यकीन कैसे ?

चुंगी अधिकारी मुझसे पूछता है, मेरा लिखा क्या क्या मेरे पास है। मैं इस जवाब पर काबू पाता हूँ कि इससे तुम्हारा कोई वास्ता नहीं, ठीक उसी तरह जैसे अपने वतन में मुझे इस जवाब पर काबू पाने की आदत पड़ गई है। मैं उसे देखकर ही समझ जाता हूँ कि वह मेरा सामान देखेगा जरूर, मेरा जवाब जो भी हो। मैं उसे अपनी कुछ पांडुलिपियाँ और तालमूद दिखाता हूँ जिसे मैंने अमेरिका में रहते पढ़ना तय किया है। उसका चेहरा दोस्ताना हो जाता है, शायद वह यहूदी है।

II

अमेरिका विशेषज्ञों द्वारा मुझे सलाह दी गई थी कि मैं कभी अपने साथ बीस डॉलर से ज्यादा लेकर न निकलूँ। और किसी भी राहज़न के माँगने पर वह उसे फ़ौरन दे दूँ। लेकिन मैं दुस्साहस से अपनी जेब में 45 डॉलर रखे हुए हूँ, और होटल की तिजोरी को चाबी भी, जहाँ बाकी रखा हुआ है, मेरे पासपोर्ट के साथ, जो अपने आप में क़ीमती है।

पहली समस्या जब मैं अगली सुबह सड़क पर आता हूँ : मुझे नहीं मालूम कि फारेनहाइट को सेल्सियस में कैसे बदलते हैं। सर्दी बहुत है लेकिन मुझे पता नहीं है कि मुझे कितना क्या ठिठुरना है। यह सिर्फ एक लतीफ़ा नहीं है। मुझे लगता है कि आदमी थर्मामीटर के मुताबिक वैसे ही ठिठुरता है जितनी घड़ी के मुताबिक उसे भूख लगती है। एक तरह का संवेदना का अवसरवाद।

साथ में लाई गई एक दूसरी सलाह : न्यूयॉर्क में तुम्हें चलना पड़ेगा, चलना पड़ेगा। शहर के पतन से मैं ग़ाफ़िल नहीं, फिर भी मुझे लगता है कि मैं एक कीर्तिमान देख रहा हूँ : जितने पतन की कल्पना की जा सकती है, उसका चरम

The customs official asks me what writings I have along with me. I suppress the answer that it's none of his damned business, as I've been accustomed for years to suppress that answer at home. I can tell by looking at him that he will inspect my luggage whatever I say. I show him my few manuscripts and the Talmud, which I decided to read while in America. His glance grows friendly, he is probably a Jew.

II

Experts on America advised me never to carry more than twenty dollars. And to hand them right over to any robber on demand. Daringly, however, I keep $45 in my pocket, and the key to the hotel safe where the rest is lying along with my passport, also an article of value. The first problem when I step out onto the street the next morning: I don't know the conversion equation from Fahrenheit to Celsius. It's cold, but I don't know how cold. I don't know whether I ought to be freezing. That's not just a joke. I suspect that one freezes according to the thermometer to the same extent that one gets hungry according to the clock. A kind of opportunism of sensations.

A second piece of advice I brought along: In New York you have to walk, walk. The degeneration of the city does not catch me unprepared. But I still have the feeling of witnessing a world's record: the most extreme example of degeneration imaginable. Even though I avoid the stretches I have been warned about. I put coins in the collection boxes that are held out to me. A young woman smiles irresistibly. I have no idea for what purpose she is collecting. For ten whole minutes I watch from a safe distance to see who else gives money. Not a single person.

wird der Spaziergang kompliziert. Ich habe die Wahl, mir entweder zwischen einer Unzahl von Mülltonnen und Abfallsäcken den Weg zu bahnen, oder aber die Straßenseite zu wechseln. Dazu müßte ich eine fast mannshohe Schneebarriere überwinden, also kehre ich um. Ich komme zurück auf den Broadway und kaufe mir einen Stadtplan. Ich finde die Stelle, an der ich mit dem Stadtplan stehe.

Nach dem Mittag laufe ich weiter, doch mit Augen, die nur noch eine Art Notdienst leisten. Als ginge der Rest des Tages sie nichts mehr an, als sei kein Platz mehr für neue Bilder. Spät abends im Fernsehen geht das Zeitalter von Muhammad Ali zu Ende, der neue Mann heißt Spinks. Ich denke, daß doch nicht ein neues Zeitalter begründen kann, wem alle Schneidezähne fehlen.

Im Bett weiß ich noch lange nicht, was New York bedeutet. Ich sage mir: Ist doch normal, du bist hier nicht in Jena. Ich finde es selbst ein bißchen lächerlich, ich komme mir verloren vor.

III

Beim Frühstück eine Show im Fernsehen. Es wird dreimal gebetet: Einmal für George Foreman, einen versunkenen Boxer, einmal für ein gelähmtes Mädchen, das blankgeputzt im Rollstuhl vor der Kamera sitzt, einmal für ganz Amerika. Hämische Urteile gehen mir im Kopf herum. Das in Mitteleuropa, denke ich, und dann Kritiker sein. Dann die Frage: Aber haben die denn nicht alles durchgerechnet? Brauchen die denn nicht einen bestimmten Standard, um den Preis für die Werbesekunde zu halten? Am Ende steht längst fest, daß so die wahre Show geht, nur bis zu uns da drüben hat es sich noch nicht herumgesprochen.

Mir fällt auf, wie oft ich plötzlich EUROPA denke. Ein Wort, daß mir zuvor kaum in den Sinn gekommen ist. Bis hierher gab ich mir immer viel detailliertere Namen: Ich war Berliner, ich war

आत्यंतिक चेहरा। हालाँकि मैंने वे रास्ते नहीं लिए जिनके बारे में मुझे चेताया जा चुका था। मैं उन चंदा पेटियों में सिक्के डालता हूँ जो मेरे सामने कर दी जाती हैं। एक नवयुवती दिलकश तरीके से मुस्कराती है। मुझे कुछ पता नहीं है वह काहे के लिए चंदा इकट्ठा कर रही है। दस मिनट तक एक सुरक्षित दूरी से मैं निगाह रखता हूँ कि और कौन पैसा देता है। कोई भी नहीं।

एक सुनसान गली में मैं दो बार मुड़कर देखता हूँ, लेकिन कोई मेरा पीछा नहीं कर रहा। इमारतो के मुहारों पर बनी आग से बचाव की सीढ़ियाँ मेरी पुरानी परिचित हैं, मैं उन्हें तब से जानता हूँ जब से सिनेमा देख रहा हूँ। अचानक मेरी सैर जटिल हो जाती है। मेरे सामने विकल्प यह है कि या तो कचरा पेटियों और कूड़े के थैलों के असंख्य के बीच से रास्ता बनाऊँ या सड़क पार कर लूँ। वैसा करने के लिए मुझे आदमी जितने ऊँचे बर्फ के अड़ंगे से पार पाना होगा लिहाज़ा मैं मुड़ लेता हूँ। वापस ब्रॉडवे आता हूँ और शहर का नक्शा खरीदता हूँ। मैं वह जगह खोज लेता हूँ जहाँ शहर का नक्शा लिए हुए मैं खड़ा हूँ।

दोपहर बाद मैं और घूमता हूँ लेकिन ऐसी आँखें लिए हुए जो सिर्फ एक तरह की आपात् सेवा निभाती हैं। जैसे बाकी दिन से उनका कोई सरोकार न हो, जैसे नए अक्सों के लिए अब और जगह न बची हो। देर शाम को टेलीविज़न पर मुहम्मद अली का युग समाप्त होता है, नए विजेता का नाम स्पिंक्स है। मैं सोचता हूँ कि किसी नए युग की स्थापना शायद ही ऐसे व्यक्ति से हो जिसके सामने के सारे दाँत टूटे हुए हों।

बिस्तर में मैं अब तक नहीं जान पाया हूँ कि न्यूयॉर्क का मतलब है क्या। मैं अपने से कहता हूँ : ठीक ही तो है, तुम यहाँ सेना में तो हो नहीं। खुद मुझे यह कुछ हास्यास्पद लगता है, लगता है मैं खो गया हूँ।

On a quiet street I turn around a couple of times, but no one is following me. The fire escapes on the building facades are old acquaintances. I've known them since I started going to movies. Suddenly my stroll gets complicated. I have the choice either of making my way through an immense number of trash cans and sacks of garbage or of going across the street. To do that I'd have to overcome a man-high barrier of snow, so I turn around. I come back to Broadway and buy a city map. I find the place where I'm standing with my city map.

After lunch I walk on, but with eyes that perform only a kind of emergency service. As though the rest of the day were of no concern to them, as though there were no more room for new images. Late in the evening on television the Age of Muhammad Ali comes to an end, the new champion is named Spinks. A new age can hardly be founded, I think to myself, by someone who has lost all his front teeth.

In bed I still am far from knowing what New York means. I tell myself: That's normal, you are not in Jena. I find it a little ridiculous myself, I feel lost.

III

At breakfast a television program. Three prayers are said: one for George Foreman, a fallen boxer, one for a crippled girl sitting all dressed up in a wheelchair in front of the camera, one for all America. Spiteful opinions whirl around in my head. Imagine that in Central Europe, I think, and then being a critic. Then the question: But haven't they figured all that out? Don't they need a certain standard to maintain the price for each second of advertising? In the end it's quite certain that that's how a real show is done, only the word about it hasn't made it back to the continent.

Köpenicker. DDR-Bürger. Ein Deutscher - das kam mir schon exotisch vor. Und auf einmal bin ich Europäer, nicht weniger.

Du mußt laufen. Wenn ich etwas kaufen möchte und viel Zeit dafür brauche mit meinem Englisch, hat man Geduld mit mir. Es ist keine Schande hier, nicht gut Englisch zu können. Im Reisebüro vor mir zum Beispiel ein steinalter Mann und seine Frau, die nach Las Vegas möchten. Ihr Englisch ist verwegen, das höre selbst ich, schlechter noch als meins. Und dabei keine Frage, daß sie Amerikaner sind, man sieht es schon an ihren Jacken.

Oben auf dem Empire-State-Building stecke ich ein paarmal 10 Cents in das Fernrohr und suche im Dunst die weltberühmten Sehenswürdigkeiten. Auf der Balustrade sehe ich ein Herz, gemalt mit dickem blauen Filzstift. Ich denke sofort an zu Hause, an Baumrinden, an Kiefern im Wäldchen hinter der Brücke, an ein bestimmtes Mädchen. Als liege meine Erinnerung auf der Lauer, als sei ihr kein Anstoß zu gering. Später lese ich die Inschrift in dem blauen Herz: 2. Februar 1978, Harry + Henry.

Laufen. Auf der Straße nach dem Mittag spricht mich eine Schwarze an, in meinem Ledermantel, mit meinem Pelzkragen. Sie lädt mich ein zu sich. Sie nennt einen Preis, der wie ein Geschenk ist, gemessen am Preis fürs Hotelzimmer. Sie ist hübsch. Ich habe noch nie eine schwarze Frau gehalten. Nur manchmal daran gedacht, zuletzt auf dem Herflug. Zweimal drehe ich mich um nach ihr, sie hat mich schon vergessen.

III

नाश्ते के वक्त टेलिविजन पर एक कार्यक्रम। तीन दुआएँ की जातीं हैं : एक बार जॉर्ज फोरमैन के लिए जो एक हारा हुआ मुक्केबाज़ है, एक बार एक अपंग लड़की के लिए जो कैमरे के सामने एक पहिएदार कुर्सी पर सजी-सँवरी बैठी हुई है, एक बार सारे अमेरिका के लिए। मेरे दिमाग़ में दुर्भावनापूर्ण विचार मँडराने लगते हैं। ऐसा मध्य यूरोप में होना, मैं सोचता हूँ और अपना आलोचक होना। फिर यह सवाल : क्या उन्होंने इस सब पर सोचा-विचारा नहीं है ? क्या विज्ञापनों की प्रति सेकंड कीमत को बनाए रखने के लिए उन्हें एक स्तरविशेष की सरकार नहीं है ? आखिर में तो यह पक्का हो जाता है कि असली कार्यक्रम इसी तरह होता है, सिर्फ यह बात वहाँ हम तक पहुँची नहीं है।

मैं गौर करता हूँ कि अचानक कितनी बार मैं यूरोप सोचता हूँ। एक ऐसा शब्द जो शायद ही पहले कभी दिमाग़ में आया हो। इससे पहले मैंने खुद विशिष्ट नाम दिए थे : मैं बर्लिनवाला था, मैं कोपेनिकाया था, जर्मन जनवादी गणतंत्री था, एक जर्मन–यह भी मुझ अजीबोग़रीब लगता था। और अचानक मैं यूरोपियन हो गया हूँ, इससे कम नहीं।

तुम्हें चलना पड़ता है। जब मैं कुछ खरीदना चाहता हूँ और अपनी अंग्रेजी में मुझे उसके लिए बहुत वक्त लगता है तो लोग मेरे प्रति धीरज रखते हैं। अंग्रेजी में अच्छी तरह न बोल पाना यहाँ कोई बदनामी की बात नहीं। उदाहरण के लिए यात्रा कार्यक्रम में मेरे आगे एक जराजीर्ण सज्जन और उनकी पत्नी, जो लास वेगस जाना चाहते हैं। मैं खुद सुन सकता हूँ कि उनकी अँग्रेजी माशाअल्ला है, मुझसे भी कहीं खराब, और कोई शुब्हा ही नहीं कि वे अमेरिकी हैं, उनके कोट देखकर ही कोई कह सकता है।

एम्पायर स्टेट बिल्डिंग की चोटी पर मैं दूरबीन में दो बार दस सेंट के सिक्के डालता हूँ और धुंध के बीच में विश्वविख्यात

I notice how often I suddenly think EUROPE. A word that previously hardly ever occurred to me. Upto this point had always given myself more specific names: I was a Berliner, a Köpenicker. Citizen of the GDR. A German - even that seemed exotic to me. And all of a sudden I'm a European, nothing less.

You have to walk. When I try to buy something and need a lot of time with my English to do it, they are patient with me. It's no disgrace here not to be able to speak English well. For example, in the travel bureau ahead of me a man as old as the hills and his wife, who want to go to Las Vegas. I myself can hear that their English is foolhardy, worse even than mine. Still, there's no question that they are Americans, you can tell just by their coats.

On top of the Empire State State Building I put ten cents in the telescope a couple of times and look through the haze for the world famous sights. On the balustrade I see a heart, drawn with a thick blue felt pen. I think of home at once, of tree trunks, of pines in the woods behind the bridge, of a certain girl. As though my memory were on lookout, as though no prod were too little for it. Later I read the inscription in the blue heart: 2 February 1978, Harry + Henry.

Walk. On the street after lunch a black girl speaks to me, in my leather coat, with my fur collar. She invites me to her place. She mentions a price that's like a gift, compared to the price of the hotel room. She is pretty. I've never held a black woman in my arms. Only thought about it at times, most recently on the flight over. Twice I look back at her, she's already forgotten me.

VI

Im Omnibus sehe ich, wie eine Frau ihre Brille mit einer Fünf-Dollar-Note putzt. Ich vermute, in New York gewöhnt man sich schneller als anderswo ab, sich über Dinge zu wundern, die man nie zuvor gesehen hat. Zum Beispiel, schon vor zwei Tagen, als ich aus dem Eishockey-Stadion kam, fand ich nichts dabei, als der Taxifahrer mich fragte, wie die Motherfucker gespielt hätten. Ich wußte sofort, daß er die New York Rangers meinte, und ich antwortete: beschissen.

Man nimmt mich mit zum Gottesdienst nach Harlem.

Sieh dich vor in Harlem. Geh nicht durch die Straßen, als hättest du Angst. Denn du weißt: gerade die Furchtsamen werden von den Hunden gebissen. Verbirg also dein klopfendes Herz. Viel lieber als in Harlem zu sein, möchtest du es doch hinter dir haben? Die in Harlem haben keine Hemmungen, vergiß das keinen Augenblick, in Harlem fühlen sie sich stark. Und dann du mit deinem Pelzkragen. Und streunende Hunde soll es geben, die sollen sich zu Rudeln zusammengetan haben, die sollen vor nichts zurückschrecken nach vierzig Tagen Frost.

Die Kirche ist ein ehemaliges Kino. Reverend Walker ist eine bekannte Persönlichkeit. Der Raum ist bunt. Die Besucher sind mit aller Kraft angezogen. Mein Bekannter sagt, sie leben von Sonntag zu Sonntag. Auf dem Podium vorne, das den Eindruck einer Bühne ohne Vorhang macht, stehen drei Chöre. In Kostümen wie College-Teams: Grün-Gold, Grün-Weiß, Braun-Braun. Ich tippe auf Braun-Braun. Ich rufe mich zur Ordung, indem ich mich daran erinnere, daß meine Schwierigkeiten mit der Kirche gewiß nicht an Harlem liegen.

Der Gesang geht los. Ich warte ungeduldig auf diese Stimmung. Ich habe Mahalia Jackson im Ohr und Little Brother Montgommery und Sister Rosetta, aber die bleiben weit. Trotzdem ganz gut,

दृश्य ढूँढता हूँ। जंगले पर मैं एक दिल देखता हूँ जो नीले मोटे फैल्ट पैन से बनाया गया है। मैं सहसा घर के बारे में सोचता हूँ, पेड़ों के तनों, पुल के पीछे वनों के चीड़ों, एक खास लड़की के बारे में। जैसे मेरी स्मृति ताक लगाए ही बैठी थी। जैसे उसके लिए कोई उकसावा छोटा न हो। बाद में उस नीले दिल के बीच की इबारत पढ़ता हूँ : 2 फरवरी 1978, हैरी + हेनरी।

घूमना। दोपहर के बाद सड़क पर एक काली लड़की चमड़े के कोट में, रोएँदार गिरेबान वाली मुझसे बात करती है। वह मुझे अपने ठिकाने का निमंत्रण देती है। जो रेट वह बतलाती है वह मेरे होटल के कमरे के किराए के सामने तोहफ़ा जैसा लगता है। वह खूबसूरत है। मैंने अब तक किसी काली औरत को बाँहों में नहीं लिया है। सिर्फ कभी कभी उस पर सोचा है, एकदम हाल में यहाँ की उड़ान के दौरान। मैं मुड़कर दो बार उसकी तरफ देखता हूँ, वह मुझे पहले ही भूल चुकी है।

IV

बस में मैं देखता हूँ कैसे एक औरत अपना चश्मा एक पाँच डॉलर के नोट से पोंछ रही है। मुझे लगता है कि दूसरी जगहों के मुकाबले न्यूयॉर्क में आदमी उन चीजों से चकित होना जल्दी बंद कर देता है जो उसके पहले उसने कभी नहीं देखी थीं। मिसाल के तौर पर दो दिन पहले जब मैं आइस हॉकी स्टेडियम से बाहर निकला तो जब टैक्सी वाले ने मुझसे पूछा कि मादरचोदों ने कैसा खेला तो मैंने ज़रा भी नहीं सोचा। मैं फौरन समझ गया कि उसका मतलब न्यूयॉर्क रेंजर्स की टीम से है और मैंने जवाब दिया : हग दिया।

मुझे हार्लेम के एक गिरजाघर में इबादत के वक्त ले जाया जाता है।

होशियार रहना हार्लेम में। सड़कों पर ऐसे नहीं चलना जैसे तुम डरे हुए हो क्योंकि तुम्हें पता है : डरने वालों को

VI

On the bus I see a woman cleaning her glasses with a five dollar bill. I suppose that in New York you quit being surprised faster than anywhere else at things you never saw before. For example, two days ago, as I was coming out of the ice hockey stadium, I didn't think anything of it when the taxi driver asked me how the motherfuckers had played. I knew at once that he meant the New York Rangers, and I answered: Like shit.

I am taken to a church service in Harlem.

Watch out in Harlem. Don't walk through the streets as though you were afraid. Because you know: It's the ones who are afraid who get bitten by dogs. So hide your pounding heart. Much rather than be in Harlem, you'd like to have it behind you. In Harlem they have no inhibitions, don't forget that for a moment, in Harlem they feel strong. And you with your fur collar. And they say stray dogs are afraid of nothing after forty days of freezing weather.

The church is a former movie theater. Reverend Walker is a well-known personality. The room is colorful. The visitors are dressed up to the hilt. My aquaintance says they live from Sunday to Sunday. On the podium at the front, which gives the impression of a stage without a curtain, stand three choirs. In costumes like college teams: green-gold, green-white, brown-brown. My bet is brown-brown. I admonish myself by reminding myself that my difficulties with churches are not due to Harlem.

The singing begins. I wait impatiently for this mood. I have Mahalia Jackson in my ear and Little Brother Montgomery and Sister Rosetta, but they remain far away. It's pretty good anyway, I think, there's a little bit of it still there, I think like a concertgoer.

denke ich, ein bißchen ist immerhin da, denke ich wie ein Konzertbesucher.

Reverend Walker predigt. Eine Weile versuche ich gar nicht erst, ihn zu verstehen. Ich sehe der Predigt zu. Er weiß, wie man sich zu bewegen hat so vorne. Er arbeitet viel mit Blicken. Seine Pausen sitzen wie Pausen in einem Musikstück. Aber die Besucher sind echt, das schwöre ich. Sie leben von Sonntag zu Sonntag.

Nach einiger Mühe finde ich dann die Eingangstür zur Predigt. Reverend Walker spricht über die Allmacht des Herrn. Er berichtet von einem Beispiel, das ich nicht verstehe. Sein zweites Bild macht mir weniger Mühe: Der Herr kann Krebs heilen. Reverend Walker kennt da einen Fall, an dem die besten Spezialisten sich die Zähne ausgebissen haben. Erst die Hinzuziehung des Herrn brachte Rettung. Er trifft sich heute noch manchmal mit der Frau, sie wohnt nicht weit. Ich denke, daß in einer Gegend, wo Arztkosten unerschwinglich sind, solche Beweise ganz überzeugend klingen.

Eindruck macht mir, daß bei der Predigt kein atemloses Schweigen herrscht. Andauernd wird dazwischengerufen. Doch nie, finde ich dann heraus, eine Ansicht, eine entgegengesetzte gar. Immer sind es Worte, die wie Rückenwind für den Reverend sein sollen: Ja, ja! Oder: Genau so ist es! Oder: Oh, Lord! Oder: Wie wahr du sprichst!

Auf einmal sagt der Reverend: Er sieht, daß wir heute eine ganze Anzahl Gäste unter uns haben. Die Gäste sollen aufstehen. Jeder von ihnen soll sagen, wer er ist und woher er kommt. Als ich an der Reihe bin, nenne ich mein Herkunftsland: Germany. Obwohl ich gar nicht weiß, was das bedeutet. Die Leute vor mir, Westdeutsche, haben auch gesagt: Germany. Und ich hatte das Gefühl, daß mein korrektes GERMAN DEMOCRATIC REPUBLIC wie eine Zurechtweisung klingen würde, die nicht hierhergehört.

ही कुत्ते काटते हैं। इसलिए अपने धड़कते दिल को छिपाओ। हार्लेम मे होने के बहुत बजाए तुम उसे अपने पीछे नहीं हुआ चाहते ? हार्लेम मे उन्हें कोई लिहाज़ नहीं है, यह एक लम्हे के लिए भी मत भूलना, हार्लेम में वे खुद को ताकतवर महसूस करते हैं। और फिर तुम अपने फर वाले कॉलर के साथ। और कहते हैं कि वहाँ आवारा कुत्ते हैं, जो कहते हैं कि झुंडों में घूमते हैं, और कहते हैं कि चालीस दिन की कड़ाकेदार सर्दी के बाद उन्हें कुछ से डर नहीं लगता।

गिरजाघर एक भूतपूर्व सिनेमा है। रेवरेंड वॉकर एक विख्यात व्यक्तित्व हैं। कमरा रंगबिरंगा है, श्रद्धालु सिर से पैर तक सजे हुए हैं। मेरा परिचित कहता है कि वे एक इतवार से दूसरे इतवार को जीते हैं। सामने चबूतरे पर, जो एक बिना पर्दे के रंगमंच जैसा लगता है, तीन गायक-समूह खड़े हुए हैं। कालेज टीमों जैसी पोशाकें : हरी-सुनहरी, हरी-सफेद, बदामी-बदामी। मुझे बदामी-बदामी जँचते हैं। मैं खुद को यह याद दिलाकर ताकीद करता हूँ कि गिरजों को लेकर मेरी दिक्कतें हार्लेम की वजह से नहीं है।

भजन शुरू होते हैं। मैं इस मनःस्थिति की अधीर प्रतीक्षा कर रहा हूँ। मेरे कानों में महालिया जैक्सन है और लिटिल ब्रदर मॉन्ट्गोमरी और सिस्टर रोज़ेटा, लेकिन वे बहुत दूर ही रहते हैं। फिर भी बहरहाल ठीक ठाक है, मैं सोचता हूँ, उसका थोड़ा बहुत तो अभी भी है, मैं किसी संगीत कार्यक्रम के श्रोता की तरह सोचता हूँ।

रेवरेंड वॉकर प्रवचन करते हैं। कुछ देर तक मैं उन्हें समझने की कोशिश नहीं करता। मैं प्रवचन को देखता हूँ। वे निगाहसाज़ी से बहुत काम लेते हैं, बीच बीच में उनका रुकना किसी संगीत रचना के विरामों की ररह होता है। लेकिन श्रद्धालुगण सच्चे हैं, इसकी मैं कसम खाता हूँ। वे एक इतवार से दूसरे इतवार जीते हैं।

कुछ प्रयास के बाद मुझे प्रवचन का प्रवेशद्वार प्राप्त होता है। रेवरेंड वॉकर ईश्वर की सर्वशक्तिमत्ता के विषय में बोल रहे हैं। वे एक ऐसे उदाहरण का ब्यौरा देते हैं जिसे मैं समझ नहीं पाता। उनका दूसरा उदाहरण मेरे लिए कम परेशानी

Reverent Walker preaches. For a while I don't even try to understand him. I observe the sermon. He knows how you have to move at the front there. He works a lot with glances. His pauses sit like rests in a piece of music. But the churchgoers are genuine, that I swear. They live from Sunday to Sunday.

After some effort I find the entrance door to the sermon. Reverend Walker is talking about the omnipotence of Lord. He reports about an example that I don't understand. His second example causes me less trouble: The Lord can heal cancer. Reverend Walker knows of a case about which the best specialists tore out their hair. Only when the Lord was called in did salvation ensue. Even today he still meets with the woman sometimes, she doesn't live far away. I think in a place where people can't afford medical costs such proofs sound quite convincing.

I am impressed that there is no breathless silence prevailing during the sermon. Shouts constantly interrupt it. But never, I find out then, an opinion, least of all one in opposition. It's always words that are supposed to be like a wind at his back for the reverend: Yes, yes! Or: That's the way it is! Or: Oh, Lord! Or: You're telling the truth!

Suddenly the reverend says he sees that we have a good number of guests with us today. The guests are supposed to rise. Each of them is to say who he is and where he comes from. When it's my turn, I name the land I come from: Germany. Although I don't know what that means at all. The people ahead of me, West Germans, also said: Germany. And I had the feeling that my correct GERMAN DEMOCRATIC REPUBLIC would sound like a reprimand that doesn't belong here.

There is singing again. Everybody holds hands. Before I can feel like a hole in the chain my two hands are taken by my two neighbours. I move my lips soundlessly because I don't

Wieder wird gesungen. Alle greifen sich an den Händen. Bevor ich mir wie ein Loch in der Kette vorkommen kann, werde ich von meinen beiden Nachbarn an meinen beiden Händen gehalten. Ich bewege lautlos die Lippen, weil ich nicht der einzige sein will, der den Text nicht kennt. Auch die Westdeutschen singen, aber sie sind Theologen. Mit meinem Tip liege ich genau richtig, Braun-Brau. sind die besten. Ich weiß, daß ich nicht hätte herkommen dürfen.

पैदा करता है। सिरजनहार कैंसर ठीक कर सकता है। रेवरेंड वॉकर एक ऐसा केस जानते हैं जिसने सभी विशेषज्ञों को लोहे के चने चबवा दिए थे। सिर्फ जब सिरजनहार को पुकारा गया तभी उद्धार हुआ। आज भी वे उस महिला से मिलते हैं जो यहाँ से दूर नहीं रहती है। मैं सोचता हूँ कि एक ऐसे इलाके में जहाँ इलाज की कीमतें लोगों के बूते के बाहर हैं ऐसे प्रमाण नितांत विश्वसनीय लगते हैं।

मैं इस बात से प्रभावित होता हूँ कि प्रवचन के दौरान कोई निःश्वास शांति नहीं रहती। चिल्लाहटें लगातार रुकावटें डालती हैं। लेकिन, मुझे पता चलता है, उनमें कभी कोई राय नहीं होती, असहमति में तो एक भी नहीं। हमेशा वे ऐसे शब्द होते हैं जो मानो रेवरेंड को पीछे से सहारा देने वाले झोंके हों : हाँ, हाँ ! यह, बिल्कुल यही बात है ! या, या मालिक ! या : सच्ची बात बोल रहे हो !

अचानक रेवरेंड कहते हैं : मैं देखता हूँ कि आज हमारे बीच खासी तादाद में मेहमान हैं। मेहमानों से खड़े होने की अपेक्षा की जाती है। उनमें से हर एक को बताना है कि वह कौन है और कहाँ से आया है। जब मेरी बारी आती है तो जिस देश से मैं आया हूँ उसका नाम बताता हूँ : जर्मनी, हालाँकि मैं नहीं जानता कि उसका कोई मतलब है भी या नहीं। मेरे आगे बैठे पश्चिम जर्मन लोगों ने भी कहा था : जर्मनी। और मुझे लगा कि मेरा सही सही **जर्मन जनवादी गणतंत्र** कहना एक ऐसी फटकार की तरह लगेगा जिसके लिए यहाँ कोई जगह नहीं है।

फिर भजन होते हैं। हर व्यक्ति दूसरे के हाथ पकड़े हुए है। इससे पहले कि मैं जंजीर की कड़ी जैसा महसूस करूँ, मेरे दोनों पड़ोसियों द्वारा मुझे मेरे दोनों हाथों से पकड़ लिया जाता है। मैं बेआवाज अपने होठ हिलाता हूँ क्योंकि मैं ही वह अकेला नहीं होना चाहता जिसे शब्द नहीं मालूम। पश्चिमी जर्मन भी गाते हैं लेकिन वे धर्मशास्त्री लोग हैं। मेरा अंदाजा ठीक था, बदामी-बदामी ही सबसे बढ़िया हैं। मुझे पता है मुझे यहाँ नहीं आना चाहिए था।

want to be the only one who doesn't know the words. The West Germans are singing too, but they are theologians. I was right about my bet, brown-browns are the best. I know I ought not to have come here.

VII

ABFAHRT

Du kommst in eine neue Stadt, du hast vorher viel gehört, dein Kopf ist voll von mitgebrachten Richtersprüchen. Du stellst fest, daß sich jedes deiner Vorurteile belegen läßt, ohne Schwierigkeiten, an jedem einzelnen ist was dran. Du sammelst Beobachtungen wie Beweise. Du willst dir zeigen, wie gut du die Stadt schon kanntest, bevor du dort gewesen bist. Du schaffst es. Das Resultat ist eine verlorene Woche, die sonstwas hätte werden können.

Im letzten Autobus fragst du dich, was dir eigentlich einfällt, mit einer Strichliste durch die Straßen zu ziehen, den Bleistift zum Abhaken in der Hand: Richtig, Armut. Richtig, Rassenprobleme. Richtig, Kriminalität. Eine tadellose Reihe von Rubriken. Was, so fragst du dich, hast du dich unentwegt abzuplagen für das längst Bewiesene? Wer hat dich beauftragt mit diesem todlangweiligen Job? Dein Gewissen? Lächerlich. Kommst hier an mit dem Vorsatz, nicht nur die Oberfläche zu sehen, und die Folge davon ist: du siehst gar nichts.

Und jetzt ärgerst du dich, daß du nicht eine Sekunde versunken bist in der aufregenden Stadt. Daß du dich nie hast fallen lassen, wo soviel Gelegenheit war. Dabei hast du sie nicht etwa übersehen, die Gelegenheiten. Jedesmal hast du den Schritt beschleunigt, bloß weg. Ohne nachzudenken, hast du gedacht: Wo soll das hinführen? Und jetzt fragst du dich, wohin das führen soll. In den langweiligen Augenblicken hast du die Augen schön offengehalten. Du wolltest immer nur sehen, was alle schon wissen, und nie, was keiner weiß. Nie warst du aufgeregt.

VII

प्रस्थान

तुम एक नए शहर मे आते हो, तुमने उसके बारे में पहले से बहुत कुछ सुन रखा है, तुम्हारा दिमाग साथ लाए हुए फैसलों से भरा हुआ है। तुमने तय कर रखा है कि तुम्हारा हर पूर्वग्रह बिना किसी परेशानी के साबित हो सकता है, उनमें से हर एक में कुछ दम है। तुम मुआयनों को सबूतों की तरह इकट्ठा करते हो। तुम खुद को बताना चाहते हो कि आने से पहले ही तुम इस शहर को कितनी अच्छी तरह से जानते थे। तुम कामयाब होते हो। नतीजा है एक बर्बाद हफ्ता, जो कुछ और भी हो सकता था।

आखिरी क्षण में तुम खुद से पूछते हो, आखिर तुम सोचते क्या हो, सड़कों पर एक फेहरिस्त लिए गुजरते हुए, हाथ में एक पेंसिल निशान लगने के लिए : गरीबी, सही। नस्लवादी समस्याएँ, सही। अपराध, सही। अनुष्ठानों की एक बेदाग़ सूची। तो तुम खुद से पूछते हो कि जो बहुत पहले सिद्ध किया जा चुका है उसकी तुम लगातार चिंता क्यों करते हो ? किसने तुम्हें यह जानलेवा उबाऊ काम सौंपा ? तुम्हारी अंतरात्मा ने ? हास्यास्पद। यहाँ आते हो यह संकल्प लेकर कि सिर्फ वही नहीं देखोगे जो सतह पर है, और नतीजा क्या है : कुछ भी नहीं देखते तुम।

और अब तुम खुद पर नाराज होते हो कि तुम इस रोमांचक शहर के साथ एक लम्हे के लिए भी यकसार नहीं हुए। कि तुम्हें कितना मौका मिला लेकिन तुमने अपने को मुक्त नहीं छोड़ा। और तुमने उन मौकों की सिर्फ अनदेखी ही नहीं की। तुमने हर बार अपनी रफ्तार बढ़ा दी, लेकिन दूसरी दिशा में। बगैर विचार किए, तुमने सोचा : यह कहाँ ले जा सकता है ? और अब तुम खुद से पूछते हो, कहाँ ले जाएगा यह सब ? तुमने उन उबाऊ लम्हों में भी अपनी आँखें

VII

DEPARTURE

You arrive in a new city, you have heard a lot about it before, your head is full of preconceived judgements that you brought along. You determine that each of your prejudices can be proven without any trouble, there's something to each one of them. You collect observations like proofs. You want to show yourself how well you already knew the city before you were there. You succeed. The result is a lost week that could have become something else.

In the last bus you wonder what you are thinking of really, traveling through the streets with a check list, in your hand a pencil for checking things off: Poverty, right. Racial problems, right. Criminality, right. An impeccable list of rubrics. So you wonder why you constantly worry yourself with what is long since proven. Who assigned you this deadly boring job? Your conscience? Ridiculous. You arrive here with the resolution to see not just what's on the surface and the result of that is: You see nothing at all.

And now you are annoyed at yourself that you didn't become absorbed for a second in this exciting city. That you didn't let yourself go when you had such opportunities. And you didn't just overlook them, those opportunities. You increased your pace every time, but in the other direction. Without reflecting, you thought: What might that lead to? And now you ask yourself where that will lead. You kept your eyes open in those boring moments. You just wanted to see what everybody knows already and never what nobody knows. You never got excited.

Plötzlich fürchtest du um deine Fähigkeit, aufgeregt zu sein. Stellst dir jemanden vor, der sich pausenlos vor dem Überraschenden hütet. Der sich alles im Voraus ausrechnet. Der dann versucht, so zu leben, daß die vorher gemachte Rechnung stimmt.

Vielleicht komme ich irgendwann nocheinmal nach New York.

Vorerst fahre ich mit dem Bus zum Flughafen La Guardia. Ich habe einen Fensterplatz erwischt und mache die Augen zu, sobald Schwarze zu sehen sind, verwahrloste Straßen, Polizisten, Weiße, Reklameschilder, Verkehrschaos.

O

खूब खोलकर रखीं। तुम हमेशा वही देखना चाहते थे जो सबको पहले से ही मालूम है, और वह कभी नहीं जो कोई नहीं जानता। तुम कभी उद्वेलित नहीं हुए।

अचानक तुम उद्वेलित होने की अपनी क्षमता को लेकर चिंतित हो जाते हो। तुम अपने सामने एक ऐसे आदमी की कल्पना करते हो जो आश्चर्यों को लेकर हमेशा चौकन्ना रहता है। जो हमेशा सब कुछ पहले ही समझ लेता है। जो फिर उसी तरह से रहना चाहता है जो पहले किए गए हिसाब के मुताबिक हो।

शायद मैं कभी किसी वक्त न्यूयॉर्क लौटूँगा।

लेकिन पहले मैं बस से ला गार्दिया हवाई अड्डे जा रहा हूँ। मुझे खिड़की के पास वाली एक जगह मिल गई है। और मैं अपनी आँखें फौरन बंद कर लेता हूँ जैसे ही दिखने लगते हैं, काले, गंदी सड़कें, पुलिसवाले, गोरे, इश्तहारों की तख्तियाँ, यातायात का प्रलय।

O

(विष्णु खरे द्वारा
ए. लेस्ली विलसन के अँग्रेजी अनुवाद की मदद से मूल जर्मन से अनूदित)

Suddenly you are anxious about your ability to become excited. You imagine someone who is always on guard against surprises. Who figures out everything in advance. Who then tries to live in a way that affirms the previously made calculation.

Perhaps I'll come back to New York sometime or other.

But first I'm taking the bus to La Guardia Airport. I managed to get a window seat and I shut my eyes as soon as Blacks can be seen, filthy streets, policemen, whites, billboards, chaotic traffic.

O

(Tr. by A Leslie Willson)

Hans Christoph BUCH

REDE DES TOTEN COLUMBUS AM TAG DES JÜNGSTEN GERICHTS

[Auszug]

Epilog

»Are U Xe Oher Tzih...«
»Aqui acaban las historias...«
(Popol Vuh)

I

Dies ist die Kunde, wie alles gewesen ist, hier wird berichtet, erzählt und offenbart, wie alles sich von Anbeginn zugetragen hat, der Ursprung und Anfang von allem, was geschah; hier wird mit Worten geschildert, erklärt und enthüllt, was im Dunkeln verborgen lag, wie die vier Himmelsrichtungen bestimmt und die vier Eckpfeiler gesetzt wurden, wie die Schnur gespannt und ausgemessen wurde die Weite des Himmels und der Erde, und wie Kukumatz und BalAm, der Meister der grünen Schüssel und der Meister der blauen Schale, das Herz des Himmels und der Erde geformt haben.

Dies ist die früheste Kunde, das erste Wort. Noch war kein Mensch da, kein Tier. Berge und Schluchten gab es nicht. Kein Gras und keinen Baum. Keine Vögel und keine Fische, keine Schlange

हांस ख़्रिस्टोफ़ बूख

॥ फैसले के दिन मृत कोलम्बस का बयान ॥

[कुछ अंश]

1

यह है समाचार, कैसी थी हर चीज, यह बताएँगे, दर्ज करेंगे और उजागर कि समय की शुरूआत से सब कुछ कैसे घटा, जो भी कुछ था उसके मूल और प्रारम्भ शब्दों में बखाना जाएगा, समझाया जाएगा, अनावृत्त किया जाएगा : अन्धकार में क्या लेटा था, कैसे चार स्वर्गीय दिशाएँ निश्चित की गईं और चारों कोनों पर आधारशिलाएँ रखी गई, कैसे आकाश और पृथ्वी का विस्तार नापने के लिए रस्सी खींची गई, और कैसे गुकुमात्स और बालआम, हरी परात के स्वामी और नीले कटोरे के स्वामी, ने आसमान और धरती का हृदय निर्मित किया।

यह सबसे पहले समाचार हैं, पहला शब्द जहाँ अभी तक कोई मानव नहीं था और न कोई पशु था। न पर्वत थे न गह्वर थे। घास नहीं, पेड़ नहीं। न पक्षी न मछलियाँ, न सर्प और न जैगुआर। सिर्फ आसमान था। कुछ आवाज न करता था,

Hans Christoph BUCH

DEAD COLUMBUS SPEAKS ON JUDGEMENT DAY

[Extract of the novel]

[EPILOGUE]

"Are U Xe Oher Tzih..."
"Aqui acaban las historias..."
(Popol Vuh)

1

These are the tidings, how everything was, these will record, narrate and reveal how all took place from the beginning of time, the origin and the commencement of all that was shall be described, explained, unveiled in words; what lay in darkness, how the four heavenly directions were determined and the four cornerstones erected, how the cord was drawn out to measure the expanse of the Heaven and the Earth, and how Gucumatz and BalAm, the master of the green tureen and the master of the blue bowl, fashioned the heart of the heaven and the earth.

und keinen Jaguar. Nur der Himmel war da. Nichts tönte, nichts regte sich, kein Laut brach das Schweigen der Welt. Noch gab es nichts Aufrechtes. Nichts ragte in die Höhe. Alles ruhte und schlief. Finster und stumm war die Nacht, unter der die Welt begraben lag. Da kamen Kukumatz und BalAm zusammen, die gefiederte Schlange und der Jaguar. Flüsternd sprachen sie miteinander und berieten sich. »Licht!«, sagte Kukumatz und sogleich erschien das Licht. Seine erste Erscheinung war der Blitz, die zweite der Donner, und seine dritte Erscheinung war die Dämmerung, bevor der Tag anbricht. Noch gab es keine Sonne, keinen Mond. »Erde!« sagte BalAm, und sogleich erhoben sich Berge aus dem Wasser, und auf den Bergen wuchsen Bäume, von denen Schlingpflanzen und Orchideen herabhingen.

Danach schufen sie die Bewohner des Waldes, die Wächter der Berge und Wälder schufen sie: den Hirsch, den Tapir, den Jaguar und den Papagei. Und als Wächter der Schlingpflanzen schufen sie Schlangen und als Wächter der Orchideen Kolibris. Und sie wiesen einem jeglichen seine Wohnung zu, dem Wild und den Vögeln: »Du, Hirsch, sollst an den Ufern der Flüsse und in den Wälden wohnen. Im Gebüsch sollst du stehen und im hohen Gras. Auf vier Beinen sollst du dich aufrechthalten.« Und so geschah es. Dann wiesen sie den Vögeln ihre Wohnstatt zu: »Auf den Zweigen der Bäume sollt ihr nisten, dort sollt ihr eure Nester bauen und eure Eier ausbrüten.« So sprachen Kukumatz und BalAm zu den Vögeln. Und den Schlangen wiesen sie die Schlingpflanzen als Wohnung zu. Es sagten nämlich die Erzeuger:»Nichts regt sich unter den Bäumen? Das ist nicht gut. Auch die Schlingpflanzen sollen ihre Wächter haben.« Und nachdem sie ihr Werk vollendet hatten, sagten Kukumatz und BalAm zu allen Geschöpfen: »Ihr sollt reden und schreien, ein jeglicher nach seiner Art. Ruft, pfeift, trillert, singt! Lobt und verehrt uns!« Darauf erhob sich ein Gebrüll unter dem Himmel. Die Schlange zischte, der Jaguar fauchte, der Hirsch röhrte und der Papagai kollerte. Nur die Fische im Wasser blieben stumm. Denn sie konnten weder singen noch sprechen.

कुछ गूँजता न था, संसार के मौन को कोई स्वर तोड़ता न था। कुछ भी सीधा खड़ा न था। कुछ भी आकाश की ओर उठता न था। सब सोते थे, सब विश्राम करते थे। रात अँधियारी और गूँगी थी, नीचे धरती लेटी हुई थी। तब गुकुमात्स और बालआम मन्त्रणा करने इकट्ठा हुए, पंखवाला सर्प और जैगुआर। वे फुसफुसाए और उन्होंने बहस की। ''उजाला !'' गुकुमात्स ने पुकार कर कहा और तुरन्त उजाला हो गया। पहले बिजली के रूप में, फिर गरज के रूप में और फिर तीसरी बार उस तरह जैसे दिन उगने से पहले प्रभात होता है। सूरज तब भी नहीं था और न चाँद।

''धरती !'' बालआम ने आदेश दिया और जल से पर्वत उभर आए और पहाड़ियों पर पेड़ उग गए, पेड़ जिनमें लताएँ और आर्किड के फूल झूलने लगे। उसके बाद उन्होंने वनों में निवास करनेवाले, पर्वतों के और वन के रक्षक रचे : हिरन, तापिर, जैगुआर और तोता। और लताओं के रक्षक के रूप में उन्होंने सर्प बनाए और आर्किड के रक्षकों के रूप में मर्मर-पक्षियों को रचा। और उन्होंने हर प्राणी को उसके घर की राह बताई, जंगली जानवरों को और चिड़ियों को। ''तुम हिरनो, नदियों के किनारे जाओ और जंगलों में रहो। अपने चार पैरों पर ऊँचे खड़े होओ, झाड़ियों में और ऊँची घास में।'' और वैसा ही हुआ। फिर उन्होंने पक्षियों को उनके घर बताए : ''तुम्हें पेड़ों की डालियों में घोंसले बनाने होंगे, तुम्हें वहाँ अपने घर बनाने पड़ेंगे और अपने अंडे सेने होंगे।'' ऐसा कहा गुकुमात्स और बालआम ने चिड़ियों से। और उन्होंने सर्पों को बिलों में उनके घरों का रास्ता दिखाया। सृजेताओं ने कहा : ''लटकती हुई बेलों में कुछ नहीं चलता ? यह तो ठीक नहीं। लताओं को भी अपने रक्षक चाहिए।'' और जब गुकुमात्स और बालआम ने अपना काम पूरा कर लिया तो उन्होंने सारे प्राणियों से कहा, ''तुम्हें अपने-अपने तरीके से बोलना और गाना चाहिए। पुकारो, सीटी बजाओ, चहचहाओ, गाओ ! हमारी स्तुति करो और हमें पूजो !'' उस पर एक जबर्दस्त गर्जना आकाश तक उठी। साँप फुफकारा, जैगुआर गुर्राया, हिरन बोकलाया और तोता कुहका। केवल जल में मछलियों ने कोई आवाज़ नहीं की। क्योंकि मछलियाँ न बोल सकती थीं और न गा सकती थीं।

गुकुमात्स और बालआम फिर मिले ओर नए सिरे से चर्चा की। ''यह ठीक नहीं है', गुकुमात्स ने कहा, ''कि पशु मानवों की तरह नहीं बोल सकते।'' और बालआम ने कहा, ''एक मानव बनाते हैं।''

There are the earliest tidings, the first word. There were still no men, nor was there beast. No mountains nor gorges. No grass, no trees. No birds and no fishes, no snake and no jaguar. Only the sky was there. Nothing sounded, nothing echoed, no tone broke the silence of the world. Nothing stood upright. Nothing rose up to the sky. All slept, all rested. Dark and mute was the night, underneath lay the earth. Then Gucumatz and BalAm came together in conference, the feathered snake and the jaguar. They whispered and they argued. "Light!" cried Gucumatz and at once there was light. First as lightning, then as thunder and then for the third time, as the dawn before the daybreak. There was still no sun, nor was there moon.

"Earth!" commanded BalAm and at once, the mountains rose out of the water and the trees grew on the hills, trees from which trailed vines and orchids. Thereafter, they created the inhabitors of the forest, the guardians of the mountains and the forest did they create: the deer, the tapir, the jaguar and the parrot. And as the guardian of the vines they created snakes, and the guardians of the orchids were the humming birds. And they directed each creature to its home, the wild animals and the birds. "You deer, go to the banks of the rivers and live in the forests. Stand tall on your four legs, in brush and tall grass." And thus it was. And they showed the birds their home: "You must nest on the branches of the trees, you must build your homes there and hatch your eggs." So said Gucumatz and BalAm to the birds. And they showed the snakes their way home to the creepers. The creators said: "Nothing moves beneath the dangling vines? That is not good. Even the vines must have their keepers." And after they had completed their work, Gucumatz and BalAm told all the creatures: "You must talk and sing, each in his way. Call, whistle, trill, sing! Praise and worship us!" Thereupon a mighty roar went up to the sky. The snake hissed, the jaguar snarled, the deer belled and the parrot cooed. Only the fishes in the water made no sound. For the fishes could neither speak nor sing.

Kukumatz und Balam kamen wieder zusammen und berieten erneut miteinander. »Es ist nicht gut«, sagt der Kukumatz, »daß die Tiere nicht wie Menschen reden können.« Und BalAm sagte: »Laß uns einen Menschen machen.«

Und sie formten einen Menschen aus Ton, aus feuchter Erde kneteten sie ihn. Und sie sahen, daß er nicht fest war, er war zu weich, er war ohne Bewegung und ohne Kraft, er konnte nicht aufrecht gehen, sein Kopf sank kraftlos zur Seite, er konnte nicht sprechen und war ohne Verstand. Er fiel ins Wasser, löste sich auf und schwand dahin. »Es ist nicht gut«, sagten Kukumatz und BalAm. Und sie verwarfen den Menschen, den sie geschaffen hatten.

Darauf schnitzten sie Wesen aus Holz. Diese Wesen sahen aus wie Menschen, sie sprachen wie Menschen, aber sie waren aus Holz. Sie hatten kein Herz und keinen Verstand, weder Blut noch Fleisch. Nichts Flüssiges war in ihnen. Trocken waren ihre Augen, trocken ihr Mund, trocken war ihr Fleisch, und ihre Gesichter waren starr und ausdruckslos. Knirschend bewegten sie sich, und wenn sie aneinander stießen, zerbrachen sie.

Und weil sie ihre Erzeuger nicht lobten, die sie aus dem Holz der Bäume geschnitzt hatten, wurden sie getötet und bestraft. Das Herz des Himmels verfinsterte sich, und schwarzer Regen fiel, Nachtregen, Blutregen. Glühendes Harz troff herab und versengte sie. Stöcke und Steine erhoben sich und schlugen ihnen ins Gesicht. Wasserkrüge, Teller, Schalen und Schüsseln, sogar die schweren Mahlsteine erhoben sich und prügelten auf sie ein. Und die Mahlsteine sagten: »Ihr habt uns geschunden und gequält. Mit harten Körnern habt ihr uns die Gesichter zerrieben. Wir haben euch genug Tribut bezahlt. Jetzt sollt ihr uns kennenlernen. Zermahlen werden wir euch, zu Staub zerreiben wir eure Knochen und euer Fleisch.« Also sprachen die Mahlsteine. Und die Schalen und Schüsseln sagten: »Schmerzen und Leiden habt ihr uns zugefügt. Auf glühenden Kohlen habt ihr uns gemartert und gequält, mit Feuer und Rauch habt ihr uns verrußt und verbrannt. Dafür rächen wir uns jetzt!«

और उन्होंने मिट्टी से एक मानव गढ़ा, उन्होंने उसे गीली धरती से गूँथ निकाला। और उन्होंने देखा कि वह मजबूत नहीं था, वह बहुत मुलायम था, उसमें कोई हरकत नहीं थी और कोई ताकत नहीं थी, वह सीधा नहीं चल सकता था, उसका सिर कमजोरी से एक तरफ लटका हुआ था, वह बोल नहीं सकता था और उसके कोई दिमाग नहीं था। वह पानी में गिर गया और घुल गया।

''यह ठीक नहीं है।'' गुकुमात्स और बालआम ने कहा। और उन्होंने उस आदमी को अस्वीकार कर दिया जिसे उन्होंने बनाया था। फिर उन्होंने लकड़ी से प्राणियों को उकेरा। यह प्राणी मानवों की तरह दिखते थे, मानवों की तरह बोलते थे। लेकिन वे काठ के बने थे। उनके हृदय और मस्तिष्क न थे, न रक्त न माँस। उनमें कुछ नहीं बहता था। उनकी आँखें सूखी थीं, उनके मुख सूखे थे और उनकी चमड़ी और उनके चेहरे भी निश्चेष्ट और भावनाशून्य थे। जब वे चलते थे तो चरमराते थे और यदि छूते थे तो वे टूट जाते थे।

और चूँकि उन्होंने अपने सृजेताओं की स्तुति नहीं की जिन्होंने उन्हें पेड़ों की लकड़ी से बनाया था, इसलिए उन्हें दंड मिला और वे मारे गए। आकाश का हृदय अँधियारा हो गया और काली वर्षा होने लगी, रात्रि वर्षा, रक्त वर्षा। गर्म दहकती हुई राल उन पर गिरने, उन्हें झुलसाने लगीं। लाठियाँ और पत्थर उठ पड़े और उनके चेहरों पर बरसने लगे। पानी के मर्तबान, थालियाँ, कटोरे और परात, चक्की के भारी पाट तक उठे और उन पर टूट पड़े। और चक्की के पाटों ने कहा, ''तुमने हमें शर्मिन्दा किया है और कष्ट दिया है। तुमने हमारे चेहरों पर सख्त दानों को रगड़ा है। हमने तुम्हें काफी नजराने दिए हैं। अब तुम हमें जान लो। हम तुम्हें दलेंगे, हम तुम्हारे माँस और हड्डियों को पीसकर धूल बना देंगे।'' चक्की के पाटों ने इस तरह कहा। और परातों और कटोरों ने कहा : ''तुमने हमें कष्ट और दुख दिए हैं। तुमने हमें सताया है, हमें यन्त्रणा दी है, तुमने हमें आग और धुएँ से जलाया और काला किया है। इसका हम बदला लेंगे !''

और कुत्ते भौंके और बोले : ''तुमने हमें कुछ खाने को क्यों नहीं दिया ? जब भी हमने खाना माँगा तुमने हमें लाठियों से मारा और लातों से भगाया। अब तुम्हें इन जबड़ों के इन दाँतों की ताकत का पता इस तरह लगेगा। चक्की के पाटों ने उन्हें पीसकर धूल कर दिया। और कुत्तों ने तोड़कर उनकी हड्डियाँ अलग कर दीं और माँस खा डाला। देवताओं का धन्यवाद

Gucumatz and BalAm came together again and conferred anew. "It is not good," said Gucumatz, "that the animals cannot speak like humans." And BalAm said, "let's make a man."

And they shaped a man out of clay, they kneaded him out of damp earth. And they saw that he was not firm, he was too soft, he was without movement and without strength, he could not walk straight, his head hung weakly to one side, he could not speak and had no mind. He fell into water and melted away.

"It is not good," said Gucumatz and BalAm. And they rejected the man they had created. Then they carved creatures out of wood. These creatures looked like men, spoke like men but they were of wood. They had no heart and no mind, neither blood nor flesh. Nothing flowed in them. Dry were their eyes, their mouths were dry and also their skin and their faces were still and expressionless. They creaked as they moved and if they touched, they broke.

And because they did not praise their creators, who made them out of the wood of trees, they were punished and killed. The heart of the heaven darkened and black rain fell, night rain, blood rain. Glowing resin dripped and singed them. Sticks and stones rose up and rained blows on their face. Water jugs, platters, bowls and tureens, even the heavy millstones rose and fell upon them. And the millstones said: "You have shamed and tortured us. You rubbed our faces with hard grains. We have paid enough tribute to you. Now you must get to know us. We shall grind you, to dust shall we grind your bones and your flesh." Thus spake the millstones. And the tureens and the bowls said: "You inflicted pain and suffering upon us. You tortured and tormented us, you blackened and burned us with fire and smoke. For that we will take revenge!"

And the dogs barked and said: "Why did you not give us anything to eat? Each time we begged for food, you hit us with sticks and kicked us away. Now will you feel the strength of the teeth in these jaws!" Thus it happened. The millstones ground them into dust. And the dogs tore apart their bones and ate the flesh. That was the punishment for not thanking the gods and for not singing a paean of praise in their honour.

Und die Hunde bellten und sagten: »Warum habt ihr uns nichts zu fressen gegeben? Immer, wenn wir um Essen bettelten, habt ihr uns mit Stöcken geschlagen und mit Fußtritten verjagt. Jetzt sollt ihr die Zähne in unseren Mäulern kennenlernen!« So geschah es. Die Mahlsteine zermahlten sie zu Staub. Die Schalen und Schüsseln verschmorten sie zu Asche. Und die Hunde zerbissen ihre Knochen und fraßen ihr Fleisch. Das war die Strafe dafür, daß sie den Göttern nicht gedankt und kein Loblied ihnen zu Ehren gesungen hatten.

Und Kukumatz und BalAm kamen zum dritten Mal zusammen. Es war nicht gut, sagten sie, es war nur ein Versuch, ein Entwurf.

Und sie schufen Menschen aus Mais. Diese Wesen redeten wie Menschen und sahen aus wie Menschen. Sie hatten Glubschaugen und Knollennasen, gelbe Gesichter und grünes Haar. Sie gründeten Städte, rodeten Wälder und besäten ihre Felder mit Mais. Und sie wurden so zahlreich, daß sie den ganzen Erdkreis bevölkerten. Da sagten die Tiere des Waldes: »Es ist nicht gut, daß die Menschen die Wälder zerstören und uns aus unseren Wohnungen vertreiben.« Und die Tiere des Waldes fielen in die Felder ein, töteten die Maismenschen und bissen ihnen die Köpfe ab. Da ließen Kukumatz und BalAm brennende Pfeile vom Himmel regnen, und sie jagten die Tiere in die Wälder zurück und lehrten die Maismenschen, das Fleisch der Tiere zu essen. Seitdem sind die Tiere des Waldes den Menschen untertan. Und zur Strafe dafür, daß sie die Tiere zu ihrem frevelhaften Tun angestiftet hatten, wurden die Dämonen des Waldes, Einskojote und Siebenpapagei, in Affen verwandelt und in die Wipfel der Bäume verbannt. Dort sitzen sie noch heute und erheben ein klägliches Geschrei, jedesmal wenn sie einen Menschen auf zwei Beinen vorbeigehen sehen. Und die Maismenschen sangen Loblieder zu Ehren von Kukumatz und BalAm, die ihnen den Mais geschenkt und die Tiere des Waldes untertan gemacht hatten; und sie bauten eine Tempelpyramide, auf deren Plattform sie die Herzen ihrer Feinde verbrannten und mit abgeschlagenen Köpfen Ball spielten. Und der süße Rauch, der von der Plattform der Pyramide in den Himmel stieg, war Kukumatz

न करने का और उनके सम्मान में स्तुति न गाने का यही दंड था।

और गुकुमात्स तथा बालआम तीसरी बार मिले। यह ठीक नहीं था, वे बोले, यह सिर्फ एक प्रयोग था, एक अभ्यास था।

और उन्होंने मकई से मानव बनाए। यह प्राणी आदमियों जैसे बोलते थे और आदमियों जैसे दिखते थे। उनकी निकली हुई आँखें थीं और मोटी नाकें थीं, पीले चेहरे थे और हरे बाल थे। उन्होंने नगरियाँ बसाईं, जंगल नष्ट कर दिए और अपने खेतों में मकई बोई और वे तादाद में इतने बढ़ गए कि जल्द ही सारी दुनिया में फैल गए। जंगल के जानवरों ने कहा : "यह ठीक नहीं है कि आदमी जंगल बर्बाद कर रहे हैं और हमें हमारे घरों से निकाल रहे हैं।" और जंगल के जानवरों ने खेतों पर हमला किया, मकई-मानवों को मार डाला और उनके सिर चबा डाले। तब गुकुमात्स और बालआम ने जलते हुए बाणों की वर्षा होने दी और उन्होंने जानवरों को जंगल में खदेड़ दिया और मकई-मानवों को जानवरों का माँस खाना सिखाया। तब से जंगल के जानवर मानवता की प्रजा हो गए।

और जानवरों को इस जघन्य हमले पर उकसाने के लिए जंगल के राक्षस इकभेड़िया और सातटुइयाँ को बन्दर बना दिया गया और उन्हें पेड़ों की चोटियों पर निष्कासित कर दिया गया। वहाँ वे आज तक बैठते हैं और जब भी कोई दो पाँववाला आदमी नीचे से गुजरता है वे अपनी मनहूस चीख चीखते हैं। और मकई-मानव गुकुमात्स और बालआम के सम्मान में स्तुतियाँ गाते, जिन्होंने उन्हें मकई दी थी और जंगलों के जानवरों को उनकी प्रजा बनाया था और उन्होंने एक पिरामिड मन्दिर निर्मित किया, जिसके ऊँचे आँगन में वे अपने शत्रुओं के हृदय जलाते थे और उनके कटे सिरों से गेंद खेलते थे। और वह मीठी लोबान, जिसकी सुगन्ध आँगन से आकाश तक उठती थी, गुकुमात्स और बालआम के आनन्द के लिए थी। चढ़ाई गई बलियों के खून को उन्होंने रात में आकाश में चमकनेवाले तारों में बदल दिया, उनके हृदयों को सूर्यों में जो प्रतिदिन पूर्व में उगते थे, और मुंडेर को चन्द्रों में जो हर शाम हवा में उछाली गई गेंदों की तरह आकाश में उठते थे। इस तरह मकई-मानवों ने देवताओं से संसार के प्रारम्भ से समय मापना और दिनों के गिनना सीखा और इसी तरह वह सर्वोत्कृष्ट था।

गुकुमात्स और बालआम ने अपने झूलनेवाले बिस्तरों को पृथ्वी के चारों कोनों से बाँध लिया और सृष्टि के सृजन से सुस्ताने

And Gucumatz and BalAm came together for the third time. It was not good, they said, that was only a trial, an exercise.

And they created men out of maize. These creatures spoke like men and looked like men. They had bulging eyes and bulbous noses, yellow faces and green hair. They built cities, ravaged forests and sowed maize in their fields. And they grew so greatly in numbers that they soon populated the whole earth. The animals of the forest said: "It is not good that men are destroying the forest and doing us out of our dwellings." And the animals of the forest attacked the fields, killed the maize-men and bit their heads off. Then, Gucumatz and BalAm let it rain blazing arrows and they drove the animals back into the forest and taught the maize-men to eat the flesh of the animals. Since then, the animals of the forest have been the subjects of mankind.

And as a punishment for instigating the animals to their heinous attack, the demons of the forest, Onecoyote and Sevenparakeet were turned into monkeys and banished to the treetops. There they sit till this day and raise a dismal cry each time a man on two legs passes. And the maize-men sang songs of praise in honour of Gucumatz and BalAm, who had given them the maize and made the animals of the forest their subjects and they erected a temple pyramid, on whose platform they burnt the hearts of their enemies and played ball with the heads they chopped off. And the sweet incense, which rose to the heavens from the platform of the pyramid, was for the pleasure of Gucumatz and BalAm. They turned the blood from the sacrifices to stars that shone on the firmament at night, their hearts into suns, that rose in the east every day and their heads into moons, that shot up in the sky every evening like balls flung up in the air. Thus the maize-men learned from the gods the art of measuring time and of counting the days since the beginning of the world. And it was best so.

Gucumatz and BalAm fastened their hammocks to the four corners of the earth and rested from the creation of the world; the monkeys chattered in the trees, the parrot cooed, the snake hissed and the jaguar snarled, while

und BalAm ein Wohlgefallen. Sie verwandelten das Blut der Geopferten in Sterne, die nachts am Firmament strahlten, ihre Herzen in Sonnen, die jeden Morgen neu im Osten auferstanden, und ihre Köpfe in Monde, die sich jeden Abend wie in die Luft geschleuderte Bälle in den Himmel hoben. So lernten die Maismenschen von den Göttern die Kunst, die Zeit zu messen und die Tage zu zählen vom Anbeginn der Welt. Und es war gut so.

Kukumatz und BalAm spannten an den vier Pfosten des Himmels ihre Hängematten auf und ruhten sich aus von der Erschaffung der Welt; die Affen lärmten in den Bäumen, der Papagei kollerte, die Schlange zischte und der Jaguar fauchte, während die Menschen säten und ernteten, Ball spielten mit abgeschlagenen Köpfen und die Herzen ihrer Feinde verbrannten. So vergingen vierzig mal vierzigtausend Tage, an denen jeden Morgen die Sonne aufging und jeden Abend der zu- oder abnehmende Mond am Himmel stand, bis die Schale der Zeit ausgelaufen war. Und hier beginnt eine andere Geschichte.

2

Am Tag 8 Ahau, 4 Katûn, 13 Baktûn nach Erschaffung der Welt stiegen die göttlichen Zwillinge Kukumatz und BalAm vom Himmel herab. Sie rollten ihre Hängematten ein, auf denen sie vierzig mal vierzigtausend Tage lang geruht hatten, schnürten die heiligen Bündel, in denen sie grüne Jade, blauen Lapislazuli, Kakaobohnen und Quetzalfedern verwahrten, und bestiegen ein Schiff, mit dem sie, der untergehenden Sonne folgend, gen Westen in See stachen. Vergebens versammelten sich die Maismenschen am Ufer und baten die göttlichen Zwillinge, sie nicht zu verlassen; vergebens warf der Herr der Menschen sich ihnen zu Füßen, und flehte sie an, zu bleiben. Weder durch Opfer noch durch Bitten oder Gebete ließen Kukumatz and BalAm sich umstimmen. Sie bestiegen ihr Schiff, und während die Sonne blutrot im westlichen Meer versank, verschwanden sie in der Dunkelheit, dem Schattenland,

लगे; पेड़ों में बन्दर किटकिटाते रहे, तोते कुहुकते रहे, सर्प फुफकारते रहे और जैगुआर गुर्राते रहे, जबकि मानव बीज बोते रहे और फसल काटते रहे, काटे गए सिरों से गेंद खेलते रहे और अपने शत्रुओं के हृदयों को जलाते रहे। इस तरह चालीस गुना चालीस हजार दिन बीत गए, जिनमें से हर दिन सुबह सूरज उगा और शाम को आकाश में चन्द्रमा बढ़ा और घटा, जब तक कि समय का पात्र सूख नहीं गया। और यहाँ एक और कहानी शुरू होती है।

पृथ्वी की सृष्टि के 8वें आहाऊ, 4 थे कातून, 13वें बाक्तून के दिन, दैवीय जुड़वाँ गुकुमात्स और बालआम स्वर्ग से उतरे। उन्होंने अपने बिस्तरे लपेटे जिन पर उन्होंने चालीस गुना चालीस हजार दिन विश्राम किया था, पवित्र पोटलियों को बाँधा जिनमें हरा जेड, नीला वैदूर्य, कोको के बीज तथा क्वेत्जाल पंख थे और एक पोत पर सवार हो गए और डूबते हुए सूर्य का अनुसरण करते हुए पश्चिन की ओर चल दिए। मकई-मानव समुद्र-तट पर इकट्ठा हो गए और दैवीय जुड़वों से उन्हें न तजने की प्रार्थना की, लेकिन कोई लाभ न हुआ। मकई-मानवों के प्रमुख ने उनके पैरों पर गिरकर उनसे रुकने की प्रार्थना की। लेकिन कोई बलि, कोई विनती, कोई दलील गुकुमात्स और बालआम का निर्णय न बदल सकीं। वे अपने यान पर सवार हो गए और जब पश्चिमी सागर में सूर्य डूब रहा था तब वे अँधेरे में अदृश्य हो गए, छायाओं के साम्राज्य में, जहाँ उलूकात्मा और चमगादड़ेश राक्षस अनंत रात्रि में राज्य करते हैं और जहाँ से कोई प्राणी जीवित नहीं लौटा है। और जब उगते सूर्य के साथ गुकुमात्स और बालआम मृत्यु के साम्राज्य से लौटे तो ये दैवीय जुड़वाँ आग जैसी दाढ़ियों और मृत्यु जैसे पीले रंगवाले राक्षसों में बदल चुके थे जो एक भयानक दृश्य था।

क्वेत्जाल पंखों और जैगुआर के चमड़े की जगह वे चींटीखोरों और कछुओं की तरह जिरहबख्तर और जूए पहने हुए थे और हरिताश्म तथा लावा-काँच के चाकुओं और कुदालों की जगह वे भाले और तलवार घुमा रहे थे जो चकमक पत्थर से भी ज्यादा सख्त और पैने थे और पंखों से ढँकी बग्घी या चमड़ों के लिपटे सिंहासन की जगह वे बिना सींगोंवाले हिरनों पर बैठकर आए थे, जिनके खुरों से आग निकलती थी और देवताओं के सुनहरे चित्रों की जगह वे एक लकड़ी

the men sowed and harvested, played balls with the heads hacked off and burned the hearts of their enemies. And thus passed forty times forty thousand days, on each one of which the sun rose in the morning and the moon waxed and waned on the firmament in the evening, till the vessel of time ran dry. And here begins another story.

2

On day 8 Ahau, 4 Katun, 13 Baktun after the creation of the world, the celestial twins Gucumatz and BalAm climbed down from the heavens. They rolled up their hammocks, on which they had rested forty times forty thousand days, fastened together the holy bundles which contained green jade, blue lapis lazuli, cocoa beans and quetzal feathers and boarded a ship and struck course towards the west by following the setting sun. The maize-men assembled at the beach and pleaded with the celestial twins not to abandon them, but to no avail. In vain, the chief of the maize-men threw himself at their feet, imploring them to stay. But not the sacrifices, nor the pleas, nor the entreaties made Gucumatz and BalAm changed their mind. They boarded their ship and while the blood-red sun sank in the western ocean, they disappeared into darkness, to the realm of shadows, where the demons Owlspirit and Batgod reigned in eternal night and from where no creature has ever returned alive. And when Gucumatz and BalAm sailed back from the Kingdom of Death upon the rising sun, the celestial twins had changed into demons with fiery beards and deathly pallor, a fearful sight.

In place of their shimmering, colourful coats of quetzal feathers and jaguar skin, they wore breastplates and harnesses like armadillos and tortoises, and instead of the knives and the axes of jade and obsidian they brandished lances and swords, harder and sharper than flintstone. And instead of riding on a sedan decorated with feathers

das die Dämonen Eulengeist und Fledermausgott in ewiger Nacht regieren; kein Sterblicher ist je lebend von dort zurückgekehrt. Und als Kukumatz und BalAm mit der aufgehenden Sonne aus dem Totenreich zurückkamen, hatten die göttlichen Zwillinge sich in Dämonen verwandelt mit feuerroten Bärten und totenblasser Haut, furchterregend anzuschauen. An Stelle ihrer leuchtend bunten Mäntel aus Quetzalfedern und Jaguarfell trugen sie Brustpanzer und Harnische wie Gürteltiere und Schildkröten, und an Stelle der Messer und Äxte aus Jade und Obsidian schwangen sie Lanzen und Schwerter, die härter waren und schärfer schnitten als Feuerstein. Und anstatt auf einer mit Federn geschmückten Sänfte oder einem mit Fellen gepolsterten Thron ritten sie auf Hirschen ohne Geweih, deren Hufe Feuer sprühten, und anstatt der goldenen Götterbilder trugen sie ein hölzernes Kreuz vor sich her, das Furcht und Schrecken verbreitete, denn die Priester hatten den Maismenschen prophezeit, die Holzmenschen werden wiederkommen, um sich an ihnen zu rächen. Und so geschah es. Sie verwüsteten die Felder, verbrannten die Häuser und plünderten die Paläste, sie drangen ins Allerheiligste der Tempel ein und stürzten die Priester von den Plattformen der Pyramiden herab. Sie töteten jeden, der sich ihnen in den Weg stellte, mit ihren Waffen, und anstatt sich mit den Herzen der Geopferten zu begnügen, wie dies die alten Götter getan hatten, verwandelten sie das vergossene Blut zu GOLD, das sie in ihren Schatzkammern horteten und auf ihre Schiffe verluden. Ihre Blutgier und ihr Golddurst waren unersättlich, sie verlangten immer mehr, und erst als der Herr der Menschen die Zimmer seines Palastes vom Fußboden bis zur Decke mit Gold gefüllt hatte, hatten die Dämonen Mitleid mit ihm und töteten den Herrn der Menschen, so wie sie ihren eigenen Gott am Kreuz geopfert hatten.

Hier endet unsere Geschichte. Es gibt nichts mehr zu erzählen. Die alte Kunde ist vergessen. Das Buch des Rates ist unsichtbar. Dies wurde geschrieben in der Zeit nach dem Ende der Zeit. Das Leben der Maismenschen ist erloschen. Alles ist zu Ende. *Ri Quizibal.*

O

का सलीब ऊपर उठाए हुए थे जो भय और आतंक उपजाता था, क्योंकि पुराहितों ने मकई-मानवों को भविष्यवाणी की थी कि काठ-मानव उनसे बदला देने लौटेंगे और ऐसा ही हुआ।

उन्होंने खेत उजाड़ दिए, घर जला डाले और महल लूट लिए, उन्होंने गर्भगृह पर आक्रमण किया और पुरोहितो को पिरामिडों के प्रांगणों से गिरा दिया। जो भी रास्ते में आया उसे उन्होंने अपने हथियारों से मार डाला, और अपनी बलियों के हृदयों से ही सन्तुष्ट न हुए, जैसे प्राचीन देवता हो जाते थे। बजाए उसके, उन्होंने खून को सोने में बदल दिया जिसे उन्होंने अपने खजानों के सन्दूकों में जमा कर लिया और अपने जहाजों पर चढ़ा लिया। उनकी खून की लालच और सोने की प्यास बुझती न थीं; वे और ज्यादा और ज्यादा चाहते थे और जब मानवों के प्रमुख ने अपने महल के कमरों को फर्श से लेकर छत तक सोने से भर दिया तभी उन्होंने उस पर दया की और मानवों के प्रमुख को उसी तरह मार डाला जिस तरह उन्होंने सलीब पर अपने देवता को मारा था।

यहाँ हमारी कथा समाप्त होती है। अब कुछ और बताने को नहीं है। पुराने समाचार भुला दिए गए हैं। ज्ञान की पुस्तक अदृश्य है। यह समय के अन्त के बाद के समय में लिखा गया था। मकई-मानवों का जीवन खत्म हो चुका है। सब कुछ समाप्ति पर है। *री किजिबाल।*

❍

(विष्णु खरे तथा पद्मा राव द्वारा अनूदित)

or a throne swathed in skins they rode on stags with no antlers, whose hooves sprayed fire and instead of the golden picture of the gods, they held aloft a wooden cross which spread fear and terror, because the priests had prophecied to the maize-men that the wooden men would return to take revenge upon them. And so it happened.

They devastated the fields, burned the houses and plundered the palaces, they stormed into the sanctum sanctorum and pushed the priests off the platforms of the pyramids. They killed everyone who crossed their path with their weapons and did not rest content with the hearts of their sacrifices, as the gods of yore did. Instead, they turned the blood into GOLD, which they hoarded in their treasure chests and loaded on their ships. Their blood-lust and their gold-thirst were insatiable; they demanded more and more and only when the chief of the men had filled the rooms of his palace from the floor to the ceiling with gold did the demons take pity on him and killed the chief of men, just as they had sacrificed their own god on the cross.

Here ends our story. There is nothing more to tell. The old tidings are forgotten. The Book of Knowledge is invisible. This was written in the Time after the End of Time. The life of the maize-men is over. Everything is at an end. *Ri Qizibal.*

❍

(Tr. by Padma Rao)

Uwe TIMM

DIE ENTDECKUNG DER CURRYWURST

[Auszug]

Die Novelle spielt in den letzten Tagen des zweiten Weltkrieges in Hamburg. Die vierzigjährige Lena Brücker hat den Deserteur Bremer aufgenommen, dem es jedoch in seinem Versteck zunehmend eng wird. Lena hat sich in ihn verliebt und versucht, das Ende des Krieges vor ihm zu verheimlichen, damit er länger bei ihr bleibt. Im Rückblick erzählt die Achtzigjährige ihre Geschichte dem Verfasser der Novelle.

Am nächsten Montag, abends, sagte Bremer zu Lena Brücker: Die Leute auf der Straße gehen schneller. Schneller? Ja, etwas, ein wenig nur, aber sie gehen schneller. Sonderbar.

Nein, ganz einfach, sagte sie, es geht wieder voran. Die Leute haben ein Ziel.

Und noch etwas war ihm aufgefallen, ein paar Frauen und Männer standen auf der Straße, vereinzelt, und sprachen die Vorbeigehenden an, wie es Nutten oder Strichjungen tun, nur daß es meist alte Männer und irgendwelche schäbig gekleideten Hausfrauen waren. Am darauffolgenden Tag sah er einen Beinamputierten an der Ecke zum Großen Trampgang stehen, den rechten Beinstummel auf die Handstütze der Krücke gestützt, bekleidet mit einer gräßlich ins Grünbraun umgefärbten Uniform, die nun wie eine fehlfarbene Forstuniform aussah. Vielleicht war der Mann ja tatsächlich in die Forstverwaltung übernommen worden. Innendienst. Hin und wieder hob er die Hand und zeigte drei Finger, als wolle er knobeln oder zeigen, was ihm fehle. Ihm fehlte aber ein Bein. Wollte er damit die

ऊवे टिम

मसालेदार गुलमे का आविष्कार

[उपन्यास-अंश]

अगले सोमवार की शाम को ब्रेमर ने लेना ब्यूकर से कहा, "सड़क पर लोग ज्यादा तेजी से चल रहे हैं।" "ज्यादा तेजी से ?" "हाँ, हल्की-सी जल्दी से, सिर्फ जरा सी, लेकिन ज्यादा तेज चल रहे हैं। अजीब है।"

"नहीं, बिल्कुल मामूली है", उसने कहा "चीजें सुधर रही हैं। लोग जान रहे हैं कि वे कहाँ जा रहे हैं।"

और एक और चीज उसके ध्यान में आई थी : कुछ औरतें और आदमी सड़क पर खड़े हुए थे, अकेले, गुजरनेवालों को टोकते हुए, जिस तरह से रंडियाँ और दलाल करते हैं, सिर्फ यही था कि वे ज्यादातर बुजुर्ग जैसे मर्द थे और कुछ फटेहाल कपड़े पहने हुए गृहिणियाँ थीं। अगले दिन उसने ग्रोमर ट्राम्पगांग के नुक्कड़ पर एक कटे हुए पैरवाले को खड़ा देखा, उसके दाएँ पाँव का ठूँठ उसकी बैसाखी के मुठिए पर टिका हुआ था; वह एक वर्दी पहने हुए था, हरे-भूरे की एक भयानक रंगत में रंगी हुई, जो वन-विभाग की फीकी वर्दी जैसी लगती थी। शायद वाकई उस आदमी को वन-विभाग में रख लिया गया था। दफ्तरी काम के लिए। बीच-बीच में वह अपना हाथ उठाता था और तीन उँगलियाँ दिखाता था जैसे गोटियाँ खेलना चाहता हो या वह दिखाना चाहता हो जो उसके पास नहीं था। लेकिन जो उसके पास नहीं था वह तो एक पैर था। क्या वह अपनी

Uwe TIMM

THE INVENTION OF CURRRIED SAUSAGE

[Extract]

The novel is set in Hamburg during the last days of World War II. Forty-year old Lena Brücker has given shelter to Bremer, an army deserter, who is increasingly getting restless in his hide-out. Lena falls in love with him and in order to make him stay longer, tries to conceal the end of the war from him. The narrator of the novel takes down the story as told by the now eighty-year old Lena Brücker in retrospective.

The following Monday evening, Bremer said to Lena Brücker: "People on the street are walking faster." "Faster?" "Yes, a bit, just a little, but they are walking faster. Strange."

"No, quite simple," she said. "Things are picking up. People know where they're going."

And something else had struck him: a few women and men were standing on the street, singly, addressing passersby, the way hookers and pimps do, except that they were mostly elderly men and some shabbily dressed housewives. The next day he saw an amputee standing at the corner of Grosser Trampgang, the stump of his right leg resting on the hand-grip of his crutch; he was wearing a uniform, dyed a horrible shade of greenish brown, that looked like an off-color forestry uniform. Perhaps the man really had been taken on by by the forestry service. Desk job. From time to time he raised his hand and showed

Zahl seiner Verwundungen andeuten? Bremer holte sich das Fernglas des Barkassenführers und sah hinunter. Kein Zweifel, der Mann sprach die Vorbeigehenden an. Aber die gingen nicht nur vorbei, die eilten vorbei. Und dann - es muß der übernächste Tag gewesen sein - entdeckte Bremer einen Mann, der, obwohl die Sonne warm, ja sogar heiß schien, einen massigen Wintermantel trug. Der Mann stand in dem überweiten dunkelbraunen Wintermantel da und öffnete ihn für die Vorbeigehenden, kurz nur, wie ein Exhibitionist. Bremer dachte an die französischen Nutten in Brest, 1941, die für ihn, es war Winter, kurz, wie einen Vorhang, ihre Pelzmäntel öffneten, um die rotgerüschten Strapse, die Seidenstrümpfe, die schwarzen oder roten Büstenheber zu zeigen. Bremer starrte durch den Feldstecher hinunter, auf den Rücken des Mannes, der eine Halbglatze hatte und sich eben, den Mantel öffnend, einer Frau zuwandte, die hinsah, ihn sogar etwas fragte, dann den Kopf schüttelte und weiterging. Endlich drehte sich der Mann um, öffnete wieder den Mantel, Bremer erschrak, er sah nacktes rosiges Fleisch und mehrere Zitzen. Der Mann trug eine Schweinehälfte auf den Leib gebunden. Schwarzmarkt, schoß es Bremer durch den Kopf, und plötzlich verstand er auch die Fingerbewegung des Amputierten. Da wurde nicht geknobelt, da wurde nicht die Zahl der Verwundungen angegeben, da wurde getauscht, da wurde die Zahl der Zigaretten angezeigt, gegen die andere Waren getauscht werden sollten.

Abends empfing er Lena Brücker: Da hat sich vor dem Haus ein Schwarzmarkt gebildet. Und während sie die Holzingersche Graupensuppe aufwärmte, erregte sich Bremer darüber, wie Ordnung und Disziplin da draußen verfielen. Was ist denn daran so schlimm, fragte Lena vom Herd her, ist doch in all den Kriegsjahren unter der Hand gehandelt worden. Es gab doch immer Schwarzmarkt. Aber nicht so offen, so dreist unter freiem Himmel. Da unten steht ein Beinamputierter und bietet sein silbernes Verwundetenabzeichen an.

Für Bremer stand die deutsche Wehrmacht, die nun schon vor acht Tagen bedingungslos kapituliert hatte, gemeinsam mit den amerikanischen und britischen Verbündeten vor Berlin. Der rechte, von den Amerikanern verstärkte Flügel hatte unter General Hoth gerade Görlitz, also die

चोटों की तादाद बताना चाहता था ? ब्रेमर ने जहाजी दूरबीन उठाई और उससे नीचे की तरफ देखा। कोई शक ही नहीं, वह आदमी गुजरनेवालों से बोल रहा था। लेकिन वे सिर्फ गुजर नहीं रहे थे, बल्कि तेज-तेज जा रहे थे। और फिर यह उसके बाद के दिन की बात रही होगी—ब्रेमर ने एक आदमी देखा जो गुनगुनी बल्कि दरअसल कड़ी धूप के बावजूद सर्दी का एक भारी कोट पहने हुए था। वह आदमी वहाँ अपने बड़े भारी गहरे भूरे ओवरकोट में खड़ा हुआ था, गुजरनेवालों के लिए वह उसे खोलता था, पल भर के लिए, किसी गुप्तांग दिखानेवाले की तरह। ब्रेमर को 1941 की ठंड की फ्रांसीसी रंडियाँ भी याद आईं। ब्रेस्ट शहर की, जो उसे दिखाने के लिए फर के कोट किसी पर्दे की तरह खोलती थीं, अपने लाल झालरदार गार्टर, रेशमी लम्बी जुराबें और नीचे से छाती को उभारनेवाली काली या लाल अँगिया की झलक दिखाने के लिए। ब्रेमर ने दूरबीन के जरिए इस नंगे होते हुए आदमी की पीठ को ताका जो उस पल अपना कोट खोलते हुए एक औरत की तरफ मुड़ा। उस औरत ने देखा, उससे कुछ पूछा भी, फिर अपना सिर हिलाया और चल दी। आखिरकार वह आदमी घूमा, उसने अपना कोट फिर खोला, और ब्रेमर को धक्का लगा; उसने नंगा गुलाबी गोश्त देखा और चूचियों की एक कतार की कतार। वह आदमी एक आधे सुअर को अपने बदन पर बाँधे हुए था। काला बाजार, कौंधा ब्रेकर के दिमाग में, और अचानक वह उस कटे हुए पैरवाले की उँगलियों की हरकत को समझ गया। वह कोई जुआ या सट्टा नहीं था, चोटों की तादाद की नुमाइश नहीं थी; यह तो चीजों की अदला-बदली थी, और जो दिखाई जा रही थी वह उन सिगरेटों की गिनती की जिन्हें दूसरे सामान के बदले में दिया जा सकता था।

उस शाम को वह लेना ब्र्यूकर से इन शब्दों से मिला : इस इमारत के सामने काला बाजार शुरू गया है। और जब वह होल्त्सिंगर का जौ का सूप गरम कर रही थी, ब्रेमर ने बाहर के व्यवस्था और अनुशासन के पतन पर अपना गुस्सा जाहिर किया। "उसमें ऐसी कौन-सी बुराई है ?" लेना ने स्टोव के पास खड़े हुए कहा, "लड़ाई के सारे सालों के दौरान हमेशा चोरी-छिपे, खरीद-बिक्री चलती रही है। काला बाजार हमेशा रहा है, हमें पता ही है।" लेकिन इतने खुल्लमखुल्ला, इतने उजड्डपन से नहीं, ठेठ सड़क पर वहाँ नीचे एक आदमी है जिसका एक पैर चला गया है और वह अपना चोटवाला चाँदी का तमगा दे रहा है।"

ब्रेकर के दिमाग में जर्मन फौज, जिसने एक हफ्ते पहले बिना शर्त हथियार डाल दिए थे, बर्लिन के दरवाजे पर अपने अमेरिकी और अंग्रेज साथियों के साथ खड़ी हुई थीं। जनरल होठ की कमान के नीचे, दक्षिणपंथी टुकड़ी, अमेरिकी फौजियों

three fingers as if wanting to play dice or display what he lacked. But what he lacked was a leg. Was he trying to indicate the number of his injuries? Bremer went for the launch-skipper's binoculars and looked down. No doubt about it, the man was addressing passersby. But they weren't merely passing by, they were hurrying by.

And then - it must have been the day after that - Bremer noticed a man who, despite the warm, in fact hot sun, was wearing a heavy winter coat. The man stood there in his voluminous dark-brown overcoat, opening it for passersby, just briefly, like an exhibitionist. Bremer was reminded of the French hookers in Brest, in the winter of 1941, who would briefly open their fur coats for him, like parting a curtain, to reveal their red frilly garters, silk stockings and black or red push-up bras. Bremer stared down through the binoculars at the back of this balding man who at that moment, opening his coat, turned toward a woman. She looked, even asked him something, then shook her head and walked on. Finally the man turned around, opened his coat again, and Bremer got a shock: he saw naked pink meat and a row of tits. The man had half a pig tied to his body. Black market, flashed through Bremer's mind, and suddenly he also understood the amputee's finger movements. There was no gambling here, no displaying of the number of injuries; this was barter, and what was being shown was the number of cigarettes to be exchanged for other merchandise.

That evening he met Lena Brücker with the words: "A black market has started up in front of this building." And while she was heating up Holzinger's barley soup, Bremer vented his annoyance at the collapse of order and discipline out there. "What's so bad about it?" asked Lena as she stood at the stove. "All through the war years under-the-counter business was being carried on the whole time. There's always been a black market, we know that." "But not so openly, not so blatantly, right out on the street. Down there is a man who's lost a leg, and he's trying to swap his silver wounds decoration."

Neiße, erreicht. Donnerwetter, sagte Bremer, das geht ja rasant. Der Russe ist ausgeblutet, einfach am Ende, sagte er, aber das alles entschuldigt nicht den Schwarzmarkt unten vor der Haustür.

Bremer saß am Tisch und aß die mitgebrachte Graupensuppe, die Lena mit kleingehacktem Kerbel verfeinert hatte. Er aß aber, als schmecke ihm die Suppe nicht. Er löffelte das in sich hinein, mit einer gleichmäßigen, ja stumpfen Gier, die sie an ihren glatzköpfigen Vater denken ließ. Schmeckt die Suppe nicht? Doch, doch.

Fehlt dir Salz? Nein, nein, sagte Bremer. Aber dieses doppelte Nein hörte sich so an, als sei es egal, ob etwas mehr oder weniger Salz in der Suppe wäre. Die werden bei Görlitz über die Neiße gehen und dann auf Breslau marschieren.

War ne schöne Zeit, genaugenommen die schönste, sagte sie, legte den blauen Faden des Himmels über den linken Zeigefinger: Wenn nur nicht immer diese dösigen Fragen nach den vorrückenden Truppen gewesen wären. Ich hatte nie was mit dem Krieg am Hut, auch nicht mit dem Militär, mag keine Uniformen, und jetzt saß zu Hause einer, der Schlachten schlug, und ich mußte immer neue Namen nennen, Städte, verstehst du, einfach verrückt, schlimmer noch, ich hatte das Ganze ja mit in Bewegung gesetzt. Die Rückeroberung des Ostens, so n Quatsch.

Manchmal hab ich überlegt, ob ich das Zeitungspapier nicht einfach früher ankommen lasse, dann ist es aus mit dem Krieg, allerdings auch mit Bremer und mir.

Und haben Sie es verkürzt?

Nee. Eben nicht.

War das nicht unfair?

Weißte, unfair ist nur das Alter. Nee. War schön. Basta. So einfach war das. Man liegt zusammen und weiß, wenn der aufsteht und weggeht, dann gibts nur noch die fünfzig-, sechzigjährigen Männer. Und die träumen dann ja auch nur wieder von ner Jüngeren. Das ist doch das Sonderbare,

की कुमुक की मदद से, अभी अभी गोर्लित्स पहुँची थी, जिसका मतलब था ओडर नदी। "ये वाकई कोई बात है।" ब्रेमर ने कहा, "क्या फुर्ती है ! रूसियों का सारा खून निकल चुका है, वे खत्म हो चुके हैं, लेकिन इस इमारत के बाहर उस काले बाज़ार के लिए यह सब कोई बहाना नहीं है।"

ब्रेमर टेबल पर बैठा हुआ जौ का सूप पी रहा था जिस पर लेना ब्यूकर ने कुछ कटी हुई केर्विल की हरी पत्ती बिखेर दी थी। लेकिन वह यूँ खा रहा था जैसे कोई स्वाद न आ रहा हो, अपने मुँह में चम्मच से दलिए को एक जिद्दी, नीरस लालच से मुँह में ठूँस रहा था जिससे लेना को अपने गंजे पिता की याद आती थी। "तुम्हें क्या दलिया पसन्द नहीं आ रहा ?" "ओह, आ रहा है !"

"क्या और नमक चाहिए ?" "नहीं, नहीं," ब्रेमर ने कहा। लेकिन वह दो बार मना करना कुछ ऐसा लगा जैसे उसे इस बात से कोई फर्क नहीं पड़ रहा था कि दलिए में नमक ज्यादा है या कम। "वो लोग गोएरलित्स से ओडर पार कर लेंगे और फिर ब्रेस्लाउ तक धावा बोल देंगे।"

"वह अच्छा वक्त था—सही पूछो तो सबसे अच्छा," आसमान के नीले धागे से अपनी बाई तर्जनी के ऊपर फन्दा डालते हुए उसने कहा : सिर्फ एक उन फौजों के कूच और तैनाती के बारे में बेवकूफी-भरे सवालों के सिवा। मेरी कोई दिलचस्पी लड़ाई में नहीं रही, न किसी भी फौजी चीज में, वर्दियाँ मुझे कभी पसन्द नहीं आईं, और अब इधर मेरे घर में ही एक आदमी था जो लड़ाइयाँ लड़ रहा था, और मुझे नए नाम, शहर गढ़ने पड़ते थे, समझते हो न—ये बिल्कुल पागलपन था और सबसे खराब बात यह थी कि मैंने ही इस सारी चीज को शुरू किया था। पूरब की दुबारा फतह, क्या बकवास थी ! कभी-कभी मैं सोचती हूँ कि क्या मुझे पहले ही अखबार नहीं आने देना चाहिए था, उससे लड़ाई का खात्मा हो जाता, लेकिन ब्रेमर ओर मेरा भी।

"और क्या आपने वैसा करने के लिए कोई जल्दी की ?"

"नहीं, वही तो बात है—मैंने नहीं की।

"क्या वह गैरवाजिब नहीं था ?"

"जानते हो, बुढ़ापा अकेली और कठिन चीज है। नहीं। वह बढ़िया था। बस सिर्फ इतना ही। तुम साथ सोते हो, और

In Bremer's mind, the German army, which a week ago had unconditionally surrendered, was standing at the gates of Berlin jointly with its American and British allies. Under the command of General Hoth, the right wing, reinforced by Americans, had just reached Görlitz, which meant, the Oder River. "It's really something," said Bremer, "the speed of it! The Russians have been bled white, they're finished, but all that is no excuse for the black market down there outside this building."

Bremer was sitting at the table eating the barley soup, which Lena had garnished with some chopped chervil. But he was eating as if without pleasure, spooning the soup into his mouth with a persistent, stolid greed that reminded her of her bald-headed father. "Don't you like the soup?" "Oh, I do!"

"Does it need more salt?" "No, no," said Bremer. But that double negative sounded as if he didn't care whether there were more salt or less in the soup. "They'll cross the Oder at Görlitz and then march on Breslau."

"It was a good time - to be exact, the best," she said, looping the blue strand of sky over her left forefinger: "If it hadn't been for all those stupid questions about troop movements. I was never interested in the war, nor in anything military, never liked uniforms, and now here was someone in my home, fighting battles, and I had to keep thinking up new names, towns, you see - it was just crazy, and the worst part was that I had helped set the whole thing in motion. The reconquest of the east, what rubbish. Sometimes I wondered if I shouldn't simply have the newsprint arrive earlier, that would have put an end to the war, but also to Bremer and me."

"And did you speed it up?"

"No. That's the point - I didn't.

"Wasn't that unfair?"

"You know, the only unfair thing is old age. No. It was good. That was all. A simple as that. You lie

ne lange Zeit ist Alter etwas, das nur für andere gilt. Und dann, eines Tages, irgendwann um die Vierzig, entdeckt man das an sich selbst: haste so n blauen Fleck, fein gesprenkelt, wie ne blaue Feuerwerksrakete, ist dir ne kleine Ader an der Innenseite vom Bein geplatzt. Am Hals, hier unterm Kinn, zwischen den Brüsten haste Falten, nicht viel, n paar, gerade morgens, und man sieht an sich selbst, man wird alt. Aber mit dem Bremer hab ich das vergessen. Ja, sagt sie, war ne rundum schöne Zeit, alles war so n bißchen schräg, aber eben das war auch schön. Bis es zu dieser Rangelei kam.

Genau siebzehn Tage nach der Kapitulation kam sie nach Hause, und er sagte nicht einmal mehr Hallo, sondern fragte gleich: Hast du ne Zeitung?
Nee.
Aber wieso. Das gibts doch gar nicht. Muß doch Zeitungen geben. Wenigstens eine Seite.
Keine Ahnung. Und das rutschte ihr ziemlich patzig raus. Sie war fertig, neun Stunden Arbeit, halbe Stunde hin und halbe Stunde zurück zu Fuß, kein Auto hatte sie mitgenommen. Und dann hatte der neue Pförtner, ein wegen seiner Nazimitgliedschaft entlassener Kriminalkommissar, ihre Einkaufstasche sehen wollen. Darin hatte sie das Kochgeschirr mit der Steckrübensuppe. Nur weil der englische Captain, der zufällig auch die Behörde verließ, sie grüßte, Bye bye sagte, war sie durchgekommen. Das war n Schreck in der Abendstunde. Sie hatte noch auf dem Heimweg überlegt, ob sie ihm erzählen sollte, die Amis bräuchten das Papier, weil sie tonnenweise Flugblätter über den russischen Stellungen abwerfen. Einfach gegenübergestellt: was am Tag der amerikanische GI und der russische Soldat zu essen bekommt. Natürlich in kyrillischer Schrift. Aber sie hatte an dem Abend keine Lust, eine Geschichte auszuschmücken, die dann ja auch wasserdicht sein mußte, weil er nachfragen und Details würde wissen wollen. Was für Flugblätter, wieso schicken die Engländer kein Papier? Er wolle endlich wissen, was genau los sei, sie solle ihm für einen Tag ein Radio besorgen. Nur für einen Tag,

तुम जानते हो कि जब वह उठेगा और चल देगा, तो तुम्हारे पास जो बचेगा वह होगा पचास और साठ साल के आदमी। और वे सिर्फ अपने से कमउम्र जवान औरतों के सपने देख रहे होंगे। यही अजीब चीज है, बूढ़ा होना एक लम्बे अरसे तक एक ऐसी चीज लगती है जो सिर्फ दूसरे लोगों को होती है। और एक दिन, कहीं चालीस के आसपास, तुम देखते हो कि वह खुद तुम्हें हो रही है; तुम एक बारीक मकड़ी जैसा निशान देखते हो, एक नीली आतिशबाजी जैसा; तुम्हारे पैर के पीछे की तरफ एक छोटी-सी नस फट जाती है। और तुम्हारी गर्दन पर, इधर तुम्हारी ठुड्डी के नीचे, तुम्हारी छातियों के बीच, सलवटें आ जाती हैं, ज्यादा नहीं, सिर्फ कुछ, खासकर सुबह और खुद को देखते हो तो मालूम पड़ जाता है कि तुम्हारी उम्र हो रही है। लेकिन ब्रेमर के साथ मैं यह सब भूल गई। "हाँ", उसने कहा, "कुल मिलाकर वह अच्छा वक्त था, हर चीज थोड़ी ऐंची-तानी थी, लेकिन वह भी अपने आप में अच्छा ही था। जब तक कि हमारे बीच वह झगड़ा नहीं हुआ था।"

फौज के हथियार डालने के ठीक सत्रह दिन बाद वह घर आई और हलो तक किए बगैर उसने उससे फौरन सवाल किया : "तुम्हारे पास अखबार है ?"

"नहीं।"

"क्यों नहीं ? यह नामुमकिन है ! अखबार तो आए होंगे कम से कम एक पन्ना।"

"कुछ पता नहीं।" और वह कुछ रुखाई से ही निकल गया। उसका धीरज छूट चुका था, नौ घंटे का काम, वहाँ पहुँचने का आधा घंटा और वापसी का आधा, किसी ने भी उसे अपनी गाड़ी पर बैठने को नहीं कहा। और फिर उस नए दरबान ने—जो पहले पुलिस कमिश्नर था और जिसकी नौकरी नात्सी पार्टी का सदस्य होने के कारण छूट गई थी—उसकी सौदे की थैली की तलाशी लेने की कोशिश की थी। उसमें कैंटीन का बन्दगोभी के सूप का एक डिब्बा था। वह इसीलिए बच सकी कि उसी वक्त अंग्रेज कैप्टेन भी दफ्तर से जा रहा था और उसे उसने "बाइ, बाइ !" किया। काम खत्म होने के बार यह एक दहशत ही थी। घर आते वक्त उसने सोचा था कि क्या वह उसे यह बताए कि अमेरिकियों को कागज चाहिए था क्योंकि वे रूसी ठिकानों पर कई टन पर्चे गिरा रहे थे। सीधी-सादी तुलना : अमेरिकी फौजी और रूसी सिपाही को खाने को रोज क्या मिलता है—बेशक रूस की किरिलियाई लिपि में, लेकिन उस शाम उसका मन ऐसी कहानी गढ़ने का नहीं हो रहा था जो असली भी लगे, क्योंकि

there together, and you know that, when he gets up and leaves, all you have left is fifty- and sixty-year-old men. And they in turn dream only of younger women. That's the strange thing, for a long time getting old is something that happens only to other people. And then one day, somewhere around forty, you find it's happening to yourself: you notice a fine blue spidery mark, like a blue fireworks rocket: a little vein has burst on the inner side of your leg. And on your neck, here under your chin, between your breasts, you have creases, not many, just a few, especially in the morning, and looking at yourself you know you're getting old. But with Bremer I forgot all that. Yes," she said, "taken all around it was a good time, everything was a bit cockeyed, but that itself was good too. Till it came to this row we had."

Exactly seven days after the surrender she came home and, without so much as a hello, he asked her right off: "D'you have a paper?"

"No."

"Why not? That's impossible! There must be newspapers. At least one sheet."

"No idea." And that slipped out rather brusquely. She'd had enough, nine hours' work, a half-hour walk to get there and half an hour back, no one had offered her a ride. And then the new doorman - a former police commissioner who had lost his job because he'd been a member of the Nazi party - had wanted to inspect her shopping bag. It contained a mess tin of turnip soup. It was only because of the British captain, who happened to be leaving the office at the same time and had said "Bye-Bye!" to her, that she got away with it. That had been a scare at the end of the day. On her way home she had wondered whether she should tell him that the Americans needed the paper because they were dropping leaflets by the ton over the Russian positions. A simple comparison: how the American GI and the Russian soldier are fed each day - in the Cyrillic alphabet, of course. But that evening she didn't feel like concocting a

irgendwo ausleihen, von einer Freundin. Als sie sagte, das ginge nicht - was sollte sie auch sagen - ranzte er sie an: sie wolle wohl nicht. Was heißt hier wohl. Du willst nicht. Ich kann nicht. Doch du kannst! Du willst nur nicht! Nein! Doch! Warum nicht? Geht nicht! Willst nicht! Ich sitz hier. Ja, und? Ich glotze auf die Straße. Ich putze. Ich laufe auf Socken rum. Da schrie er schon. Verstehst du, es geht um mein Leben. Ja, O.K., sagte sie. Er stutzte, sah sie entgeistert an, einen Augenblick. Wie kam das Wort in ihren Kopf? Für ihn geht es um Kopf und Kragen, und sie sagt O.K. Er tat ihr plötzlich leid, wie er dastand mit einem hochroten Gesicht, wie ein trotziges Kind. Es ging ja schon nicht mehr um sein Leben, schon seit Tagen nicht mehr. Und weil er ihr leid tat, machte sie genau das Falsche, sie sagte die Wahrheit. Sie sagte: Es ist gar nicht so schlimm, wie du denkst. Da begann er zu brüllen, und desto lauter, je öfter sie Pscht machte. Die Nachbarn. Scheißegal! Was?! Können mich mal. Du läufst rum, aber auf mich warten draußen die Kettenhunde. Unsinn. Du sagst Unsinn? Die stellen mich an die Wand! Und du sagst einfach Unsinn. Du sagst O.K. Er wischte mit dem Arm über den Tisch. Er machte reinen Tisch, wischte den Atlas runter, die Teller, die Tassen, die Messer, Gabeln, auch die Gläser zersplitterten am Boden. Er lief zur Tür, die sie, wie immer, ganz selbstverständlich abgeschlossen hatte, er wollte raus, und da sie den Schlüssel abgezogen hatte - nie zuvor war ihr aufgefallen, daß sie den Schlüssel, als hielte sie ihn gefangen, abzog - schlug er - außer sich vor Wut - mit der Faust gegen die Türklinke und nochmals und nochmals, mit aller Wucht. [...]

वह सवाल पूछता और ब्यौरे जाना चाहता। कैसे पर्चे, अंग्रेज कुछ कागज क्यों नहीं भेज रहे ? उसने जोर देकर जानना चाहा कि आखिर चल क्या रहा है, मेहरबानी करके क्या वह उसे एक दिन के लिए रेडियो लाकर देगी ? सिर्फ एक दिन के लिए, कहीं से माँगकर लाए, शायद अपने किसी दोस्त से ? जब उसने उसे बताया कि वह असम्भव था—और क्या कह सकती थी वह ?—तो वह बदतमीजी पर उतर आया। "लगता है कि तुम चाहती नहीं—नहीं, लगता नहीं, तुम चाहती ही नहीं हो !" "नहीं !" "हाँ !" "तुम क्यों नहीं कर सकतीं ?" "करना मुमकिन नहीं है !" "तुम करना चाहती नहीं ! मैं यहाँ दड़बे में बंद हूँ !" "तो क्या हुआ ?" "मैं सड़क ताकता रहता हूँ। मैं सफाई करता हूँ। मैं मोजे पहने घूमता रहता हूँ।" अब वह चिल्लाने लगा था। "तुम्हें समझ में नहीं आता ? मेरी जिन्दगी अधर में लटकी हुई है !" "हाँ, ठीक है", उसने कहा।

वह सन्न रह गया, एक क्षण-भर उसे हक्का-बक्का देखता रहा। उसके दिमाग में यह शब्द आया कैसे ? उसकी जिन्दगी दाँव पर लगी है और वह कहती है ठीक है। जब वह एक जिद्दी बच्चे की तरह लाल मुँह लिए खड़ा हुआ था तो वह अचानक उसके लिए तरस से भर गई। उसके लिए अब जिन्दगी और मौत का मामला नहीं था, कई दिनों से नहीं रहा था। और क्योंकि वह उसके लिए दुखी थी, इसलिए उसने सारी गलत चीजें कीं। "उतनी बुरी हालत नहीं है जितनी तुम सोचते हो", वह बोली। अब वह गरजने लगा और जितनी बार उसने श् श् श् कहा वह उतनी ही जोर से गरजता गया। "पड़ोसी !" "मैं झाँट परवाह नहीं करता !" "क्या ?" "ऐसी की तैसी कराएँ साले अपनी। तुम चाहे जहाँ जाने के लिए आजाद हो, लेकिन मैं ? फौजी पुलिस मेरी ताक में है।" "बकवास।" "तुमने कहा बकवास ? वो मुझे दीवार के सहारे खड़ा कर देंगे और तुम सिर्फ बकवास कह सकती हो, ठीक है कहती हो !" उसने अपना हाथ टेबल पर इस पार से उस पार रगड़ता हुआ चला दिया और उस पर से सारी चीजें बुहार दीं—एटलस, रकाबियाँ, कप, छुरियाँ, काँटे और गिलास जो फर्श पर आवाज के साथ बिखर गए। वह दरवाजे की तरफ लपका जिसे हमेशा की तरह उसने आदतन चाबी से बन्द कर दिया था। वह बाहर जाना चाहता था और क्योंकि उसने चाबी निकाल दी थी—तब तक उसे कभी इसका भान न हुआ था कि वह मानो उसे कैद रखने के लिए चाबी निकालकर रख लेती थी—इसलिए वह गुस्से से बदहवास अपनी पूरी ताकत से दरवाजे के कब्जे पर बार-बार घूँसा मारने लगा।
[...]

(विष्णु खरे द्वारा अनूदित)

story that must also hold water, because he would ask questions and want to know details. What leaflets, why aren't the British sending any paper? He insisted on knowing what exactly was going on, would she please get hold of a radio for him for a day? Just for one day, borrow it from someplace, maybe from one of her friends? When she told him that that was impossible - what else could she say? - he became abusive. "You don't seem to want to - no, not *seem*, you just *don't* want to!" "I can't." "Yes you can! You just don't want to!" "No!" "Yes! *Why* can't you?" "Can't be done!" "You don't want to! I'm cooped up here." "So what?" "I stare down at the street. I clean up. I walk around in socks." By this time he was shouting. "Can't you understand? My life is on the line!" "Yes, okay," she said.

He was stunned, looked at her aghast for a moment. How did that word enter her head? His life is at stake, and she says okay. She suddenly felt sorry for him as he stood there crimson in the face, like a stubborn child. It was no longer a matter of life or death for him; it hadn't been for days. And because she felt sorry for him, she did exactly the wrong thing: "It's not as bad as you think," she said. Now he began to roar, and the more often she said "Sshh" the louder he roared. "The neighbors!" "I don't give a shit!" "What?" "They can kiss my ass. You're free to go wherever you like, but me? The MPs are waiting outside for me." "Nonsense." "Nonsense, you say? They'll put me up against a wall! And all you can say is nonsense, you say okay!" He swept his arm across the table, clearing everything off it - atlas, plates, cups, knives and forks, and glasses that shattered on the floor. He dashed to the door which, as always, she had automatically locked. He wanted out, and since she had removed the key - it had never occurred to her till then that she removed the key as if to keep him prisoner - he beat his fist, beside himself with rage, against the door handle, again and again, with all his might.
[...]

(*Tr. by Leila Vennewitz*)

Gottfried BENN

WAS SCHLIMM IST

Wenn man kein Englisch kann,
von einem guten englischen Kriminalroman zu hören,
der nicht ins Deutsche übersetzt ist.

Bei Hitze ein Bier sehn,
das man nicht bezahlen kann.

Einen neuen Gedanken haben,
den man nicht in einen Hölderlinvers einwickeln kann,
wie es die Professoren tun.

Nachts auf Reisen Wellen schlagen hören
und sich sagen, daß sie das immer tun.

Sehr schlimm: eingeladen sein,
wenn zu Hause die Räume stiller,
der Café besser
und keine Unterhaltung nötig ist.

Am schlimmsten:
nicht im Sommer sterben
wenn alles hell ist
und die Erde für Spaten leicht.

O

गॉटफ़्रीद बेन

॥ बुरा क्या है ॥

अंग्रेजी न जानना
और उस अच्छे जासूसी उपन्यास का जिक्र सुनना
जिसका अनुवाद तुम्हारी भाषा में नहीं हुआ है

देखना जब तुम्हें गर्मी लग रही हो
एक बियर को जिसके वास्ते तुम्हारे पास पैसे नहीं हैं

दिमाग में एक नए विचार का आना
लेकिन उसे रवीन्द्रनाथ ठाकुर की एक पंक्ति जैसा
न बना पाना
जैसा कि प्रोफेसर लोग करते हैं

रात में एक यात्रा के दौरान लहरों के थपेड़े सुनना
और सोचना : ये वे हमेशा करती हैं

बहुत बुरा : कहीं बाहर निमंत्रित होना
जबकि घर में ज्यादा शान्ति है
कॉफी बेहतर है
और तुम्हें मनोरंजन की कोई दरकार नहीं है

सबसे बुरा :
गर्मियों में न मरना,
जब सब कुछ इतना चटख है
और बेलचे के लिए धरती आसान है
❍

(जर्मन से अनूदित : विष्णु खरे)

WHAT'S BAD

When you do not know English
and hear of a good English detective novel
that has not been translated into German.

To see when you're hot
a beer that you can't afford.

To have a new thought without being able
to make it sound like a line by Hölderlin
as the professors do.

On a journey by night to hear waves beating
and to think: they do that all the time.

Very bad: to be invited out
when at home it is quieter,
the coffee is better,
and you've no need to be amused.

Worst of all:
not to die in summer,
when everything is bright,
and the earth is easy on the spade.
❍

(Tr. by Christopher Middleton)

EIN WORT

Ein Wort, ein Satz -: Aus Chiffren steigen
erkanntes Leben, jäher Sinn,
die Sonne steht, die Sphären schweigen
und alles ballt sich zu ihm hin.

Ein Wort - ein Glanz, ein Flug, ein Feuer,
ein Flammenwurf, ein Sternenstrich -
und wieder Dunkel, ungeheuer,
im leeren Raum um Welt und Ich.
O

॥ एक शब्द ॥

एक शब्द, एक वाक्यांश : संकेत लिपि से
अचानक उभरता है अर्थ, जीवन, देखा जिसे
सूर्य अचल खड़ा रहता है, चुप हैं नक्षत्र
सारी वस्तुएँ उसमें खिंची हो जाती हैं एकत्र

एक शब्द—एक दमक, एक उड़ान
एक मशाल, एक गिरता हुआ तारा—
और फिर एक विराट अँधियारा
शून्य में, संसार और मेरे दरमियान
○

(जर्मन से अनूदित : विष्णु खरे)

A WORD

A word, a phrase -: from cyphers rise
Life recognized, a sudden sense,
The sun stands still, mute are the skies,
And all compacts it, stark and dense.

A word -, a gleam, a flight, a spark,
A thrust of flames, a stellar trace -,
And then again - immense - the dark
Round world and I in empty space.
○

(Tr. by Richard Exner)

KREISLAUF

Der einsame Backzahn einer Dirne,
die unbekannt verstorben war,
trug eine Goldplombe.
Die übrigen waren wie auf stille Verabredung
ausgegangen.
Den schlug der Leichendiener sich heraus,
versetzte ihn und ging für tanzen.
Denn, sagte er,
nur Erde solle zur Erde werden.
O

॥ सिलसिला ॥

गुमनाम मरी उस रंडी की
अकेली दाढ़ में
सोना भरा था
बाकी सारे जैसे एक चुप्पे समझौते के तहत
चम्पत हो गए थे
उस भराई को निकाल लिया मुर्दाघर के नौकर ने,
उसे गिरवी रख दिया और नाच-गाने के लिए चल दिया
क्योंकि, जैसा उसका कहना था,
सिर्फ मिट्टी को ही मिट्टी में मिलना चाहिए
O

(जर्मन से अनूदित : विष्णु खरे)

CYCLE

The solitary molar of a whore
who had died incognito
wore a gold filling.
(The rest had decamped
as if by silent agreement.)
That filling was swiped by the mortician's mate
and pawned, so he could go to a dive
and dance, for, as he put it:
"Earth alone should return to earth."
O

(Tr. by Francis Golffing)

Bertolt BRECHT

ICH SAGE JA NICHTS GEGEN ALEXANDER

Timur, höre ich, nahm sich die Mühe, die Erde zu erobern.
Ich verstehe ihn nicht:
Mit etwas Schnaps vergißt man die Erde.
Ich sage ja nichts gegen Alexander.
Nur
Habe ich Leute gesehen, bei denen
War es sehr merkwürdig
Eurer Bewunderung höchst würdig
Daß sie
Überhaupt lebten.
Die großen Männer sondern zu viel Schweiß ab.
Ich sehe in allem nur den Beweis
Daß sie nicht allein sein konnten
Und rauchen
Und trinken
Und so.
Und sie müssen zu armselig sein
Als daß es ihnen genügen könnte
Bei einer Frau zu sitzen.

❍

बेर्टोल्ट ब्रेख्ट

॥ मैं सिकन्दर के ख़िलाफ़ तो कुछ नहीं कह रहा ॥

तैमूर ने, सुनता हूँ, ज़ेहमत उठायी, धरती जीतने के लिए।
वह मेरी समझ में नहीं आता :
ज़रा-सी दारू भुला देती धरती को।
मैं सिकन्दर के ख़िलाफ़ तो कुछ नहीं कह रहा।
बस
मैंने देखे हैं लोग, जिनकी रिस्बत
ग़ौर करने लायक था यह
तुम्हारी सराहना के लायक वाक़ई
कि वे
सचमुच ज़िन्दा भी थे।
बड़े लोग बड़ा ही पसीना उलचते हैं
मैं देखता हूँ इस सबमें बस यह सबूत
कि अकेले वे कर नहीं पाए बसर
और धूम्रपान
और मद्यपान
वग़ैरह-वग़ैरह।
और वे इतने अभागे रहे होंगे
कि उनके लिए काफ़ी न होता
बैठना साथ एक औरत के।
O

(अनुवाद : गिरधर राठी और रायनर लौट्ज़)

I'M NOT SAYING ANYTHING AGAINST ALEXANDER

Timur, I hear, took the trouble to conquer the earth.
I don't understand him;
With a bit of hard liquor you can forget the earth.
I'm not saying anything against Alexander
Only
I have seen people
Who were remarkable -
Highly deserving of your admiration
For the fact that they
Were alive at all.
Great men generate too much sweat.
In all this I see just a proof
That they couldn't stand being on their own
And smoking
And drinking
And the like.
And they must be too mean-spirited
To get contentment from
Sitting by a woman.
O

(Tr. by Humphrey Milnes)

SCHLECHTE ZEIT FÜR LYRIK

Ich weiß doch: nur der Glückliche
Ist beliebt. Seine Stimme
Hört man gern. Sein Gesicht ist schön.

Der verkrüppelte Baum im Hof
Zeigt auf den schlechten Boden, aber
Die Vorübergehenden schimpfen ihn einen Krüppel
Doch mit Recht.

Die grünen Boote und die lustigen Segel des Sundes
Sehe ich nicht. Von allem
Sehe ich nur der Fischer rissiges Garnnetz.
Warum rede ich nur davon
Daß die vierzigjährige Häuslerin gekrümmt geht?
Die Brüste der Mädchen
Sind warm wie ehedem.

In meinem Lied ein Reim
Käme mir fast vor wie Übermut.

In mir streiten sich
Die Begeisterung über den blühenden Apfelbaum
Und das Entsetzen über die Reden des Anstreichers.
Aber nur das zweite
Drängt mich zum Schreibtisch.

❍

॥ प्रगीत के लिए बुरा वक़्त ॥

सो मैं जानता हूँ : सिर्फ़ सुखी
होता है लोकप्रिय। उसकी आवाज
आती है पसंद। उसका मुख सुन्दर।

आँगन मे अपंग पेड़
दिखला रहा है ख़राब है ज़मीन, पर
राहगीर उसे गाली देते अपंग की
और ठीक भी है।

खाड़ी की हरी-हरी नावें और मस्त पाल
मैं नहीं देखता। उनमें
देखता हूँ बस फटे जाल मछुओं के।
क्यों बात करता मैं केवल इसी की
कि चालीस की देहातिन झुकी-झुकी चलती है ?
स्तन लड़कियों के
सदा की तरह गर्म हैं।

मेरे गीत में एक भी तुक
लगेगी मुझे दुस्साहस जैसी।

मुझमें है खींच-तान
सेब के फूलते पेड़ों से उछाह
और पुतैया के बयानों से वहशत।
लेकिन यह दूसरी बात ही
धकेलती है मुझे लिखने की मेज़ की तरफ़।
O

(अनुवाद : गिरधर राठी और रायनर लौट्स)

BAD TIME FOR POETRY

Yes, I know: only the happy man
Is liked. His voice
Is good to hear. His face is handsome.

The crippled tree in the yard
Shows that the soil is poor, yet
The passers-by abuse it for being crippled
And rightly so.

The green boats and the dancing sails on the Sound
Go unseen. Of it all
I see only the torn nets of the fishermen.
Why do I only record
That a village woman aged forty walks with a stoop?
The girl's breasts
Are as warm as ever.

In my poetry a rhyme
Would seem to me almost insolent.

Inside me contend
Delight at the apple tree in blossom
And horror at the house-painter's speeches.
But only the second
Drives me to my desk.
O

(Tr. by John Willett and Ralph Manheim, with Erich Fried)

AN DIE NACHGEBORENEN

I

Wirklich, ich lebe in finsteren Zeiten!
Das arglose Wort ist töricht. Eine glatte Stirn
Deutet auf Unempfindlichkeit hin. Der Lachende
Hat die furchtbare Nachricht
Nur noch nicht empfangen.

Was sind das für Zeiten, wo
Ein Gespräch über Bäume fast ein Verbrechen ist
Weil es ein Schweigen über so viele Untaten einschließt!
Der dort ruhig über die Straße geht
Ist wohl nicht mehr erreichbar für seine Freunde
Die in Not sind?

Es ist wahr: ich verdiene noch meinen Unterhalt
Aber glaubt mir: das ist nur ein Zufall. Nichts
Von dem, was ich tue, berechtigt mich dazu, mich sattzuessen.
Zufällig bin ich verschont. (Wenn mein Glück aussetzt, bin ich verloren.)

Man sagt mir: Iß und trink du! Sei froh, daß du hast!
Aber wie kann ich essen und trinken, wenn
Ich dem Hungernden entreiße, was ich esse, und
Mein Glas Wasser einem Verdurstenden fehlt?
Und doch esse und trinke ich.

Ich wäre gerne auch weise.
In den alten Büchern steht, was weise ist:
Sich aus dem Streit der Welt halten und die kurze Zeit
Ohne Furcht verbringen
Auch ohne Gewalt auskommen

॥ अनुजों से ॥

1

सचमुच, मैं जी रहा अँधेरे ज़माने में !
निष्कपट शब्द है विदूषकता । चिकना ललाट
जताता है निष्ठुरता। हँस रहा जो उसको
ख़बर ख़ौफ़नाक
बस अभी मिली नहीं।

कैसा ज़माना है ये, जहाँ
पेड़ों पर बातचीत गोया गुनाह है
क्योंकि निहित है उसमें चुप्पी ढेरों अपकर्मों पर।
वहाँ जो आराम से सड़क पार कर रहा
अब न हो शायद अपने मित्रों की पहुँच में
जो हैं संकट में ?

सच है : कमाता हूँ अब भी गुज़ारे भर
लेकिन विश्वास करो : यह बस संयोग है। कुछ नहीं ऐसा
जो मैं करूँ और मुझे हक़ पहुँचे भर-पेट खाने का।
संयोग से बचा हूँ। (यदि मेरा भाग्य थमा, मैं गया।)

मुझसे कहा जाता है : अरे तू तो पी ! मौज कर कि है
तेरे पास !
पर मैं कैसे खाऊँ और पियूँ अगर
छीनता हूँ भूखे से, जो मैं खाता हूँ, और
मेरा पानी का ग्लास एक प्यास से मरते को चाहिए ?
फिर भी खाता हूँ मैं और पीता हूँ मैं।

मैं भी हो जाता सयाना।
पुरानी किताबों में दिया है, क्या है सयानापन :
दुनिया की झिकझिक से बचना और यह थोड़ा-सा वक़्त
निर्भय बिता लेना

TO THOSE BORN LATER

I

Truly, I live in dark times!
The guileless word is folly. A smooth forehead
Suggests insensitivity. The man who laughs
Has simply not yet had
The terrible news.

What kind of times are they, when
A talk about trees is almost a crime
Because it implies silence about so many
horrors?
That man there calmly crossing the street
Is already perhaps beyond the reach of his friends
Who are in need?

It is true I still earn my keep
But, believe me, that is only an accident. Nothing
I do gives me the right to eat my fill.
By chance I've been spared. (If my luck breaks, I
am lost.)

They say to me: Eat and drink! Be glad you have it!
But how can I eat and drink if I snatch what I eat
From the starving, and
My glass of water belongs to one dying of thirst?
And yet I eat and drink.

I would also like to be wise.
In the old books it says what wisdom is:
To shun the strife of the world and to live out
Your brief time without fear
Also to get along without violence
To return good for evil

Böses mit Gutem vergelten
Seine Wünsche nicht erfüllen, sondern vergessen
Gilt für weise.
Alles das kann ich nicht:
Wirklich, ich lebe in finsteren Zeiten!
[...]

हिंसा के बिना निभा लेना भी
बदी का बदला नेकी से चुकाना
निज वासनाओं की तृप्ति नहीं, बल्कि विस्मरण
माना जाता है सयानापन।
ये सब मैं कर नहीं सकता :
सचमुच, मैं जी रहा अँधेरे ज़माने में !
[...]

(अनुवाद : गिरधर राठी और रायनर लौट्स)

Not to fulfil your desires but to forget them
Is accounted wise.
All this I cannot do:
Truly I live in dark times.
[...]

(Tr. by John Willett and Ralph Manheim, with Erich Fried)

FAHREND IN EINEM BEQUEMEN WAGEN

Fahrend in einem bequemen Wagen
Auf einer regnerischen Landstraße
Sahen wir einen zerlumpten Menschen bei Nachtanbruch
Der uns winkte, ihn mitzunehmen, sich tief verbeugend.
Wir hatten ein Dach und wir hatten Platz und wir fuhren vorüber
Und wir hörten mich sagen, mit einer grämlichen Stimme: Nein
Wir können niemand mitnehmen.
Wir waren schon weit voraus, einen Tagesmarsch vielleicht
Als ich plötzlich erschrak über diese meine Stimme
Dies mein Verhalten und diese
Ganze Welt.

O

॥ एक आरामदेह कार में जाते हुए ॥

एक आरामदेह कार में जाते हुए
एक बरसाती चौड़े मार्ग पर
हमने देखा एक ख़स्ता-हाल आदमी शाम के समय
हमें हाथ देता नीचे झुक-झुककर, ले चलें उसे साथ।
हमारे पास छत थी और हमारे पास जगह थी और हम बढ़ गए आगे

और हमने सुना मुझे कहते, एक झुँझलाए स्वर में : नहीं
हम नहीं ले सकते किसी को साथ।
हम आ चुके थे काफ़ी आगे, एक दिन पैदल सफ़र के बराबर
जब मैं अचानक चिहुँक पड़ा इस अपने स्वर
इस अपने बर्ताव और इस
सारी दुनिया पर।
❍

(अनुवाद : गिरधर राठी और रायनर लौट्ज़)

TRAVELLING IN A COMFORTABLE CAR

Travelling in a comfortable car
Down a rainy road in the country
We saw a ragged fellow at nightfall
Signal to us for a ride, with a low bow.
We had a roof and we had room and we drove on
And we heard me say, in a grumpy voice: no
We can't take anyone with us.
We had gone on a long way, perhaps a day's march
When suddenly I was shocked by this voice of mine
This behaviour of mine and this
Whole world.
❍

(*Tr. by Michael Hamburger*)

DER RAUCH

Das kleine Haus unter Bäumen am See.
Vom Dach steigt Rauch.
Fehlte er
Wie trostlos dann wären
Haus, Bäume und See.
O

॥ धुआँ ॥

वह छोटा-सा घर पेड़ों के नीचे झील पर।
छत से उमड़ रहा धुआँ।
इसके बग़ैर
कितने नीरस होते
घर, पेड़ और झील।
○

(अनुवाद : गिरधर राठी और रायनर लौट्स)

THE SMOKE

The little house among trees by the lake.
From the roof smoke rises.
Without it
How dreary would be
House, trees and lake.
○

(*Tr. by Derek Bowman*)

Paul CELAN

ESPENBAUM

Espenbaum, dein Laub blickt weiß ins Dunkel.
Meiner Mutter Haar ward nimmer weiß.

Löwenzahn, so grün ist die Ukraine.
Meine blonde Mutter kam nicht heim.

Regenwolke, säumst du an den Brunnen?
Meine leise Mutter weint für alle.

Runder Stern, du schlingst die goldne Schleife.
Meiner Mutter Herz ward wund von Blei.

Eichne Tür, wer hob dich aus den Angeln?
Meine sanfte Mutter kann nicht kommen.

❍

पाऊल त्सेलान

॥ एस्पनच्या झाडा ॥

एस्पनच्या झाडा, तुझ्या पानांची पांढरी
नजर पडते काळोखात
माझ्या आईचे केस कधी पांढरे झालेच नाही।

डँडेळायन, किती हिखागार आहे युक्रेन।
माझी सोनेरी केसांची आई धरी आलीच
नाही परतून।

पाऊसभरल्या ढगा, कशाळा बनतोयस तू
विहिरींचा काठ ?
माझी अस्फुट बोलणारी आई रडतेय
सगळयांसाठीच

गोल तारा, तू बांधतोस सोनेरी अंबाडा।
माझ्या आईच्या ह्रदयाला होतं लागळेळं शिसं।

ओकच्या दरवाजा, कोणी उखडळी तुझी बिजागरं ?
माझी मायाळू आई आता परतणार नाही।
❍

(अनुवाद : दिलीप चित्रे, लोथार लुट्से)

ASPEN TREE

Aspen tree, your leaves glance white into the dark.
My mother's hair was never white.

Dandelion, so green is the Ukraine.
My yellow-haired mother did not come home.

Rain cloud, above the well do you hover?
My quiet mother weeps for everyone.

Round star, you wind the golden loop.
My mother's heart was ripped by lead.

Oaken door, who lifted you off your hinges?
My gentle mother cannot return.
❍

(Tr. by Michael Hamburger)

DEIN HAAR ÜBERM MEER

Es schwebt auch dein Haar überm Meer mit dem goldnen Wacholder.
Mit ihm wird es weiß, dann färb ich es steinblau:
die Farbe der Stadt, wo zuletzt ich geschleift ward gen Süden ...
Mit Tauen banden sie mich und knüpften an jedes ein Segel
und spieen mich an aus nebligen Mäulern und sangen:
'Oh komm übers Meer!'
Ich aber malt als ein Kahn die Schwingen mir purpurn
und röchelte selbst mir die Brise und stach, eh sie schliefen, in See.
Ich sollte sie rot dir nun färben, die Locken, doch lieb ich sie steinblau:
O Augen der Stadt, wo ich stürzte und südwärts geschleift ward!
Mit dem goldnen Wacholder schwebt auch dein Haar überm Meer.
❍

॥ तुझे केस अध्धर समुद्रावर ॥

अध्धर आहेत तुझे केस समुद्रावर सोबत सोनेरी ज्युनिपर।
त्याच्यासोबत पांढरे होतायत, तर मी त्यांना कळप ळावीन
        दगड निळा :
तो शहराचा रंग, जिथून मागल्या खेपेळा
                मला फरफटत नेळ होतं दक्षिणेळा
दोरखंडानं बांधून जखडून एकेक टोक शीडाळा
आणि धुकाळळेल्या तोंडांमधून माझ्यावर थुकून ते गायले :
"ये ऽ ऽ रे ऽ ऽ समुद्रावरून !"

पण मी पडाव होऊन रंग दिळा माझ्या पंखांना जांभळा
आणि स्वतः गुदमरून झालो एक झुळूक त्यांना झोप ळाग गया
        पूर्वी किनारा सोडून
आता मी रंगवून ळाळ करायळा हव्या तुझ्य
बटा पण मळा आवडतात त्या दगडनि।
शहराच्या डोळयांनो, जिथं मी कोसळलो आणि फरफटत नेळा
        गेळो दक्षिणेळा
सोबत सोनेरी ज्युनिपर अध्धर शिवाय तुझे केससुध्दा समुद्रावर।
○

(अनुवाद : दिलीप चित्रे, लोथार लुट्ट्से)

YOUR HAIR ABOVE THE SEA

Your hair too hovers above the sea with the golden
        juniper.
Together with it turns white, but I dye it stone-
        blue:
that city's colour where last I was dragged to the
        south...
With ropes they bound me and knotted a sail to
        each one
and spat at me from their misty mouths and sang
        out:
"O come over the sea!"
But I as a dinghy painted my pinions purple
and wheezed a breeze for myself and before they
        slept sailed away.
Now it is red I should dye them, your locks, but I
        like them stone-blue:
O eyes of the city where, felled, I was dragged to
        the south:
With the golden juniper now your hair too hovers
        above the sea.
○

(Tr. by Michael Hamburger)

Günter EICH

EN ATTENDANT

Am Dienstag stellten wir noch
die Abfälle vors Haus,
am Mittwoch
boten wir das Haus an,
am Donnerstag uns,
aber die Müllabfuhr ließ uns aus.
So bleiben wir und hoffen
auf bessere Wochen und
die Bestechlichkeit der Träger.

O

ग्युंटर आइष

॥ सेवा में ॥

मंगलवार को भी हम
अपना कूड़ा दरवाजे के सामने रखते हैं,
बुधवार को
हम अपना घर बिक्री के लिए उठाते हैं,
बृहस्पतिवार खुद को,
लेकिन कूड़ा उठानेवाले हमें
छोड़ देते हैं
तो हम रुके रहते हैं और उम्मीद करते हैं
बेहतर हफ्तों की और
उन सफाईवालों की जिन्हें घूस दी जा सकती हो
○

(अनुवाद : विष्णु खरे)

EN ATTENDANT

On Tuesday we still
put our garbage in front of the door,
on Wednesday
we put the house on the market,
on Thursday ourselves,
but the refuse collectors
missed us out.
So we stay and hope
for better weeks and
dustmen who can be bribed.
○

(Tr. by Michael Hamburger)

TAUBEN

Taubenflug über die Äcker hin, -
ein Flügelschlag, der schneller ist als die Schönheit.
Sie holt ihn nicht ein, sondern bleibt mir
als Unbehagen zurück im Herzen.

Als wäre auch Taubengelächter vernehmbar
vor den Schlägen, den grün gestrichenen Zwerghäusern,
und ich beginne nachzudenken,
ob der Flug ihnen wichtig ist,
welchen Rang die Blicke zum Erdboden haben
und wie sie das Aufpicken des Korns einordnen
und das Erkennen des Habichts.

Ich rate mir selbst, mich vor den Tauben zu fürchten.
Du bist nicht ihr Herr, sage ich, wenn du Futter streust,
wenn du Nachrichten an ihre Federn heftest,
wenn du Zierformen züchtest, neue Farben,
neue Schöpfe, Gefieder am Fuß.
Vertrau deiner Macht nicht,
so wirst du auch nicht verwundert sein,
wenn du erfährst, daß du unwichtig bist,

daß neben deinesgleichen heimliche Königreiche bestehen,
Sprachen ohne Laut, die nicht erforscht werden,
Herrschaften ohne Macht und unangreifbar,
daß die Entscheidungen geschehen im Taubenflug.
O

॥ कबूतर ॥

जुते हुए खेतों के ऊपर से कबूतरों की उड़ान
पंखों की एक फटकार सुन्दरता से भी ज्यादा तेज
वह उन्हें पकड़ नहीं सकती, हालाँकि मेरे दिल में रहती है
वापस बेचैनी की तरह।

मानों कबूतरों की हँसी भी सुनी जा सकती हो
हरे पुते हुए उनके उन बौने घरों, मड़वों के सामने
और मैं विचारना शुरू करता हूँ कि
क्या उड़ान उनके लिए जरूरी है
जमीन की तरफ निगाह करने को वह कौन-सा स्थान देते हैं
और दानों को चुगने की क्या कीमत आँकते हैं,
बाजों को पहचानने की क्या।

मैं खुद को कबूतरों से डरने की सलाह देता हूँ।
तुम उनके मालिक नहीं हो, मैं कहता हूँ, जब तुम उन्हें
चुग्गा डालते हो,
जब तुम उनके पैरों में संदेसे बाँधते हो
जब तुम उनकी अजीब नस्लें पैदा करते हो, नए रंग,
नई कलगियाँ, या पैरों के ऊपर पंखों के नए लच्छे।
अपनी शक्ति में कोई विश्वास न रखो
तब जब तुम्हें यह मालूम होगा तो कोई अचम्भा नहीं होगा
कि तुम्हारी कितनी कम वकत है,

कि तुम्हारी तरह के अलावा भी छिपे हुए राज्य हैं,
बिना ध्वनियों की भाषाएँ जिनका अध्ययन नहीं किया जा
सकता,
सत्ताहीन और अजेय उपनिवेश,
कि कबूतरों की उड़ान में निर्णय लिए जाते हैं।
○

(अनुवाद : विष्णु खरे)

PIGEONS

Flight of pigeons over the ploughed fields -
a wingbeat more swift than beauty
that cannot catch up with such speed
but remains in my heart as discomfort.

As if the laughter of pigeons too could be heard
in front of the dovecotes, dwarf dwellings painted
green,
and I begin to consider
whether flight is important to them,
what rank they accord to the earthward glance
and how they value the pecking of grain,
how the recognition of hawks.

I advise myself to be afraid of pigeons.
You are not their master, I say, when you throw
them food,
when you fasten messages to their legs,
when you breed curious variants, new colours,
new crests, or tufts of feathers above the feet.
Put no trust in your power,
then you'll not be astonished
when you discover how little you count,

that besides your kind there are hidden kingdoms,
languages without sounds that cannot be studied,
dominions without power and unassailable;
that decisions are made by the pigeon's flight.
○

(*Tr. by Michael Hamburger*)

IN ANDEREN SPRACHEN

Wenn der Elsternflug mich befragte,
das Wippen der Bachstelze,
in allen Jahrhunderten vor meiner Geburt,
wenn das Stumme mich fragte,
gab mein Ohr ihm die Antwort.

Heute erinnert mich
der Blick aus dem Fenster.
Ich denke in die Dämmerung,
wo die Antwort auffliegt,
Federn bewegt,
im Ohr sich die Frage rührt.

Während mein Hauch sich noch müht,
das Ungeschiedne zu nennen,
hat mich das Wiesengrün übersetzt
und die Dämmerung denkt mich.

❍

॥ दूसरी भाषाओं में ॥

पाखीउड़ान ने मुझसे पूछा,
पंखों के ऊपर नीचे होने ने,
मेरे जन्म से पहले की सारी सदियों में,
जब चुप्पी ने मुझसे सवाल किया
तो मेरे कान ने उत्तर दिया।

मुझे याद दिलाता है आज
खिड़की से दिखता दृश्य।
मैं सान्ध्यवेला में सोचता हूँ
उत्तर उड़कर जहाँ जाता है,
पंखों को स्फुरित करता है,
मेरे कान में प्रश्न सुगबुगाता है।

जब मेरी साँस परिश्रम करती है
अवर्गीकृत को नाम देने की
चरागाह के हरेपन ने मेरा अनुवाद कर दिया है
और सान्ध्यवेला मुझे सोच रही है।
O

(अनुवाद : विष्णु खरे)

IN OTHER LANGUAGES

When the magpie's flight questioned me,
the wagtail's flicking,
in all the centuries before my birth,
when silent things questioned me
my ear gave the answer.

What reminds me today
is the view from my window.
I think into the twilight
where the answer flies up,
sets feathers into motion,
the question stirs in my ear.

While my breath still labours
to name the undifferentiated
the meadow's green has translated me
and the twilight thinks me.
O

(*Tr. by Michael Hamburger*)

Hans Magnus ENZENSBERGER

ZUKUNFTSMUSIK

Die wir nicht erwarten können,
wirds lehren.

Sie glänzt, ist ungewiß, fern.

Die wir auf uns zukommen lassen,
erwartet uns nicht,
kommt nicht auf uns zu,
nicht auf uns zurück,
steht dahin.

Gehört uns nicht,
fragt nicht nach uns,
will nichts von uns wissen,
sagt uns nichts,
kommt uns nicht zu.

War nicht,
ist nicht für uns da,
ist nie dagewesen,
ist nie da,
ist nie.
O

हांस माग्नुस एंत्सेंसबर्गर

॥ भविष्य रागिणी ॥

नाही धरवत धीर आता जिच्यासाठी
ती शिकवील ते।

दूर अनिश्चित चमकतंय ते।

देतो येऊ आपल्या दिशेनं आपण जिला
आपली अपेक्षा नाही तिला,
नाही येत नी आपल्या दिशेनं,
परतून येत नाही ती आपल्या दिशेने
राहाते खिळून।

ती आपली नसतेच,
नसते विचारत आपल्याला,
नसते काहीही कळून घेणार आपल्या विषयी
सांगत नसते काहीही आपल्याला,
नसते येत आपल्या दिशेनं।

नव्हतीच,
नाहीच आपल्यासाठी ठेवलेली,
नव्हती कधीच ठेवलेली,
नसतेच कधीही,
नसतेच मुळी।
○

*(लोठार लुत्से यांच्या साहाय्याने मूळ जर्मनवरून
अनुवाद : दिलीप पुरुषोत्तम चित्रे)*

DREAMS OF THE FUTURE

What we cannot wait for
will teach us to.

Bright, unknown, distant.

What we take as it comes
does not anticipate us
await us,
does not get back to us,
remains to be seen.

Does not belong to us,
does not ask after us,
will hear none of us,
tells us nothing,
does not befit us.

Was not,
is not there for us,
has never been,
is never there,
is never.
○

(Tr. by Padma Rao)

Erich FRIED

VIELLEICHT ALLENDE

Ich bin der Niederlagen müde
und müder noch
der Freunde die kommen nach jeder Niederlage
und beweisen: 'Eigentlich war sie ein Sieg'

Dabei reden sie so
um nicht selber der Niederlagen
so müde zu werden daß sie ihnen erliegen
Doch solche Reden
Führen zu solchen Siegen

Ich weiß: Noch immer hing der Sieg des Neuen
am Ende einer Kette von Niederlagen
(von denen dies eine ist) als letztes Glied
Das könnte ein Trost sein
aber die Glieder bluten

Wenn ich tot bin können sie sagen:
'Er hat sich selbst getötet'
fast wie man sagen könnte
wenn ich das wirklich täte:
'Die ihn getötet haben das waren sie'

Aber wenn ich auch müde bin des Erlebenmüssens
ihrer Verbrechen und des Zeitungsgeschwätzes
diese Niederlage beweise die Vergeblichkeit unserer Sache
und müde meines Zualtseins um selbst noch die Kräfte
zu sammeln zum neuen Kampf
ich bin nicht müde des Kampfes
gegen die die eines Tages sterben
an meinem Tod
❍

एरिष फ्रीट

॥ नहीं थका हूँ ॥

मैं थक चुका हूँ पराजयों से
और और भी ज्यादा थक चुका हूँ
उन दोस्तों से जो हर पराजय के बाद आते हैं
और सिद्ध करते हैं : 'दरअसल वह विजय थी'

वे इस तरह इसलिए कहते हैं
कि पराजयों से थक न जाएँ इतने
कि उनके आगे दम तोड़ दें
लेकिन उस तरह की बात
उसी तरह की विजयों की तरफ ले जाती है

मैं जानता हूँ : नए की विजय
हमेशा आई है पराजयों की एक कड़ी के अन्त में
(जिनमें से यह एक है) अन्तिम कड़ी के रूप में
इससे कुछ राहत मिल सकती है
लेकिन कड़ियों से खून गिरता है

जब मैं मरूँ तो वे कह सकते हैं
उसने खुद को मारा'
जिस तरह से तुम कह सकते हो
यदि मैं वाकई वैसा करूँ तो
'यह वे लोग थे जिन्होंने उसे मारा'

लेकिन भले ही मैं थक चुका हूँ बर्दाश्त करने से
उनके जुर्म और अखबारों की अफवाहबाजी
कि यह पराजय हमारे लक्ष्य की नाउम्मीदी का सबूत है
और थक चुका हूँ अब इतनी उम्र का हो जाने से
कि खुद इतनी ताकत जुटा नहीं सकता
नए संघर्षों के लिए
लेकिन मैं उनके खिलाफ लड़ाई से नहीं थका हूँ जो एक
दिन मरेंगे मेरी मौत से
❍

(अनुवाद : विष्णु खरे)

ALLENDE PERHAPS

I am tired of defeats
but tireder still
of friends who come after each defeat
and prove: 'Actually it was a victory'

They talk like that
so as not to be so tired of defeats
that they succumb to them
But that kind of talk
leads to that kind of victory

I know: The victory of the new
has always come at the end
of a chain of defeats
(of which this is one) as the last link
That might be some comfort
but links bleed

When I am dead they can say:
'He killed himself'
just as you could say
if I really did so:
'They were the ones who killed him'

But even if I am tired of having to endure
their crimes and the newspaper gossip
that this defeat is proof
of the hopelessness of our cause
and tired of being too old
to summon up the strength myself
for new struggles
I am not tired of the fight
against those who one day will die
of my death
❍

(*Tr. by Stuart Hood*)

FRAGEN NACH DER POESIE SEIT AUSCHWITZ

Ob sie aufstieg als braunes Vöglein
aus dem Rauch der Verbrennungsöfen
und dann Rast hielt auf einer der Birken
von Birkenau

Ob sie näherflog
angelockt von den Schreien der Mädchen
und bei der Vergewaltigung zusah
und dann

dem Staub der Ruinenstädte
ihr Lied sang von stiller Liebe
und den Verhungernden
die Ballade vom reifenden Korn

Ob sie aufwuchs im Schatten des Geldes
und ihm ihre Stimme lieh
weil es längst schon zu groß war
um noch klimpern zu können

Ob sie die Welt durchflog
und ihren Sinn für das Schöne
von den bunten Farben
der zerrissenen Körper lernte

vom hellen Brand der Dorfhütten
oder von Spiegelungen
des wechselnden Tageslichtes
in glasigen Augen

Ob sie in einem chemisch entlaubten Baum
zuletzt ihr Nest aus verschont gebliebenen Haaren
Papierfasern Kleiderresten
und blutigen Federn baute

und nun auf Paarung wartet
auf das Sitzen auf ihren Eiern

॥ आउश्वित्स के बाद कविता के बारे में सवालात ॥

क्या वह एक नन्हीं भूरी चिड़िया के रूप में
शवदाह भट्टियों के धुएँ से उभरी
और फिर बिर्केनाउ के भूर्जों में से एक पर
सुस्ताने के लिए उतरी

क्या वह नजदीक उड़कर गई
लड़कियों की चीखों से खिंचकर
और उन पर बलात्कार होते हुए देखा
और फिर

तबाह शहरों की धूल के लिए
मूक प्रेम का अपना गीत गाया
और भूखे मरते हुओं के लिए
पकती फसल की गाथा

क्या वह पैसे की छाया में बड़ी हुई
और उसे अपनी आवाज उधार दे दी
क्योंकि पैसा इतना बड़ा हो गया था
कि खनखनाना उसके लिए कठिन हो गया था

क्या वह विश्व के बीच से उड़ी
और अपना सौन्दर्यबोध सीखा
चटख रंगों से
चिन्दा-चिन्दा लाशों से

गांव की झोंपड़ियों की उजली लपटों से
या विस्फारित आँखों में
दिन के बदलते उजाले की दमक से

QUESTIONS ABOUT POETRY SINCE AUSCHWITZ

Whether it rose up as a small brown bird
out of the smoke of cremation ovens
and then rested in one of the birchs
of Birkenau

whether it flew closer
drawn by the screams of the girls
and saw them raped
and then sang

to the dust of the ruined cities
its song of quiet love
and to the starving
the lay of the ripening corn

whether it grew up in the shadow of money
and lent it its voice
for money had grown too big
to be able to jingle

whether it flew through the world
and learned its sense of beauty
from the vivid colours
of bodies torn to pieces

from the bright flames of village huts
or from the glint
of the changing daylight
in glazed eyes

whether at last in a tree
stripped by defoliants
it built its nest of hair
of paper shreds of rags and bloody feathers

und auf das Ausschlüpfen ihrer
immer wieder unschuldigen Jungen

das wissen nur lyrische Dichter
die unentwegten
Rufer zum Vogelschutz
in der bald wieder heilen Welt.
❍

क्या आखिरकार रसायनों से पत्रहीन किए गए किसी पेड़ पर
आखिर में उसने बालों
कागज की चिंदियों चिथड़ों
और खूनी पंखों का अपना घोंसला बनाया

और अब सहवास की प्रतीक्षा करती है
अपने अंडों को सेने के वक्त की
और उनसे अपने
हमेशा के लिए निर्दोष चूजों के निकलने की

यह सिर्फ गीतकार ही जानते हैं
जो अदम्य आह्वान करते हैं
जंगली पक्षियों की सुरक्षा के लिए
जल्द दुबारा संपूर्ण होनेवाली दुनिया में।
O

(अनुवाद : विष्णु खरे)

कविता का शीर्षक ठेओडोर अडोर्नो के उस प्रसिद्ध वक्तव्य का हवाला देता है जिसमें कहा गया था कि (नात्सी यातना-शिविर) आउश्वित्स (में हजारों निरपराध यहूदियों की हत्या) के बाद कोई कविता संभव नहीं है।

and now waits for mating
for the time to sit on its eggs
and for the hatching of
its eternally innocent young

that only lyric poets know
who steadfastly call
for wild bird protection
in a world soon to be whole again.
O

(*Tr. by Stuart Hood*)

The title is a reference to the statement by Theodor Adorno that no poetry is possible after Auschwitz.

RÜCKBLICK

Ich wollte
meiner Zeit
Flamme sein
oder
Teil ihrer Flamme

Ich war
ihr Schatten
oder
ein Teil
ihres Schattens

Meine Zeit
war die Zeit
der Wut:
Schatten der Wut.

Meine Zeit
war die Zeit
der Ohnmacht:
Schatten der Ohnmacht

die Zeit
der Tyrannei:
Schatten der Tyrannei

Ich wollte
meiner Zeit
Fahne sein
oder ein
Fetzen der Fahne

Fahne
der Flamme
der Wut
der Ohnmacht

॥ पुनरावलोकन ॥

मैं चाहता था
अपने समय की
लपट होना
या
उस लपट का अंश होना

मैं उसकी
छाया था
या
एक अंश
उसकी छाया का

मेरा समय
समय था
उन्माद का
उन्माद की छाया का

मेरा समय
समय था
लाचारगी का
लाचारगी की छाया का

समय
तानाशाही का
तानाशाही की छाया का

मैं चाहता था
अपने समय
का परचम होना
या उस परचम का एक रेशा

RETROSPECT

I wanted
to be the flame
of my time
or
part of its flame

I was its shadow
or
part
of its shadow

My time
was the time
of fury --
shadow of fury

My time
was the time
of helplessness --
shadow of helplessness

the time
of tyranny --
shadow of tyranny

I wanted
to be the banner
of my time
or a shred of its banner

Banner
of flame
of fury
of helplessness

der Tyrannei
oder ihr Fetzen
oder ein Teil
seines Schattens
❍

परचम
लपट का
उन्माद का
लाचारगी का
तानाशाही का
या उसका एक रेशा
या हिस्सा
उसकी छाया का
○

(अनुवाद : विष्णु खरे)

of tyranny
or its shred
or part
of its shadow
○

(*Tr. by Stuart Hood*)

Günter GRASS

ZUNGE ZEIGEN

[Auszug]

1

Schwarz ist die Göttin, Fledermäuse
lösen sich schwarz aus Bäumen,
die schwarz vorm Mond stehn.

Nicht mehr ach, weh und oh und: Jeder
Engel ist schrecklich. Kein Gedanke
steht an, Poren zu schließen.
Überfluß muß es sein, den anderes Klima
auf Eis gelegt hat.
Hier, hieß es zu Haus, wo niemand sich einläßt
auf was, extrem nichts sein darf
und einzig Ausgleich
als Terror erlaubt ist,
hier wird nicht geschwitzt!

Alle Schleusen gesprengt. Fließt,
tropft aufs Blatt,
macht sich mit Tinte gemein: Ich bin,
feuchte durch, lauf über
und setze lachend
schweißgetriebene Wörter, die eng stehn,
verschachtelt wie wir in den Pendelzügen
nach Ballygunge.

Der die das. Im allgemeinen Geschiebe wird
jeder Artikel gestrichen. Eigener
leckt fremden Schweiß. Was griffig,
entzogen (nun auch der Teppich, das Erbstück
unter den Füßen weg). Einander
abhanden gekommen, greifen wir über uns
und ins Leere; es sei denn,
einer der praktischen Griffe - notfalls
für jedermann - gäbe Halt.

Stille, nur schmatzende Geckos,
bis von der Straße der Bus nach Calcutta,

ग्युंटर ग्रास

॥ जीभ दिखाना ॥

[कुछ काव्यांश]

1

काली है देवी, चमगादड़ें
छूटती हैं काली पेड़ों से,
जो चाँद के सामने काले खड़े हैं।

अब और आह, हाय और नहीं और : हर
फ़रिश्ता ख़ौफ़नाक है। कोई विचार
कतार में खड़ा नहीं होता रोमकूप बंद करने के लिए
समृद्धि ही होगी जिसे दूसरी आबहवा ने
बर्फ़ पर रख दिया है।
यहाँ, जैसा देस में कहते हैं, जहाँ कोई
कुछ से नहीं उलझता, अति नहीं होनी चाहिए
और सिर्फ़ ख़म्याज़े के तौर पर
दहशत की इजाज़त है,
यहाँ कोई पसीना नहीं बहेगा !

सारे जलकपाट खुल जाते हैं। बहता है,
चादर पर गिरता है,
यकसार हो जाता है स्याही के साथ : मैं,
पूरा सील जाता हूँ,
और पसीना-चालित शब्दों से हँसा दिया जाता हूँ,
जो भिंचे खड़े हैं,
हमारी तरह बालीगंज की शटलगाड़ी में गुँथे।

स्त्री नपुंसक पुल्लिग। सब अलग अलग
फाँकों मे कट जाएँगे। दूसरे का
पसीना चाटता है एक। जो छूने में अच्छा है,
छूट गया (अब गलीचा भी, पैरों तले की विरासत,
गया)। एक दूसरे को खोए हुए, हम अपने ऊपर
और शून्य में पकड़ते हैं; तब यह होता है
कि अभ्यस्त पकड़वाला कोई–ज़रूरत हो तो हर एक को–
सहारा देता है।
चुप्पी, सिर्फ जीभ चटखारती छिपकलियाँ,

SHOW YOUR TOUNGE

[Verse-extracts]

1

Black, the goddess. Loosing themselves
black from trees, bats
black before the moon.

No more ah, alas, and every
angel is terrible. No thought
stands in line to close the pores.
It must be overabundance that another climate
has put on ice.
Here, they say at home, where no one
gets involved, nothing should be
extreme and only as compensation is terror
permitted. No sweat here!

All sluices open, it flows, drops
onto the sheet, makes
common cause with ink: I am
sopped through and set laughing by
sweat-driven words in tight ranks
encapsulated like us in our
commuter train to Ballygunge.

The, a, an get canceled.
The drift is general
when one licks another's sweat.
The old good grip gone, and the carpet too,
the heirloom underfoot, gone. We
have mislaid one another.

Silence, only the lip-smacking
of geckos, until the bus to Calcutta,
the resounding horn, the oncoming traffic,
and the neighbor's radio bawls love
like everywhere else.

die Dauerhupe, der Gegenverkehr...
Und aus des Nachbarn Radio plärrt Liebe
wie überall.

Das jede Nacht.
Doch heute der Mond
als Zugabe voll.

6

Müll unser. Täglich, wenn nicht ein Streik
allen Rädern und auch der Zeit
in die Speichen fällt, karren Kipplader,
was die Stadt erbricht, nahe der Straße
zum Flughafen (VIP-Road genannt)
immer höher zuhauf, daß Landschaft entsteht,
die ihren Horizont täglich ändert
und vielen Kinderhänden, die wie die Kinder
müllfarben sind, Nährmutter,
Fundgrube ist.

Denn alles, ob Knopf oder Tube,
fällt auf, wird gesichtet, bleibt habhaft,
damit nichts, kein Coca-Deckel, kein Nagel,
die Ampulle, die Dose aus Dosen,
auch nicht die Scherbe von Scherben
verlorengeht.

Wer nennt Gerüche Gestank!
Was riecht, das sind wir.
Unser täglicher Nachlaß; nicht nur vom Reichen
fällt ab, selbst Mangel wirft hinter sich.
Das alles vermengt und gesiebt
gärt unterm nächsten Monsun und riecht:
Müll unser.

Doch gegraben in tausend
und etwas mehr Jahren,
wo unterm Schwemmland
nach letzter Sintflut das sagenhafte
Calcutta zu liegen verspräche,
fände sich nichts, nicht Tube, nicht Knopf,
kein Nagel, kein Coca-Deckel,
die Dose aus Dosen und die Ampulle,
die Scherben der Scherbe nicht.
Nichts wäre gesprächig:
stummer Müll nur.

बस की सड़क से कलकत्ता तक,
लम्बे हार्न, आता हुआ यातायात...
और पड़ोस के रेडियो से चीखता है प्यार
सब जगह की तरह।

यह हर रात।
फिर भी आज चाँद
घलुए में पूरा है।

6

कूड़ा हमारा। प्रतिदिन, यदि कोई हड़ताल
सभी पहियों और समय में भी
कोई अड़ंगा न डाल दे, ठेले ले जाते हैं
वह जो शहर वमन करता है, हवाई अड्डे जाने वाली
सड़क के (जो वी.आइ.पी. रोड कहलाती है) नज़दीक
लगातार ऊँचा होता जाता है, परिदृश्य निर्मित करता है, जो
अपने क्षितिज को प्रतिदिन बदलता है
और कई बच्चाहाथों के लिए, जो बच्चों की तरह
कूड़े के हैं, दाई माँ,
खजानों की खान है।

सभी कुछ, बटन हो या ट्यूब
खोज लिया जाता है, देखा जाएगा, झपटा जाता है।
साथ में कुछ भी, कोई कोला-कैन,
कोई कील, इंजैक्शन की शीशियाँ,
डिब्बों के डिब्बे, टुकड़ों के टुकड़े तक
बर्बाद नहीं जाते।

बू को बदबू कौन कहता है !
जो बदबू देता है, वह हम हैं।
हमारी दैनिक पूँजी; यह सिर्फ़ अमीरों से ही
नहीं टपकती, गरीब भी इसमें योगदान देते हैं।
यह सब एकमेक होता है और निथरता है
ख़मीर उठाता है अगली मान्सून के तले और गँधाता है :
कूड़ा हमारा।

फिर भी हज़ार से कुछ ज़्यादा बरस बाद
खोदे जाने पर
जहाँ पिछले जलप्रलय के बाद
मिट्टी के मैदान के तले
पौराणिक कलकत्ता अपने होने की आशा बँधाएगा,
कुछ नहीं मिलेगा, ट्यूब नहीं, बटन नहीं,
न कोई कील, न कोला-कैन,

This, every night. Yet today
the moon is full for an encore.

6

Garbage, our own. Daily, provided a strike
doesn't put a stick in the wheel.
Dumpsters take the city's vomit
along the road to the airport, VIP road,
creating landscape, changing the horizon daily,
and for many children the garbage is
foster mother, treasure quarry.

Everything is found, grabbed. Nothing,
from bottle cap to nail to vial to fixture to tube,
not even the refuse of the refuse is lost.

The stink, it comes from us,
our daily remains. Not just from the rich
does it dribble, the poor contribute too.
Mingled and sieved, it ferments
beneath the next monsoon. Our stink.

Yet, in excavations a thousand years from now
in alluvial flats from the last Great Flood,
the site of legendary Calcutta, nothing
will be found, no bottle cap, no nail, no avil,
no fixture or tube, not even
the refuse of the refuse, only silent garbage.

In the present garbage already
turning to humus, promising vegetables, we found
a school hidden in a shed, children
crouched over slates, practicing Bengali letters.
The exercise, written over and over,
in translation: Life is beautiful.

The vultures here know too much, know
what will be in the paper tomorrow.
Soon that computer, the one
the son of a sweeper,
say the vultures,
developed in his free time,
says the paper,
will regulate garbage collection. But
the stink won't be so easy to...

Gegenwärtig jedoch
fanden wir mitten im Müll, wo er geebnet
schon Humus zu werden
und Gemüse zu treiben verspricht,
eine Schule in einem Schuppen versteckt.
Still hockten Müllkinder über Schiefertafeln
und übten bengalische Schrift.
Das Leben ist schön, hieß (für uns) übersetzt,
was sie zur Übung wieder und wieder
schrieben.

Vögel darüber. Gesichtet aus Vogelschau
ist alles möglich, sich nah.
Die Geier hier wissen zu viel
und plaudern aus, was morgen erst
in der Zeitung steht: Demnächst soll jener Computer,
den dem Sohn eines Sweepers,
sagen die Geier,
in seiner Freizeit entwickelt hat,
steht in der Zeitung,
die Müllabfuhr steuern; nur der Gestank
lasse sich nicht...

11

Dahin bringt das Leben sich
über kurz oder lang: in krummes Geäst
gebettet, mit Knüppeln bedeckt,
die auf Schalen gewogen,
wie sie beim Jüngsten Gericht (aus kaufmännisch
frommer Sicht) in Gebrauch sein werden.
Hat seinen Preis, rötliches Brennholz,
gefällt in den fiebrigen Sundarbans,
darf nicht geringer ausschlagen
als der Kadaver.

Auf diversen Brandstätten - alle
an den mündenden Arm des Ganges,
aus Hooghlyufer gerückt - qualmen Stöße
über lustlosen Feuern, immer noch feucht
vom Wasser, das niederkam, wiederholter
Sturzgeburt gleich (und die Stadt
als Meldung in aller Welt Zeitung brachte).
Noch zögern die teuren Hölzer
und müssen belebt, mit Reisstroh
belebt, durch Gutzureden
belebt werden.

बक्सों के बक्से और इंजैक्शनों की शीशियाँ,
न टुकड़ों के टुकड़े।
कुछ नहीं बोलेगा : सिर्फ़ गूँगा कूड़ा।

फिलहाल फिर भी
हम पाते हैं कूड़े के बीच, जहाँ वह
खाद बन रहा है और सब्जियों की
उम्मीद बँधा रहा है, एक स्कूल
एक शेड के नीचे छिपा हुआ।
चुपचाप उकडूँ झुके हुए हैं कूड़े के बच्चे स्लेटपट्टियों पर
जीवन सुन्दर है, (हमारे लिए) अनुवाद किया जाता है,
जो वे अभ्यास के रूप में बार बार
लिख रहे हैं।

उसके ऊपर पक्षी। पक्षीआँख से देखो
तो सभी संभव है, स्वयं के समीप है।
गीध यहाँ बहुत जानते हैं और वह
गपियाते हैं जो सुबह अखबारों में छपता है :
शीघ्र ही एक कम्प्यूटर,
जिसे एक भंगी के बेटे ने,
गीध कहते हैं,
अपने छुट्टी के वक्त में बनाया था,
छपा है अख़बार में,
कूड़ा इकट्ठा करने को नियंत्रित करेगा; सिर्फ बदबू
इतनी आसानी से...

11

यहाँ तक जीवन ले ही आता है स्वयं को देर-सवेर :
आड़ी-टेढ़ी डालियों का बिस्तरा, टहनियों से ढका हुआ,
तौली गई टहनियाँ जैसे (बहीख़ाते नुमा)
आख़िरी फैसले में इस्तेमाल की जाने वाली हों।
अपनी कीमत है ललछौंही जलाऊ लकड़ी की
जिसे भफाते हुए सुंदरबन में काटा गया था,
लकड़ियाँ लाश से लम्बी होनी चाहिए।

विभिन्न शमशान घाटों पर—जो
गंगा की बहती हुई धारा के बराबर
हुगली के किनारे तक चले गए हैं –
बेजान आग पर धुँआते हैं ढेर लकड़ियों के, जो पानी से
अभी तक सीली हैं, बार बार पैदा की गई
जैसे अचानक प्रसूति में (और शहर को
दुनिया भर के अखबारों में सुर्खियाँ बनाते हुए)
अभी भी हिचकिचाती है कीमती लकड़ी
और उसे उकसाना पड़ता है धान के पुआल से

11

Life comes to this sooner or later.
Bedded in branches, covered with sticks,
sticks weighed (as in a businessman's
Last Judgement), because wood costs,
reddish firewood felled in feverish sundarbans,
and the sticks must not be longer
than the cadaver.

At the burning ghats along the Ganges,
down to the banks of the Hooghly,
woodpiles smoldering, still damp
from water delivered again and again
like sudden birth (turning the city
into headlines around the world).
Reluctant still´, that costly wood,
it needs to be coaxed with rice straw,
encouraged with words, revived.
Melted butter greases the dead.
Flowers on top, sweet of breath, cheerful.
Red paint on the soles of unaligned feet.
Leaves on dead eyes. But the phrases
we find obituarily handy - passed on,
sleeping the last sleep, went
to his reward - are unavailable.
The dead here are dead in earnest.

The wood takes them, the stump-toothed
fire gnaws through
Renewed, elsewhere, perhaps, the soul.
Ashes and charred scraps belong to the river,
to which everything is added: excrement,
petals, chemicals, the bather's fragile nakedness,
the sweat of faded cloth.

But today Durga and Lakshmi and company
are carted with hoopla and rat-a-tat
to the Hooghly.
The feast is over. For seven days
the gods have visited.
Straw puppets, to which clay (dried and lacquered)
lends the aspects of flesh.
Displayed: the lion and hoot owl,
the rat, peacock, and swan. And on ten arms

Geschmolzene Butter fettet die Leichen.
Drauf Blumen, wie sie, gleich süß von Atem,
zu lustigem Anlaß gebräuchlich.
Rot eingestrichen die Sohlen verdrehter Füße.
Blätter decken den Sterbeblick. (Jene Wörter jedoch,
die uns als Nachruf zur Hand - dahingegangen,
entschlafen, abgerufen in eine bessere Welt -,
sind nicht im Handel). Die Toten hier
sind besonders tot.

Leergelebt nimmt Holz sie gefangen.
Mit stumpfen Zähnen frißt Feuer sich durch.
Mag die Seele woanders aufs neue,
Asche und Reste verkohlt kriegt der Fluß,
dem alles beigemengt wird: Scheiße
Blüten, Chemie, der Badenden
nackte Gebrechlichkeit, der Schweiß
verwaschener Tücher.

Doch heute werden Durga and Lakshmi, wer noch,
mit Trara und Getrommel zum Hooghly gekarrt.
Das Fest ist aus. Auf sieben Tage
kam Götterbesuch: Strohpuppen, denen Tonerde
(getrocknet bemalt) fleischiges Aussehen gibt.
Zur Schau gestellt mit Getier: Löwe und Eule,
Ratte, Schwan, Pfau. Und an zehn Armen
glitzert in Händen Gewalt, damit das Gute
über das Böse und andere
dumme Geschichten.

In jedem Slum: selbst die ärmsten
der Armen türmen ihren Altar.
Seht, wie altgediente Marxisten
sechstausend Bettler raus aus der Stadt
ins Abseits treiben, solange die Gottheit
ihr Fest gibt.

Gebete und Priester haben wie anderswo
ihren Preis; Schrecken verteilt sich
umsonst. Käme doch Zorn auf
und hielte an.

❍

उकसाना पड़ता है भले शब्दों से
पुनर्जीवित करना होता है।

घी शवों को चिकनाता है
ऊपर से फूल, साँस में सुगँधित,
सामान्यतः प्रसन्न अवसर के लिए।
अस्तव्यस्त पैरों के तलुओ पर लाल आलता।
मृत आँखों पर पत्तियाँ। (लेकिन वे मुहावरे
जो हम यूरोपियों को मृत्युलेख के लिए आसानी से मिल जाते हैं—
दिवंगत, चिरनिद्रा, श्रेष्ठतर संसार को निमंत्रित—
उपलब्ध नहीं हैं।) मृतक यहाँ
गंभीरता से मृत हैं।
लकड़ी शवों को पकड़े रखती है।
ठूठों के दाँतों से आग भकोस डालती है,
आत्मा शायद कहीं और नई,
राख और जले हुए हिस्से नदी के हैं
जिसमें सभी कुछ मिलता है : मल,
पंखुड़ियाँ, रसायन, स्नानार्थियों की नाजुक
नग्नता, फीके कपड़ों का पसीना।

लेकिन आज दुर्गा और लक्ष्मी और जाने कौन
भजन-कीर्तन और ढोल-ताशे के साथ हुगली ले जाए जाएँगे।
त्यौहार समाप्त हो गया है। सात दिन तक
देवता उतरे : पुआल के पुतले जिन्हें (सूखी
और रंगी हुई) मिट्टी ने शरीर दे दिया है।
प्रदर्शन के लिए पशुलोक प्रस्तुत है : सिंह और उलूक
मूषक, हंस, मयूर। और दस भुजाओं पर
दमकती है शक्ति, ताकि पुण्य पाप पर
तथा अन्य मूर्खतापूर्ण कहानियाँ।

हर गंदी बस्ती में : ग़रीब से ग़रीब भी
अपनी वेदी ऊँची उठाते हैं।
देखो कैसे खुर्राट मार्क्सवादी
छः हजार भिखारियों को निगाह से परे
शहर के बाहर खदेड़ देते हैं, जब तक कि
पूजा उत्सव समाप्त न हो जाए।
पूजाओं और पुजारियों की, हर जगह की तरह
एक कीमत होती है; भय मुफ्त में बँटता है। काश
गुस्सा भी आए और ठहरे।
O

(जर्मन से अनुवाद : विष्णु खरे)

glistening power, so that good
may defeat evil, and similar nonsense.

In every slum even the poorest
of the poor raise high their altar,
Veteran Marxists drive six thousand beggars
out of town, out of sight, for as long
as divinity holds its feast.

Prayers and priests, as everywhere, have
their price. The price is fear. We could do
with a little anger.
O

(Tr. From German by John E. Woods)

Sarah KIRSCH

KALT

Aus teerschwarzem Meer steigt der
Mond auf. Solltest nun
Unter ein Dach gelangen verehrtes
Herz. Sonst greint die Sehnsucht
Ihren verlorenen Traum von der
Schönheit der Welt die so
Verkommen darnieder
Liegt. Blatt geht weil Frost
Andere Zeit macht.
❍

सारा किर्श

॥ गाराठा ॥

मधून डांबरकुट्ट समुद्राच्या येतोय वर
चंद्र। अडोशानं राह्यला पाहिजे
खाली एखाद्या छपराच्या, माननीय
हृदया। एरव्ही ही केकाटत राहातेय आस
तिचं हरपलेलं स्वप्न
सौंदर्याचं जगाच्या जे
कुजून खाली खितपत
पडलंय। पान जातं कारण हिम
वेगळा काळ करतं।
○

(लोठार लुत्से यांच्या साहाय्याने मूळ जर्मनवरून अनुवाद : दिलीप पुरुषोत्तम चित्रे)

FERNE

Niemals wird auf den
Armen Gefilden Herrlichkeit
Liegen wie in der Kindheit als noch die
Fichten grün und licht lebten.
Schwarzes
Wissen beugt mir den Hals.
O

॥ दूरत्व ॥

नव्हेच कधीही वर
दरिद्री क्षेत्रांच्या प्रभा
पसरणार जशी लहानपणीच्या अजूनही
फरच्या हिरव्या झाडांवर प्रकाश जिवंत।
काळं
ज्ञान मोडायळा ळावतं मला मान।
○

(लोठार लुत्से यांच्या साहाय्याने मूळ जर्मनवरून अनुवाद : दिलीप पुरुषोत्तम चित्रे)

DER CHRONIST

Es quellen aus der Feder zartgeschnäbelt
So schwarze Tintenzüge dunkel erglänzend.

Ein Strom von Wiederholungen. Und Grauen
Entspringt der zitternden Hand. Sie wandert

Bei Tag und bei Nacht elend übers Papier,
Zu preisen gibt es heut nicht mehr viel.

Und deshalb ist des Schreibens müde die Hand.

O

॥ बखरकर्ता ॥

उचंबळून येतात लेखणीतून कोवळ्या चोचीचे
काळ्याभोर शाईचे कित्ते काळसरपणे चमकत।

झरा पुनरावर्तनांचा। आणि बीभत्स
पाझर फुटतो थरथरणाऱ्या हाताळा तो भरकटतो

दिवस अन् रात्रभर वणवण भणंग कागदभर।
स्तुती करावंसं उरलेलं नाही आज फारसंकाही।

आणि म्हणून लिहायला शिणून गेलाय हात।
○

(लोठार लुत्से यांच्या साहाय्याने मूळ जर्मनवरून अनुवाद : दिलीप पुरुषोत्तम चित्रे)

WACH

Die Bruchweide jammert im Wind.
Der volle Mond hat sich
Auf meinen Mühlstein gesetzt.
Unter der Milchstraße jagt der
Schatten des Schwans.

Ich male mir Wiedersehen aus.
So ist die Nacht schlaflos.
Während ich mir den
Buckel vollüge entdeckt das
Lachen der Elster den Tag.
❍

॥ जागी ॥

ठिसूळ वाकुंजी आक्रोशते वाऱ्यात
पूर्ण चंद्र येऊन
बसलाय माझ्या उरावरल्या दगडावर।
खाली आकाशगंगेच्या
पाठलाग करणारी सावली राजहंसाची।

मी मनाशीच रंगवते परतभेट।
अशी आहे बिनझोपेची रात्र।
मी स्वतःशी भरपूर खोटंनाटं बोलत असतानाय
मॅगपाय पक्ष्याच्या हसण्याला लागतो दिवस झाल्याचा शोध।
○

(लोठार लुत्से यांच्या साहाय्याने मूळ जर्मनवरून अनुवाद : दिलीप पुरुषोत्तम चित्रे)

FLÜCHTIG

Ich ging vor mir
Auf und davon sprach
Auf mich ein: ver-
Giß! Und mache dich
Hart. So kannst du

Von Erde berichten. Den
Schwerbeschreiblichen
Bäumen Anfang des
Sommers.
O

॥ पलायमान ॥

मी गेले पुढे माझ्याच
निघून आणि तिथून आर्जवलं
आपल्यालाच : वि–
सरून जा ! आणि कर स्वतःला
कठिण। म्हणजे तू कळवू शकशील
पृथ्वीला बातमी। ती
वर्णनदुर्लभ
झाडं ज्यांनी सुरू होतो
उन्हाळा।
o

(लोठार लुत्से यांच्या साहाय्याने मूळ जर्मनवरून अनुवाद : दिलीप पुरुषोत्तम चित्रे)

Tadeus PFEIFER

SPAZIERGANG IM WINTER

Am 1. Jänner
spazierten wir über Rauhreifkristalle
Das Wort
glitt auf dem Atemdampf in die zersprungene Luft
und riß die Lippe auf.

Im Acker hielt das Rund der Krähen schwarzen Rat.
Eine folg auf. Schrie ihren Schrei,
der sich schlitternd in meinen Vers krallte,
während die andern mit schweren Flügeln
den trägen Flug im Kreise nachvollzogen.
○

टाडेऊस फ़ाइफ़र

॥ सर्दियों में घूमना ॥

पहली जनवरी को
हम पतले काँच-जैसे बर्फ पर घूमने गए
वह शब्द
साँस की भाप से तिड़की हुई हवा में फिसला
और होंठ को चीर गया।

मैदान में कौओं का गोल मंत्रणा कर रहा था।
एक उड़ गया।
उसकी चीख़ चीख़ी
और उसने फिसल कर मेरी कविता में अपने पंजे गाड़ दिए
जबकि दूसरों ने भारी पँखों से
एक गोल में उसकी मद्धिम उड़ान का अनुसरण किया
○

(जर्मन से अनुवाद : विष्णु खरे)

A WALK IN WINTER

On 1 January
we walked upon hoar-frost crystals.
The word
slid from the breath vapour in the cracked air
and tore the lips apart.

In the fields a round of crows holds a conference.
One flew away.
Its cry screamed
and, sliding, clawed into my poem
while the others with heavy wings
imitated its indolent flight in a circle.
○

(Tr. by Vishnu Khare)

SAMMLER TOTER GEDICHTE

Tote Gedichte, du findest sie überall
überfahren, gefoltert, verhungert,
einige haben sich selbst umgebracht.

Gestern der ärgste Fund, tot in der Sonne
mit offenem Mund, der Blick
gebrochen,
Ameisen über die Zunge,
letzte Verse
gekotet.

Ein Eimer Wasser, weißes Papier,
wir säuberten behutsam das tote Gedicht.
Mit geschlossenen Augen,
gewaschenem Leib,
hochgebundenem Kiefer
liegt es jetzt,
das tote Gedicht,
ordentlich da.
O

॥ मृत कविताओं का संकलनकार ॥

मृत कविताएँ–तुम उन्हें पाते हो हर जगह,
कुचली हुईं
यातना दी गईं
भूखी मारी गईं;
कुछ ने खुद को मार डाला है

कल मिली सबसे ख़राब हालत में, सूरज के तले मुर्दा
खुला मुँह
आँखें निकली हुईं
जीभ पर चींटियाँ रेंगती हुईं
आखिरी कविता ग़लाज़त में

एक बाल्टी पानी, सफ़ेद काग़ज,
हमने सावधानी से मरी कविता को नहलाकर साफ़ किया।
बंद आँखें
धुले बदन,
भिंचे जबड़ों के साथ
वह लेटी हुई है अब, मृत कविता, करीने से।
O

(जर्मन से अनुवाद : विष्णु खरे)

COLLECTOR OF DEAD POEMS

Dead poems - you find them everywhere,
Run over, tortured, starved,
some have killed themselves.

Yesterday, the worst discovery, dead under the sun
with open mouth, the eyes
staring.
Ants crawling on the tongue,
with its last lines
Soiled in muck.

A pail of water, white paper,
we washed the dead poem cautiously clean.
With closed eyes,
washed body,
closed jaws,
it lies now,
the dead poem,
tidy there.
O

(Tr. by Vishnu Khare)

A,B,C...

Muß die Sprache
etwas heißen?
Könnte sein,
sie wär' nur Sprache?

Müssen meine Worte
dir erzählen,
was du ohne sie
nicht hörst?

Stünde ein Wort
vor deinen Augen,
das nichts als klares
Zeichen zeigt,

was tun damit?
Es nicht
lesen,
haben.

O

॥ क ख ग ॥

क्या भाषा का
कोई अर्थ होना ही चाहिए ?
क्या ऐसा हो सकता है
कि वह केवल भाषा ही रहे ?

क्या मेरे शब्दों का
तुम्हें वह बखानना ही होगा
जो तुम उसके बिना सुन नहीं सकते ?

एक ऐसे शब्द को अपनी आँखों के आगे रखो
जो साफ संकेतों में कुछ नहीं दिखाता

क्या करें उसका ?
उसे पढ़ें नहीं,
पाएँ।
O

(जर्मन से अनुवाद : विष्णु खरे)

A,B,C...

Must the language
mean something?
Could it be
that it were only a language?

Must my words
describe to you
what you do not hear
without them?

Place a word before your eyes
which shows nothing
in clear signs,

what does one do with it?
Not to read it,
to possess it.
O

(Tr. by Vishnu Khare)

EINS UND ANDERES

Schweigen. Nichts sagen.
Verschweigen,
was du weißt.
Was vieles heißt,

darüber reden,
diskutieren,
soviel du kannst,
ist die Kunst.
O

॥ एक और दूसरा ॥

चुप रहना। कुछ न कहना।
जो तुम जानते हो
उसे छिपाना।
जो बहुत मालूम है,

उसकी चर्चा करना,
बहस करना,
जितना तुम कर सकते हो
यह कला है।
○

(जर्मन से अनुवाद : विष्णु खरे)

ONE AND THE OTHER

To keep silent. Not to say.
To conceal,
What you know.
What is much known,

To speak about it,
To discuss
As much as you can
Is the art.
○

(Tr. by Vishnu Khare)

AN AFTERWORD

In October 1992, when I once again took charge of the Delhi office of the South Asia Institute, I realized that here was perhaps my last opportunity to present contemporary Indian literature, both in the original and in German translation, to an interested Delhi public. The circumstances were favourable to such an audacious undertaking: in the Max Mueller Bhavan, without whose participation it would have been impossible to organize such a programme, I found Georg Lechner and Petra Matusche, both of them well-known for their open-mindedness and imaginativeness. Perhaps even more important, I was confident that I could rely on advice and assistance from my Indian friends (who have been my teachers as well), in particular Vishnu Khare.

Thus, the idea and concept of the Living Literature series were born, and in many a session the details of individual programmes were worked out. Now, in retrospect, I am happy and proud to say that most of the programmes were well attended; in fact, they even attracted Indians not used to visiting foreign cultural institutes, mainly because they could not, or would not, participate in English-medium functions.

In the whole series, the organizers naturally were at the receiving end, and I am pleased to express my gratitude first of all to the authors, many of them recognized throughout India, for having agreed to present their recent productions to mixed Delhi audiences. In return, South Asia Institute and Max Mueller Bhavan could, however modestly, provide a first international trial ground with regard to the acceptability and translatability of these writings outside their linguistic regions.

In a culture where 'shabda', word sound, is so important in literary appreciation, authors and audiences were given an opportunity to experience how the sounds of the Indian original were echoed, both strangely familiar and familiarly strange, in a foreign idiom - a multilingual event in a multilingual society. On this background, but also for other, more personal reasons, the programme most memorable for me is the one organized on the occasion of my departure from Delhi in September 1994. It was devoted to Hindi Yuva Kavita; besides some established poets in their thirties, Vishnu and I had invited two teen-agers from Madhya Pradesh, both of them in Delhi for the first time in their lives and at the beginning of a very uncertain poetic career. They heard the translation of their poems into two European languages: besides German, Krzysztof Byrski's resounding Polish.

My commitment to Indian languages and literatures will certainly not end before I do, even if now I am trying to practice the art of timely withdrawal (so essential in Indian culture). I do so reassured by the fact that this work is continued by a successor like Barbara Lotz.

Lothar Lutze
Berlin

NOTES ON CONTRIBUTORS

INDIAN AUTHORS

AHTESHAM, Manzoor
Born in Bhopal in 1948. After studies in engineering, he worked in a medical shop and runs now his own business of interior and furniture design in Bhopal. His first short story appeared in 1973, followed by several collection of short stories, including *Ramzan mein ek maut* (1982), and three novels, *Kuch din aur* (1976), *Sukha Bargad* (1986) and *Dastan-e-lapata* (1995). In collaboration with Satyen Kumar, he wrote several theatre plays, amongst them *Ek tha badshah* (1980). His novel *Sukha Bargad* won him the *Shrikant Verma Smriti Samman* as well as the *Bharatiya Bhasha Parishad Puruskar*, Calcutta. In 1995 he received the Pehal Award for his entire writing. His works were translated into several languages. At present, he is working on his fourth novel.

AMBUJ, Kumar
Born in Mangwar, Madhya Pradesh, in 1957. He is a post-graduate in Botany, and is studying for his Master's degree in Law. In 1988, he published his first 24 poems in an associated issue of the journal *Vasudha*, and published his first collection of poems, *Kiwar*, in 1992. His second collection of poems, *Krurta*, appeared in 1996. Having published widely in major Hindi magazines, his poems are translated into several Indian languages, German and Russian. In 1988 he received the *Bharat Bhushan Agarwal Puruskar*, and in 1992 the *Makhanlal Chaturvedi Puruskar* of the M.P. Sahitya Parishad for his poetry. He has participated in numerous readings organized by the Sahitya Akademi and other important literary organisations, and has edited the supplement of contemporary poetry for *Vasudha* in 1995. He lives in Indore, M.P., where he works for the State Bank of Indore.

ANANTHA MURTHY, U.R.
Born in Melige, Karnataka, in 1932. He received his M.A. in 1956 in Mysore, and his Ph.D. in English and Comparative Literature from University of Birmingham, U.K. During his professional career, he was appointed to a vast number of academic posts, amongst them as Professor for English at Mysore from 1980-92, and as a Visiting Professor at JNU New Delhi, at Kolhapur University, at Tuft's University, at Tübingen University (Germany) and as a Fulbright Visiting Professor in Iowa. He was the Chairman of the National Book Trust of India from 1992 to 1993, a Visiting Writer at the International Writing Program, University of Iowa in 1985, and a Writer in Residence, University of Texas at Austin in 1995. He has published four novels in Kannada, *Samskara* (1965), *Bharathipura* (1974), *Avasthe* (1978) and *Bhava* (1994), several collections of short stories including *Akasha battu bekku* (1983), *Mooru dasakada kathegalu* (1989) and *Suryana kudure* (1995), a number of poetry collections, the latest being *Ajjana hegala sukkagalu* (1989) and *Mithuna* (1992), besides numerous volumes of essays in Kannada and English and a play. He conducted interviews for the TV and written several film scripts for feature films. A renowned scholar, he delivered numerous lectures and talks all over the globe. Amongst his many honours are the Homi

Bhabha Fellowship 1972-74, the Fiction Award of the Karnataka Sahitya Akademi 1983, the Award for Literary Distinction, Government of Karnataka in 1984, the Harmony Award in 1990, the Masti Award in Literature in 1994 and the Jnanpith Award in 1995. His novel *Samskara* was translated into English (by A.K. Ramanujan), Russian, French, Hungarian and German besides all major Indian languages, and made into a film. Since 1993, he is the President of the Sahitya Akademi in New Delhi.

ANWAR, Shaista
Born in 1974. She was educated in Bhopal and obtained her B.Sc. in 1995, followed by her M.Sc. in 1997. She published numerous poems in the Hindi daily *Bhaskar*, as well as in the book *Konpal*, an anthology of poems compiled during a workshop for creative writing, organised and sponsored by the Ministry for Human Resource Development, the NCERT and the Poetry Society for the youth of Madhya Pradesh, in which she participated in 1994. Her literary interest focusses on the writings of Ghalib and Nirala. She lives and studies in Bhopal.

CHATURVEDI, Sanjay
Born in Etawah, Uttar Pradesh, in 1958. He obtained his MBBS and MD from King George's Medical College, Lucknow. He has so far published two collections of his poetry, *Savera tab bhi hoga* in 1985, and *Prakashvarsh* in 1993. Many of his poems have appeared in anthologies, literary supplements and leading journals of Hindi. He also translates foreign poetry into Hindi. In 1992, he received the *Bharat Bhushan Smriti Puruskar*. He has a wide experience of travelling in remote areas, and his interests include the philosophy and sociology of science. He is living in New Delhi, where he presently works as a reader in the Deptt. of PSM, in the University College of Medical Sciences & GTB Hospital.

CHITRE, Dilip Purushottam
Born in 1938. Grew up in Baroda and Bombay, and studied English literature at Bombay University. In the early 1960's, he lived and worked as a school teacher in Ethiopia. Since then he has mainly lived in Bombay and Pune, working in advertising and as an editor, painter, film-maker and free-lance writer. In the 1980's he also served as the director of Bharat Bhavan Bhopal. He has published poetry, fiction, criticism and travel and journalistic writing in English and Marathi. He has translated extensively from Marathi into English, and from German into Marathi, together with L. Lutze. His publications include *Travelling in a Cage* (1980), poems in English; *Kavite nantarchya kavita* (1978), poems in Marathi; *An Anthology of Marathi Poetry 1945-65* (1967) and *Says Tukaram* (1991), both volumes of translation. His latest book is his translation of the mystical Marathi poem *Anubbhavamrut - The Immortal Experience of Being*. Among his honours are the Maharashtra Government Poetry Award in 1960-61, the *Karad Puruskar* and the Godavareesh Memorial Award, both in 1981. He won the national Sahitya Akademi Award in 1994 as well as the Sahitya Akademi prize for translation, and the Indira Gandhi Fellowship in 1997. He was a visitor at the Iowa International Writing Program in 1975-7. Chitre's Hindi feature film *Godam* (1983) won the Jury's Special Prize at Nantes, France in 1984. He recently co-directed and scripted a film for Second German Television (ZDF), *Bombay: Geliebter Moloch*.

DABRAL, Mangalesh
Born in Kafalpani, Tehri Garhwal, Uttar Pradesh in 1948. A renowned poet, journalist and translator, he has been working as an editor with several dailies, and has so far published three collections of his poems, *Pahar par laltein* (1981), *Ghar ka rasta* (1988) and *Ham jo dekhte hain* (1995), as well as a travel diary *Ek baar Iowa* (1996). His poetry has won him several awards including the *Omprakash Smriti Samman* (1982), the *Shrikant Verma Puruskar* (1989), the *Shamsher Samman* (1995) and the *Pahal Samman* in 1996. His poems have been translated and published in all major Indian languages and in English, Russian, German, Polish, Spanish and Bulgarian. Many of his poems have been included in various anthologies, such as *Periplus* (ed. D. Weissbort / A.K. Mehrotra), *Survival* (ed. D. Weissbort / G. Rathi), *Gestures*, an anthology of poems from SAARC-countries, and *Signatures* (ed. K. Satchidanandan). He has translated extensively from English into Hindi works by B. Brecht, H.M. Enzensberger, Yannis Ritsos, E. Cardenal, P. Neruda, S. Pencheva and Zbigniew Herbert, amongst others. He was a co-translator of Hermann Hesse's novel *Siddharta* and edited an anthology of teacher-poets of Rajasthan, *Ret ghari*. He visited Iowa as a Fellow of the International Writing Programme at the University of Iowa. At present, he is the editor of the Sunday magazine of *Jansatta*, a Hindi daily published by the Indian Express Group. He lives in New Delhi.

DASGUPTA, Alokeranjan
Born 1933. Studied in Shantiniketan and Calcutta University, from where he obtained his M.A. and Ph.D. In 1957 he became professor of Bengali literature at Jadavpur University, went to Germany with a Humboldt Fellowship in 1971, and was teaching as a visiting professor for Bengali at the South Asia Institute Heidelberg from 1971 to 1992. He was key advisor at the German Book Fair 1986 and at the Indian Festival in Germany in 1991, besides being advisor in several national and international editorial boards. At present he is cultural co-ordinator for *Bildung und Wissen* in Nürnberg. A committed literary translator from German into Bengali, he has published nearly thirty volumes of German poetry, plays and prose translated into Bengali, including authors as Goethe, Kleist, Hölderlin, Rilke, Biermann, Kirsch, Weiss, Kroetz, Strauss and many others, besides translating works from French and Hindi into Bengali. Furthermore he has co-translated and edited many volumes and anthologies from Bengali into German. Besides ten books of literary essays and literary history, he has published eighteen collections of his own poetry. Some of his latest publications include *Gelobt sei der Pfau* (Contemporary Indian Poetry in German translation, 1986), *Der andere Tagore* (Selected writings of Tagore in German translation, 1987), *Rangamaya panchamukhi* (dramatic collages of five German writers, 1995), *Der König und der Barde* (A literary encounter with India in German, 1994), *Sarah Kirscher Kavita* (1996) and *My Tagore* (1997). Some of his more recent poetry collections are *Dhunuri Diechhe Tangkar* (1988), *Kabita samagra* (1988), *Marami Karat* (1990), *Rakta Megher Skandapuram* (1993), *Jwarer cihore taraju kempe jaye* (1994), *Asta sunya enke dilo tempera* (1996), *Tuhser jure trishul chinha* (1996), and *The Mystical Saw and other poems* (translated into English by Roland Hindmarsh, 1996). His honours include the Calcutta University Literary Prize 1983, the Ananda Literary Award 1985, the Goethe Medal awarded by the Goethe Institute Munich in 1985, the Rabindranath Tagore Literature Prize 1987 of German-Indian Society, the Shiromani Award 1992 and the Sahitya Akademi Award 1992. He lives in Hirschberg, Germany.

FAZLI, Nida
Born in Delhi. A renowned Urdu poet, he has published three collections of his poetry, *Lafzon ka pul*, *Mor nach* and *Aankh aur khvab ki darmiyan*. Besides being an outstanding poet, he is the author of a book of literary criticism, *Mulakaten*, and has a novel, *Divaren*, to his credit. His poems are widely anthologized and translated into many languages. His honours and awards include the *Khusro Puruskar* (M.P.), the *Marwar Kala Sangam Puruskar* of Jodhpur, the prize of the Punjab association, the *Kala Sangam Puruskar* of Ludhiana, the *Hindi Urdu Sangam Puruskar* of Lucknow, the prize of the Urdu Akademi of Maharashtra and of Bihar, as well as the prize of the Urdu Akademi of Uttar Pradesh. An engaged and sought-after participant in innumerable national and international poetry readings, he is currently active in the field of filmscripts and is involved as script writer and advisor in a number of TV productions. He lives in Mumbai.

GILL, Gagan
Born in New Delhi in 1959. She received an M.A. in English from the University of Delhi. She works as a journalist in Hindi and Punjabi, and has been the sub-editor of the Hindi magazine *Vama* and the literary editor of the Hindi *Sunday Observer*. She was a visitor at the Iowa International Writing Program in 1989-90, and in 1992-93 she was a Nieman Fellow for journalism at Harvard University. Her first collection of poetry, *Ek din lautegi ladki*, appeared in 1989, and her second collection, *Andhere mein Buddha*, in 1996. She edited and translated the poetry of the Punjabi poet Haribhajan Singh into Hindi, *Jangal mein jhil jagti* (1989), and edited an art volume on the Indian painter Ram Kumar, *A Journey Within* (1996). In 1996, she also edited a special number of *Yatra*, a literary magazine, on *New Women Writing in Hindi*. Her poems have been translated into English, German, Russian and Chinese besides several Indian languages, and appeared in all major anthologies of modern Indian writing, as well as in international literary magazines. She has given readings of her works in various cities of the US, UK, Germany and China. She worked on contemporary women poets of India as part of a Senior Fellowship for the Dept. of Culture, Govt. of India, and is regularly contributing book reviews, essays, travelogues and literary comments to all major magazines in Hindi and English. She regularly participates in literary panels and was invited recently to Berlin for a lecture on *Three Generations of Women Writing in India* as part of the celebrations for India's 50 years of Independence. At present she is working on her third book of poems.

KAUNSWAL, Pramod
Born in Tehri Garhwal in 1966. M.A. in Economics from Jamia Milia Islamia, New Delhi. He is a poet, writer, journalist and art critic in Hindi. His first collection of poetry, *Apni hi tarah ka admi*, was published in 1991. He is also the author of the book *Itihas sandarbh kosh*. His poems were published in various leading journals and magazines and translated into several Indian languages. He also edited an anthology of contemporary Hindi poets of Chandigarh, and is presently preparing a book on contemporary painters and sculptors of Punjab. For three years he was working for the paper *Amar Ujala* in Meerut, after that for the Chandigarh edition of *Jansatta*. He has directed the film *Kandi ki kahani* on environment issues of the Shivalik Hills in the Himalayas, and works at present as Senior Producer (News) in Television International (TVI). He lives in New Delhi.

KHARE, Vishnu
Born in Chhindwara, Madhya Pradesh, in 1940. M.A. in English Literature from Indore in 1963. Between 1962 and 1975, he worked under various teaching and journalistic assignments, including as sub-editor of *Cinema Express* and *Indore Samachar*, Lecturer in English in Colleges at Indore, Ratlam, Rampura and Mhow, M.P. as well as in Delhi University. From 1976 to 1984 he was the Dy. Secretary (Programme) at Sahitya Akademi New Delhi. Between 1985 and 1993, he worked as Res. editor for *The Navbharat Times* in Lucknow, Jaipur and New Delhi. He was Senior Fellow at the Nehru Memorial Museum and Library from 1993 to 1995. Since 1995, he is the film critic in *The Pioneer*, and contributes as political and cultural columnist to various dailies and journals in Hindi and English. He began writing in 1956 with short stories, poems and satire, and has published three volumes of his own poetry, *Vishnu Khare ki kavitaen* (1971), *Khud apni ankh se* (1978) and *Sab ki Awaz ke parde mein* (1994). He has extensively translated and published poetry from and into Hindi, including *Maru pradesh aur anya kavitaen* (T.S. Eliot's Waste Land a.o.poems, 1960), *The People and the Self* (English tr. from Hindi poets, 1983), *Der Ochsenkarren* (Hindi poetry tr. into German with L. Lutze, 1983), *Ham sapne dekhte hain* (tr. of poems by M. Radnoti, 1983), *Yah chaku samay* (tr. of writings by A. Jozsef, 1980), *Ham cheekhte kyon nahin* (German poetry, 1983), *Kalevala* (Finnish National epic, 1990), *Ham is dharti ke namak hain* (Swiss poetry, 1990) and *Jeebh dikhana* (Günter Grass' *Zunge Zeigen*, 1994). He received the Delhi State Award for Literature 1991-92, the Madhya Pradesh Bhawani Prasad Mishra Award for Poetry in 1994 and the Raghuvir Sahay Award for poetry in 1994.

KUMAR, Satyen
Born in Delhi in 1944. He was educated in Delhi and Sagar, and has studied upto M.Pharm. After various assignments in this field, he was teaching for ten years in the Medical College Bhopal. He now runs his own printing press in Bhopal and is actively involved in various projects of painting, graphics, theatre and photography. He has published four collections of short stories, including *Jahaz tatha anya kahaniyan* (1973), *Barf* (1983), *Sherni* (1987) and *Ek nam aur* (1995), as well as a play together with Manzoor Ahtesham, *Ek tha badshah* (1980), and two novels, *Chutti ka din* (1986) and *Nadi ko yad nahin* (in press).Three of his books in Hindi have won various awards, including the *Yashpal Puruskar* in 1979, the *Subhadra Kumari Chauhan Puruskar* in 1983 and the *Vagishwar Puruskar* in 1986. He published and edited the Hindi magazine *Kahaniyan* for five years.

MAHAPATRA, Sitakant
Born 1937. Educated at Allahabad University and at Cambridge University, England. He was a member of the Indian Administrative Service in Orissa for over thirty years. A renowned anthropologist, he has lectured in Universities of Harvard, Chicago and California. He has published more than two dozen books in Oriya and English, among them collections of his Oriya poems as *Samudra* (1977), *Chitranadi* (1979) and *Drushya* (1981), and English translations of his own poetry, as *Quiet Violence* (1970), *The Other Silence* (1973), *The Old Man in Summer* (1975), *The Jester and Other Poems* (1979), *The Songs of Kubja and Other Poems* (1980), *Selected Poems* (1986), *The Death of Krishna and Other Poems* (1991) and *A Morning of Rain and Other Poems* (1991). He has edited several anthologies of Oriya tribal poems in English translation, among these *The Empty Distance Carries* (1972), *The Wooden Sword* (1973), *Staying is Nowhere* (1975), *Forgive the Words* (1976), *Bakhen* (1979), *Men, Pattern of Dust* (1981), *The Awakened Wind* (1983), *The Endless Weave* (1991) and *Unending Rhythms* (1992). He is the author of a number of volumes of literary criticism, and has translated and edited poetry from Oriya, Sanskrit and Vietnamese. His poem-

anthologies have been published in Romanian, French, German, Swedish and Danish. He is a winner of the National as well as the Orissa Sahitya Akademi Award, the Kumaran Asan Poetry Award, the Soviet Land Nehru Award and the Bhartiya Jnanpith Award (1993).

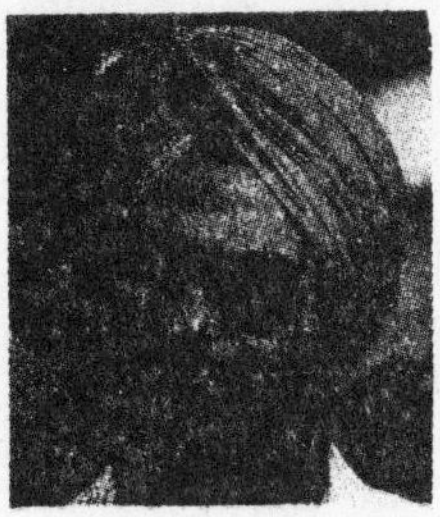

MOHANJEET
Born in 1938.Obtained his M.A. and Ph.D. in English and Punjabi, and is presently Reader in Punjabi at Desh Bandhu College, University of Delhi. So far he has published six anthologies of his poetry, including *Sehkda Shehir* (1964), *Varvrik* (1976) and *Ki Nari Ki Nadi* (1994), and has edited two volumes of Punjabi poetry. Additionally he has translated and published numerous books of history, fiction and prose into Punjabi, including the works of international poets such as Bertolt Brecht, Pablo Neruda and Nazim Hikmat. He also translated Garcia Lorca's play *Yerma* into Punjabi. His own poems appeared in Bulgarian translation in an anthology edited by Sati Kumar, and were translated into major Indian languages. An active writer and journalist, he participated in several National Poetry Meets, as well as in an International Seminar organized by Columbia University in 1994. He scripted and voiced about ten documentaries in Punjabi for the National Television *Doordarshan*, and was for many years the editor of the literary journal *Charcha*. He is the recepient of the Best Poetry Awards of Punjabi Akademi in 1987 and in 1997.

NARAYAN, Kunvar
Born in 1927 in Faizabad, Uttar Pradesh. He received a master's degree in English literature from Lucknow University in 1951. He is a businessman by profession and lives in Lucknow. He appeared as one of the contributors to the anthology *Tisra Saptak* (1959), edited by Ajneya. His short stories are collected in *Aakaaron ke aaspaas* (1971) and among his volumes of poetry are *Chakravyuh* (1956), *Parivesh: Ham tum* (1961), *Apne saamne* (1979) and *Koi dusra nahin* (1993). His short epic *Atmajayi* was published in 1965. He was a member of the editorial board of the magazines *Yugchetna*, *Naya Pratik* and *Chhayanat*, and has served as vice-chairman of the Uttar Pradesh Sangeet Natak Akademi between 1976 and 1979. He has published essays and art reviews in all leading Hindi literary magazines, and his honours include the *Hindustani Akademi Puruskar* in 1971, the Uttar Pradesh Government's *Premchand Puruskar* for fiction in 1972-3, the Kumaran Asan Award in 1982, the *Tulsi Puruskar* in 1982, and a special prize from the *Hindi Sansthan* Uttar Pradesh in 1987. For *Koi dusra nahin* he received the *Vyas Samman*, the Bhawani Prasad Mishra Award, the Shatdal Award and the Sahitya Akademi Award, all in 1995. He has translated several foreign authors into Hindi, amongst them C. Cavafy and J.L. Borges, and his own works have been translated into English, German and Italian. He visited Czechoslovakia, Poland, Russia and China as part of a cultural delegation in 1955, and participated in literary meetings with N. Hikmet, A. Slonimiskie and P. Neruda. In 1994, he was invited to the University of Venice for a lecture series on *Mythology and Modern Hindi Poetry*.

NOOR, Sutinder Singh
Born in Kotakpura, Punjab, in 1940. He obtained his M.A. and his Ph.D. in English and Punjabi, and is professor at the Department of Punjabi at the University of Delhi. He has published four collections of his own poetry, *Birkh nipatre* (1969), *Kavita di jalawatni* (1990), *Sardal de ar par* (1995) and *Siraf kavita nahin* (1997). His essays of literary criticism are collected in six volumes, *Navin kavita seema te sambhavana* (1972), *Mohan Singh da kavjagat* (1976), *Navin Punjabi alochna* (1978), *Sahit sidhant te vihar* (1980), *Adhunik kavita* (1982), and *Sabhiachar te sahit* (1990). He has also two volumes of poetry translations

into Punjabi to his credit, *Cherry de phul* (Modern Japanese Poetry, 1972) and *Suraj te mesiha* (Modern European Poetry, 1986). He has travelled widely and participated in numerous national and international poetry readings and seminars. His essays and books of literary criticism were awarded with the Criticism Award of Punjabi Akademi, New Delhi. He is also the recipient of the Shiromani Lekhak Award of the Language Department Punjabi in 1994, as well as the IAPA Award (Canada) in 1997 and the Warishah Award (Denmark) in 1996.

PATAR, Surjeet

Born in 1944 in Punjab. He is at present an associate professor of Punjabi in the Department of Journalism, Languages and Culture at Punjab Agricultural University, Ludhiana (Punjab). He has so far published three collections of his poetry: *Hava vich likhay haraf, Birkh arz karay* and *Hanerayvich sulagdi varanmala.* A prolific translator of theatre plays, he has translated and adapted several plays by international authors into Punjabi, such as *Agg de kaleeray* (Lorca's *Blood Wedding*), *Eh koyee reet nahin* (Brecht's *Exception and the Rule*), *Shehar mere di pagal aurat* (Giraudoux' *The Mad Woman of Chaliot*), *Yerma* (Lorca's *Yerma*), *Haithh Vagay Darya* (Kamal Kapoor's *Clytemnestra*), *Nag Chhaya* (Girish Karnad's *Nagmandala*) and *Fida* (Racine's *Phaedra*). He has been associated with the National Television *Doordarshan* for many years, and has scripted and presented a serial *Sooraj da sarnawan*, depicting the history of Punjabi poetry in about 30 episodes. He has also scripted and presented about twenty programmes on Punjabi Folk Poetry and Music for *Doordarshan, Lok Rang*. A renowned poet, he is participating in many national and international poetry readings, meetings and seminars. His many awards include the Punjabi Sahitya Akademi Award in 1978, the Musafir Poetry Award by the Bhasha Vibhag Punjab in 1979, the Kartar Singh Dhaliwal Award of the Punjabi Sahit Akademi in 1985, the *Pash Puruskar* in 1992, the *Dashabadi Kavi Puruskar* of the Punjabi Akademi Delhi in 1992 and the Sahitya Akademi Award in 1993.

PRAKASH, Uday

Born in a village in Madhya Pradesh in 1951. M.A. in Hindi Literature from Sagar University, M.P. Research Scholar in Jawaharlal Nehru University, New Delhi, with a vast working experience in the field of academics, journalism, administration and audi-visual media. He was co-editor with several leading Hindi journals, as *Dinman* and *Poorvagraha*, and regularly contributes reports, news analysis and comments on political affairs, cinema and various forms of art to dailies and journals. His published collections of poetry are *Suno Karigar* (1980) and *Abootar Kabootar* (1984), besides several collections of short stories, amongst them *Dariyayi Ghoda* (1982), *Tirich* (1990), *Aur ant mein Prarthna* (1994) and *Paul Gomra ka scooter* (1997). He has translated extensively, and published *Kala anubhav* (*Art Experience* by Prof. Hariyanna, 1982), *Amritsar: Indira Gandhi ki akhiri ladai* (*Amritsar: Indira Gandhi's Last Battle* by Tully/Jacob, 1985), two volumes from R. Rolland's *Inde* tr. into Hindi, *Lal ghas par neele ghode* (Russian play by M. Shatrov, 1988), *Ek purush dedh purush* (Kannada play by Prasanna), besides numerous translations of poems by P. Neruda, F.G. Lorca, H.L. Borges, P. Aluar, Hernandez and other international poets, which were published in reputed literary magazines. His own poems and short stories were translated into major Indian languages and English, Spanish, Russian, Japanese, German and Italian, and included in many anthologies. He received the *Bharat Bhushan Agarwal Puruskar* in 1980, the *Om Prakash Samman* in 1984, the Shrikant Verma Award in 1990, the Best Author of the Year Award by the Union Bank of India in 1989 and the *Muktibodh Samman* by the M.P. Sahitya Parishad in 1996.

RAWAT, Bhagwat

Born in Teharka, Madhya Pradesh, in 1939. From 1959 he taught in Bhopal, and completed his studies up to an M.A. B.Ed. degree. From 1969, he taught in the Regional College of Education, Bhopal, and was posted to the Regional College of Mysore from 1972-1975. Between 1983 and 1992 he served as a reader of Hindi at the Regional College, Bhopal. He has published widely in all leading Hindi literary magazines and his poems were translated into several Indian languages. He has published five collections of his poetry, including *Samudra ke bare mein* (1977), *Di hui Duniya* (1981), *Hua kuch is tarah* (1988), *Suno Hiraman* (1992) and *Sach puchho to* (1996). A collection of his essays, *Kavita ka dusra path* was published in 1993. His biography on the poet Kedarnath Agrawal was awarded with the *'Jiunga jindagi abhi aur' Samman*. Other awards include the *Madhya Pradesh Sahitya Puruskar* in 1977 and the *Vagishwar Puruskar* in 1988. He was last working as Director of the M.P. Hindi Granth Akademi. Between 1981 and 1994, he was the president of the Progressive Writer's Association, M.P., and the editor of its journal *Vasudha*.

SACHDEVA, Padma

Born in Jammu in 1940. She joined All India Radio in 1969. Deeply influenced by the cruelties of partition and the rediscovery of Dogri with its rich oral tradition of folktales and songs, she published her first collection of poems in 1969 which won her the Sahitya Akademi Award in 1971. She has published several volumes of poetry in Dogri, *Meri kavita meri geet* (1996), *Tawi te chanhan* (1976), *Nherian galian* (1982), *Pota pota nimbal* (1987), *Uttar vahini* (1992), and *Tainthian* (1996). Her works in Hindi including prose, poetry and interviews are *Sabad milawa* (1987), *Diwankhana* (1988), *Mitwa ghar* (1991-95) and *Amrai* (1996). She published a Hindi short story collection *Godh Bhari* (1990) and two novels, *Ab na banegi dehri* (1992) and *Nausheen* (1995) in Hindi, as well as a travelogue *Main kahti hun aankhin dekhi* (1995). She has translated extensively from Dogri into Hindi and vice versa, from Hindi to Punjabi, and English into Hindi and Dogri. She was honoured with the Jammu and Kashmir Cultural Academy Award (1983), the Soviet Land Nehru Award (1987), the Hindi Akademi Award, U.P. (1987-88), the J&K Robe of Honour (1989), the *Sauhardra Samman* of U.P. Akademi (1989), the Harmony Award (1990), the *Raja Rammohan Roy Kalashri Puruskar* (1993) and the Mata Kusum Kumari International Hindi Award (1996). She recorded a Dogri music album with Lata Mangeshkar and is the convener of the Dogri Advisory Board at the Sahitya Akademi New Delhi.

SHUKLA, Prayag

Born in Calcutta in 1940. A poet, art critic, fiction writer and journalist of Hindi, he has worked with several dailies and literary magazines such as *Navbharat Times*, *Vama*, *Kalpana*, *Parag*, *Dinman* amongst others. He has edited a book on art appreciation *Dekhna* (1993), as well as a book for the Lalit Kala Akademi (Academy of Fine Arts) Delhi, *Kala samay samaj*, besides being the guest editor for two issues of their journal *Samkaleen*. He has organized and documented several exhibitions on fine arts and painting such as *Drawing '94*, besides covering the works of several leading Indian painters and visual artists. His literary work includes several short story collections, *Akeli Akritiyan*, *Iske bad*, *Veh antardeshiya*, *Chhayayen*, *Ghar aur bahar* (1995) and *Kai* (1995), as well as two novels, *Gathri* and *Kal aur aaj* (1993). He published seven collections of his poetry, including *Kavita sambhav*, *Yeh ek din hai*, *Rat ka ped*, *Adhuri chizen tamam*, *Yeh jo hara hai*, *Bite kitne baras* (1992) and *Yeh likhta hun* (1995). A complete collection of his poetry upto 1995, *Yani kai varsh*, was published in 1995. He visited Germany, France, Britain, and covered the Festival of India in the then USSR in 1987. He translated the works of Jibanandan

Das fom Bengali into Hindi, as well as several foreign authors such as Octavio Paz. In 1984, he participated in the International Writing Programme in Iowa. As a journalist, he writes on films, theatre and dance, as well as on literary events. He lives in New Delhi.

SINGH, Kedarnath
Born in Chakia, U.P. in 1934. He was educated at Banaras Hindu University, from where he received an M.A. in Hindi literature in 1956 and a Ph.D. in 1964. He has taught at U.P. College, Varanasi, and St. Andrew's College, Gorakhpur, and has served as the principal of U.N. Postgraduate College, Pandrauma, Uttar Pradesh. Since 1976 he has been a professor of Hindi at the School of Languages, Jawaharlal Nehru University, New Delhi. His works appeared first in the anthology *Tisra Saptak* (1959), edited by Ajneya. He has published three books of scholarly criticism on modern Hindi literature, *Kalpana aur Chhayavad*, *Adhunik Hindi kavita mein bimb vidhan* and *Mere samay ke shabda*, as well as several volumes of poetry, including *Abhi bilkul abhi* (1960), *Zamin pak rahi hai* (1980), *Pratinidhi kavitaen* (1985), *Akal mein saras* (1988), *Uttar Kabir aur anya kavitaen* (1995) and *Bagh* (1996). He has co-edited several books and is the editor of the Hindi literary magazine *Sakhi*. Amongst the many prizes he received are the *Sahitya Akademi Puruskar*, the *Maithili Sharan Gupt Samman*, the *Kumaran Ashan Puruskar*, the *Dinkar Puruskar*, the *Jivan Bharti Samman*, the *Dayavati Modi Kavi Shekhar Samman* and the Joshua Prize. He was invited for poetry readings to the US, Russia, Kazaksthan, Trinidad and Germany.

SINGH, Varyam
Born in Banjar Valley, District Kullu, Himachal Pradesh in 1948. School education in Banjar. Completed Russian studies at the Institute of Russian Studies, New Delhi in 1969. Did his specialization in Russian Literature from Moscow State University and was appointed Assistant Professor at Jawaharlal Nehru University in 1972. At present he is professor in the Centre of Russian Studies, JNU. He writes poetry in Hindi and Siraji (Pahari or Himachali). He has published three collections of poems in Hindi and two collections in Pahari. He has been actively translating Russian poetry into Hindi and published about 16 collections of poetry translations. He was awarded for his Pahari poetry by the Himachal Academy of Arts, and for his translations by the *Madhya Pradesh Sahitya Parishad*. He is the General Secretary of the *Roerich Adhyayan Parishad* and the editor of the magazine *Agnichetna*.

SOBTI, Krishna
Born in 1925 in Gujarat (now Pakistan). She came to India after partition and had her early education in Lahore, Shimla and Delhi. An outstanding writer, editor and participant in the literary scene of Hindi and Urdu, she has published a number of novels and novelettes in Hindi, including *Dar se bicchudi* (1958), *Mitro Marjani* (1966), *Yaron ke yar* (1986), *Surajmukhi andhere ki* (1972), *Ham Hashmat* (1977), *Tin Pahad* (1968), *Jindaginama* (1979) and *Ai Ladki* (1991). After her first short stories *Lama* and *Nafisa*, published in 1944, she wrote several well known short stories, amongst them *Sikka badal gaya* (1948), *Badli baras gayi* (1952), *Na gulma na chamantha* (1953), *Dadi Amma* (1954), *Badlon ke ghere* (1955, also the title of a short story collection in 1980), *Tillo hi tillo* (1955) and *Kuch nahin, koi nahin* (1955). A book of her selected writings, *Sobti ek sohabat*, appeared in 1989. Her works have been translated into many Indian and foreign languages, and her *Badlon ke ghere*, *Dar se bicchudi* as well as *Mitro Marjani* were adapted for the theatre and staged successfully, while *Sikka badal gaya* was made into a film. She was also the advisor for a TV serial on partition, *Buniyad*. She has travelled widely and her writing has won her numerous awards, including the Shiromani Award in 1980 and 1981, the Sahitya Akademi

Award in 1980, and the *Hindi Akademi Puruskar* in 1982. She was a Writer in Residence at the Bharat Bhavan, Bhopal in 1982. A committed and engaged writer, she is regularly contributing to journals, literary seminars and writer's meets. Based in Delhi, she is at present associated with the Institute for Advanced Studies in Shimla.

SUBODH, Nitin Nema
He published his poems first in the book *Konpal*, an anthology of poems compiled during a workshop for creative writing, organised and sponsored by the Ministry for Human Resource Development, the NCERT and the Poetry Society for the youth of Madhya Pradesh, in which he participated in 1994. He lives in Madhya Pradesh.

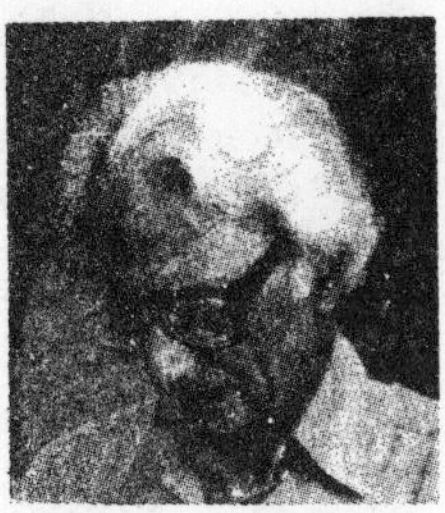

VAID, Krishna Baldev
Born at Dinga, Punjab (former Pakistan), in 1927. M.A. from Punjab University and Ph.D. from Harvard University in 1961. Came to India in 1947 after partition and taught English Literature at Delhi, Chandigarh, and the State University of New York, Pottsdam. He was a visiting professor at Brandeis University in 1968 and at the IIT in Delhi in 1981. He was president of the Nirala Srijanpith, Bhopal, in 1985. A prolific writer of novels, short stories and essays in Hindi and English, his first novel *Uska bachpan* appeared in 1957, followed by *Bimal urf jayen to jayen kahan* (1974), *Nasreen* (1975), *Dusra na koi* (1978), *Dard ka dawa*, (1980), *Guzra hua zamana* (1981), *Kala kolaj* (1989) and *Nar Nari* (1996) His short story collections include *Beech ka darwaza* (1963), *Mera dushman* (1966), *Dusre kinare se* (1970), *Lapata* (1973), *Uske bayan* (1974), *Meri priya kahaniyan* (1978), *Voh aur main* (1979), *Khamoshi* (1986) *Aalaap* (1986), *Pratinidhi kahaniyan* (1990), *Lila* (1993), *Charchit kahaniyan* (1995), *Pita ki parchhaiyan* (1997) and *Das pratinidhi kahaniyan* (1997). Several of his works appeared in his own English translation, such as *Steps in Darkness* (tr. of *Uska Bachpan*, 1962), *Silence* (1972), *Bimal in Bog* (1974), *Dying alone* (novel, 1992) and *The Broken Mirror* (novel, 1994). Apart from his own works, he has translated *Godot ke intezar mein* (*Waiting for Godot*), *Aakhiri khel* (*Endgame*), *Phaedra* (*Phaedre*) and *Alice ajoobon ki duniya mein* (*Alice in Wonderland*), besides the works of other Hindi writers as *Days of Longing* (*Veh din* by Nirmal Varma) and *Bitter Sweet Desire* (*Dusri bar* by Shrikant Varma). *Technique in the Tales of Henry James* (1964) is a book of literary criticism. Among his many honours is the *Shiromani Award* in 1993.

VAJPEYI, Ashok
Born in Durg, Madhya Pradesh in 1941. He was educated at Sagar University, received his M.A. in English from Delhi University in 1963 and was teaching at Dayal Singh College for two years. In 1965 he was appointed to the IAS, and is since working under different assignments such as Special Officer for Culture at the M.P. Government in Bhopal, and is presently Joint Secretary Culture at the Ministry of Human Resource Development. A noted poet, editor, critic and translator, he has published several volumes of his own poetry, *Shahar ab bhi sambhavna hai* (1966), *Ek patang anant mein* (1984), *Tatpurush* (1988), *Kahin nahin wahin* (1990), *Bahuri akela* (1992), *Thodi si jagah* (1994), *Ghas mein dubka aakash* (1994), *Hona prithvi na hona aakaash* (1994 and *Punarapi* (1995). He has several books of literary essays to his credit, including *Philhal* (1970), *Kuch purvagrah* (1884) and *Kavita ka galp* (1997), and edited two volumes of essays, *Tisra Sakshya* (1979) and *Kavita*

ka janpad (1992). *All but Alone*, a selection of his poems in English translation, appeared in 1996. He was the founder of several prestigious cultural institutions such as the *Bharat Bhavan* in Bhopal, and has been the editor of the journals *Samvet*, *Pehchan*, *Purvagrah*, *Samas*, *Bahuvachan* and *Kavita Asia*. His works have been translated into Russian, Czech, French, German, Bulgarian, Nepali, Arabic and Norwegian, besides all major Indian languages. He has given poetry readings in many countries and is the recipient of the Sahitya Akademi Award in 1993 and the first *Dayavati Modi Kavi Shekhar Samman* in 1994.

VERMA, Nirmal
Born in Shimla in 1929. M.A. in History from St. Stephen's College, Delhi. Between 1959 and 1986 he lived in Prague, studying and translating Czech literature. For some years, he worked as a reporter for the *Times of India* in London, from where he returned in 1972. He was a fellow at the Institute for Advanced Studies in Shimla, and a participant in the International writer's programme in Iowa in 1977. He was the president of the *Nirala Srijanpith*, Bhopal (1982-83) and the *Yashpal Srijanpith*, Shimla (1989). He lives in New Delhi. He has published four novels, *Ve din* (1964), *Lal tin ki chhat* (1979), *Ek chitda sukh* (1979) and *Rat ka reporter* (1989), besides eight collections of short stories, including *Parinde* (1959), *Jhalti jhadi* (1965), *Pichhli garmiyon mein* (1968), *Kavve aur kala pani* (1994), *Pratinidhi kahaniyan* (1987), *Meri priya kahaniyan*, *Bich behas mein* (1972) and *Sukha* (1995). He has two travelogues, *Chidon par chandni* (1964) and *Har barish mein* (1970), as well as numerous collections of his essays to his credit, such as *Shabd aur smriti* (1976), *Kala ka jokhim* (1981), *Dhalan se utarte hue* (1991), *Bharat aur Europe: Pratishruti ke kshetr* (1991) and *Shatabdi ke dhalte varshon mein* (1995). He as also written three plays. Numerous short stories and novels have been translated into English such as the novels *Days of Longing*, *Dark Despatches* and *A Rag called Happiness*; the short story collections *Hill Station*, *Crows of Deliverance* (1988), *The World Elsewhere* (1987), *Maya Darpan* (1986), and *Such a Big Yearning* (1995), besides *Word and Memory* (Essays, 1988). He is the co-editor of the literary journal *Yatra*, and is regularly contributing to national and international seminars and writer's meets. His works have been translated into all major Indian and European languages. Amongst his many prestigious awards are the Sahitya Akademi Award (1985), the *Sadhna Samman* in 1983, the *Sarvocch Rammanohar Lohia Samman* in 1995 and the *Murtidevi Puruskar* of Bhartiya Jnanpith in 1997. The film on his short story *Maya Darpan* won the *Hindi Film Puruskar* in 1973.

GERMAN AUTHORS

BECKER, Jurek
Born on September 30th, 1937 in Lodz, Poland, Becker spent a part of his childhood in the Lodz Ghetto as well as in the concentration camps of Ravensbrück and Sachsenhausen. 1945 he came to East Berlin, learnt German and later studied philosophy at Humboldt University, but was expelled in 1960 for political reasons. In 1977 he was granted a unique two years exit visa after his protest against the expatriation of Biermann, and quietly shifted to West Germany. His novels reflect both the Jewish experience as well as his experiences with the East German state. International recognition came in 1969 with the publication of his novel *Jakob der Lügner* (*Jakob the Liar*, 1975), which has been translated into twelve languages. His other works include: *Irreführung der Behörden* (1973), *Der Boxer* (1975), *Schlaflose Tage* (1978), *Nach der ersten Zukunft* (1980), *Aller Welt Freund* (1985), *Bronsteins Kinder* (1986), *Amanda Herzlos* (1992), *Wir sind auch nur ein Volk* (1994/95) and his last work *Ende des Größenwahns* (1996). He was a writer-in-residence at Oberlin College, Ohio,

in 1987, lectured at Cornell University, Ithaca, New York in 1984 and was a guest professor at the University of Texas in Austin in 1987. He also lectured at the Universities of Essen (1878) and Frankfurt (1989). Among the prizes he has received are the Heinrich-Mann-Prize (1971), the Charles-Veillon-Prize (Zurich, 1971), the City of Bremen Prize (1974), the National Prize of the German Democratic Republic (1974) and the Adolf-Grimme-Prize for the TV-series *Liebling Kreuzberg*, 1986. Becker died on March 14th, 1997.

BENN, Gottfried

Born in 1886. Generally acknowledged to be one of the most outstanding German lyric poets of the twentieth century, Gottfried Benn studied medicine in Marburg and Berlin and published in 1912 the cycle of poems *Morgue und andere Gedichte* (*Morgue and other Poems*). These often brutal and grotesque poems established Benn's reputation as a poet of uncompromising modernity. He published in major expressionist journals and his second volume of poems *Söhne (Sons)* appeared in 1913. He was *Kommissarischer Leiter* (Acting leader) of the Poetry Section in the Prussian Academy of Arts and a director of the new Union of National Writers, and published the essay collection ***The New State and the Intellectuals*** in 1933. Though Benn never joined the National Socialist party, he ardently declared and supported the "New State". In 1936 however, the Nazis declared his earlier work as "immoral". Eventually, his work was banned and he was expulsed from the Reich's Literature Chamber. During World War II he rejoined the army and served as a doctor throughout the war.The concept of the 'absolute poem' became important during this time: his poem *Ein Wort* (1943) emphasizes the impact and the transience of articulate utterance. Benn remained in Germany after the war, and documented the dislocation and suffering of the post-war period in the novella *Die Ptolemäer* (1947). A famous lecture on writing lyric poetry, which he gave at Marburg in 1951, was later quoted and discussed by T.S. Eliot. His works are collected in eight volumes of *Gesammelte Werke*, in *Sämtliche Erzählungen* and in four volumes of *Das Hauptwerk*. Benn died in 1956.

BRECHT, Bertolt

Born in Augsburg in 1898. His first plays, such as *Baal* (1918) and *Trommeln in der Nacht* (1923), created theatrical scandals by their reluctance to conform to accepted standards, with their anarchic tendencies, cynical tones and balladesque structure. With *Im Dickicht der Städte* (1923), Brecht turned increasingly to a marxist interpretation of life. His greatest success during the years of the Weimarer Republic were his plays *Die Dreigroschenoper* (1928), *Mann ist Mann* (1926) and *Aufstieg und Fall der Stadt Mahagony* (1928-9). His first book of poetry, *Die Hauspostille* (1927), parodies the style of popular anthologies with their moralizing homilies. In the early '30s, his flight from the Nazis became inevitable (he was fifth on their blacklist). After his dramatic cantata *Die Massnahme* (1930), the adaptation of Gorki's *Mutter* was performed in 1932 under great difficulties; his film *Kuhle Wampe* (1932) was immediately banned. After the burning of the Reichstag he fled to Vienna and then moved on to Denmark (Svendborg), from where he commented the events in Germany and wrote some of his most impressive poems, as *Schlechte Zeiten für Lyrik*, as well as several plays, including *Die Rundköpfe und die Spitzköpfe* (1933-4), *Die Horatier und die Kuratier* (1934) a.o. In 1940, he left for America, and in 1941 his play *Mutter Courage und ihre Kinder* was staged in Zurich. The year 1943 saw a performance of two of his plays in Zurich, *Der gute Mensch von Sezuan*, and *Das Leben des Galilei*, both amongst his masterpieces. Other plays of that time include *Der aufhaltsame Aufstieg des Arturo Ui* (1941), *Herr Puntila und sein Knecht Matti*, as well as the famous *Der Kaukasische Kreidekreis* (1944-5). He returned to Europe at the end of 1947. After his return to East Berlin, he wrote nothing of original merit for the theatre, but adapted, produced and modified

plays a.o. *Waiting for Godot*. He withdraw again into poetry and wrote, in the *Buckower Elegies*, some of his finest serene and silent poems far from the turmoil of Berlin. Besides his plays, which had an enormous influence on the theatre, his poetry is collected in *Die Hauspostille* (1927), *Svendborger Gedichte* (1939) and *Buckower Elegien* (1953). His narrative prose is best exemplified by the short stories *Kalendergeschichten* (1949) and *Geschichten von Herrn Keuner* (1958). In several editions, his theoretical writings on theatre, prose and poetry are collected, such as *Schriften zum Theater* in seven vols. (1963). Brecht died in then East Berlin in 1956.

BUCH, Hans Christoph

Hans Christoph Buch was born in Wetzlar, Germany, in 1944. He published his first book *Unerhörte Begebenheiten. Sechs Geschichten* in 1966, followed by numerous publications including *Jammerschoner. Sieben Nacherzählungen* in 1982, *Karibische Kaltluft. Berichte und Reportagen* in 1985, *Der Herbst des großen Kommunikators. Amerikanisches Journal* in 1986, *Waldspaziergang. Unpolitische Betrachtungen zu Literatur und Politik* in 1987 and *Die Nähe und die Ferne. Bausteine zu einer Politik des kolonialen Blicks* as part of the prestgious *Frankfurter Poetikvorlesungen* in 1991. His first novel, *Die Hochzeit von Port-au-Prince* (tr. into English by Ralph Manheim) is the story of a French officer sent to Haiti by Napoleon to arrest a leader of the slave revolt, as well as a historically documented account of a quarrel between Haitian police and a German colonist. After his second novel, *Haiti Chérie,* he thematizes again five hundert years of colonial rule in America in his latest novel *Rede des toten Kolumbus am Tag des jüngsten Gerichts* (1992), with Columbus not figuring as the historic discoverer but as the narrator, reincarnated in several characters who came to Haiti under different circumstances in search of fortune and paradise, but found hell and destruction instead, the last being a Jewish immigrant whose flight from the Nazis ends in the Voodoo-Dictatorship of Papa Doc. Buch lives presently in Berlin.

CELAN, Paul

Paul Celan was the pseudonym of Paul Anczel, who was born in the German-Jewish cultural enclave Romania Bukovina in 1920. His home town was occupied by Russian troops in 1940 and by the Germans in 1942. Both his parents were deported to an extermination camp, and Celan himself was sent to a labour camp. He survived and moved to Paris, where he lived and worked as a teacher at the *École Normale Superieure* until his death. The awareness of the Holocaust is at the centre of his work, and his approach to the problems of language and communication is linked to the impossibility of conveying the extreme physical and existential exposure of the persecuted, which he expresses in a distorted and reversed syntax. A man of mystical tendencies, his religious concept of enlightenment can be traced in references to the Bible and esoteric Judaism. His first book of poems *Der Sand aus den Urnen* (1948) was withdrawn after publication; his main work is contained in the collections *Mohn und Gedächtnis* (1952), *Von Schwelle zu Schwelle* (1955), *Sprachgitter* (1959), *Die Niemandsrose* (1963), *Atemwende* (1967), *Fadensonne* (1968), *Lichtzwang* (1970) and *Schneepart* (1971). These, together with translations of twenty-one sonnets by Shakespeare and poems by Char, Supervielle, Michaux, Yessenin, Mandelstam, Block a.o. were assembled in the provisional *Gesammelte Werke* (1983) in five volumes. Some of his speeches, letters and essays provide some aid to the understanding of his poems, such as *Der Meridian* (1960), *Der Traum vom Traume* (1948) or *Gespräch im Gebirg* (1959). His early poem *Todesfuge* is widely anthologized. He also published translations of Rimbaud and Valéry. Paul Celan committed suicide in 1970.

EICH, Günter
Eich was born in 1907. He studied Sinology, then served in the German army in World War II and was interned in an American prisoner of war camp, an experience which inspired the much-anthologized poem of *Inventur (Inventory)*. His lack of ideological commitment made him dependent during the Third Reich on the few outlets for work in which Nazi policy was not rigidly enforced, such as the periodical *Die Kolonne* and radio drama. His first collection of poems appeared in 1930 and for some time he remained loyal to nature lyric, but most of his post-war poetry in the volumes *Abgelegene Gehöfte* (1948), *Untergrundbahn* (1949), *Botschaften des Regens* (1955), *Zu den Akten* (1964) and *Anlässe und Steingarten* (1966) is characterized by an exploratory approach to reality and language's relation to it, which breaks with the romantic tradition. He wrote the witty *Maulwürfe* (*Moles*) in 1968, *Ein Tibeter in meinem Büro* and *49 Maulwürfe* in 1970, consisting of aphorisms, proverbs, nonsensical fantasies prompted by gossip and verbal clichés. He returned to poetry with *Nach Seumes Papieren* (1972). In 1953 he married the writer Ilse Aichinger. An outstanding poet and playwright for radio, he initiated the renaissance of radio drama and wrote at least forty-six radio plays between 1932 and 1972, including *Der Tiger Jussuf* (1952), *Die andere und ich* (1951), *Die Mädchen aus Viterbo* (1953) and *Die Brandung vor Setúbal* (1957). He was awarded the Büchner Prize, and an edition of his works appeared in four volumes in 1973. He died in 1972.

ENZENSBERGER, Hans Magnus
Enzensberger was born 1929 and grew up in Bavaria, studied in France and Germany from 1949 to 1954 and worked for South German Radio. He has lived as a free-lance writer and as a lecturer in Norway, Rome and the USA. A stay in Cuba inspired him to the documentary play *Das Verhör von Habana* in the late sixties. He published the poetry collections *verteidigung der wölfe* (1957), *landessprache* (1960) and *blindenschrift* (1964). After these, *Mausoleum. 37 Balladen aus der Geschichte des Fortschritts* (1975) presents portraits of major politicians, revolutionaries, scientists and inventors. The darker aspects of the development of humanity received an allegorical treatment in *Der Untergang der Titanic* (1978). The collection *Gedichte 1955-1970* adds thirty-three poems to the first three volumes. This book, together with *Die Furie des Verschwindens* (1980) and *Zehn Lieder für Ingrid Caven* are assembled in *Die Gedichte* (1983), followed by a poetry collection *Gedichte 1950-1985* (1986). Schooled in the dialectics of Hegel, Marx and Adorno, he edited the highly influential periodical *Kursbuch* from 1965-1975 and presided over the notorious issues in 1968, which rejected the mainstream of literary criticism and of politically uncommitted imaginative writing. Later on he edited the magazine *Transatlantik*. His journalistic writings are collected in numerous volumes such as *Politik und Verbrechen* (1964), *Politische Kolportagen* (1966) or *Politische Brosamen* (1982), the seven travel reports *Ach Europa!* (1987) and the compendium *Mittelmaß und Wahn* (1988). A Hispano-American complex is formed by *Das Verhör von Habana*, *Der kurze Sommer der Anarchie. Buanoventura Durrutis Leben und Tod* (1972), *El Cimarron* (1970) and *La Cubana* (1975). Five prose biographies appeared as *Der Weg ins Freie. Fünf Lebensläufe* (1975), and *Der Menschenfeind* (1979) and *Der Menschenfreund* (1984) both focus on intellectuals whose actions reflect the contradictions of their social group. His latest poetry collection, *Zukunftsmusik*, appeared in 1991.

FRIED, Erich
Fried was born 1921 in Vienna, an emigrated to London after his Jewish father had been killed by the Gestapo in 1938. He remained in Britain until his death, employed for a time by the BBC World Service and active as a translator of Shakespeare, Dylan Thomas, Wilfried Owen and T.S. Eliot. His first collections, *Deutschland* (1944) and *Österreich* (1945) were typical products of exile literature, while *Reich der Steine. Zyklische Gedichte* (1963) incorporated the non-specific imagery characteristic of certain modernist trends. A political dimension emerges in the laconic word play of *Warngedichte* (1965) and becomes dominant in *und Vietnam und* (1966). He produced eighteen volumes of poetry, four collections of

short stories and the novel *Ein Soldat und ein Mädchen* (1960). His relation to Brecht and several other poets emerges in numerous quotations from them. The principle of paradox is refined and extended to include puns and word games, phonetic experiments, along with a pragmatic analysis of clichés and slogans from all sections of the political spectrum. From 1963 onwards, he was member of the "Gruppe 47". In 1977, he received the *Prix International des Editeurs*, for his book *Hundert Gedichte ohne Vaterland*, which was translated into seven languages. His poetry collection *Liebesgedichte* appeared in 1979, and in 1986 he published his memoirs *Mitunter sogar lachen*. His collected works were published from Verlag Klaus Wagenbach, Berlin, in 1993. Amongst his awards are the *Bremer Literaturpreis*, the *Österreichischer Staatspreis* and the *Georg-Büchner-Preis*. He died in 1988.

GRASS, Günter
Born in Danzig (now Poland) in 1927. At the end of World War II, he was forced to leave his birthplace and became a POW, then worked in a china clay mine before training as a monumental mason. Between 1948 and 1956, he studied sculpture and graphic art in Düsseldorf and Berlin, joining the "Gruppe 47" shortly before the appearance of his first poems and plays. In 1956, he moved to Paris, where he completed *Die Blechtrommel* in 1959, which marked a turning point in the literature of the FRG and made him internationally famous. Sharing a single setting, but differing in length and narrative technique, the other two titles of the so called Danzig trilogy are *Katz und Maus* (1961) and *Hundejahre* (1963). The novel *örtlich betäubt* (1969) deals with the challenges of the student movement, while in *Aus dem Tagebuch einer Schnecke* (1972) the experiences of a campaigner for the SPD are narrated. In his masterpiece *Der Butt* (1977), nine female cooks between the stone age and the present are made the vehicles of a pro-feminist view of history. In *Das Treffen in Teltge* (1979) he focusses on the limited power of the artist-intellectual during a fictional poet's meet at the end of the Thirty Year War. *Kopfgeburten oder die Deutschen sterben aus* (1980) as well as *Zunge zeigen* (1988), bring out the contrast between the West and the Third World, the second being a more direct account of his stay in India between August 1986 and January 1987. His novel *Die Rättin* appeared in 1986. Grass' early plays include *Hochwasser* (1957), *Noch zehn Minuten bis Buffalo* (1959) and *Die Plebejer proben den Aufstand* (1966) a.o. His poetry collections *Die Vorzüge der Windhühner* (1956), *Ausgefragt* (1967) and *Gleisdreieck* (1960) are collected in *Gesammelte Gedichte* (1971). His entire works are collected in a *Werkausgabe* in ten volumes (1987). A novellette, *Unkenrufe*, appeared in 1992. After 1990, the process of unification in Germany dominates both his political speeches and the topic of his latest novel, *Ein weites Feld* (1995).

KIRSCH, Sarah
Sarah Kirsch, whose original name was Ingrid Bernstein, was born in 1935, studied at the *Literaturinstitut* in Leipzig and wrote her first works in collaboration with her then husband Rainer. After protesting with many other GDR writers against the expatriation of Wolf Biermann, she was allowed to move to West Berlin in 1977 and now lives in Schleswig-Holstein, Northern Germany. Her work is best seen in relation to the tradition of German nature poetry originating with the Romantics. The identifiable landscape of her verse include the GDR countryside in *Landaufenthalt* (1967), *Zaubersprüche* (1973), *Rückenwind* (1976); or Italy in *Drachensteigen* (1979); Provence in prose poems of the intimate diary *La Pragerie* (1980); USA in *Erdreich* (1982) and Schleswig-Holstein in *Erdreich* und *Katzenleben* (1984). Water plays an important role and can be related to her preoccupation with metamorphosis and her predilection for flowing verse forms with sparing use of punctuation. Two selections appeared in 1985, containing poems from the years 1967-79 (*Hundert Gedichte)* and 1980-85 (*Landwege*). Her collection *Erlkönigs Tochter* appeared in 1992, and her latest collection *Bodenlos* in 1996.

PFEIFER, Tadeus
Pfeifer was born 1949 in Freiburg, Germany, and grew up in Basel, Switzerland, where he works and lives today as a writer, art and literary critic and filmmaker. From 1972 till 1985 he published the literary magazine *Poesie* and wrote numerous monographs on contemporary artists, as well as essays on modern art. His works include several novels, short stories and poetry collections as *Im Gras kreischt freundlich der Affe* (1989), *Das Echo von Bois Rateau* (1992) and *Die Architektur der Liebe* (1997). His experiences on four extensive trips to India between 1985 and 1995 are reflected in many of his poems. As a special contribution to contemporary writing in India, he edited the poetry collection *Indische Lyrik. Poesie 51* in 1985, consisting of several modern Indian authors in German translation. In collaboration with Ludy Kessler, he produced several TV-Films on romanic churches in Europe. He recently produced a number of experimental video films with Enrique Fontanilles, amongst these two on the river Ganges in Benares: *A Hundred Years and Ten Minutes* (1995) and *It's an Absolutely Wonderful Place* (1996).

TIMM, Uwe
Born in 1940 in Hamburg, Timm studied philosophy and German literature in Munich and Paris, then sociology and economics, and obtained his Ph.D. in 1971. Resident in Munich, he has been involved in a publishing venture, the *Autoren-Edition*, and a literary group, the *Wortgruppe München*. His first novel *Heißer Sommer* (1974) is an authentic fictional treatment of the student movement. In *Morenga* (1978) he turned his attention to the uprising of the Hottentots against German colonial rule in South-West-Africa (Namibia). The novels *Kerbels Flucht* (1980) and *Der Mann auf dem Hochrad* (1986) were followed by *Der Schlangenbaum* (1986), in which a German engineer is forced to abandon the construction of a paper factory in the South American jungle, a novel which combines several of Timm's earlier themes. His approach to social realism is defined in the important essay *Realismus und Utopie* (1976). His novel *Die Entdeckung der Currywurst* appeared in 1993 and deals, as his novel *Kopfjäger*, with the clash of reality and narration. Many of his books bear the impression of his intense travel experiences. Besides his novels, he has film scripts and children's books to his credit.

TRANSLATORS

BAKHT, Baidar
An engineer by profession, Baidar Bakht lives in Canada. He has extensively translated twentieth-century Urdu poetry from India and Pakistan with collaborators Leslie Lavigne and Kathleen Grant Jaeger. With Jaeger he has edited and translated *An Anthology of Modern Urdu Poetry* (1984) in two volumes.

BANDOPADHYAY, Manohar
Born 1941. Edits an English monthly of the Ministry of Railways in New Delhi. He has published over ten volumes poetry and short stories, and translated the modern Hindi epic *Kamayani* into English. As a reviewer he has been associated with numerous newspapers and magazines.

BOWMAN, Derek
A well-known translator of several German authors, such as U. Bräker and Th. Fontane.

DAS, Jagannath Prasad
Born in 1936. Was educated at Allahabad University, and worked for several years in the Indian Administrative Service. Since the late 1960's he has published a dozen books, including collections of his poems and plays

in Oriya, as well as translations of his own and other Oriya poet's works into English and other languages. Among his collections of poems are *Anya sabu mrityu* (1976) and *Je jahara nirjanta* (1978). A selection of his poems in English translation is *Love is a Season* (1978). *Under a Silent Sun* (1992) is an anthology of recent Oriya women poetry, translated and edited with Arlene Zide.

DIXIT, R.K.

Born 1940. Received his M.A. degree from Kanpur University in 1961, and his M.A. in Linguistics from Lancaster, U.K. in 1977. Obtained his Ph.D. from Bhopal University in 1983 on E.E. Cummings. Worked as Head of Department of Languages at RCE, Bhopal and is presently Professor of English at the NCERT in New Delhi.

DUBEY, Ashutosh

A young Hindi poet. He is presently living in Indore, M.P., where he teaches English at the University.

EXNER, Richard

A translator of several works of Benn, he is also the author of "Gottfried Benn (1886-1956)" in: *Books Abroad XXX, 4* (1956). Has also translated works of E. Kästner.

GOLFFING, Francis

Apart from works of Gottfried Benn, he has translated many other German authors, including Friedrich Nietzsche.

GROVER, Teji

Born 1955. Poet, novelist and translator. She received the Bharat Bhushan Agarwal Award for the best poem (1989). At present she teaches English Literature at Chandigarh. She edited books for children and published two collections of poems and a novel.

HAMBURGER, Michael

Born in Berlin, he came to Britain with his family in 1933. A distinguished poet and renowned translator, he has been awarded the Schlegel-Tieck Prize and the Goethe Medal for his services to German literature. His many volumes of translation include the works of Rilke, Huchel, Celan and Grass. His *Collected Poems* was published in 1984. He is the Winner of the European Literature Prize for Translation, 1990.

HARDER, Hans

Born 1966. Studied Indology and Anthropology in Hamburg and Heidelberg. Since 1995 he is a lecturer and research assistant at the Department for Indology, University of Halle/Wittenberg. His recently completed Ph.D. thesis is on Bankimchandra Chatterjee.

HINDMARSH, Roland

Born 1922. Studied Philosophy, Psychology and Literature and did his M.A. at the University of Cambridge in 1952. He taught English in Sweden and Uganda, served as an inspector of schools in East Africa, as the Director of Studies at the Bell Scholl of Languages in Cambridge, and with the British Council Division at Calcutta, Tehran, London and Brussels. He was awarded the OBE in 1982.

HOOD, Stuart

Previously controller of BBC TV, a distinguished broadcaster, journalist, novelist and latterly Professor of Film and Television at the Royal College of Arts. He has been a close friend of Erich Fried's for many years and published a collection of his poetry in English translation.

HUECKSTEDT, Robert A.

He did his AB at Brown University and his Ph.D. at Harvard University in Sanskrit and Indian Studies. He currently teaches Hindi, Sanskrit, Urdu and South Asian Civilizations at the University of Manitoba,

Winnipeg, Manitoba. His translations from the Hindi have appeared in *Concerning Poetry*, *raddle moon*, *Pig Iron*, *Paintbrush*, *Indian Literature*, *Other Voices* and *Nimrod*. His translation *The Hunted*, of Mudra Rakshasa's Hindi novel *Dandavidhan* was published by Penguin in 1992. He is the author of *The Style of Bana: An Introduction to Sanskrit Prose Poetry* (1985) and *Nearness and Respective Correlation* (1995) in the field of Paninian linguistics.

JAIDEV
Professor of English at the University of Himachal Pradesh, Shimla.

JOSHI, Madhu B.
Translator and freelance writer. She has been associated with educational radio since 1981. She has published two collections of folktales and short stories for children. She has also translated American and Canadian fiction into Hindi.

LOTZ, Barbara
Born 1957. Studied Indology and Hindi Literature in Heidelberg and New Delhi. M.A. in Hindi Literature from Delhi University. From 1992 to 1994 she taught at South Asia Institute Heidelberg. Works as the representative of the Institute at their Branch Office in New Delhi since 1994. Translated and published several short stories from Hindi into German, and is currently working towards her Ph.D. in Indology on the Hindi poet G.M. Muktibodh.

LOTZ, Rainer
Born in 1953. Ph.D. on the reception of Brecht's poetry in Hindi literature. Worked as DAAD-lecturer for German language and translation studies at Jawaharlal Nehru University, New Delhi and Mumbai University between 1985 and 1997. Presently engaged in several projects of the Centre of Literary Translation.

LUTZE, Lothar
Born in 1927. Studied Anglistics, German Literature and Russian Philology in Berlin. Ph. D. in 1956, Habilitation in 1983. Since 1960, he has been visiting and working in India on several sojourns, and continued his studies of Hindi-Urdu and Bengali. He established the Department of Modern Indology at the South Asia Institute, Heidelberg University, and was the founder of the publication series for direct translations from Indian languages into German, the *Neue Indische Bibliothek*. He has published mainly in the field of Sociology of Literature and Comparative Literature, such as *Hindi Writing in Post-Colonial India* (1985). He has translated a vast number of authors from Hindi, Marathi and Bengali, and published several Hindi poetry anthologies in German translation, including *Als wär die Freiheit wie ein Stein gefallen* (1968) and *Der Ochsenkarren* (1983). He served twice as the representative of the South Asia Institute in New Delhi. He now lives in Berlin.

MANHEIM, Ralph
A renowned translator of German authors, he has rendered numerous titles of authors such as Brecht, Buch, Canetti, Cassirer, Freud, Grass (12 titles), Handke, Heidegger, Hesse, Jaspers, Remarque and many others into English. Amongst his honours is the *Schlegel-Tieck-Preis* for translation in 1989.

MATUSCHE, Petra
Born in 1944. Studied Philosophy and French Literature. She joined the Goethe Institute in 1971 and spent several years in Korea and Japan, before coming to India in 1991. As the programme officer of Max Mueller Bhavan from 1991-1997, she was one of the organisers of the series *Living Literature*. Transferred to the head office in Munich in 1977, she is currently working as a programme co-ordinator for the celebration of Goethe's 250th anniversary in 1999.

MEHROTRA, Arvind Krishna
Born 1947 in Lahore Pakistan and educated at Allahabad University and the University of Bombay. He has taught at the University of Hyderabad and is currently professor of English at Allahabad. Published poetry

and criticism in English as well as translations of poetry from Hindi and Prakrit. His recent books are *Middle Earth* (1984) and *The Absent Traveller* (1991). He has edited *The Oxford India Anthology of Twelve Modern Indian poets* (1992) and co-edited *Periplus*, a volume of and about poetry in translation.

MERRIL, Christie

Christi Merril is a student and translator of Hindi in the University of Iowa's Comparative Literature Doctoral Program.

MIDDLETON, Christopher

A reputed translator of German authors, he has translated works of Canetti, Celan, Grass (poems), G. Hofmann, Kafka, Trakl, Walser and Wolf, a.o. In 1986, he received the *Schlegel-Tieck-Preis* for translation.

OESTERHELD, Christina

Born 1952. Studied Indology and Anglistics at Humboldt University, Berlin. From 1976 till 1990 she worked as a lecturer and research assistent at Humboldt University. Ph.D. thesis on the novels of the Urdu writer Qurratulain Hyder. Since 1990 she works at the Department of Modern Indology, South Asia Institute Heidelberg, where she conducts research work and courses on contemporary Urdu language and literature. She has translated and published prose and poetry by several Urdu writers into German, and has co-edited and published her translations in several anthologies, amongst them *Erkundungen. 23 Short stories from India* (1990) and *Gesteht's! Die Dichter des Orients sind größer.* (Poetry and prose in Urdu by Indian and Pakistani writers, 1991).

POSTERO, Nancy

She is a radio journalist and a translator. She has worked extensively with the Native Americans in Peru and other Latin American countries for a radio documentary series entitled *Vanishing Homelands.* At present, she is working towards her Ph.D. in Anthropology at the University of Berkeley.

PRASAD, G.J.V.

Prasad is a writer and an academician. He has published a novel, *A Clean Breast* (1993), and a collection of poems, *In Delhi Without a Visa* (1996). He also translates from Indian languages (mainly Tamil and Hindi) into English. He is presently Assistant Professor of English at Jawaharlal Nehru University, New Delhi.

RAMANUJAN, A.K.

A.K. Ramanujan (1929-1993) taught at the University of Chicago and at various institutions in the US and India for forty years. His books include *The Striders* (1967), *Speaking of Shiva* (1973), *Samskara* (1976), *Hymns for the Drowning* (1981), *Poems of Love and War* (1986) and *Folktales from India* (1990), all works of translation. His posthumous *Collected Poems* and *Collected Essays* will be published by OUP New Delhi. An outstanding scholar, poet and translator, he was honoured with many awards, including the prestigious MacArthur Award.

RAO, Padma

Born 1959. Graduated in English literature from Delhi University, and studied German and French at the Max Mueller Bhavan and the Alliance Francaise in New Delhi. Has co-authored a travel guide on South India for Merian, Hamburg and coordinated GEO magazine's 1994 India special issue. Has been a translator and research assistant with Radio Deutsche Welle, Cologne, a news editor with Deutsche Presse Agentur (dpa), and worked in New York for *Outlook* magazine, the ARD, the German Radio and the ZDF. Presently a special correspondent with *The Pioneer*, New Delhi.

RATHI, Girdhar

Born 1946. He has a vast working experience in the field of journalism, administration, writing and research. Has edited a weekly newspaper and has long been associated with *Alternatives* as its managing editor. Published around forty books, amongst them three collections of his own poetry, *Bahar-bhitar* (1979), *Uninde ki lori* (1985) and *Nimitt* (1995), as well as numerous essays on literary and cultural criticsm, book reviews and

a travelogue on China. Besides translating a large number of Indian prose and poetry into English, he translated the works of Brecht, Guillen, Bonnefoy, Ritsos, Pesoa and Pu Yi and others into Hindi, and published several books of prose and poetry translations, amongst them *Adhunik Hungari kavitaen* (Hungarian Poetry) and *Har shai badalti hai* (Poems by Bertolt Brecht.) He is the co-editor of *Survival*, a collection of modern Hindi poetry in English translation (1994), and the editor of *Shabd Setu. Das Bharatiya Kavi* (1994). He received the *Omprakash Sahitya Samman* for *Bahar-bhitar* in 1980. He is currently the editor of the Sahitya Akademi bimonthly Hindi journal *Samkalin Bharatiya Sahitya.*

SHIVANATH

Shivanath is a Dogri writer. He has written books on the history of Dogri literature and has worked on the *Encyclopaedia of Indian Literature* and the *History of Indian Literature* projects of the Sahitya Akademi. A retired civil servant, he now lives in Delhi.

SINGH, Kuldip

Kuldip Singh has translated some thirty short stories and a documentary novel, *An Island of Salt*, working from both Hindi and Punjabi into English. His translations and his original English-language poems have been widely published in India. He also works as a Reader in Physiology at the Gandhi Medical College in Bhopal, and deputy director of medical education in the state government service there.

SINGH, Khushwant

Khushwant Singh (82) is a novelist, historian and journalist. His three weekly columns are reproduced by over 50 journals in India and abroad. His first book was the award-winning bestseller *Train to Pakistan.* In 1966, he published a two-volume *History of the Sikhs*. His four recent books are *Sex, Scotch & Scholarship, Need for a New Religion in India and Other Essays, Delhi* and *Women and Men in My Life.* Over the years, he has travelled widely and has written and lectured extensively on history, culture and philosophy.

SNELL, Rupert

Born in 1951. Ph.D. and presently Reader in Hindi at the Department of the Languages and Cultures of South Asia at SOAS, London. Formerly Head of Dept. of South Asia. His publications include *Hindi. A Complete Course for Beginners* (with S.C.R. Weightman, 1989), *Hindi and Urdu since 1800: a Common Reader* (with C. Shackle, 1990), *The Hindi Classical Tradition: a Braj Bhasha Reader* (1991) as well as numerous editions and articles published in the field of classic and modern Indology.

TRIVEDI, Harish

Born 1947. He was Commonwealth Scholar at the University of Wales and an honorary research fellow at the University of Birmingham, England. He has translated Premchand's biography *Premchand: His Life and Times* (1982) and Muktibodh's novel from Hindi into English. He has edited three books of criticism, including *Colonial Transactions: English Literature and India.* He is Professor of English at the University of Delhi.

VENNEWITZ, Leila

A well-known translator from German into English, she has more than ten titles of H. Böll to her credit, besides works of A. Kluge, M. Walser and U. Timm.

WEISS, Christian

Born 1959. Studied German Literature, History and Indology in Heidelberg. Since 1989 free-lancing as author, journalist and translator. He is co-editor of the book *Religion-Macht-Gewalt. Religiöser Fundamentalismus und Hindu-Moslem-Konflikte in Südasien* (1996).

WEISSBORT, Daniel

Born 1935 in London. Professor of English and Comparative Literature at the University of Iowa, where he directs the M.A. Program in Translation. With British poet Laureate Ted Hughes in 1965 he founded

the magazine *Modern Poetry in Translation.* He has published four volumes of his own poetry, as well as numerous translations, mostly of poetry from Russian. In addition he has edited three anthologies, most recently, *The Poetry of Survival: Post-War Poets of Eastern and Central Europe.*

WILLETT, John.

A renowned translator of numerous titles of prose, poetry and plays by Bertolt Brecht.

WILLSON, Leslie A.

He is the founder-editor of the bi-lingual journal *Dimension: Contemporary German Arts and Letters,* and serves on the editorial board of Dimension². The prestigious Goethe-Medal in 1981 is only one of the honours he received for his untiring efforts in translating German literature for the American reader. He served for two years as the President of the American Translators Association and is now Professor Emeritus at the University of Texas of Austin.

WOODS, John E.

Besides *Zunge Zeigen* by Grass, he has translated works of several German authors, including A. Schmidt and P. Süskind (*Das Parfum*).

ZIDE, Arlene

Born 1940 in New York. Ph.D. in Linguistics and South Asian Languages. A linguist, poet and translator, her poetry has appeared in numerous journals in India and the US. In collaboration with the poet J.P. Das, she published a book of translations of contemporary Orya women poets, *Under a Silent Sun* (1992). She has edited and translated a volume of poems by Indian women, *In their own voice* (Penguin 1993). At present, she teaches at a college in Chicago and edits the journal *Primavera,* devoted to writings by women.

ACKNOWLEDGEMENTS AND COPYRIGHT STATEMENTS

Following are the bibliographical details of the sources used. The editors and publishers thank the authors, translators and publishers for permission to reprint material which they published originally, or for which they hold copyright. Copyright-holders who could not be contacted because of lack of information are requested to correspond with Vani Prakashan, New Delhi. The listing follows the table of contents.

Manzoor Ahtesham: Excerpt in Hindi from the novel *Daastaan-e-laapataa.* New Delhi, Rajkamal Prakashan 1995.

U.R. Anantha Murthy: Excerpts in Kannada from the short story "Suryana Kudure" in: *Suryana Kudure* (short story collection, 1995). "A Horse for the Sun" tr. by Manu Shetty and A.K. Ramanujan in: *India International Centre Quarterly,* Monsoon 1992. New Delhi, IIC 1992.

Satyen Kumar: Excerpts in Hindi of the short story "Aayaam" in: *Ek nam aur tatha anya kahaniyan.* New Delhi, Rajkamal Prakashan 1995.

Uday Prakash: Excerpts in Hindi from the short story "Chhappan tole ka kardhan" in: *Tirichh. Uday Prakash ki nau kahaniyan.* New Delhi, Vani Prakashan 1989. "The Golden Waist Chain" appeared earlier, tr. by Sara Rai in: Sara Rai (ed.): *The Golden Waist Chain. Modern Hindi Short Stories.* New Delhi, Penguin 1990.

Krishna Sobti: Excerpts in Hindi from the novel *Mitro Marjani.* New Delhi, Rajkamal Prakashan 1992 (1st ed. 1966). English translations of *Mitro Marjani* appeared earlier in: *Indian Literature 22, 4,* tr. by R.S. Yadav. Sahitya Akademi, 1979. Excerpts tr. by Aditya Behl in: Behl/ Nicholls (eds.): *The Penguin New Writing in India.* Penguin India 1992.

Krishna Baldev Vaid: The Hindi short story "Andhere ki aatmaa" in: *Lila aur anya kahaniyan.* New Delhi, Rajpal Publishers 1993. "The Soul of Darkness" in: Krishna Baldev Vaid: *Dying Alone. A Novella and Ten Short Stories.* New Delhi, Penguin 1992.

Nirmal Verma: Excerpts in Hindi from the short story "Landan ki ek raat" in: *Jalti Jhadi.* New Delhi, Rajkamal Prakashan 1976. (1st ed. 1965). "A Night in London" in: Nirmal Verma: *Such a Big Yearning and Other Stories.* New Delhi, Indus (Harper Collins) 1995.

Kumar Ambuj: "Naye aparadhi" and "Akasmat ek din" in: *Krurta.* New Delhi, Radhakrishna Prakashan 1996. "Bijli ka khamba" in: *Kivad.* New Delhi, Aadhaar Prakashan 1992.

Shaista Anwar: All three poems in Hindi in: *Konpal. Yuva Kavita Karmshala.* Bhopal, Regional College of Education 1993.

Sanjay Chaturvedi: "Paise ke dant" in : *Samkalin Tisri Duniya* (1991) and in *Prakshvarsh,* New Delhi, Aadhaar Prakashan 1993. "Lutere bankar itihas" in: *Pahal*-37, and in *Prakashvarsh,* s.a.

Dilip P. Chitre: "Chavtha Brandenburg kancerto" and "Andhalchala disanare dekhave" in: *Ekun kavita-1,* Bombay, Popular Prakashan 1992. "The House Of My Childhood" in: *Travelling in a Cage.* Bombay, Clearing House 1980.

Mangalesh Dabral: "Patton ki mrityu" and "Shahar-1" in: *Pahad par laltein,* New Delhi 1981. "Sapna" in: *Ghar ka rasta,* New Delhi 1988. "Kuch deer ke liye" in: *Ham jo dekhte hain,* New Delhi 1995. "City", "Dream" and "The Death of Leaves" in: Weissbort/Rathi (eds.): *Survival.* New Delhi, Sahitya Akademi 1994.

Alokeranjan Dasgupta: All four poems in Bengali included here in: *Dhunuri Diyechhe Tangkar*, Calcutta, M.C. Sarkar and Sons 1988. All English translations in: Alokeranjan Dasgupta: *The Mystical Saw and Other Poems.* Edited and translated by Roland Hindmarsh. New Delhi, Sahitya Akademi 1996. All German translations by Harder/Weiss in: *Indien in der Gegenwart*, Bd.1, Nr.2, New Delhi, ICCR 1996.

Nida Fazli: All four poems in Urdu in: *Mor nach.* Bombay, New Writers Publ. 1978. "A Page from the New Diary" appeared earlier in: Dharwadker/Ramanujan (eds.): *The Oxford Anthology of Modern Indian Poetry.* OUP Delhi 1994.

Gagan Gill: All three poems in Hindi in: *Andhere mein buddha.* New Delhi, Rajkamal Prakashan, 1996. "Migraine" in: Bhalla/Gill (eds): *Yatra 6.* New Delhi, Harper Collins 1996. "Somebody Else's Love" in: *Indian Literature 173*, New Delhi, Sahitya Akademi 1996. "The Fish" in: Weissbort (ed.): *Poetry in Translation 11.* 1997.

Pramod Kaunswal: Both poems in Hindi in: *Apni hi tarah ka aadmi.* New Delhi, Aadhaar Prakashan 1992.

Vishnu Khare: Both poems in Hindi in: *Sab ki aawaaz ke parde mein.* New Delhi, Radhakrishna Prakashan 1994. "Single Wicket Series" in: *The Book Review Vol. XVIII, No.5.* New Delhi, May 1994.

Sitakant Mahapatra: All three poems in Oriya in: *Chadei re to ki janu* (1990) and *Shresta Kavita* (1992). All English translations in: Sitakant Mahapatra: *The Sky of Words and Other Poems.* New Delhi, Sahitya Akademi 1996, and in: *The Ruined Temple and Other Poems*, New Delhi, Harper Collins 1996. "Dhangras Liebeslied" tr. by Heinrich v. Stietencron appeared earlier in: Sitakant Mahapatra: *Hahnenkampf.* NIB 7. Frauenfeld, Verlag im Waldgut 1991.

Mohanjeet: Both poems in Punjabi in his poetry collection *Kinar ki nadi.* New Delhi, Arsee Publications 1994.

Kunvar Narayan: All three poems in Hindi in: *Koi duusra nahin.* New Delhi, Rajkamal Prakashan 1993.

Sutinder Singh Noor: All three poems in Punjabi in: *Sardal de ar par*, New Delhi, Sonal Prakashan 1996.

Surjeet Patar: "Ek pashu katha" and "Kavi saheb" in his collection *Birkh arz karey.* The other two poems in his collection *Haneray Vich Sulagdi Varanmala.*

Bhagwat Rawat: All three poems in Hindi in: *Sach puchho to.* New Delhi, Radhakrishna Prakashan 1996.

Padma Sachdeva: "Raja ke mahal" appeared in Hindi first in *Dharmyug* in 1967. "The Raja's Palaces" was first published in *Indian Literature*, Sahitya Akademi. "Kabutar" is included in a collection in press, as well as its English translation "Pigeons".

Prayag Shukla: All four poems in Hindi in: *Yeh likhta hun.* New Delhi, Vani Prakashan 1995.

Kedarnath Singh: All three poems in Hindi in: *Yeh dharti rahegi. Kedarnath Singh ki chuni hui kavitaen. Dayawati Modi Kavi Shekhar Samman 1996 ke awsar par.* New Delhi, Modi Kala Bharti 1996. "Banaras" in: Weissbort/ Rathi (eds.): *Survival.* New Delhi, Sahitya Akademi 1994. "On reading a Love Poem" tr. by V. Dharwadker appeared earlier in Dharwadker/ Ramanujan (eds.): *The Oxford Anthology of Modern Indian Poetry.* OUP Delhi 1994. Copyright for "What is poetry" with Rupert Snell.

Varyam Singh: "Boli" and "Katab" in: *Paryashi apne.* Banjar (Kullu), Apne Bol Prakashan."Urdi rauhai" in: *Uchtti marni biya*, Banjar (Kullu), Apne Bol Prakashan 1983.

Nitin Nema Subodh: All three poems in Hindi in: *Konpal. Yuva Kavita Karmshala.* Bhopal, Regional College of Education 1993.

Ashok Vajpeyi: "Deh ki pukar sunte hi deh hi" in: *Thodi si jagah.* New Delhi, Radhakrishna Prakashan 1994. "Talash" and "Sambhavna" in: *Ghas mein dubka aakaash.* New Delhi, Vani Prakashan 1992. All English translations in: *All But Alone.* New Delhi, Har-Anand Publications 1996.

Jurek Becker: Excerpts in German from "New Yorker Woche" and in English from "A Week in New York", both published in the bilingual journal *Dimension*, volume 11, 1978. Copyright for the German and English version by kind permission of A. Leslie Willson, Editor, *Dimension. Contemporary German Arts and Letters*, Austin, USA.

Hans Christoph Buch: Excerpts in German from the novel *Rede des toten Kolumbus am Tag des Jüngsten Gerichts*, Frankfurt, Suhrkamp Verlag 1992. Copyright for the excerpt "Epilog" by kind permission of Suhrkamp Verlag, Frankfurt.

Uwe Timm: Excerpts in German from the novel *Die Entdeckung der Currywurst*. Köln, Verlag Kiepenheuer & Witsch 1993. (7. Aufl. 1994). Excerpts in English from *The Invention of Curried Sausage* (Translated by Leila Vennewitz). New York, New Directions Publishing Corporation 1995. Copyright for the German reprint obtained by Verlag Kiepenheuer & Witsch, Köln. The English version is reprinted by kind permission of New Directions Publishing Corp. Copyright 1995 by Leila Vennewitz.

Gottfried Benn: All three poems in German and in English from: Gottfried Benn: *Primal Vision. Selected Writings.* Bilingual volume edited by E.B. Ashton. London, Marion Boyars Publishers Ltd., 1976. The copyright for "Was schlimm ist" and "Kreislauf" was obtained from Verlag Klett-Cotta, Stuttgart. The source is quoted as: Gottfried Benn. *Sämtliche Werke.* Stuttgarter Ausgabe. In Verb. mit Ilse Benn hrsg. von Gerhard Schuster. Band I: Gedichte1. Klett-Cotta, Stuttgart 1986. Copyright for "Ein Wort" was obtained from Arche Verlag Zurich. The source is quoted as: Gottfried Benn. *Statische Gedichte.* Hg. von Paul Raabe. Copyright 1948, 1983 by Arche Verlag AG, Raabe + Vitrali, Zürich.

Bertolt Brecht: All five poems in German from: Bertolt Brecht. *Werkausgabe edition Suhrkamp*, Bd. 8, 9 und 10. Frankfurt 1967. All English translations from: Bertolt Brecht. *Poems 1913-1956.* Edited by John Willett and Ralph Manheim. London, Eyre Methuen Ltd., 1976. First Indian reprint 1981 by Radhakrishna Prakashan, New Delhi. Copyright for the German reprint obtained from Verlag Suhrkamp, Frankfurt. Copyright for the English reprint obtained from Random House UK Limited, London.

Paul Celan: Both poems in German in: *Mohn und Gedächtnis.* Stuttgart, Deutsche Verlags-Anstalt, 1968. "Aspen Tree" in: *Paul Celan. Selected Poems.* Tr. by Christopher Middleton and Michael Hamburger. London, Penguin, 1972. Reprint of the German poems by kind permission of Deutsche Verlags-Anstalt, Stuttgart. Copyright for both English translations by kind permission of Michael Hamburger.

Günter Eich: All three poems in German and English in: *Pigeons and Moles.* Translated with an introduction by Michael Hamburger. Skoob Books, London 1991. (Bilingual edition). Copyright of the German poems by kind permission of Verlag Suhrkamp, Frankfurt. Reprint of the English translation by kind permission of Michael Hamburger.

Hans Magnus Enzensberger: "Zukunftsmusik" in: *Zukunftsmusik.* Frankfurt, Verlag Suhrkamp 1991. Copyright by kind permission of Suhrkamp Verlag, Frankfurt.

Erich Fried: "Vielleicht Allende" in: *Gegengift.* Verlag Klaus Wagenbach, Berlin 1974. "Fragen nach der Poesie..." in: *100 Gedichte ohne Vaterland.* Verlag Klaus Wagenbach, Berlin 1978. "Rückblick" in: *Die bunten Getüme.* Verlag Klaus Wagenbach, Berlin 1977. Reprint by kind permission of Verlag Klaus Wagenbach, Berlin. Copyright of "Allende perhaps", "Retrospect" and "Questions about Poetry" with John Calder Publishers, London.

Günter Grass: German version in: *Zunge zeigen.* Darmstadt, Luchterhand Literaturverlag GmbH 1988. English translation in: *Show Your Tongue.* Tr. by John E. Woods. London, Secker and Warburg 1989. Hindi translation in: *Jibh dikhana.* Tr. by Vishnu Khare. New Delhi, Radhakrishna Prakashan 1994. *Zunge Zeigen* in: Günter Grass, Gedichte und Kurzprosa. (Studienausgabe Bd.11). Steidl Verlag, Göttingen 1994. Reprint by kind permission of Steidl Verlag, Göttingen. Reprint of the English translation by kind permission of Random House U.K. Ltd. London, for Secker and Warburg. Copyright for the Hindi translation rests with Vishnu Khare.

Sarah Kirsch: All five poems in German in: *Erlkönigs Tochter.* Stuttgart, Deutsche Verlags-Anstalt, 1992. Reprint by kind permission of Deutsche Verlags-Anstalt Stuttgart.

Tadeus Pfeifer: All poems in German in: *Das Echo von Bois-Rateau.* Karlsruhe, von Loeper Literaturverlag 1992. Reprint by kind permission of the author.

FOLLOWING SOURCES ARE ACKNOWLEDGED FOR NOTES ON TRANSLATORS AND AUTHORS:

BENN, Gottfried: *Primal Vision. Selected Writings.* Edited by E.B. Ashton. London, Marion Boyars, 1976.

BHALLA, A./ GILL, G. (eds.): *Yatra 6.* Harper Collins India, 1996.

CELAN, Paul: *Selected Poems.* Translated by Michael Hamburger and Christopher Middleton. Introduction by Michael Hamburger. Penguin Books 1972.

DHARWADKER, V./ RAMANUJAN, A.K. (eds.): *The Oxford Anthology of Modern Indian Poetry.* OUP Delhi, 1994.

EICH, Günter: *Pigeons and Moles.* Translated with an Introduction by Michael Hamburger. London, Skoob Books 1991.

FRIED, Erich: *100 Poems without a Country.* Translated with an Introduction by Stuart Hood. London, John Calder 1978.

FURNESS, R./ HUMBLE, M.: *A Companion to Twentieth Century German Literature.* London, Routledge 1991.

MAX MUELLER BHAVAN: *Jurek Becker: An Introduction.* New Delhi 1993.

WEISSBORT, D./ RATHI, G. (eds.): *Survival. An Experience and Experiment in Translating Modern Hindi Poetry.* New Delhi, Sahitya Akademi 1994.

WILLETT, J. / MANHEIM, R. (eds.): *Bertolt Brecht. Plays, Poetry and Prose. Poems 1913-1956.* London, Eyre Methuen 1976. First Indian Reprint: New Delhi, Radhakrishna Prakashan 1981.

Gesamtverzeichnis der Übersetzungen deutschsprachiger Werke (GVÜ) 1954-1990. Bearb. v. Willi Gorzny, 12 vols. München, New Providence, London, Paris, K.G. Saur 1995.

o

LIST OF EVENTS

23.11.1992	*Uday Prakash and Hans Christoph Buch.* Prose readings in Hindi and German with translations.
15.12.1994	*"Har Shai Badalti Hai".* Book Release of the Hindi translations of B. Brecht's poetry by Girdhar Rathi and Rainer Lotz.
16.3.1993	*Alokeranjan Dasgupta.* Poetry reading in Bengali and German with translations.
8.4.1993	*Nida Fazli and Kedarnath Singh.* Poetry Reading in Urdu and Hindi, followed by German translations.
28.10.1993	*Dilip Chitre.* Poetry reading in Marathi, English and German with translations.
2.12. 1993	*Nirmal Verma and Jurek Becker.* Prose readings in Hindi and German with translations.
8.12.1993	*"The Indian Response to Rushdie's Midnight Children".* Lecture by Prof. Dieter Riemenschneider.
10.12.1993	*Sitakant Mahapatra.* Poetry reading in Oriya, with English and German translations.
7.2.1994	*"Sab Ki Awaaz Ke Parde Mein".* Book release and poetry reading in Hindi by Vishnu Khare, with German translations.
4.3.1994	*"Triveni":* Ashok Vajpeyi, Mangalesh Dabral and Kunvar Narayan. Poetry reading in Hindi, followed by German and Polish translations.
30.8.1994	*U.R. Anantha Murthy.* Prose reading in Kannada, English and German.
28.9.1994	*"Yuva Hindi Kavita".* Kumar Ambuj, Sanjay Chaturvedi, Shaista Anwar, Pramod Kaunswal and Nitin Nema Subodh. Poetry reading in Hindi, followed by German and Polish translations.
24.10.1997	*"Jibh Dikhana".* Book release of the Hindi translation of G. Grass' *"Zunge Zeigen"* by Vishnu Khare.
10.2.1995	*Krishna Baldev Vaid and Tadeus Pfeifer.* Poetry and prose in Hindi and German, with German, Hindi and English translations, followed by discussion.
28.4.1995	*"Poetry in music and dance - Songs of Vidyapati and Chandidas".* Poetry in Bengali with German translations. Odissi dance by Kabita Dvivedi, Manipuri dance by Vijayantibala Devi.
5.5.1995	*"Mitro Marjani".* Prose reading by Krishna Sobti in Hindi with German translation and slides from the theatre play.

20.10. 1995 *"Ek Din Lautegi Ladki"*. Poetry reading in Hindi by Gagan Gill, with German translations.

22.12. 1995 *"Punjabi Poetry"*. Poetry reading in Punjabi by Surjeet Patar, Mohanjeet and Sutinder Singh Noor, followed by German and Hindi translations.

13.1.1996 *Uwe Timm*. Readings from his novels in German with Hindi and English translations, followed by discussion.

26.4.1996 *"Yeh Likhta Hun"*. Poetry reading in Hindi by Prayag Shukla with German translations.

15.11.1996 *"Voices from Bhopal"*. Prose and poetry reading in Hindi by Manzoor Ahtesham, Satyen Kumar and Bhagwat Rawat, with German translations.

7.1.1997 *"Writing in Lesser Known Languages"*. Poetry and prose reading in Siraji, Dogri, Bangani, Maithili and tribal languages from Andhra Pradhesh and Orissa, with German and English translations.

11.2.1997 *"Distant Relationship: Kabir and Angelus Silesius"*. Lecture by Prof. Lothar Lutze.

3.3.1997 *"Aspects of Absurdity: Kabir, Rabindranath and Vinodkumar Shukla"*. Lecture by Prof. Lothar Lutze.

7.3.1997 *"The Traveller in Germany: In Memory Of Ajneya"*. Lecture by Prof. Lothar Lutze.

OOO